Opting for the Best

OXFORD MORAL THEORY

Series Editor
David Copp, University of California, Davis

Opting for the Best

Oughts and Options

DOUGLAS W. PORTMORE

OXFORD
UNIVERSITY PRESS

Oxford University Press is a department of the University of Oxford. It furthers
the University's objective of excellence in research, scholarship, and education
by publishing worldwide. Oxford is a registered trade mark of Oxford University
Press in the UK and certain other countries.

Published in the United States of America by Oxford University Press
198 Madison Avenue, New York, NY 10016, United States of America.

Library of Congress Cataloging-in-Publication Data
Names: Portmore, Douglas W., author.
Title: Opting for the best : oughts and options / Douglas W. Portmore.
Description: New York : Oxford University Press, 2019. |
Includes bibliographical references and index.
Identifiers: LCCN 2018046823 (print) | LCCN 2019014471 (ebook) |
ISBN 9780190945367 (updf) | ISBN 9780190945374 (epub) |
ISBN 9780190945381 (online content) | ISBN 9780190945350 (cloth : alk. paper)
Subjects: LCSH: Conduct of life. | Decision making. | Choice (Psychology) | Values.
Classification: LCC BJ1595 (ebook) | LCC BJ1595.P835 2019 (print) |
DDC 170/.42—dc23
LC record available at https://lccn.loc.gov/2018046823

9 8 7 6 5 4 3 2 1

Printed by Sheridan Books, Inc., United States of America

For my parents:
Linda Hills, Pakinee Portmore, and Ralph Portmore

CONTENTS

PREFACE

IT'S OFTEN UNCLEAR what we ought to do. Much of the time this is because it's unclear what matters. Suppose, for instance, that we're poultry farmers wondering whether we ought to put our chickens in cages or let them roam free. We know that we'll make more money if we put them in cages but also that they'll suffer more if we do. Still, if we want to know what we ought to do, we need to know whether their suffering matters, and, if so, how much it matters as compared to our profits.

Sometimes, though, we know exactly what matters and by how much, and it's still unclear what we ought to do. To illustrate, suppose that what matters is my health and that what would be best for my health is my quitting smoking and eating less (JACKSON & PARGETTER 1986). Assume, though, that if I were to quit smoking, I would eat more, not less. It's not that I couldn't quit smoking and eat less; it's just that I wouldn't. And assume that my weight is such a concern that I would be better off maintaining the status quo than quitting smoking and eating more. So, should I quit smoking? On the one hand, I must quit smoking to do what's best, which is to quit smoking and eat less. On the other hand, my quitting smoking would result in my eating more, which is worse than the status quo. So, figuring out what I ought to do can require knowing more than just what matters. I must also know how what matters determines what I ought to do. Should I, for instance, do what's entailed by my doing what's best in terms of what matters even if this would, as it happens, result in something worse than the status quo?

This book seeks to address the issues that remain after setting aside the question of what matters. These issues include, What are our options? Do I, for instance, have the option of typing out the cure for cancer if that's what I would in fact do if I were to have the right intentions at the right times (e.g., the intention to type the letter T at t_1, the intention to type the letter H at t_2, the intention to type the letter E at t_3, etc.)? Which options do we assess

in terms of their own goodness and which do we assess in terms of the goodness of the options that entail them? How do the things that matter determine which options we ought to perform? If, for instance, one of the things
that matters is my not violating anyone's rights, do we assess a given option in
terms of whether it entails my violating someone's rights or do we first assess
its prospect (i.e., its possible outcomes and their associated probabilities) in
terms of this and then assess the option in terms of how its prospect compares
to those of its alternatives? And what if there is uncertainty or indeterminacy
concerning whether an option would involve my violating someone's rights?

In this book, I argue that we should set aside the issue of what matters if
we want to solve certain puzzles concerning what we ought to do, including
puzzles concerning supererogation, indeterminate outcomes, overdetermined
outcomes, predictable future misbehavior, and good acts that entail bad acts.

* * *

Throughout this book, I'll be abiding by the following conventions. Tables,
figures, sections, and subsections will be numbered according to the chapter
in which they appear. Thus, Table 8.2 is the second table in Chapter 8, §4.6 is
the sixth section of Chapter 4, and §4.6.1 is the first subsection of §4.6. Major
propositions will initially be set off from the rest of the text by indentation on
the left and additional line spacing above and below. These propositions will
either be given a name or will be numbered according to the chapter in which
they first appear. Thus, 2.11 refers to the eleventh numbered proposition of
Chapter 2. Long quotations will be set off by indentation on the left and right,
a smaller font size, and additional line spacing above and below. And where
it would otherwise be unclear or ambiguous what the scope of something is,
I'll use the symbols < and >. Thus, the claim "<φ-ing> and <φ-ing and ψ-ing>
are both options" means that the following are both options: (1) φ-ing and
(2) jointly φ-ing and ψ-ing.

References in the text and footnotes are given by the author's last name
and year of publication, both appearing in small capitals. For instance, "GERT
2012" refers to Josh Gert's *Normative Bedrock*, which was published in 2012.
If I need to cite more than one work published in a given year by the same
author, I will differentiate them with letters. Thus, GERT 2007B refers to the
second of Gert's 2007 publications as listed in the references given at the back
of the book. You'll find complete bibliographic information for all references
there. When I refer to an author rather than his or her work, the name will
not appear in small capitals.

Technical terms and phrases will be defined as they come up and will often be set off by italics when they're initially defined. Note, though, these initial definitions do not always match up exactly with those given in the glossary. This is because whereas the initial definitions often paper over certain complications that are not addressed until later in the book, the glossary definitions represent my final formulations. Readers should consult the glossary if either they need to be reminded of a definition or they want to know its final formulation.

Examples will be given easy-to-remember titles and set off by italics: e.g., *Arm Raising, Getting Groceries*, and *Slice and Patch Go Golfing*.

I will typically use "she," "her," and "hers" as generic personal pronouns whenever the gender of the referent is unspecified, although I will occasionally use "he," "him," and "his" as generic personal pronouns, as when I must do so to remain consistent with some quoted passage. I realize that this is far from ideal, but all the alternatives seem to me to be at least as bad.

Rather than use only Anglo-American names such as "John Smith" and "Jane Jones," I have chosen to use names that reflect the diversity of the society in which I live. These names are mostly chosen from among my friends, students, and acquaintances. But sometimes, the name is chosen because it has a certain meaning that makes it particularly apt. For instance, in one case, I call the bad person Apollyon (meaning "the destroyer") and the good person Alexandra (meaning "the defender").

ACKNOWLEDGMENTS

MY GREATEST DEBT is owed to Fred Feldman, Holly M. Smith (previously Holly S. Goldman), and Michael J. Zimmerman. Their pioneering work on some of the same topics have shaped my ideas in more ways than can be adequately documented in the references to follow. I've been especially influenced by Feldman's *Doing the Best We Can* (1986) and even more so by Goldman's "Doing the Best One Can" (1978).

Special thanks are also owed to those who provided me with detailed comments on drafts of one or more chapters: Andreas Brekke Carlsson, Richard Yetter Chappell, John Doris, Dale Dorsey, David Estlund, Andrew T. Forcehimes, Johann Frick, Liz Harman, Brian Hedden, Paul Hurley, Hrishikesh Joshi, Andrew Khoury, Seth Lazar, Jörg Löschke, Berislav Marušić, Ellie Mason, Kian Mintz-Woo, Shyam Nair, Philip Pettit, Sam Preston, Susanna Rinard, Tina Rulli, David Shoemaker, Michael Smith, David Sobel, Daniel Star, Steve Sverdlik, Matthew Talbert, Christian Tarsney, Travis Timmerman, Peter Vallentyne, and an anonymous reviewer for Oxford University Press.

For helpful comments and/or discussions on some of the ideas for this book, I thank Per Algander, Chrisoula Andreou, Brad Armendt, Christian Barry, Marius Baumann, Robert Beddor, David Boonin, Elizabeth Brake, David O. Brink, Campbell Brown, Cheshire Calhoun, Kendra Chilson, Eric Chwang, Stew Cohen, Yishai Cohen, Brad Cokelet, Mary Coleman, Stephanie Collins, David Copp, Peter de Marneffe, Jamie Dreier, Julia Driver, Gerald B. Dworkin, Adam Elga, James Fanciullo, Sarah Fine, Josh Gert, Peter A. Graham, Preston Greene, Pat Greenspan, Johan E. Gustafsson, Matthew Hammerton, Chris Heathwood, Jonathan Herington, Pamela Hieronymi, Brad Hooker, Adam Hosein, Eric Hubble, Frank Jackson, Karen Jones, William Kilborn, Alex King, Victor Kumar, Eden Lin, Thomas Mautner, Simon May, David McElhoes, Conor McHugh, Thaddeus Metz,

Gene Mills, Dan Moller, Christopher Morris, Rick Morris, Howard Nye, Graham Oddie, Hille Paakkunainen, Tom Parr, Martin Peterson, Ángel Pinillos, Felix Pinkert, Abelard Podorski, Jonathan Quong, Jason Raibley, Andrew Reisner, Massimo Renzo, Steve Reynolds, Melinda Roberts, Toni Rønnow-Rasmussen, Connie Rosati, Marya Schechtman, Mark Schroeder, Luke Semrau, Dan C. Shahar, Peter Singer, Walter Sinnott-Armstrong, Justin Snedegar, Nic Southwood, Julia Staffel, Eric Swanson, Larry Temkin, Michael Tooley, Jacob Velasquez, Jean-Paul Vessel, Steve Wall, Ralph Wedgwood, Stephen J. White, David Wiens, Bill Wringe, Erik Zhang, Jake Zuehl, the students in my Spring 2018 seminar entitled "Control and Responsibility," and audiences at Princeton University, Syracuse University, Arizona State University, Australian National University, University of Colorado at Boulder, University of Maryland at College Park, the 2014 Rocky Mountain Ethics Congress, the Arizona Center for the Philosophy of Freedom, the 2015 Workshop on Supererogation (Concept and Context) in Basel, Switzerland, the 2017 Princeton Workshop on Professor Procrastinate, the 2017 DEthiX Conference at UC Davis, the 8th Annual New Orleans Invitational Seminar in Ethics, the 2014 Pacific Division Meeting of the American Philosophical Association, the 2018 Bled Philosophy Conference on Ethical Issues, the 2018 Feasibility and Collectives Workshop at the Australian National University, the 2018 Dartmouth Ethics Institute's Workshop on Moral and Political Philosophy, and the 2017 Conference on Neutrality (Reasons, Values, and Times) at Nanyang Technological University.

For financial and institutional support, I thank Arizona State University, the RSSS Visiting Fellows Program, School of Philosophy, Australian National University, and the Laurance S. Rockefeller Visiting Faculty Fellowship Program at the University Center for Human Values, Princeton University. ANU and Princeton are by far the two most intellectually stimulating places I've had the pleasure of visiting.

For assistance in publishing this book, I thank the people at Oxford University Press (New York) and especially Peter Ohlin. And I thank David Copp for including this book in his series entitled "Oxford Moral Theory."

For their love and support, I thank my wife Erin and my daughter Fiona as well as my parents.

Last, some kernels of the ideas that are further developed here have appeared in the following previously published work:

- "Perform Your Best Option," *Journal of Philosophy* 110 (2013): 436–459.
- "Maximalism versus Omnism about Permissibility," *Pacific Philosophical Quarterly* 98 (2017): 427–452.

- "Maximalism versus Omnism about Reasons," *Philosophical Studies* 174 (2017): 2953–2972.
- "Transitivity, Moral Latitude, and Supererogation," *Utilitas* 29 (2017): 286–298.
- "Uncertainty, Indeterminacy, and Agent-Centered Constraints," *Australasian Journal of Philosophy* 95 (2017): 284–298.
- "Maximalism and Moral Harmony," *Philosophy and Phenomenological Research* 96 (2018): 318–341.
- "Control, Attitudes, and Accountability," forthcoming in the fifth volume of *Oxford Studies in Agency and Responsibility*.

For permission to borrow material from these publications, I thank the editors and publishers of these journals.

Opting for the Best

CHAPTER 1

Opting for the Best

ONE OF THE most important questions is how we ought to live. Unfortunately, there's little agreement on what the answer is. Some say that we should maximize our own happiness. Others say that we should maximize overall happiness. Still others say that we should abide by certain rules—such as the Golden Rule, the Ten Commandments, or Kant's categorical imperative. Perhaps, though, we can all agree that we should do our best—best, that is, in terms of whatever ultimately matters. So, even if there's little agreement on what ultimately matters (Is it maximizing happiness, obeying God's commands, doing unto others as you would have them do unto you, treating humanity always as an end and never merely as a means, all of these, some of these, or none of these?), we should all agree that we each ought to opt for what's best in terms of whatever ultimately matters.

This book is an attempt to formulate this idea as precisely and plausibly as possible and to address some questions that remain after setting aside the issue of what ultimately matters. In particular, I'll address the following three questions. First, what are our options? Even if we know both what ultimately matters and that we each ought to opt for what's best in terms of what ultimately matters, we still need to know what our options are. For suppose we want to know whether what I'm doing now—that is, typing out this introductory chapter—is my best option. It won't be enough for us to know what ultimately matters. For regardless of what ultimately matters, there will always be other possible events that are better than what I'm doing now. So we need to know which of these possible events are, in the relevant sense, options for me. To illustrate, suppose that what ultimately matters is the production of aggregate happiness. Given that my typing out and sending an email to the National Institutes of Health that credibly explains how to cure cancer is going produce much more aggregate happiness than my typing out this introductory chapter, it follows that I'm performing my best option in typing out this introductory chapter only if I don't have the alternative option of typing out and sending such an email. And some have suggested that I have such an option.[1] After all, my typing out and sending such an email just consists in my making a certain series of keystrokes. And regardless of what the first keystroke in this series is, I have at present both the ability and the opportunity to make that keystroke. And regardless of what the second keystroke in that series is, I will, subsequent to making the first keystroke, have both the ability and opportunity to make the second keystroke. And so on and so forth for all the remaining keystrokes in the series. Thus, it's not enough for me to know that, say, the production of aggregate happiness is what ultimately matters. I also need to know which of the events that would produce aggregate happiness are options for me.

The second question is, When assessing what we ought to do, which options are we to assess in terms of their own goodness and which are we to assess in terms of the goodness of other options—for example, the options of which they are, say, a proper part? To illustrate, suppose again that what ultimately matters is the production of aggregate happiness and that, therefore, the more aggregate happiness I produce, the better. And assume that what's best in terms of the production of aggregate happiness is my raising both my arms at time t, that a distant second best is my raising neither of my arms at t, and that worst of all is my raising only one of my arms at t. And let's assume that I have all the following distinct options: raising both my arms at t, raising neither of my arms at t, raising my left arm at t, raising my right arm at t, raising *only* my left arm at t, and raising *only* my right arm at t.[2] Last, assume that, because, prior to t, I'm going to irrationally form the intention to make things go as badly as possible, I would not raise my right arm at t if I were to raise my left arm at t. And, likewise, I would not raise my left arm at t if I were

---

1. See, for instance, CARLSON 1999A (p. 91), FELDMAN 1986 (pp. 24–25), WILAND 2005, and ZIMMERMAN 1996 (p. 91). Others disagree—see, for instance, DORSEY 2013B and HOWARD-SNYDER 1997.

2. Raising my right arm at t isn't an alternative to raising *only* my right arm at t, but the two are distinct options. For whereas two options, φ and ψ, are *alternative options* if and only if <φ-ing and ψ-ing> is not an option, two options, φ and ψ, are *distinct options* if and only if it is not the case that each entails the other. The two are distinct, then, because although raising *only* my right arm at t entails raising my right arm at t, raising my right arm at t does not entail raising *only* my right arm at t.

Table 1.1 My Options in *Arm Raising*

Option	Outcome	Ranking
Raise my left arm at *t*	Produces the least aggregate happiness	Worst
Raise my right arm at *t*	Produces the least aggregate happiness	Worst
Raise only my left arm at *t*	Produces the least aggregate happiness	Worst
Raise only my right arm at *t*	Produces the least aggregate happiness	Worst
Raise both my arms at *t*	Produces the most aggregate happiness	Best
Raise neither of my arms at *t*	Produces the 2nd most aggregate happiness	2nd Best

to raise my right arm at *t*. Let's call this case *Arm Raising*, which I depict in Table 1.1.[3]

Now, the question is this: In *Arm Raising*, are we to assess the option of raising my left arm at *t* in terms of its own goodness or in terms of the goodness of the best option that includes raising my left arm at *t* as a proper part? If it's the former, then I should not raise my left arm at *t*, for this is one of my worst options in terms of the production of aggregate happiness given that I would not raise my right arm at *t* if I were to raise my left arm at *t*. But if it's the latter, then I should raise my left arm at *t*, for doing so is a proper part of my best option: raising both of my arms at *t*. Thus, we need to know whether we are to assess all or only a proper subset of a subject's options in terms of their own goodness.

The third and last question that I'll address is, Which, if either, are we to assess directly in terms of what ultimately matters—our options or their prospects?[4] To illustrate, suppose that one of the things that ultimately matters

---

3. This case is borrowed from JACKSON 2014 (p. 645).

4. If there is just one way that the world would turn out if a subject, S, were to φ, then this is the *outcome* of S's φ-ing. But there may not be one way that the world *would* turn out, but only several different ways that it *could* turn out. And, in that case, we need to talk about the *prospect*, not the outcome, of S's φ-ing. The prospect of S's φ-ing is the probability distribution consisting in the mutually exclusive and jointly exhaustive set of possible worlds that could be actualized by her φ-ing, with each possibility assigned a probability such that the sum of those probabilities equals 1. And, of course, if there is only one possible world that could be actualized by her φ-ing such that the probability that this world would be actualized if she were to φ is 1, then the prospect of S's φ-ing is just the outcome of S's φ-ing. Thus, strictly speaking, there is no need to talk about outcomes at all. We can just talk about the prospect of S's φ-ing, which in certain instances will be the outcome of S's φ-ing.

to a subject is that everything she does has the property of determinately not violating anyone's rights. But now suppose that one thing she could do is to φ and that, unfortunately, her φ-ing doesn't have this property. For there is, we'll suppose, no determinate fact as to whether her φ-ing would violate anyone's rights. What's true is only that there is a good chance that it wouldn't violate anyone's rights but some very small chance that it would. Now, if we were to evaluate the option directly in terms of this property, we would be forced to say that her φ-ing would be wrong, given that it doesn't have the property of determinately not violating anyone's rights. But this seems like a mistake if the probability that her φ-ing would violate someone's rights is extremely low. We may think, then, that whether she ought to φ depends not on whether it has the property of determinately not violating anyone's rights but on whether it has a sufficiently low probability of violating someone's rights. So, the question is, Do we assess a given option directly in terms of whether it has the property of determinately not violating anyone's rights, or do we first evaluate the option's prospect in terms of the probability that it would violate someone's rights and then assess the option in terms of how its prospect ranks in comparison to those of its alternatives? And, as we've just seen, the answer to this question is especially important when it comes to situations in which it is indeterminate whether a subject's option would constitute violating someone's rights.

My hope is that by setting aside the question of what ultimately matters we can better make progress in answering these three important questions. Moreover, I'll argue that it is only by answering these questions that we can make headway in solving certain puzzles concerning what we ought to do, including some involving supererogation, indeterminate outcomes, overdetermined outcomes, predictable future misbehavior, and good options (e.g., my raising both my arms at t) that entail bad options (e.g., my raising my left arm at t).

I admit, of course, that there are many issues concerning what we ought to do that can't be resolved but by addressing the question of what ultimately matters. We can't, for instance, resolve the issue of whether to adopt either a population policy that will result in a larger population with a lower average level of well-being or one that will result in a smaller population with a higher average level of well-being unless we address the question of whether bringing more happy people into existence is something that ultimately matters—that is, something we should ultimately care about. Nevertheless, there are, I'll argue, other issues concerning what we ought to do that can be resolved only by setting aside the issue of what ultimately matters and addressing these other three important questions. Consider *Arm Raising* again. There's no question that the only thing that matters in this instance is my producing as much aggregate happiness as possible. Consequently, we won't be able to resolve the issue of whether I ought to raise my left arm at *t* simply by figuring out whether I should care about anything besides, or in addition to, the production of aggregate happiness. Indeed, we know that (1) I'll produce less aggregate happiness if I raise my left arm at *t* than if I don't, that (2) I'll produce the most aggregate happiness possible only if I raise both my arms at *t*, and that (3) raising both my arms at *t* necessitates raising my left arm at *t*. So, the only way that we're going to resolve the question of whether I ought to raise my left arm at *t* is by figuring out whether this option should be assessed in terms of whether performing it would produce more aggregate happiness than not performing it or in terms of whether performing it is necessitated by performing the option that would produce the most aggregate happiness. And, as I'll argue throughout this book, there are many other such puzzles that can best be resolved by setting aside the issue of what ultimately matters in order to address them.

§1.1 The Opting-for-the-Best View

It is, I believe, fairly uncontroversial to suppose both that (1) whether an event has a deontic status (such as that of being obligatory, permissible, supererogatory, or that which ought to be performed) depends, in part, on whether it is an option for some subject, and that (2) if it is an option for that subject, which specific deontic status it has depends on how it compares to the alternative options.[5] For instance, whether I ought to run a mile in under six minutes depends both on whether it's an option for me and, if it is, on whether it's better than all my alternative options. And so, the following should seem fairly uncontroversial, for it basically says that for any subject and any member of at least a certain subset of her options, that subject ought

---

5. A *deontic status* is any status such as the following: wrong, optional, obligatory, permissible, supererogatory, and that which ought to be performed. All options are either permissible (i.e., right) or impermissible (i.e., wrong). Permissible options are either optional or obligatory. An obligatory option is a permissible option whose alternatives are all impermissible. And all obligatory options ought to be performed. An optional option is one that it is both permissible to perform and permissible to refrain from performing. Some, but not all, optional options ought to be performed. Those optional options that are better than all of their alternatives ought to be performed. And those optional options that are better than some permissible alternative are supererogatory.

to φ if and only if φ is her best option—best, that is, in terms of whatever ultimately matters. As a slogan, we might put it this way: *your options are a proper subset of all possible events, and you ought always to perform the best member of some (not necessarily proper) subset of your options.*[6] But, to put things more precisely, the view is as follows.

> **The Opting-for-the-Best View (incomplete formulation):** There is a set of events, which is a proper subset of all possible events and which I call the set of S's options (or 'O' for short) such that, for any subject S and any possible event *e*, whether S's *e*-ing has a deontic status depends on whether *e* is a member of O. And, if it is a member of O, then what particular deontic status it has depends on how it compares to the *alternative members*[7] of O such that, for any member φ of a certain subset (perhaps, a *proper subset*) of O, S ought to φ if and only if φ is the best member of this subset of O in terms of whatever ultimately matters.[8]

To understand why this should seem fairly uncontroversial, we need to take note of the following nine points.

§1.1.1 Perhaps, some options that ought to be performed are suboptimal

The opting-for-the-best view doesn't assume that, for any subject and any option of hers φ, she ought to φ if and only if φ is her best option. Rather, it says that, for any subject and any member φ of a certain subset (perhaps, a proper subset) of her options, she ought to φ if and only if φ is her best option. In other words, it doesn't say that you ought always to perform *your best option,*

---

6. For any two sets, A and B, if every member of A is also a member of B, then A is a *subset* of B (i.e., A⊆B). Note that this allows that A can be a subset of B even if A and B contain all the same members (i.e., even if A=B). However, if every member of A is also a member of B, but not every member of B is also a member of A, then A is a *proper subset* of B (i.e., A⊂B).

7. For any two members, *x* and *y*, of the set O, <my *x*-ing> and <my *y*-ing> are *alternative members* of O if and only if <my jointly *x*-ing and *y*-ing> is not itself a member of O. Thus, <my walking at *t*> and <my chewing gum at *t*> are not alternative members of the set of my options given that <my jointly walking and chewing gum at *t*> is a member of the set of my options. But <my walking at *t*> and <my running at *t*> are alternative members of the set of my options given that <my jointly walking and running at *t*> is not a member of the set of my options.

8. I leave implicit the relevant grounding claim: the claim that, if a subject ought to φ, this is in virtue of the fact that φ is the best member of this subset of O in terms of whatever ultimately matters.

but only that you ought always to perform *the best member of some subset of your options.* This allows, then, for the possibility that not all of a subject's options are to be assessed in terms of their own goodness. I formulate the view in this way, because, in some cases, it's reasonable to suppose that a subject ought to perform a suboptimal option. To illustrate, recall *Arm Raising.* Raising both my arms at *t* is best, raising neither of my arms at *t* is second best, and raising just one of my arms at *t* is the worst. And recall that, as a matter of fact, I would not raise my right arm at *t* if I were to raise my left arm at *t.* So, raising my left arm at *t* is not my best option. After all, we're assuming both that raising only my left arm at *t* would produce one of the worst possible outcomes and that I would in fact raise *only* my left arm at *t* if I were to raise my left arm at *t.*[9] But although raising my left arm at *t* is suboptimal, some will, nevertheless, claim that it's what I ought to do (see, e.g., JACKSON 2014, p. 646). After all, it's entailed by my best option, which is raising both my arms at *t.* So, if the opting-for-the-best view is to be as uncontroversial as possible, it must allow for the possibility that some options, such as raising my left arm at *t,* ought to be performed despite their being suboptimal. And this is why the opting-for-the-best-view is formulated so as to be neutral regarding whether all or only a proper subset of a subject's options are to be assessed in terms of their own goodness.[10]

§1.1.2 Not all possible events are eligible for deontic status

It's not just any possible event that can have a deontic status. Take, for instance, the possible event of my walking on water. Or take the possible event of *your* going for a run. Or take the possible event of Halley's comet colliding with Earth. None of these are eligible for the status of being what *I* ought to do, nor for any other deontic status that takes me as its subject. Halley's comet's colliding with Earth isn't even something that someone can opt for. Your going for a run isn't something that *I* can opt for. And even though my

---

9. We're also assuming, merely for the purposes of illustration, that the goodness of an act is purely a function of the goodness of its outcome and that an act's outcome just consists in what would be the case were the agent to perform it, where what would be the case depends on what the agent would in fact simultaneously or subsequently do if she were to perform it.

10. This is also why I don't define "S's best option" as "the option that S has most reason to perform." After all, it seems reasonable to suppose that, in *Arm Raising,* I have most reason to raise my left arm at *t* even though this is not my best option. I'll have much more to say about this and related issues in Chapter 6.

walking on water is something that it's possible, in some sense, for me to opt for, the sense of "possibility" that's relevant in determining whether an event is eligible for deontic status seems to be much narrower than this. So, it seems that the opting-for-the-best view is correct in supposing that only a proper subset of all possible events is eligible for deontic status.

§1.1.3 Alternatives matter

Of course, just because some event is eligible for deontic status doesn't mean that it will have the status of being what I ought to do. So, what sets the option that I ought to perform apart from the other events that are also eligible for this status? The only reasonable answer is that the option that I ought to perform is better than all those alternatives. For why else would it be that I ought to perform it as opposed to one of them?

Admittedly, I'm assuming that what particular deontic status an option has depends on how it compares to its alternatives. But this, I believe, is fairly uncontroversial. What's more, I'm not the only one who thinks so. Here's Justin Snedegar.

> Nearly everyone accepts that in ethics, and normative philosophy more generally, alternatives matter. Whether what you did was wrong, or was what you ought to have done, or whether you even had any reason to do it depends on what the alternatives were. Suppose you run into the burning building, scoop up [baby Nestor, and only baby Nestor], and carry him out to safety. Is this what you ought to have done? Maybe so. But what if an alternative, one that you could have just as easily performed, was to run in, scoop up both [baby Nestor and baby Ángel]—who was right next to [baby Nestor]—and carry both of them to safety? If this was an alternative, what you did was not what you ought to have done. If this was not an alternative, what you did may well have been what you ought to have done. So the claim that alternatives matter is uncontroversial, in the following sense: The *availability* of certain alternatives can affect the normative status [or what I'm calling the deontic status] of an action. (2015, p. 379)[11]

---

11. Recall that, as I've defined alternatives (see note 2), alternatives are mutually exclusive. So, although saving both baby Nestor and baby Ángel isn't an alternative to saving baby Nestor, saving both baby Nestor and baby Ángel is an alternative to saving *only* baby Nestor. And, thus, whether you did what you ought to have done in saving *only* baby Nestor depends on whether

Further evidence for the uncontroversial nature of this assumption lies with the fact that there are very few theories that deny it, and those that do are widely acknowledged to be problematic for this very reason, and sometimes even by their initial proponents. Consider, for instance, the following view.

> **Absolute Level Satisficing Utilitarianism:** There is a number, n, such that an option is morally permissible if and only if the result of performing this option would be either (R1) at least n units of happiness or (R2) less that n units of happiness but no fewer units than would result from performing any alternative option. (BRADLEY 2006, p. 98)

The problem lies with R1, which implies that so long as an option would produce at least n units of happiness, the alternatives are irrelevant in assessing its moral permissibility. To illustrate, imagine that n equals 200 and that among my options are (1) doing nothing, in which case Olga will save three lives, resulting in 300 units of happiness and (2) paying Olga $100 to save only two of the three, resulting in only 200 units of happiness. Absolute level satisficing utilitarianism implies that my paying Olga $100 to save only two of the three is morally permissible even though I have the option of doing nothing, which would be better for me, worse for no one, and much better for the person who would otherwise die.[12] This implication is quite counterintuitive; it seems morally impermissible for me to go out of my way, sacrificing my own interests, to prevent an additional life from being saved (BRADLEY 2006, p. 103). The lesson, then, is that whether one is permitted to do something that results in 200 units of happiness depends on whether there is a better option. Of course, this is to assume that there are certain ends (such as the production of happiness) that we ought, other things being equal, to promote, but I take this assumption to be fairly uncontroversial. And, if we accept this assumption, the deontic status of an option will depend on how it compares to the agent's other options in terms of the promotion of such ends.

---

you had the alternative of saving both baby Nestor and baby Ángel. In holding that alternatives must be mutually exclusive, I follow BERGSTRÖM 1966 and depart from CARLSON 1999B. Carlson holds that a subject's set of alternatives consist in what I'm calling her set of options (see p. 255). Thus, on Carlson's view, saving both baby Nestor and baby Ángel is an alternative to saving baby Nestor since they're distinct options.

12. Assume that Olga is indifferent between (1) saving all three and receiving $0 and (2) saving only two and receiving $100. Consequently, she will fare no worse if I do nothing.

And it's not just the moral status, but also the rational status, of an option that depends on how it compares to its alternatives. To illustrate, consider Josh Gert's earlier view concerning objective rational status, where an act has the status of being objectively irrational (i.e., objectively rationally impermissible) if and only if it is one that absolutely should not be performed, all things considered (GERT 2003, p. 137). His view was as follows.

> **Gert's Earlier View:** An act is objectively irrational if and only if it will bring some harm to the agent without bringing any compensating benefit to anyone, including, but not limited to, the agent. (GERT 2007A, p. 544)

On this view, the objective rational status of an act does not depend on what the alternatives are. Indeed, in defending this view, Gert had insisted that "to ask what the objective rational status of an action is, *given the existence of a certain alternative*, is to make a mistake [emphasis in the original]" (GERT 2007B, p. 467). But this failure to consider alternatives is the view's downfall, as even Gert now acknowledges (GERT 2012, pp. 117–118). To illustrate, consider *Postal Worker*. Assume both that, for each $200 donation that Oxfam receives, forty children will be saved and that someone's $200 cash donation to Oxfam is about to get ripped to shreds in a mail-sorting machine. A nearby postal worker named Imelda could prevent this from happening by throwing herself into the machine to jam it, thereby sacrificing her life to ensure that Oxfam receives this particular cash donation. But if Imelda refrains from throwing herself into the machine, she can continue to work for the rest of the day, thereby earning a check for $200, which she could then sign over to Oxfam. So, she can ensure that Oxfam gets an additional $200 either by throwing herself into the machine or by continuing to work and signing over the resulting earnings to Oxfam.

Strangely, according to Gert's earlier view, it is not objectively irrational for Imelda to sacrifice her life to save the specific forty children that this particular cash donation would save, for Gert holds that saving those forty children compensates for the harm of her losing her life.[13] But it's absurd to think that Imelda's sacrificing her life is rationally permissible when there is a way

---

13. Assume that the forty children who would be saved if she were to throw herself into the machine are distinct from the forty who would be saved if she were to refrain from doing so and sign over the resulting earnings to Oxfam. Nevertheless, assume that there is no way for Imelda to identify who the forty saved are in either case.

for her to save just as many unidentifiable children without sacrificing her life. So, again, we see that alternatives matter because there are certain ends that we ought, other things being equal, to promote. In this case, it's the end of minimizing one's self-sacrifices. And if we accept this, we must also accept that the deontic status (in this case, the objective rational status) of an option depends on what the alternatives are and on how these alternatives compare to the option in question in terms of the promotion of such ends.[14]

So, it seems that, as the opting-for-the-best view holds, what particular deontic status an option has depends on how it compares to its alternatives. For instance, whether an option has the status of being what the subject ought to do depends on whether it is better than all its alternatives. For if there was an alternative that was just as good as it, it wouldn't be that she ought to perform it as opposed to this equally good alternative. Rather, it would just be that she ought to perform one of the two. Likewise, whether an option is supererogatory (i.e., whether it goes beyond the call of duty) depends on whether it is better than what's minimally required—that is, better than the alternatives that constitute doing the bare minimum required. For if the given option were no better than what's minimally required, it wouldn't go *beyond* the call of duty.

§1.1.4 Oughts versus obligations

Admittedly, satisficers would deny that a subject is obligated to φ if and only if φ is her best option. But I haven't claimed that a subject is *obligated* to perform her best option but only that she *ought* to perform her best option. And there's an important difference between what a subject is obligated to do and what she ought, but is not obligated, to do. For one, it is only when a subject fails to do what she is obligated to do that she is blameworthy (or otherwise accountable) absent suitable excuse. For another, although we often have the right to demand that subjects do what they're obligated to do, we never have the right to demand that they do what they ought, but are not obligated, to do. Consequently, the two can come apart. For instance, although I ought to

---

14. This sort of objection to Gert's view was first pressed by Tenenbaum (2007) and was then further pressed by me in my 2012, where I argued that Gert's response to Tenenbaum in his 2007B was inadequate. In more recent work, Gert has come to acknowledge the problem and has, consequently, revised his view. On his current view, "the objective rationality of an action depends on the harms and benefits of the action *and of its salient alternatives* [emphasis in the original]" (GERT 2012, p. 118).

send my mother flowers for Mother's Day, the most that I'm obligated to do is to send her a card—or so we'll assume.

So, although we should think that a subject ought to φ if and only if φ is her best option, we should think that a subject is obligated to φ if and only if φ is her only sufficiently good option—that is, her only option that's sufficiently good to count as permissible. And since one can either accept or deny that only those options that are no worse than any alternative count as sufficiently good, both satisficers and maximizers should be happy to accept the opting-for-the-best view.

§1.1.5 Best option versus best outcome

It's quite controversial to suppose that a subject ought to φ if and only if her φ-ing would bring about the (impersonally) best outcome. But the opting-for-the-best view doesn't suppose this. For the best *option* needn't be the one that would bring about the best *outcome*. By "best option," I just mean the option that's best in terms of whatever ultimately matters.[15] And what *ultimately matters* for a given subject at a given time is just whatever she ought to care about noninstrumentally at that time.[16] Thus, if one of the things that a subject should ultimately care about at present is that she doesn't take any present opportunity to violate someone's rights, then one thing that ultimately matters

---

15. The reader may wonder what makes an option best in terms of what ultimately matters. On this issue, I will, for the most part, remain neutral. But I can say this much: if the only thing that ultimately matters is how much utility there is, then it would, I think, be plausible to suppose that the best option is just the one that would produce more utility than any alternative option would. But things might be more complicated, for, perhaps, whether a subject treats a person as a mere means also ultimately matters. And, given this, it could be that an option is best only if it doesn't treat a person as a mere means, so it won't be best even if performing it would minimize the total instances in which the given subject treats a person as a mere means. Thus, it may be that what makes an option best in terms of something that ultimately matters isn't simply maximizing or minimizing that thing.

16. To illustrate, let's suppose that the utility of an option consists in how much aggregate happiness it produces. And let's suppose that the production of utility is the only thing that ultimately matters. In that case, the expected utility of an option would matter, but it wouldn't be something that *ultimately* matters. For it seems that performing the option with the greatest expected utility matters only because doing so gives one the best chance of maximizing utility. Moreover, choosing always to perform the option with the greatest expected utility matters only because doing so is instrumental to maximizing utility over time. Thus, expected utility isn't something that ultimately matters; it matters only insofar as it is instrumental with respect to maximizing utility. By contrast, those who think that fairness matters tend to think that it is something that ultimately matters. For they tend to think that even if the only option for making the distribution of utility fairer is one that fails to maximize utility, it may still be that we ought to opt for that option.

(at least, relative to her at this moment) is that she doesn't take any present opportunity to violate someone's rights. And this view is to be contrasted with, say, the view that what she should ultimately care about at present is her minimizing her rights violations over time such that she should perform now an option that would violate someone's rights if this would minimize her rights violations over time. On this contrasting view, then, what ultimately matters for her at present is not that she doesn't take any present opportunity to violate someone's rights but that she acts now so as to minimize her rights violations over time.

Next, consider one other view. On this view, two things ultimately matter for her at present: that (1) she doesn't take any present opportunity to violate someone's rights and that (2) the world contains as much aggregate happiness as possible. On this view, her best option in terms of what ultimately matters is the one that produces the most aggregate happiness without her taking any present opportunity to violate someone's rights. And this would be true even if she could bring about a much better *outcome* (impersonally speaking) by taking some present opportunity to violate someone's rights, thereby both minimizing her rights violations and maximizing aggregate happiness. Thus, the best option needn't be the one that would produce the best outcome.[17] Of course, it could be the one that would produce the best outcome, as it would be if, say, aggregate happiness was the only thing that ultimately matters. But it needn't be. For it could be, for instance, that never taking the present opportunity to violate someone's rights also matters. Or it could be that never taking the present opportunity to violate someone's rights is the only thing that matters—in which case, every option that didn't entail taking some present opportunity to violate someone's rights would be tied for best.

When thinking about what ultimately matters, it's important to note that I'm not assuming that only voluntary acts can be options. Recall that, as I've stipulatively defined the word "option," an option is just that which is eligible for deontic status. And, arguable, it's not just voluntary acts that are eligible for deontic status. For it seems, for instance, that a subject can be prohibited from believing a proposition on insufficient evidence or required to want what's best for her children. Yet believing and desiring are not (at least, not

---

17. To say that a subject ought to do what's best is ambiguous. It could mean either that (1) a subject ought to do what would bring about the impersonally best outcome or that (2) a subject ought to do what it would be best for her to do. The opting-for-the-best view concerns the latter: a subject ought to do what it would be best for her to do, which may or may not be what would bring about the impersonally best outcome. For more on this, see HURLEY 2017.

typically) voluntary acts—that is, acts that we perform at will. So although I'll often talk both about what a subject ought to "do" and about what option she ought to "perform," I'm intending for these verbs to be interpreted broadly such that believing, desiring, and intending all count as things that a subject "does" and "performs."[18] Thus, 'φ' ranges over whatever constitutes a subject's options, and this may include, say, believing some proposition, desiring some state of affairs, or intending to perform some action. Moreover, a subject's options may include conjunctive options. For instance, a subject may have the conjunctive option of asserting p while believing that it's not the case that p, which, of course, would in many contexts constitute lying. And if there can be different types of options, then there may be different sorts of things that ultimately matter in assessing these different types of options. For instance, it may be that, when it comes to assessing the option of forming a belief, what ultimately matters is whether the belief is true. Yet, when it comes to assessing the option of performing a voluntary act, it may be that what ultimately matters is whether the act maximizes happiness. Thus, it could be that what makes an option best in terms of what ultimately matters is that it contains only true beliefs and contains all and only those voluntary acts that maximize aggregate happiness. And, so, assessing whether some conjunctive option is best may involve assessing different conjuncts in terms of different criteria—for example, assessing beliefs in terms of the truth and voluntary acts in terms of the production of aggregate happiness.[19]

§1.1.6 The best must be sufficiently good

As I'll be using the term "best," the *best option* must be sufficiently good in addition to being better than every alternative. Of course, this is to do some violence to our ordinary usage of the word "best," but I'm willing to do so for the sake of preventing the opting-for-the-best view from having the controversial

---

18. So, the relevant *doings* include all things that are done in response to reasons, such as touching one's nose, thinking of potential problems for one's view, and forming the belief that it's raining as a result of feeling raindrops on one's head. They exclude, however, things that are not done in response to reasons, such as fainting, digesting, and perspiring. I'll have much more to say about this in §3.2.

19. Of course, it could also be that we should assess all options (regardless of type) according to the same criteria. For instance, Susanna Rinard (2018) has argued that we should assess believing that p in the same way that we assess performing an act x, such that if whether a subject ought to perform x just depends on whether her performing x would maximize aggregate happiness, then whether a subject ought to believe that p just depends on whether her believing that p would maximize aggregate happiness.

implication that a subject ought to perform an option so long as it is better than every alternative.

To see why this implication is controversial, consider *Incompatible Promises*. In this case, I've negligently made two promises—namely, P1 and P2—despite not having the option of keeping them both. Consequently, my options are (1) to break just P1, (2) to break just P2, and (3) to break both promises. Further suppose that it would be better if I were to break just P2 than if I were to break just P1, and better if I were to break just one than if I were to break both. Thus, my breaking just P2 is better than every alternative. Yet, despite this, some may deny that I ought to perform this option. They may claim that I'm in a dilemma such that I have no option that I ought to perform given that each of my options entails breaking a promise.

So, if we want to make the opting-for-the-best view as uncontroversial as possible (and I do), we'll need to understand "best" such that an option is best if and only if it is both sufficiently good and better than every alternative. Moreover, we'll need to understand "sufficiently good" to mean "good enough both in terms of how it compares to the alternatives and in terms of whatever the relevant noncomparative standards are." This way, the opting-for-the-best view can accept that, in the above case, there is no option that I ought to perform, because, in this case, I have no best option. For, according to the relevant noncomparative standards, none of my options in this case count as sufficiently good given that each constitutes breaking a promise. And this is true even though one of my options—namely, breaking just P2—is better than every alternative.

I should also note that I mean to allow for the possibility that a sufficiently good option could be truly awful. For there can be some situations in which all of a subject's options are truly awful. And although some will say that in such cases there is no option that the subject ought to perform, others will say that she ought to perform her least awful option. So, I mean for "sufficiently good" to be interpreted such that it's compatible both with the view that there are some situations in which no option is sufficiently good (because none of them meet the relevant noncomparative standards—for example, that of not constituting the breaking of a promise) and with the view that there are some situations in which some truly awful options are sufficiently good (because some of them meet the relevant comparative standards—for example, that of being less awful than the alternatives). And this is, in part, why I define *the best option* as the one that is both sufficiently good and better than every alternative and also why I define *a sufficiently good option* as one that meets both the relevant comparative standards and the relevant noncomparative standards.

Another reason for my insisting that the best option be sufficiently good to be permissible is that, if I didn't, I would have to allow either that some options that ought to be performed are impermissible or that an option can be both impermissible and what ought to be performed. And neither seems acceptable to me.

§1.1.7 "Option" versus "can"

There is a fair bit of controversy concerning whether "ought" implies "can."[20] But there can be no controversy concerning whether "ought" implies "option." For I'm using the word "option" as a term of art with a stipulative definition. By stipulation, an option is just whatever is eligible for deontic status such that, necessarily, an event has a deontic status only if it's an option for some subject. Or, to put things a bit more carefully, an *option* for a subject, S, just is any member of the set such that, for any possible event *e*, S's *e*-ing can have a deontic status only if it is a member of this set. So, even if it's coherent to suppose that a subject ought to *e* even though she can't *e*, it's incoherent to suppose that a subject ought to *e* even though she doesn't have the option of *e*-ing. Thus, even those who are skeptical about whether "ought" implies "can" should have no difficulty accepting the opting-for-the-best view.

The problem with the word "can" is that it isn't up to the task of helping us to differentiate between those things that are eligible for deontic status and those things that are not. To see why, consider that whereas the word "obligated" is able to take a far future event as its object, the word "can" isn't. Consequently, whereas it makes perfect sense to say "I am at present obligated to help my friend move six months from now," it's infelicitous to say "I can at present help my friend move six months from now." This is because, helping my friend move six months from now is something that I'll be able to do, if at all, only six months from now. And given that a far future event can be the object of a deontic status but not the object of the word "can," the word "can"

---

20. Regarding this controversy, see, for instance, SINNOTT-ARMSTRONG 1984 and STREUMER 2003. Personally, I find this issue rather uninteresting. It simply turns on whether there is any ordinary sense of the word "ought" and any ordinary sense of the word "can" such that "ought" implies "can." By contrast, the issues of whether "S ought to φ" implies "S has control over her φ-ing" and, if so, what type of control it implies that she must have seem much more interesting. And these are issues that I'll take up in chapters 2 and 3.

is ill-suited for doing the important philosophical work of distinguishing between what is and isn't eligible for deontic status. Thus, finding no ordinary word that does the job, I've had to co-opt the word "option" for this purpose, stipulating that I'll use it to mean "that which is eligible for deontic status."

In any case, it's clear enough that the set of a subject's options isn't coextensive with the set of things that she can do. For one, the set of things that she can do includes things that are not options for her. For instance, I can unintentionally knock over a glass of wine (indeed, clumsy people like myself do so all the time). Yet, this isn't an option for me. For even if the fate of the world depended on my unintentionally knocking over a glass of wine, I couldn't be obligated to do so. I could, of course, be obligated to perform an *intentional* act that would increase my chances of unintentionally knocking over a glass of wine (say, the intentional act of concussing myself after placing several glasses of wine around me). But I couldn't be obligated to perform the unintentional act of accidentally knocking over a glass of wine. For it seems that I can be obligated to do only that over which I exert some direct control. And I exert no direct control over whether I knock over a glass of wine unintentionally. It seems, then, that there are things that I can do that are not options for me.

Another reason to think that the set of a subject's options isn't coextensive with the set of things that she can do is that some of a subject's options include things that she can't do—at least, not by intending to do them. For instance, I can't seem to bring myself to form the intention to exercise. Nevertheless, I'm obligated to do so. For although I can't form this intention simply by intending to do so, I can and ought, it seems, to form it in (nonvoluntary) response to my awareness of the facts that constitute decisive reason for me to do so—that is, the facts linking exercising with leading a long and healthy life. So it seems that I can have an obligation to form this intention, and so I must have the option of forming this intention even though it isn't something I can do simply by intending to do it. (I'll have more to say about this in Chapter 3.)

§1.1.8 *Objective oughts versus subjective oughts*

The word "ought" has both an objective (or fact-relative) sense and a subjective (or evidence-relative) sense, and what makes the opting-for-the-best view fairly uncontroversial is that it concerns "ought" in the objective sense. I'll explain why this is shortly, but first, let's get clear on the two senses. To do so, it will be helpful to consider the following example.

Table 1.2 Pablo's Options in *Mine Shafts*

Option	Actual Lives Saved	Expected Lives Saved
Close gate 1	100	$(0.5 \times 100) + (0.5 \times 0) = 50$
Close gate 2	0	$(0.5 \times 0) + (0.5 \times 100) = 50$
Close gate 3	0	$(0.5 \times 90) + (0.5 \times 90) = 90$
Close no gate	0	$(0.5 \times 0) + (0.5 \times 0) = 0$

Mine Shafts: A hundred miners are trapped underground in one of two mine shafts. Floodwaters are rising, and the miners are in danger of drowning. Pablo can close only one of three floodgates. Closing gate 1 will save all 100 if they're in shaft A and 0 if they're in shaft B. Closing gate 2 will save 0 if they're in shaft A and all 100 if they're in shaft B. And closing gate 3 will save ninety (i.e., the ninety highest up in the shaft) regardless of which shaft they're in. Pablo can also close no gate in which case none of the miners will survive. Pablo knows that the miners are in either shaft A or shaft B, but he has no idea which. As a matter of fact, they're in shaft A. See Table 1.2.[21]

In thinking to himself and deliberating about what to do, Pablo should conclude that he ought (in some sense) to close gate 3—and let's assume that he knows all the relevant facts except those indicating which shaft the miners are in. His guessing which shaft they're in and then closing either gate 1 or gate 2 based on that guess would be too risky. He would thereby risk saving no one, whereas he is guaranteed to save ninety if he closes gate 3. And having concluded that he ought, in this sense, to close gate 3, he will, if conscientious, form the intention to do so.[22] Thus, we can rightly expect (in the normative, and not necessarily the probabilistic, sense of "expect") him to close gate 3. Moreover, if he fails to do so, we can rightly blame him—assuming,

---

21. This sort of example originates with REGAN 1980 (pp. 264–265, n. 1) and has been made famous, in this particular form, by Parfit in his 2011A (p. 159).

22. Strictly speaking, a subject's both being conscientious and believing that she subjectively ought to φ isn't sufficient to ensure that she intends to φ. She must also believe that she will φ if she intends to φ. For, if she doesn't believe this, it would be irrational for her to form the intention to φ. See BROOME 2013 (p. 25). And note that a *conscientious* person is one who is appropriately concerned with what ultimately matters.

at least, that he lacks any suitable excuse.[23] The sense in which Pablo ought to close gate 3 is what's known as the *subjective sense* of "ought," and the defining feature of this sense of "ought" is that we can legitimately (normatively) expect subjects to do what they ought to do in this sense. Moreover, we can legitimately hold them accountable (absent suitable excuse) for failing to do what they ought to have done in this sense, at least where this was, as it was with Pablo, also what they were obligated to do.[24]

What makes this sense of "ought" subjective is that what a subject ought to do in this sense depends on her subjective position—specifically, on her epistemic position concerning what her options are, how they relate to each other, which features of them ultimately matter, and how they compare with respect to these features.[25] Thus, someone, who (like Pablo) has no more reason for thinking that the miners are in shaft A than for thinking that they're in shaft B subjectively ought to close gate 3. But someone for whom the evidential probability that the miners are in shaft A is greater than 0.9 subjectively ought to close gate 1.[26] And someone for whom the evidential probability that the miners are in shaft B is greater than 0.9 subjectively ought to close gate 2. (I'm assuming that each of these three subjects is otherwise relevantly informed.)

---

23. Strictly speaking, the reason that it would be legitimate for us to blame Pablo if he were to fail to close gate 3 is that, in addition to this being what he subjectively ought to do, it's what he is subjectively obligated to do.

24. Thus, the subjective ought is the one that's "most immediately relevant to action" (JACKSON 1991, p. 472). And, following Michael Smith, I take the idea to be that the acts that subjectively ought to be performed "are those we can legitimately expect agents to do and criticize them for failing to do" (M. SMITH 2006, p. 142). Smith is, I believe, using "ought" to mean "obligated" here, for it is only when we fail to do what we are subjectively obligated to do that it is legitimate to criticize us. For a subject to be *accountable* for having φ-ed is for her to be praiseworthy or blameworthy for having φ-ed, thereby making her the appropriate target of either retributive attitudes (such as guilt and indignation) or meritorious attitudes (such as pride and admiration) in virtue of her having φ-ed. I'll have much more to say about this in Chapter 2.

25. As indicated above, this ought is sometimes called the *evidence-relative ought* because it is relative to the subject's evidence. Admittedly, there may be other subjective oughts, such as a *belief-relative ought*—an ought that's relative to the subject's beliefs. But these other subjective oughts will not concern us here. See PARFIT 2011A.

26. For any proposition p, the *evidential probability* that p for a given subject is the degree to which her body of evidence supports p. If the evidential probability that the miners are in shaft A is greater than 0.9, then the expected value of closing gate 1 will be greater than either that of closing gate 2 or that of closing gate 3. For if we take any number greater than 0.9 and multiply it by 100 lives, the product will be greater than 90 lives, which is the expected value of closing gate 3. And it will also be greater than the expected value of closing gate 2, which will be less than 10 lives given that the evidential probability that the miners are in shaft B is, in that case, less than 0.1.

So, as we've just seen, which act a subject subjectively ought to perform depends on what her evidence is. And the same holds for which attitude a subject subjectively ought to form. For instance, Pablo subjectively ought to believe that there's a significant chance that he'll save no one if he closes gate 1, because that's what his evidence suggests is very likely true. And, in general, a subject subjectively ought to believe what her evidence suggests is very likely true. Similarly, a subject subjectively ought to fear what her evidence suggests is very likely a danger to her, subjectively ought to admire those who her evidence suggests are very likely admirable, and subjectively ought to blame those who her evidence suggests are very likely blameworthy.

Of course, there is also an objective sense of "ought," which is, for the most part, independent of the subject's epistemic position.[27] Indeed, what differentiates the objective ought from the subjective ought is just the degree to which the subject's epistemic position is relevant to the latter but not the former. So, these two oughts coincide just when the given subject has full knowledge of what her options are, how they relate to each other, what ultimately matters, and how they compare in terms of what ultimately matters. Thus, in the objective sense, a subject ought to believe what is true, fear what is a danger to her, admire those who are admirable, blame those who are blameworthy, and choose the most choice-worthy of her options—and do so regardless of what her evidence is concerning who or what has these properties. Similarly, a subject objectively ought to perform what is in fact her best option regardless of what her evidence suggests is her best option.[28]

---

27. I'm not claiming that what a subject objectively ought to do is entirely independent of her epistemic position. For, perhaps, the acquisition of certain kinds of knowledge is something that ultimately matters. And if that's right, then, other things being equal, a subject who lacked such knowledge objectively ought to do what would lead to its acquisition. Thus, I haven't defined what a subject objectively ought to do in terms of what she would do if she were both conscientious and fully informed. Such a definition would commit the conditional fallacy (see JOHNSON 1999) and, consequently, wrongly disallow the possibility that a subject objectively ought to acquire the kinds of knowledge whose acquisition ultimately matters. It would be committed to wrongly disallowing this possibility since anyone who is fully informed would have no reason to acquire the knowledge that, being fully informed, she already has. So, instead, I hold that what a subject objectively ought to do is just a function of what her options are, how they relate to each other, what ultimately matters, and how they compare in terms of what ultimately matters. Such a view rightly leaves open the possibility that a subject's epistemic position may be relevant in determining what she objectively ought to do, allowing that a subject objectively ought to do what would lead her to acquire certain kinds of knowledge.

28. I'm papering over an important potential complication here. As noted in §1.1.1, there may be instances in which a subject should not perform her best option but should instead perform

Thus, Pablo objectively ought to close gate 1, and this holds even if his evidence erroneously suggests that the miners are in shaft B. Closing gate 1 is Pablo's best option, for what matters is his saving all one hundred miners, and his closing gate 1 is the only way for him to do this given that the miners are in shaft A. The fact that Pablo objectively ought to close gate 1 holds even if he has no way of knowing that closing gate 1 is his best option. For what a subject objectively ought to do just depends on the actual features of her options and not on what she takes those features to be, nor on what her evidence suggests that they are likely to be.

The idea that a subject ought to perform her best option (i.e., the option that is, in fact, best in terms of what ultimately matters) is plausible only if we interpret the ought in question to be the objective one. This is because there are several ways for it to turn out that a subject subjectively ought to perform something other than what is, in fact, her best option. First, the subject may be nonculpably ignorant of, or have misleading evidence regarding, some of the relevant nonnormative facts. Suppose, for instance, that, from Pablo's epistemic position, there is a greater than 0.9 evidential probability that the miners are in shaft B. In that case, closing gate 2 is his *best bet*—that is, it's what it would make most sense for a conscientious person of his abilities, capacities, and epistemic position to do in the circumstances. And so, he subjectively ought to close gate 2. Second, the subject may be nonculpably ignorant of, or have misleading evidence regarding, what her options are. Suppose, for instance, that Pablo has no idea that he has the option of closing gate 3. Perhaps, although easily accessible, the lever for closing gate 3 is hidden and unmarked. Consequently, he has no reason for thinking that he has the option of closing gate 3. And assume that he doesn't have time to go looking for any hidden levers. Given all this, it seems that he subjectively ought to close either gate 1 or gate 2, these being what, from his epistemic position, seem to be his only two options for saving some miners. Third, the subject may be nonculpably ignorant of, or have misleading evidence regarding, some of the relevant normative facts.[29] Suppose, for instance, that Pablo's evidence suggests that what

---

a suboptimal alternative that is entailed by her best option. Strictly speaking, then, I should say instead that a subject objectively ought to perform what is in fact *appropriately related to* her best option. (One possibility is that φ's being appropriately related to her best option consists in φ's being identical to her best option, but another possibility is that φ's being appropriately related to her best option consists in φ's being entailed by her best option.)

29. I reject the view that a subject can be only *culpably* ignorant of (or uncertain about) the relevant normative propositions given that they are knowable a priori. For it seems to me that a

ultimately matters is his packing heaven with more fresh souls. In that case, it seems that he subjectively ought to close no gate so as to pack heaven with more fresh souls. Fourth, Pablo may have certain cognitive limitations that prevent him from drawing certain helpful inferences. Suppose, for instance, that Pablo is cognitively disabled and so, is unable to figure out more than just the fact that the only way for him to have any chance of saving some of the miners is to close one of the three gates. In that case, it seems that he subjectively ought to arbitrarily select one of the three gates and close it. For we cannot legitimately expect someone who lacks the capacity for recognizing the reasons for choosing to close gate 3 over either gate 1 or gate 2 to act on those reasons.

So, we've seen that even though closing gate 1 is in fact Pablo's best option, this needn't be what he subjectively ought to do. And, in general, a subject may be nonculpably ignorant of what her best option is and consequently be subjectively required to do something else. To know what one's best option is, one must know what ultimately matters, what one's options are, how one's options relate to each other, which option is best in terms of what ultimately matters, whether every option is to be assessed in terms of its own goodness, etc. Moreover, one would have to be free of any significant cognitive impairments. But since a subject can be cognitively impaired and/or nonculpably ignorant of, or uncertain about, such things, it won't necessarily be that she *subjectively* ought to perform what is, in fact, her best option. Pablo's best option (viz., closing gate 1) is, then, only what Pablo objectively ought to do, not what he subjectively ought to do. And this is why

---

subject can be less than 100 percent confident in certain relevant normative propositions, and nonculpably so, even if these propositions are knowable a priori. After all, some a priori truths are far from obvious. Indeed, it seems that subjects should be less than 100 percent confident in the sorts of a priori normative propositions over which we find considerable disagreement among those seemingly in the best possible epistemic position to judge. Here, I'm thinking of normative problems such as those involving how to solve the nonidentity problem, which (if any) axioms of orthodox decision theory to reject, which (if any) axioms of standard deontic logic to reject, and whether we should assess an act such as my raising my left arm at t in terms of its own goodness or in terms of the goodness of the options that entail it. These seem to be truly difficult normative problems such that individuals can be nonculpably ignorant of (or uncertain about) their solutions. Indeed, it seems to me that people are required to be uncertain about their solutions given that there is considerable disagreement about their solutions even among those seemingly in the best epistemic position to judge. (Note that I'm not claiming that these people with differing judgments *are* epistemic equals, but only that they can *appear* to us to be so and that this is relevant in terms of what our credences in their judgments should be.) For more on these issues and for some other suggested truly difficult normative problems, see STAR 2015 (pp. 6–7). For a skeptical position regarding the relevance of at least one type of normative uncertainty (viz., moral uncertainty), see HARMAN 2015.

we should interpret the opting-for-the-best view as saying that subjects *objectively* ought to perform their best option. Indeed, we should, throughout this book, interpret all oughts and deontic statuses as being objective unless I explicitly say otherwise.

Of course, even if we deny that a subject subjectively ought to perform her best option, it may seem that she subjectively ought to perform the option with the greatest expected deontic utility, where *deontic utility* is a measure of how good an option is in terms of whatever ultimately matters and *expected deontic utility* is a probability distribution consisting in the set of mutually exclusive and jointly exhaustive possibilities concerning its deontic utility, with each possibility assigned an evidential probability such that the sum of these probabilities equals 1. But I doubt that even this much is true. For one, the subject may not know that the option with the greatest expected deontic utility is an option for her. And if she doesn't even know (and nonculpably so) that it's an option for her, I don't see how we could legitimately (normatively) expect her to perform it or blame her for failing to perform it. For another, the subject may not know (again, nonculpably so) that the option with the greatest expected deontic utility is her best bet. She may think—in accordance with her evidence—that her best bet is to perform the option that is most likely her best option. And in that case, I don't see how we could legitimately expect her to perform the option with the greatest expected deontic utility instead of what she thinks is most likely her best option. Nor it seems could we rightly blame her if she performs what she thinks is most likely her best option. Of course, as philosophers like Parfit (2011A, p. 159), Regan (1980, pp. 264–265, n. l), and Jackson (1991, pp. 462–463) have argued, she is mistaken in thinking that her best bet is to choose what's most likely her best option. For, as *Mine Shafts* demonstrates, an agent's best bet can sometimes be an option that has no chance of being her best option. After all, Pablo's best bet is to close gate 3 even though this has no chance of being his best option. But if a person is unaware (and nonculpably so) of such cases and, consequently, the reasons that Parfit, Regan, and Jackson have for thinking that an agent's best bet may have no chance of being her best option, it could be that her evidence supports the contention that her best bet is to choose what's most likely her best option. And since we're talking about what a subject subjectively ought to do, we must look at what it makes most sense for her to do from her epistemic position, not from the epistemic position of others who have made discoveries (admittedly, a priori discoveries) that she has not made. Last, it could be that the given subject lacks the cognitive abilities necessary to make the precise calculations needed to determine what her expectably best option is. And if she can't make these precise calculations, it would be unreasonable for us to expect her to act as the conclusions of these merely possible calculations would support her acting. Moreover, it would be inappropriate to blame her for acting contrary to what, from her epistemic position, is her best bet.

§1.1.9 Directive oughts versus evaluative oughts

As we've just seen, the opting-for-the-best view concerns whether an option *objectively* ought to be performed. Given this, some will worry that it's merely an evaluative view that tells us only how it would be desirable for a subject to respond, and not a practically useful view that directs her to respond in some way.[30] But this worry is misguided. The objective ought, although objective, is still a *directive ought* in that it directs its subject to perform some option, implying that she has a reason to perform that option. It is not, then, merely an *evaluative ought*, which tells her only that it would be good if some event were to occur—without implying that anyone could perform that event or has any reason to perform it.

To illustrate the difference between these two oughts, consider that although it makes perfect sense to claim that it ought to be (where this is the evaluative ought) both that Pablo closes gate 1 and that some hurricane turns south so as to miss the most populated areas, it makes sense only to claim that Pablo ought (where this is the directive ought) to close gate 1. It makes no sense to claim that the hurricane ought (where this is the directive ought) to turn south, for it makes no sense to claim that it has a reason to turn south. And whereas claiming that it ought to turn south implies that it has a reason to turn south, claiming that it ought to be that it turns south doesn't.

The reason it doesn't make sense to claim that the hurricane has a reason to turn south is that a reason for a subject to φ must be the sort of thing that she can respond to by φ-ing, but a hurricane cannot turn south in response to the fact that it would miss the most populated areas by doing so. Although it can physically respond to such things as changes in the ocean temperature, it cannot rationally respond to facts, for it lacks the capacity to cognize

---

30. John Gibbons presses this sort of objection against objective theories of practical and theoretical rationality in his 2013 (chap. 6).

facts as well as the capacity to rationally respond to such cognitions. It seems, then, that we should accept the following constraint on what can count as a reason.

> **The Response Constraint:** For any option φ, any subject S, and any proposition *p*, the fact that *p* constitutes a reason for S to φ only if both (1) S has the capacity to know or otherwise adequately cognize this fact and (2) her adequately cognizing this fact could, via the exercise of her rational capacities, *directly* cause her to φ—that is, without causing her to form the intention to do something that will, in turn, cause her to φ.[31]

We should accept this constraint, because, for one, it explains why a genuine normative reason to φ must be the sort of thing that can cause its subject to φ, such that, if it does, this will explain why she φ-ed (B. WILLIAMS 1995, p. 39). That is, any fact that constitutes a reason for her to φ must be one that she can apprehend and then, as a consequence of that apprehension's effects on her rational capacities, come to φ.[32] And for another, we should accept this constraint because it provides the best explanation for why some facts that make it desirable to φ constitute a reason to do so while others don't. Those that don't fail to meet the response constraint. To illustrate, consider the following three facts. First, consider the fact that the only way for Vojko to make it across the lake in time to rescue those on the other side is by walking across its liquid surface. Now, in virtue of this fact, it's certainly desirable for him to do so. But this fact is not one such that his coming to know it could, via the exercise of his rational capacities (or anything else), cause him to walk across its surface. Thus, it does not constitute a reason for him to do so.

Second, consider the fact that my forming the belief that I have an immortal soul would considerably lessen the anxiety that I have concerning death. Clearly, this fact makes it desirable for me to form this belief. Moreover, my coming to know this fact could, via wishful thinking, directly cause me to

---

31. This constraint has, in one form or another, been endorsed by many philosophers, see GIBBONS 2013, KELLY 2002, KIESEWETTER 2016, KOLODNY 2005, PARFIT 2011A (p. 51), RAZ 2011 (p. 28), SHAH 2006, and B. WILLIAMS 1981.

32. Here, I've been influenced by work such as GIBBONS 2013. But, unlike Gibbons, I don't think that a fact that constitutes a reason for a subject S to φ has to be in her ken. It just has to be one such that, were it in her ken, she could apprehend it and whose apprehension could in turn directly cause her to φ via her rational capacities.

form this belief. But to form this belief via wishful thinking is not to form it via my rational capacities. Indeed, I could not, *via my rational capacities*, form it as a result of my coming to know (or otherwise adequately cognizing) the fact that it would be beneficial to do so—at least, not without its first causing me to form the intention to do something that will, in turn, cause me to form this belief. But if I cannot, via my rational capacities, form this belief without going through the intermediary step of forming the intention to do something else, my forming this belief is not something that I have a reason to do—and this holds despite the fact that it would be desirable for me to do so.

Third, consider the fact that Rima could prevent millions of people from dying from cancer if she were to make the following keystrokes: D, e, a, r, SPACE, N, I, H, SPACE, D, i, r, e, c, t, o, r, : (and so it continues with the remaining 50,000 or so keystrokes needed to compose an email to the director of the National Institutes of Health that explains how to cure cancer in such a way that he or she will have to take it seriously). This fact, of course, makes it desirable for Rima to make this specific series of keystrokes, but it cannot constitute a reason for her to make them—at least, not if we accept the response constraint and acknowledge that she lacks the capacity to adequately cognize this fact.

Let me explain. To adequately cognize a given set of facts, one must be able to hold that set before one's mind (by, say, knowing them, perceiving them, visualizing them, or otherwise mentally apprehending them) in such a way that the formation of these mental states can then cause one, via the exercise of one's rational capacities, to φ. Thus, for the fact that p to constitute a genuine reason for a subject to φ, she must have the conceptual apparatus and cognitive capacities required to apprehend that p. Yet, the fact described (incompletely) above will, we'll assume, refer to terms, concepts, equations, and chemical formulae that are well beyond Rima's current abilities to apprehend. Moreover, the fact will refer to many more keystrokes than it's possible for someone with her limited human cognition to hold before the mind (by, say, memorizing them). Perhaps, if Rima had a photographic memory and was shown a visual representation of the entire series, she could hold the entire series before her mind. And, perhaps, if she were some sort of savant with respect to remembering complex sequences of characters, she could hold the entire series before her mind as some complex belief that she acquired via memorization. But we'll assume that she lacks such capacities. And, thus, the best that she can do is to form the much simpler belief that there is some unknown and complex sequence of characters that she could type into her computer that would constitute her disseminating the cure for cancer. But this mental state couldn't, via the exercise of her rational capacities, cause her to disseminate the cure for cancer. For this mental state lacks the specific content regarding what the characters need to be, which is information that she needs in order to execute this complex series of keystrokes—or so we'll assume.

The point, then, is that when it comes to our determining what a subject objectively ought to do, we are to hold her capacities fixed. For a subject's obligations are meant to be obligations to which she could respond, not obligations to which some more cognitively sophisticated version of herself could respond. Thus, what a person is objectively obligated to do coincides with what she, given her capacities, would be subjectively obligated to do if she were to possess all the relevant knowledge that she is, given her capacities, capable of possessing. And this explains why Rima is not obligated to disseminate the cure for cancer by typing out a certain series of keystrokes even though it would be desirable for her to do so. For the problem for her with respect to typing out this series of keystrokes is not merely that she doesn't know what the series is. Rather, it's that she lacks the capacities needed to possess such knowledge. And since she lacks the capacity to possess such knowledge she cannot have an obligation (not even an objective one) to act as she might act if she were to possess such knowledge.[33]

So, we've now seen three instances in which a fact in virtue of which it would be desirable for a subject to φ doesn't constitute a reason for her to φ. And, given this, we should conclude that to say that a subject objectively ought to φ is to say more than just that it would be desirable for her to φ. This is because the claim that a subject objectively ought to φ necessarily implies that she has a reason to φ. And, as we've just seen, there are many instances in which it would be desirable for a subject to φ even though, given the response constraint, she doesn't have a reason to φ. So, although it makes perfect sense to claim that it would be desirable for me to walk on water, it makes no sense to claim that I objectively ought to walk on water given that I could not respond to this fact by walking on water. Therefore, contrary to the worry in question, the objective ought is not merely an evaluative ought, but a directive ought. Consequently, the opting-for-the-best view isn't making the trivial claim that it is, in some sense, desirable for a subject to opt for her best option, but is instead making the nontrivial claim that she objectively ought to opt for her best option and, consequently, has a reason to do so. And that reason

---

33. For more on such cases, see CARLSON 1999A, HOWARD-SNYDER 1997, and HOWARD-SNYDER 1999.

is one that she could respond to provided she were to acquire the necessary knowledge—knowledge that she has the capacity to acquire.[34]

Admittedly, when engaged in our first-person practical deliberations, our end-goal is to figure out what we subjectively ought to do, not what we objectively ought to do. But this is not to say that the objective ought is irrelevant to our first-person deliberations. Indeed, it's quite relevant. For our deliberations about what we subjectively ought to do depend on our judgments about what we objectively ought to do. For instance, Pablo's judgment that he subjectively ought to close gate 3 is based on such judgments as the following: (1) that he objectively ought to save all the miners; (2) that, of all the options that he objectively ought not to perform, his closing gate 3 is the least bad; (3) that, of all the options that he objectively ought not to perform, closing the gate that would save no miners is, by far, the worst; and (4) that in closing either gate 1 or gate 2 he would be taking a very substantial risk of closing the gate that would save no miners. Thus, it's important to investigate what we objectively ought to do to ensure that these judgments on which we base our first-person practical deliberations are themselves justified.[35]

Of course, my response to the above worry has presupposed the response constraint, which is not uncontroversial. So, let me respond to two worries about it. One worry is that it's supposedly subject to the following sort of counterexample. Nate hates all parties except for successful surprise parties, which he loves.[36] It seems, then, that the fact that there is a surprise party that he knows nothing about waiting for him at home is a reason for him to go home. Yet Nate's adequately cognizing this fact couldn't, via the exercise of his rational capacities, directly cause him to go home, because if he knew that there was a surprise party waiting for him at home, it wouldn't be a successful one, so it wouldn't be one that he had any reason to attend.

I'm not exactly sure what to say about such cases. Nevertheless, I deny that the fact that there is a surprise party waiting for Nate at home is a reason for him to go home. Of course, this is not to deny that he has a reason to go home. Indeed, the fact that his life would go better if he were to go home is a reason for him to go home. And the response constraint would certainly

---

34. The opting-for-the-best view is clearly not a trivial view, as there are views that are incompatible with it, such as Gert's earlier view, absolute level satisficing utilitarianism, and, as we'll see below, a certain kind of rule-consequentialism.

35. See PORTMORE 2011 (chap. 1) for more on this.

36. This example is adapted from SCHROEDER 2007 (p. 33).

allow this to be so. But suppose that Nate was unable to adequately cognize any fact other than the fact that there's a surprise party waiting for him at home. In that case, I must deny that Nate has any reason to go home. But I don't find this counterintuitive. It would, of course, be counterintuitive to deny that it would be good for Nate to go home. But no one denies this. I deny only that Nate has a reason to go home, a reason to which he's incapable of responding. This, it seems to me, is no more counterintuitive than denying that the hurricane has a reason to turn south, a reason to which it's incapable of responding.[37]

Others worry about the response constraint on the grounds that it's inextricably tied to Bernard Williams's internalism about reasons (1981). But the two are not inextricably tied together. For although Williams relies on the response constraint as a premise in his argument for internalism, it constitutes but one premise in his argument. Consequently, we can accept this premise without accepting his conclusion (i.e., internalism). And this is important because internalism is quite controversial. According to *internalism*, a subject has a reason to φ only if she could come to φ via a sound deliberative route from the motivations that she already has in her actual motivational set. And this view implies (implausibly, I believe) that a person who is kicking her pet dog may have no reason to stop doing so. For there may be nothing in her motivational set that could lead her to stop doing so—perhaps she just doesn't care at all whether her dog suffers. To some like myself, this is an unacceptable implication of internalism. But the proponent of the response constraint needn't accept this implication. For the proponent of the response constraint can just deny that reasons must appeal to the agent's actual motivational set as opposed to the motivational set that she would have if she had all and only the motivational states that she ought to have. Thus, the proponent of the response constraint could point out that this woman is capable of cognizing the fact that her dog's suffering is bad, and that if she were to respond appropriately to this cognition via her rational capacities, she would then come to desire that her dog not suffer, and, as a result, she would be moved to stop kicking her dog.

I HAVE NOW clarified many aspects of the opting-for-the-best view, explaining what I mean by such notions as "best," "ought," and "option." The hope is that, as a result, you'll recognize just how uncontroversial the view is. Indeed, this view should seem

---

37. I'm not alone in thinking that such putative counterexamples to the response constraint are far from conclusive—see, for instance, KIESEWETTER 2016 (p. 769).

no more controversial than the thought that whether an event has a deontic status, and, if it does, what particular deontic status it has, depends both on whether it's a member of some proper subset of possible events and on how it compares to the alternative members in this set in terms of what ultimately matters. So long as you accept this thought, you should accept the opting-for-the-best view. But to ensure that you see the view as uncontroversial as I do, I will in the next section explain just how ecumenical it is.

But before I do, I need to add to it. For, as it stands, the opting-for-the-best view concerns only one kind of deontic status: the status of being what ought to be done. There are, of course, several other distinct deontic statuses: permissible, impermissible, obligatory, optional, and supererogatory. So, if we want to provide a more complete account of an option's possible objective deontic statuses, we need to adopt the following expanded version of the opting-for-the-best view.

> **The Opting-for-the-Best View:** There is a set of events, which is a proper subset of all possible events and which I call the set of S's options (or 'O' for short) such that, for any subject S and any possible event e, whether S's e-ing has a deontic status depends on whether e is a member of O. And, if it is a member of O, then what particular deontic status it has depends on how it compares to the alternative members of O such that, for any member φ of a certain subset (perhaps, a proper subset) of O,
> - (OUGHT) S ought to φ if and only if φ is the best member of this subset of O;
> - (PERMI) S is permitted to φ if and only if φ is one of the sufficiently good members of this subset of O; and
> - (SUPER) S's φ-ing is supererogatory if and only if there is some alternative member of this subset of O, ψ, such that (1) she is both permitted to φ and permitted to ψ and (2) her φ-ing is better than her ψ-ing.[38]

It's important to note that, in the above formulation and elsewhere in this book, I leave implicit that the word "objectively" should modify each deontic status. Thus, strictly speaking, "S ought to φ" should read

---

38. I don't personally find that it's necessary, but if we wanted to, we could add some further conditions to SUPER, such as that φ-ing would be contrary to S's self-interest and/or that S would be morally praiseworthy for φ-ing.

"S objectively ought to φ," "S is permitted to φ" should read "S is objectively permitted to φ," and "S's φ-ing is supererogatory" should read "S's φ-ing is objectively supererogatory." I also leave implicit that for each bi-conditional, the right side grounds the left side. For instance, I leave implicit that if a subject ought to φ, this is in virtue of the fact that φ is the best member of this subset of O.

Even this expanded formulation of the opting-for-the-best view doesn't itself tell us whether an act is wrong, optional, or obligatory, but it needn't do so. For we can derive such verdicts from the opting-for-the-best view given that these three additional statuses are all interdefinable with that of being permissible. Here's how: (OPTIO) a subject's φ-ing is *optional* if and only if she is both permitted to φ and permitted to refrain from φ-ing, (WRONG) a subject's φ-ing is *wrong* (or impermissible) if and only if φ is an option that she's not permitted to perform, and (OBLIG) a subject is *obligated* to φ if and only if she is permitted to φ but not to perform any alternative to φ.[39]

Importantly, I take the two added clauses—PERMI and SUPER—to be just as uncontroversial as OUGHT. So, I have not made the view more controversial in expanding upon it as I have. Consider, first, that PERMI seems incontrovertible. After all, to say that an option is sufficiently good is just to say that it's good enough to count as permissible. Thus, for at least a certain subset of a subject's options, that option is permissible if and only if it is sufficiently good.[40] And consider, second, that SUPER seems relatively uncontroversial. For, to say that an act is supererogatory is just to say it goes beyond the call of duty and so exceeds what's minimally required. Thus, for the performance

---

39. Others may suggest that we should instead define "obligatory" such that a subject is obligated to φ if and only if all the alternatives to her φ-ing are impermissible. The problem with this is that it forces us either to rule out, on mere definitional grounds, the possibility of there being a situation in which all a subject's options are impermissible or to accept that, in such situations, each of these impermissible options is obligatory. Both seem problematic. See VALLENTYNE 1992.

40. Note that I'm not claiming that, for *any* option, an option is permissible if and only if it is sufficiently good. That's false. To see why, consider the case in which two children, baby Nestor and baby Ángel, are trapped inside a burning building and you're the only one who could possibly rescue one or both them. It seems that safeguarding your own welfare by rescuing neither child is sufficiently good to count as permissible. Moreover, it seems that your going into the building and rescuing just one of the two is better than your rescuing neither. And, yet, it's clearly impermissible for you to enter the burning building and rescue just one of the two even though this is better than the sufficiently good option of rescuing neither. This is known as the *all or nothing problem*, and I'll have much more to say about it in §6.4.

of an option to exceed what's minimally required, it must, as SUPER states, be better than some permissible alternative.[41]

And before moving on to the next section, let me note that I mean for the opting-for-the-best view to be neutral among various qualified and unqualified interpretations of ought/permissible/supererogatory. Thus, if we leave the opting-for-the-best view as it is, then we leave "ought," "permissible," and "supererogatory" unqualified. And, in that case, the opting-for-the-best view is telling us that what a subject just plain ought to do—that is, what she ought to do, all things considered—is perform her best option.[42] But if we want, we can add whatever qualifier we like in front of "ought," "permissible," and "supererogatory" in the above formulation (be it "morally," "rationally," "prudentially," "aesthetically," or whatever) so long as we also add that same qualifier in front of "best," "good," and "better." Thus, the moral version of the opting-for-the-best view tells us that a subject *morally* ought to perform the *morally* best member of the relevant set, and the rational version of the opting-for-the-best view tells us that S's φ-ing is *rationally* supererogatory if and only if there is some alternative member of that set, ψ, such that (1) she is both *rationally* permitted to φ and *rationally* permitted to ψ and (2) her φ-ing is *rationally* better than her ψ-ing.

Note, then, that I want to allow not only for the possibility that some options are *morally* supererogatory but also for the possibility that some options are *rationally* supererogatory. Of course, the idea that some options are rationally supererogatory may seem strange at first, but I think that we should accept that there could be such options. After all, suppose that I rationally ought to order the lobster bisque because (1) pleasing others is one of my ends, (2) my ordering the lobster bisque would slightly please the waiter who recommended it to me, (3) ordering the lobster bisque is otherwise just as rationally good as ordering the alternative (viz., the turtle soup),

---

41. Some act-utilitarians (e.g., HARWOOD 2003 and VESSEL 2010) have denied this, claiming that an optional act that produces more happiness for others than some permissible alternative is morally supererogatory even if it is not any morally better than that permissible alternative. For instance, suppose that I can maximize utility by either φ-ing or ψ-ing, and assume that the only relevant difference between the two is that whereas my φ-ing will produce 10 units of happiness for me and 0 units for you, my ψ-ing will produce 0 units for me and 10 units for you. Some act-utilitarians claim that, in such a case, my ψ-ing is morally supererogatory even though it isn't any morally better for an agent to act so as to ensure that others receive more of some maximal quantity of utility. I find this implausible and explain why elsewhere—see PORTMORE 2011 (pp. 91–93).

42. Some reject the idea that there is such a thing as what a subject ought to do, all things considered—see, for instance, COPP 1997B. But see DORSEY 2016 for a persuasive reply.

and (4) furthering my ends is something that ultimately matters vis-à-vis my acting rationally. Still, we might think that I'm not rationally obligated to order the lobster bisque. We may think that the fact that my ordering the lobster bisque would further some minor end of mine and to such a trivial extent is merely an *enticing reason*—a reason that favors the option in a way that doesn't open me up to criticism should I ignore it.[43] And, if so, we should think that this is a case where my ordering the lobster bisque is rationally supererogatory given that there is the alternative of ordering the turtle soup, which is such that (1) I am both rationally permitted to order the lobster bisque and rationally permitted to order the turtle soup, and (2) my ordering the lobster bisque is rationally better than my ordering the turtle soup.

§1.2 The Ecumenical Nature of the View

The opting-for-the-best view is quite ecumenical. Apart from its commitment to the things that ultimately matter being such that we can rank some options as better than others in terms of them, the view is almost entirely neutral with respect to substantive issues—the one exception, we'll see, is the issue of whether there can be obligation dilemmas. To illustrate just how ecumenical it is, consider the following six points.

First, the view is neutral both regarding what ultimately matters and regarding how many things ultimately matter. For, as far as the opting-for-the-best view is concerned, the things that ultimately matter may include utility, justice, fidelity, fairness, beneficence, self-improvement, obedience to God, justifiability to others, respect for autonomy, or any set of such things. Moreover, if it turns out that several things ultimately matter, the view will be neutral on how these things function together to determine what's best. Some considerations may trump, silence, intensify, or undermine others in the determination of what's best (or sufficiently good). And it may even be that some of these considerations make an option permissible but not obligatory. This is important, because some philosophers think that whereas the fact that an option is significantly less harmful to *the agent* than the alternatives can make it obligatory, the fact that it is significantly less harmful to *others* than the alternatives cannot. They hold that the fact that an option is significantly

---

43. For more on the notion of an enticing reason, see DANCY 2004.

less harmful to *others* than the alternatives can only make an option permissible.[44] The opting-for-the-best view allows for such possibilities.

Second, as far as the opting-for-the-best view is concerned, it may be that several of the things that ultimately matter are incommensurable with each other. And when two options are better than all the others but incommensurable with each other, the view will allow either that they are both permissible or both impermissible. The view could even hold that it's just indeterminate whether they're permissible or not.

Third, as far as the view is concerned, it may be that which options are sufficiently good or best depends on facts about the subject in question. It could be, for instance, that what matters most relative to me (i.e., what I should be most concerned about) is that *I* not kill anyone, but that what matters most relative to you (i.e., what you should be most concerned about) is that *you* not kill anyone. And it could be that what matters most relative to me is that I not kill anyone now as opposed to sometime in the future. Also, it could be that I'm permitted to perform certain types of acts given that my culture condones such acts but that you are prohibited from performing such acts given that your culture condemns them. So, as far as the opting-for-the-best view is concerned, what an agent ought to do can be time-relative, agent-relative, culture-relative, or any other sort of relative.

Fourth, the opting-for-the-best view is compatible with most normative theories and with all plausible normative theories. Indeed, the only theories that it's incompatible with are those that, like absolute level satisficing utilitarianism, implausibly deny that whether a subject ought to φ can depend on whether there is a better alternative. Yet, every plausible normative theory accepts, explicitly or implicitly, that the availability of better alternatives matters—that, for instance, whether you did what you ought to have done in saving only baby Nestor depends on whether you had the option of just as easily saving both baby Nestor and baby Ángel. Clearly, maximizing act-consequentialist theories (which hold that an act is permissible if and only if there is no alternative whose outcome is better than its outcome) explicitly endorse the view that alternatives matter. But most nonconsequentialist theories (and, indeed, all plausible ones) endorse some version of the principle of beneficence, which makes alternative options relevant by holding that

44. This is analogous to Josh Gert's claim that whereas some considerations (e.g., those involving harm to oneself) play both a requiring role and a justifying role in determining the deontic statuses of one's actions, other considerations (e.g., those involving benefits to others) have only a justifying role to play. See GERT 2004 and 2012.

a subject ought, other things being equal, to provide the greatest benefit possible.[45] Clearly, Rossian pluralists accept such a principle (W. D. ROSS 1930), as do virtue ethicists (e.g., FOOT 1985). And even Kantians hold that there is an imperfect duty of beneficence (see, e.g., HILL 2002). It seems, then, that all plausible theories accept (at least, implicitly) that alternatives matter.

In any case, so long as a theory accepts that alternatives matter, we can formulate it as a version of the opting-for-the-best view. To illustrate, suppose that a theory holds that a subject's φ-ing is permissible if and only if φ is F, where 'F' stands for some fundamental permissible-making feature of options, such as "productive of maximal aggregate happiness," "in accordance with Kant's categorical imperative," or "how a virtuous person would characteristically act in the situation." To formulate this theory as a version of the opting-for-the-best view, we need only supplement it with the relevant views concerning what's best, better, and sufficiently good. Thus, to accommodate PERMI, we simply need to supplement it with the view that an option is sufficiently good if and only if it is F. And if the theory holds that a subject's φ-ing is supererogatory if and only if φ is G, then we simply need to supplement it with the view that 'G' stands for something such as "productive of more than the maximal amount of aggregate happiness," "productive of more aggregate happiness than is required by the categorical imperative," or "productive of more aggregate happiness than a virtuous person would characteristically produce in the situation."[46] Thus, the opting-for-the-best view is compatible with any normative theory that acknowledges the normative significance of alternatives.

---

45. It's not only by endorsing the principle of beneficence that nonconsequentialist theories commit themselves to the relevance of alternatives. Any nonconsequentialist theory that holds that some acts are supererogatory (and thus better than some permissible alternatives) is committed to the relevance of alternatives. The same holds for any nonconsequentialist theory that adopts Kamm's principle of secondary permissibility, which permits an agent to push an innocent bystander in front of a trolley to save five lives at the cost of this bystander's leg, but only if an alternative is to save the five lives at the cost of this bystander's life by redirecting the trolley away from the five and toward the bystander (see KAMM 2007, p. 26). And the same holds for any nonconsequentialist theory that accepts that an act that is mutually beneficial (beneficial both to the agent and the patient) can be wrong because it's exploitive, as where there is an alternative that is also mutually beneficial but that more fairly distributes these benefits between the agent and the patient.

46. Admittedly, no option can produce more than the maximal amount of aggregate happiness. But the point is that even though maximizing act-utilitarianism doesn't allow for supererogatory acts, we can still formulate it as a version of the opting-for-the-best view by taking 'G' to stand for something that ensures that no option will be supererogatory, as I've done here by suggesting that it could stand for "productive of more than the maximal amount of aggregate happiness."

Fifth, the opting-for-the-best view is compatible with both maximizing and satisficing theories and, relatedly, with both theories that allow for supererogatory acts and theories that don't. For instance, it can take a maximizing form that doesn't allow for supererogatory acts by holding that only those options that are no worse than any alternative count as sufficiently good. In which case, no option could go beyond the call of duty, for no option could, then, be any better than one that is sufficiently good. But the opting-for-the-best view could, instead, take a satisficing form by allowing that some sub-optimal options are sufficiently good and, thus, permissible. And this would leave room for supererogatory acts—acts that are better than the ones that are merely sufficiently good.

Sixth, the opting-for-the-best view is compatible with *prohibition dilemmas*, situations in which each of a subject's options is prohibited such that she has no permissible course of action (VALLENTYNE 1989). To illustrate, recall *Incompatible Promises*, the case in which I've negligently made two promises, P1 and P2, despite not having the option of keeping both. As far as the opting-for-the-best view is concerned, it could be that none of my options are permissible and that, therefore, I face a prohibition dilemma. For it could be that on the relevant noncomparative standard, an option counts as sufficiently good only if it doesn't constitute breaking a promise. And since each of my mutually exclusive and jointly exhaustive options constitute breaking a promise, none of them will be sufficiently good. Alternatively, it could be that there is no such noncomparative standard for being sufficiently good and that I'm therefore permitted (indeed, obligated) to perform the option that's better than every alternative: namely, breaking just P2. The opting-for-the-best view is neutral regarding such issues.[47]

Nevertheless, the opting-for-the-best view is incompatible with *obligation dilemmas*, situations in which a subject is both obligated to φ and obligated to ψ and yet doesn't have the option of both φ-ing and ψ-ing (VALLENTYNE 1989). For the opting-for-the-best view is committed to what's known as *joint satisfiability*: if a subject is both obligated to φ and obligated to ψ, then she has the option of both φ-ing and ψ-ing (KIESEWETTER 2018). This commitment,

---

47. Although the view is compatible both with the view that there are prohibition dilemmas and with the view that there are no prohibition dilemmas, we should think that there are no prohibition dilemmas if we take an obligation to perform an act to necessitate an obligation to form the intention to perform it. For take the above case concerning the two incompatible promises. In that case, it seems much more plausible to suppose that I'm obligated to form the intention to perform the option that constitutes my breaking just P2 than to suppose that I'm not obligated to intend to perform any of my options.

however, should be neither surprising nor worrying given that the opting-for-the-best view limits the sorts of events eligible for deontic status to only those that count as options for the subject. And it does so precisely because the relevant practical obligations are meant to be *intention-guiding* in the sense that each obligation to act necessitates an obligation to intend to perform that act—or, at least, to intend to do something that entails performing that act.[48]

Joint satisfiability follows from the intention-guiding nature of practical obligations given that there is a consistency requirement on beliefs and intentions. "There is, in particular, a rational demand that one's intentions, taken together with one's beliefs, fit together into a consistent model of one's future" (BRATMAN 2009, p. 29). We can state this demand more precisely if we stipulate that when someone intends to φ the propositional content of her intention is the proposition that she φs. The requirement, then, is that a subject must be such that the set consisting of the propositional contents of all her beliefs and all her intentions is logically consistent (J. ROSS 2009, p. 244).[49] Thus, if the set consisting of the propositional contents of all her beliefs and all her intentions is logically inconsistent, then that's a set of beliefs and intentions that it's irrational for her to have. So, the possibility of an obligation dilemma would imply that believing what's true while having the intentions that one is required to have is logically incompatible with one's being as one is required to be—that is, consistent. And that's just absurd. Being knowledgeable couldn't be incompatible with fulfilling one's obligations.[50]

---

48. Thus, from the fact that I'm obligated to refrain from killing my daughter, it doesn't follow that I'm obligated to form the specific intention to refrain from killing her. It's enough that I form the more general intention to do right by my family given that this entails my refraining from killing her.

49. Besides Bratman (2009) and J. Ross (2009), Wedgwood (2007, p. 109) endorses this view. And note that this is not the metaphysical view that intending to φ involves believing that one will φ. Rather, it is the normative view that intending to φ requires one to believe that one will φ. For a defense of this view, see BRATMAN 1987.

50. For more on this, see both Chapter 4 and KIESEWETTER 2015 (pp. 929–934). What Kiesewetter says is along similar lines to what I say in PORTMORE 2011 (pp. 181–183). The main difference is that whereas Kiesewetter's argument is based on the procedural rational requirement that a subject be such that, if she believes that she's obligated to φ, she intends to φ, my argument in my 2011 is based on the substantive rational requirement that she intends to φ if she is obligated to φ. But both arguments argue against the plausibility of conflicting obligations on the basis of this sort of connection between being (or believing that one is) obligated to φ and having a substantive (or procedural) rational requirement to intend to φ along with the idea that rationality requires that a subject to be such that, if she believes she will not both φ and ψ, then she does not both intend to φ and intend to ψ.

So we should deny the possibility of obligation dilemmas and accept joint satisfiability.[51]

More formally, the argument for joint satisfiability (and against obligation dilemmas) is as follows:

(1.1) It is not the case that <if a subject is both obligated to φ and obligated to ψ, then she has the option of both φ-ing and ψ-ing>. In other words, there is a subject who is both obligated to φ and obligated to ψ but doesn't have the option of both φ-ing and ψ-ing. [Assumption for *reductio*]

(1.2) Thus, if this subject believes what's true, then she'll believe that she's both obligated to φ and obligated to ψ but doesn't have the option of both φ-ing and ψ-ing. [From 1.1]

(1.3) For all actions x and all subjects S, if S is obligated to do x, then she is obligated to intend to do something that entails her doing x. [From the fact that practical obligations are intention-guiding]

(1.4) Thus, if this subject intends to do all that she is obligated to intend to do, she will both intend to do something that entails her φ-ing and intend to do something that entails her ψ-ing. [From 1.1 and 1.3]

(1.5) Thus, if this subject believes what's true and intends to do all that she is obligated to intend to do, she'll believe that she doesn't have the option of both φ-ing and ψ-ing while both intending to do something that entails her φ-ing and intending to do something that entails her ψ-ing. [From 1.2 and 1.4]

(1.6) A subject who believes that she doesn't have the option of both φ-ing and ψ-ing while both intending to do something that entails her φ-ing and intending to do something that entails her ψ-ing has an irrational set of beliefs and intentions. [From the consistency requirement on beliefs and intentions]

---

51. Even those who endorse obligation dilemmas admit that they're not using "obligation" in the same intention-guiding sense that I'm using it—the sense that's tied to intention formations. For instance, Tessman (2015, p. 8) is explicit in saying that because it is impossible to fulfill an obligation to jointly φ and ψ when this is not option, such an obligation demands no action or intention. Thus, she is using "obligation" in what we might call the action-assessment sense, where "one can say that a moral agent both makes a correct action-guiding decision [that is, forms the correct intention] and yet, in acting on that decision, commits an act that one can assess as morally bad, or in some sense wrong" (2015, p. 32, n. 37).

(1.7) Thus, if this subject believes what's true and intends to do all that she is obligated to intend to do, then she'll have an irrational set of beliefs and intentions. [From 1.5 and 1.6]

(1.8) It's not the case that <if this subject believes what's true and intends to do all that she is obligated to intend to do, she'll have an irrational set of beliefs and intentions>. For it's implausible to suppose that a subject who believes what's true and intends to do all that she is obligated to intend to do has an irrational set of beliefs and intentions. [Assumption]

(1.9) Therefore, if a subject is both obligated to φ and obligated to ψ, then she has the option of both φ-ing and ψ-ing. [From 1.1–1.9 by *reductio*][52]

The two most controversial premises are, I believe, 1.3 and 1.6. I'll take each in turn. Premise 1.3 is, I believe, intuitively plausible. If you're required to perform an action, then, given that no one could be required to perform an action unintentionally, you must be required to form the intention to perform it—or, at least, the intention to perform something that entails performing it, which is what's required for performing it intentionally. But there may seem to be counterexamples to the view that practical obligations are intention-guiding. First, it may seem that I could be obligated to act spontaneously even if I'm not obligated to form the intention to do so given that such an intention would only be self-defeating. But we should deny that I'm obligated to act spontaneously if this isn't something that I can do intentionally. We should hold, instead, only that I am obligated to perform (intentionally) some distinct act that would increase the chances that I'll act spontaneously—for example, the act of consuming a few stiff drinks. Second, it may seem that I'm obligated to refrain from torturing children even though I'm not obligated to form the intention to refrain from torturing children. After all, if I need to form the intention to refrain from torturing children to prevent myself from doing so, something has gone terribly wrong. But although I admit that something has gone wrong if this is so, it seems that I should form some intention that entails my refraining from torturing children—perhaps, the general intention to refrain from hurting others.[53] In any case, if I do find myself

---

52. This argument is, in part, inspired by one found in KIESEWETTER 2018, which is a response to WHITE 2017, which argues against joint satisfiability. This argument differs from Kiesewetter's, though, in that it concerns the objective (i.e., fact-relative) sense of obligation.

53. See note 48.

tempted to torture children, I should certainly resolve (and thereby intend) to refrain from doing so. So there seems to be no good counterexample to 1.3.

I also find 1.6 intuitively compelling. But, as with 1.3, there may seem to be counterexamples to it. One putative counterexample is the preface paradox. Imagine that a nonfiction writer apologizes in the preface to her book for the inevitable fact that at least one of the other claims in the book is false, and false despite her best efforts to carefully research each one. So, either she ought not to believe all these other claims or the consistency requirement (i.e., 1.6) is false. And it may seem that since it's not at all subjectively irrational for her to believe all these other claims given how carefully she's researched them, we must reject the consistency requirement.

But this is, in fact, no counterexample to the consistency requirement. For although it may be subjectively rational for her to believe all these other claims, she ought not to believe all of them. For we're assuming that some are false, and one (objectively) ought not to believe false claims. So, although she's right to believe that not all the other claims in the book are true, she's wrong to believe all of them—specifically, she's wrong to believe the false ones.

Nevertheless, there are other putative counterexamples to the consistency requirement. Consider, for instance, the Cathedral Paradox.

> Susan is planning her trip to Europe. There are 20 cathedrals she would like to visit. Each one has a fee. She really would like to see each one. . . . [But] she can only afford 19 cathedrals. . . . Let the cathedrals number 1 through 20. And let ϕ_n be the action of visiting cathedral n. Susan intends ϕ_1, intends ϕ_2, . . . and intends ϕ_{20}. However, Susan knows that it is impossible for her to perform the conjunctive action ϕ_1, . . . and ϕ_{20}. She simply doesn't have the cash. And so Susan plans to skip at least one cathedral, intending the action: not ϕ_1 or . . . or not ϕ_{20}. (GOLDSTEIN 2016, p. 2)[54]

Either Susan ought not to have all these intentions or the consistency requirement is false. And since there seems to be nothing subjectively irrational

---

54. Shpall (2016) offers a similar example. Both Shpall and Goldstein are concerned with the following subjective version of the consistency requirement: a subject is subjectively obligated to be such that the set consisting of the propositional contents of all her beliefs and all her intentions is logically consistent. By contrast, I'm concerned with the following objective version: a subject is objectively obligated be such that the set consisting of the propositional contents of all her beliefs and all her intentions is logically consistent.

about her having all these intentions, it may seem that we must reject the consistency requirement. But this too is no counterexample to the consistency requirement. For although it is subjectively rational for her to have all these intentions, she ought not have them all. After all, she will not, in fact, visit all twenty cathedrals. And she objectively ought not to intend to visit whichever cathedral it is that she won't visit even if she intends to visit it.

But what if we suppose that there is no fact of matter as to which cathedral she'll skip. Suppose, then, that there is, for each cathedral, a 1-in-n objective chance that she'll have to skip it. In that case, it may seem that given the low probability that she'll have to skip any given cathedral, she should intend to visit each one—and if you deny that the probability that she'll skip a given cathedral is low enough to make her intending to visit it rational, then just change the example so that n equals, say, twenty billion. It would certainly be low enough then. And, perhaps, doing this makes for a more plausible counterexample. But I don't think so. In this case, we have to acknowledge that it's not entirely up to Susan which cathedral she skips or which cathedrals she visits. Consequently, we should deny that she objectively ought to intend to visit each one. Instead, we should hold only that she objectively ought, for each cathedral, to intend to *try* to visit it. For what's up to her is not whether she visits it but only whether she *tries* to visit it.[55]

So, we've seen that the opting-for-the-best view is quite ecumenical. The only substantive positions that it can't accommodate are (1) the view that there are obligation dilemmas and (2) the view that alternatives don't matter. And these views are so implausible that they should not concern us. Consequently, people of all theoretical stripes should be happy to embrace the opting-for-the-best view. Yet, as I explain in the next section, there is one type of theorist that can't.

§1.3 A Potential Objection to the Opting-for-the-Best View

I've claimed that the opting-for-the-best view is fairly uncontroversial. Admittedly, though, some must reject it. In particular, rule-consequentialists must. Given that they're *consequentialists*, they must hold that the only thing that ultimately matters is the goodness of consequences, which in turn commits them to the view that the best option is always the one with the best

---

55. I'll have more to say in defense of this sort of view in Chapter 3.

consequences. But, given that they're *rule*-consequentialists, they must insist that subjects ought to abide by the ideal code of rules (i.e., the set of rules whose internalization by the vast majority would have the best consequences) even when their doing so wouldn't have the best consequences. Thus, rule-consequentialists must deny that subjects ought always to perform their best option.[56]

Of course, Brad Hooker would likely object to this characterization. He claims that although rule-consequentialism "selects *rules* by whether their internalization could reasonably be expected to maximize the good, [it] does not . . . evaluate *acts* this way. Rather, it evaluates acts by reference to the rules thus selected" (2000, p. 102). But while I'm willing to concede that rule-consequentialism can assess the *deontic* statuses of our acts by reference to such rules, I deny that it can assess the *evaluative* statuses of our acts in this way. For the evaluative status of an act (i.e., its goodness) is, by definition, a function of whatever ultimately matters, and, according to consequentialism, what ultimately matters is not whether our acts accord with certain rules, but whether our acts maximize the good.

Hooker may still object. After all, he seems to suggest that what ultimately matters is that we "behave in ways that are impartially defensible" rather than in ways that maximize the good (2000, p. 102). But it seems to me that if one thinks that what ultimately matters is not the maximization of the good but that our actions our impartially defensible to each other, then one should self-identify as a contractualist, not as a consequentialist. Of course, this may just be a terminological dispute. Indeed, Hooker insists that this is the type of "consequentialist" theory that he's exploring (2000, p. 104). But if that's right, then let me just flag that I'll be understanding "consequentialism" differently from the way he does. As I understand it, consequentialism (whether it be an act version or a rule version) is, by definition, committed to the maximization of the good being what is best in terms of what ultimately matters. In any case, it's only on this understanding of consequentialism, that rule-consequentialism turns out to be incompatible with the opting-for-the-best view. The relevant question for our purposes, then, is whether

---

56. Technically, the proponent of the opting-for-the-best view may also deny that subjects ought always to perform their best option, for she may deny that we are to assess all options in terms of their own goodness. Nevertheless, the proponent of the opting-for-the-best view will insist that the only exceptions are instances in which the subject must perform a suboptimal option in order to perform some optimal option that entails it. Since such exceptions needn't concern us here, I'll ignore this complication.

this incompatibility between the two is a problem for the opting-for-the-best view or for rule-consequentialism so understood.

Unsurprisingly, I think that it's a problem only for rule-consequentialism so understood. After all, if what ultimately matters is producing good consequences, it just seems crazy to insist that subjects follow the rules even when they know that their doing so will have bad consequences. To do so is to insist that a subject perform an option that is worse than some alternative in terms of what ultimately matters simply because that option and not the alternative is in accord with the set of rules that is better than any alternative set of rules in terms of what ultimately matters. But what ultimately matters is, of course, doing what's best in terms of what ultimately matters, not doing what's in accordance with the set of rules that's best in terms of what ultimately matters. And this is why the rule-worship objection to rule-consequentialism had seemed such a devastating objection to the view until Brad Hooker came along to claim that the rule-consequentialist can be a consequentialist and hold that what ultimately matters is behaving in ways that are impartially justifiable to others rather than in ways that would maximize the good.

But if, like me, you insist that, by definition, it's the goodness of consequences and not anything else that ultimately matters on consequentialism, then it should seem strange to you that a consequentialist theory might insist that we ought to follow certain rules even when we know that our doing so would have worse consequences than our not following them. Of course, rule-consequentialists could respond to this worry by arguing that their theory is correct all the same. That is, they could argue, as Brad Hooker has, that the correct moral theory is the one that "does a better job than its rivals of matching and tying together our moral convictions" (2000, p. 101) and that rule-consequentialism does a better job than its rivals. But the fact that rule-consequentialism denies that subjects ought always to perform their best option is a powerful reason for thinking that it doesn't do a better job. After all, one of our most entrenched moral convictions is that subjects (morally) ought always to perform their (morally) best option.[57]

Nonetheless, rule-consequentialists could argue that despite rule-consequentialism's inability to accommodate this particular conviction, the theory is, all things considered, superior to its rivals in terms of matching and tying together all of our various convictions. But I very much doubt

---

57. Technically, what's counterintuitive is rule-consequentialism's denial that subjects should only perform a suboptimal option if doing so is necessary for performing an optimal option. See note 56.

this. Note, first, that the opting-for-the-best view is, as we've seen, quite ecumenical. Indeed, we've seen that the opting-for-the-best view can match the verdicts of any plausible theory. If, for instance, a theory holds that a subject ought to φ if and only if φ is F, then, to match its verdicts, the opting-for-the-best view need only insist that a subject's option is best if and only if it's F. So, if the proponent of the opting-for-the-best view wants to match rule-consequentialism's verdicts, she need only insist that a subject's option is best if and only if the ideal code requires her to perform it. Indeed, the only thing that the proponent of the opting-for-the-best view can't do is hold that (1) a subject ought to φ if and only if the ideal code requires her to φ while denying that (2) her φ-ing is best if and only if the ideal code requires her to φ. Of course, that's precisely what rule-consequentialists must do—that is, they must insist upon clause 1 while denying clause 2. They must deny clause 2, because they're *consequentialists*. And they must accept clause 1, because they're *rule*-consequentialists. Consequently, they're forced to deny our conviction that subjects ought always to perform their best option. And yet, in doing so, they don't gain the ability to accommodate any verdicts that the opting-for-the-best view can't accommodate. Thus, it seems that, if anything, the opting-for-the-best view has a leg up on rule-consequentialism when it comes to matching our convictions.

Second, it seems that the opting-for-the-best view can do at least as good a job of tying these convictions together. For whereas the rule-consequentialist will attempt to show that we can derive our moral convictions from the idea that we ought to follow the ideal code, the proponent of the opting-for-the-best view will attempt to derive them from the idea that we ought to perform our best option. And I see no reason for thinking that the opting-for-the-best view will fare any worse than rule-consequentialism does in this regard.

So, although the existence of a rival that does a better job of matching and tying together our moral convictions would be a significant objection to the opting-for-the-best view, I don't yet see any reason to think that there is such a rival.

§1.4 Remaining Controversies and the Plan for the Rest of the Book

The opting-for-the-best view is, I've argued, fairly uncontroversial. Nevertheless, there are several controversies concerning how best to understand and formulate it. These are controversies that proponents of the view must face regardless of what their position is concerning what ultimately matters.

The first issue concerns which options are to be assessed in terms of their own goodness and which, if any, are to be assessed in terms of the goodness of the options that entail them. The issue arises, because sometimes the best option is a more specific version of a suboptimal (perhaps, bad) option. To illustrate, consider *Quitting Smoking*. In this case, Tamar has the option of quitting smoking as well as the more specific option of quitting smoking and eating less. And quitting smoking and eating less is a *version* of quitting smoking in that quitting smoking and eating less entails quitting smoking. Now, suppose that we've come to the conclusion that all that ultimately matters is how much aggregate happiness there is and that, consequently, the more aggregate happiness an option produces, the better it is. Assume, then, that the property of maximizing aggregate happiness is the only property that we should be concerned with whether or not our options have. So let's assume that Tamar's best option is to quit smoking and eat less, as this is her only option that would maximize aggregate happiness. But now let's assume that if Tamar were to quit smoking, she would eat more, not less. This is not because she couldn't quit smoking and eat less, but rather because she stubbornly refuses to ever go hungry and her appetite is going to increase if she quits smoking. Last, let's assume that, given her type 2 diabetes, it would be better for her to continue smoking than to quit smoking and eat more— that is, she would produce more aggregate happiness if she were to continue smoking than if she were to quit smoking. So, quitting smoking is not her best option. Interestingly, then, although quitting smoking is not her best option, her best option—quitting smoking and eating less—is a version of this sub-optimal option.

Now, if we hold that a subject ought to φ if and only if φ is her best option while letting the variable 'φ' range over all her options, the implication is that Tamar ought not to quit smoking (given that there is a better alternative—that is, the option of not quitting smoking) but ought to quit smoking and eat less (given that there is no better alternative). Yet, she cannot quit smoking and eat less if she doesn't quit smoking. So, if we hold this sort of view, we commit ourselves to holding that it can be that an agent (1) ought to refrain from φ-ing, (2) ought to jointly φ and ψ, but (3) lacks the option of both refraining from φ-ing and jointly φ-ing and ψ-ing. And that seems like a problem, given that we're assuming that the relevant ought is intention-guiding such that joint satisfiability must hold. This problem is known as the *problem of act versions*, and it's a problem that I'll discuss in much greater detail in Chapter 4. But the point for now is that it raises the issue of whether we should restrict the range of the variable 'φ' in the opting-for-the-best view to a proper subset of the agent's options, for this could potentially solve the problem. If we did this, we could, for instance, assess only those options that are not entailed by any other option in terms of their own goodness. All other options would, then, be assessed in terms of whether they are entailed by the best option that is not entailed by any other option. Of course, not everyone agrees that this is the best way to solve the problem. But I'll take up these issues in chapters 4 and 5.

To understand the next issue for proponents of the opting-for-the-best view, note that, according to this view, whether a subject's *e*-ing (where *e* is some possible event) has a deontic status at all depends on whether it's an option. And if it is an option, what specific deontic status it has depends on how it compares to her alternative options (or, at least, on how the more specific versions of this option compare to the agent's other similarly specific alternative options). Thus, it's absolutely crucial to get clear on which events constitute her options. This will let us know both what sorts of events can have a deontic status and what sorts of events we are to compare an option to in determining its specific deontic status.

So the second controversy concerns what sorts of events count as a subject's options. Perhaps it's only those events that are under her *volitional control*—that is, only those events that she can make happen by trying, deciding, intending, or otherwise willing to perform them. This would mean that my forming a belief—say, the belief that I've just typed the word "the"—wouldn't necessarily count as an option for me. For the formation of such a belief is not (at least, not typically) something that I can make happen by intending to form that belief—that is, it's not something that I can do at will (at least, not typically). Of course, I can make it happen by typing the word "the." For that will cause me to have the perception of having typed the word "the," which will in turn cause me to form the belief that I have done so. But I can't form the belief that I've just typed the word "the" simply by intending to form that belief and thus without my first typing the word "the." Another possibility, though, is that an event counts as an option for a subject so long as it is responsive to her awareness of facts that constitute reasons for and against that option. In that case, my forming a belief could count as an option so long as I could do so in response to my awareness of certain facts that constitute reasons for my doing so—perhaps, in response to my perception of having typed the word "the." I'll take up these issues in chapters 2 and 3.

A third controversy for proponents of the opting-for-the-best view concerns how reasons figure into all this. Consider that the performance of one option can entail the performance of another, because, as we've seen, one option can be a more specific instance of another. For instance, I have the option of baking a pumpkin pie as well as the option of baking a pie, and the former entails the latter given that baking a pumpkin pie is just a more specific instance of baking a pie. Now, suppose that I have both reason to bake a pie and reason to bake a pumpkin pie. Which, if either, grounds the other? Do I have a reason to bake a pie in virtue of my having a reason to perform some instance of pie-baking—perhaps, pumpkin-pie baking? Or do I have a reason to bake a pumpkin pie in virtue of my having a reason to bake a pie? Or does neither ground the other, as would be the case if, say, I had a reason to do each because each would have good consequences? So, one possibility is that how much reason I have to bake a pie is just a function of how good the consequences of my baking a pie would be. But another possibility is that how much reason I have to bake a pie depends not on how good its consequences would be but on how good the consequences of my baking a pumpkin pie would be. And if it's the latter, we have to ask whether it also depends on the extent to which my baking a pie makes it probable that I'll bake a pumpkin pie. Last, we have to ask whether what I ought to do is always what I have most reason to do or whether sometimes it's only what is entailed by what I have most reason to do. I'll take up these issues in Chapter 6.

The fourth and final issue concerns how the things that ultimately matter determine the evaluative status of an option (e.g., best or sufficiently good).[58] Suppose, for instance, that one of the things that ultimately matters to a subject is her not violating anyone's rights. The issue, then, is whether we are to assess an option directly or indirectly in terms of such things. And we would do so directly if we were to take an option to be sufficiently good only if its performance has no chance of constituting the violation of someone's rights. But we would do so indirectly if we were instead to use the things that ultimately matter to determine how that option's prospect ranks in comparison to those of its alternatives and then take the option to be sufficiently good just in case its prospect is not outranked by that of some alternative. And this issue becomes particularly salient in cases where it is uncertain or indeterminate

---

58. An *evaluative status* is any status such as the following: good, bad, better, worse, best, worst, sufficiently good, insufficiently good, etc.

whether an option would constitute a rights violation. I'll take up this issue in Chapter 7.

Finally, I'll conclude the book in Chapter 8 by reviewing the conclusions from the previous chapters and showing how these conclusions culminate in a coherent and plausible version of the opting-for-the-best view. And I'll show how this version of the opting-for-the-best view has many virtues, which allow it to solve various puzzles concerning what we ought to do, including some involving overdetermined outcomes, indeterminate outcomes, predictable future misbehavior, and good acts that are more specific versions of bad acts.

CHAPTER 2

What Are Our Options?

IN THE LAST chapter, I argued for the following view:

> **The Opting-for-the-Best View (short version):** For any subject S and
> any member φ of a certain subset of S's options, S ought to φ if and only
> if φ is the best member of this subset in terms of whatever ultimately
> matters.[1]

This view leaves a lot unspecified. It doesn't tell us what ultimately matters.
Nor does it tell us what the relevant subset of S's options is. It doesn't even tell
us what counts as an option. Perhaps, only voluntary acts count as options.
But, perhaps, the nonvoluntary formation of an attitude (such as a belief)
also counts as an option. It may even be that the conjunction of the two—for
example, believing p while asserting not-p—counts as an option.

In this and Chapter 3, I'll argue for what I take to be the most plausible
account of our options. I'll start in this chapter by arguing that a subject's
having the relevant sort of control over whether she φs is both necessary and
sufficient for φ's being an option for her. And in Chapter 3, I'll argue that the
relevant sort of control is what I call *rational control*, which is the sort of control that we exert over our beliefs, desires, and intentions.

---

1. For the complete version, see either the glossary or the end of §1.1.

§2.1 The Need to Restrict What Can Count as an Option

Everyone seems to agree that not just any possible event can be something that a subject is obligated to perform such that she would be accountable for failing to perform it.[2] For instance, I cannot legitimately be held accountable for a meteor's hitting the Earth or for your freely choosing to hit a child. I'm not even accountable for all my own bodily movements. For instance, I cannot legitimately be held accountable for the irregular beating of my heart or for the nonvoluntary kick of my leg that occurs when the doctor taps my patellar ligament with her reflex hammer. As noted in Chapter 1, it seems that only some possible events are events that a subject could be obligated to perform and accountable for failing to perform. These events are what I've stipulatively called *the subject's options*.

What sets a subject's options apart from other possible events, it seems, is the fact that they are under her control. Since I don't have the relevant sort of control over either the irregular beating of my heart or your freely choosing to hit a child, I cannot be obligated to refrain from these things, nor accountable for "doing" them. But since I do have the relevant sort of control over whether *I* hit a child, I can be both obligated to refrain from doing so and accountable should I do so. The reason that control is necessary both for having obligations and for being accountable for violating them is that obligations have two important roles to play: a directive role and an inculpatory role.[3] And these are roles that they can play only if their application is restricted to events over which their subjects exert control. Moreover, these two roles are what distinguishes obligations from mere evaluations (such as the evaluation that some event is good, bad, or neutral).

So let's look at these two roles more closely, starting with the directive role. In order for obligations to fulfill this role, they must direct us to respond

---

2. Recall that, throughout this book, I use the verbs "do" and "perform" such that believing, desiring, and intending count as things that a subject "does" and "performs."

3. To be clear, I hold that a genuine obligation must be able to play both of these two roles. But one could instead hold that it is enough that a genuine obligation plays at least one of these two roles. Take, for instance, some of the versions of hybridism discussed in TIMMERMAN & COHEN 2016. On these versions of hybridism, there are two types of genuine obligations, where one type plays the directive role and the other type plays the inculpatory role. The main motivation for adopting such a hybrid view (thereby postulating two types of obligations) is the thought that this is the only way to adequately account for certain intuitions. But, as I'll argue in Chapter 5, we can account for such intuitions without resorting to such a nonparsimonious view.

to our situation in only those ways that we are capable of responding. Mere evaluations, by contrast, needn't be so restricted, for mere evaluations don't direct us to do anything. Evaluations tell us whether some event or situation is good, bad, or neutral, but they don't tell us what, if anything, we ought to do about it. To illustrate, the fact that I'm suffering may be bad, but this mere evaluation doesn't direct me to do anything about it. For there may be nothing that I can do about it. So mere evaluations don't presume that I have control over what's being evaluated. But obligations do. If I'm obligated, say, to take some painkillers, then I must have control over whether I do or not. Thus, obligations must be restricted in a way that mere evaluations needn't be.

I must have control over whether I'm to fulfill my obligations, because all obligations are grounded in reasons and reasons are facts to which their subjects must be able to respond. We should, then, take the response constraint that we discussed in Chapter 1 to apply to obligations as well as to reasons. That is, we should accept the following expanded version of that constraint.

> **The Response Constraint (expanded): (RC1)** For any option φ, any subject S, and any proposition p, the fact that p constitutes a reason for S to φ only if both (1) S has the capacity to know or otherwise adequately cognize this fact and (2) her adequately cognizing this fact could, via the exercise of her rational capacities, *directly* cause her to φ—that is, without causing her to form the intention to do something that will, in turn, cause her to φ. And (RC2), for any principle P that directs a subject to φ based on certain facts that putatively constitute decisive reason for her to φ, P states a genuine obligation only if both (1) she has the capacity to know or otherwise adequately cognize these facts and (2) her adequately cognizing these facts could, via the exercise of her rational capacities, directly cause her to φ.

Given this constraint, we must restrict the events that are eligible for being obligatory to those that could be caused by a subject's recognizing and responding to the facts that make their occurrence something that the subject ought to desire. Thus, if the elimination of all suffering couldn't be caused by my recognizing and responding to the facts that make this something that I ought to desire, I cannot be obligated to bring this about. For, in that case, it would be pointless to direct me to do so, as there would be no way for me to do what I've been directed to do. We see, then, that given the directive role of obligations their application must be restricted to those events over which their subjects exert control. And since options are just those possible events that are eligible for being obligatory, we must likewise restrict a subject's options to those events over which she exerts control.

Besides this directive role, obligations play an inculpatory role, for there is a necessary connection between a subject's failing to respond as some obligation directs her to respond and her being accountable for so failing.[4] Of course, no one thinks that the connection is so simple that if a subject fails to respond as she's objectively obligated to respond, she's necessarily accountable for that failure. A subject can lack accountability on the grounds of either being ignorant of certain relevant facts or having some other suitable excuse. But, absent some suitable excuse, a subject is accountable for any failure to abide by her objective obligations.[5] And since, as I'll argue below, it's inappropriate to hold people accountable for events that weren't under their control, we must restrict their options to those events that were under their control.

So I've argued that obligations play two important roles: (1) they direct us to respond to our situation in certain ways and (2) they inculpate us when we fail to do so without some suitable excuse. Yet, neither role can be fulfilled without restricting what counts as an option, for it would be illegitimate both to direct us to respond in ways that we're incapable of responding and to fault us for responding in ways for which we had no alternative way of responding. Thus, what counts as an option must be restricted. And, as I've already suggested, I believe that our options must be restricted to all and only those possible events over which we exert the relevant sort of control. In sections 2.2 and 2.3, I'll argue, first, that a subject's having control over whether she φs is necessary for φ's being an option for her, and second, that it is also sufficient. So this chapter will show that a subject's options consist in all and only those events that are under her control in some relevant sense. And in Chapter 3, I'll argue that the relevant sense of control is rational control—the sort of control that we exert over our beliefs, desires, and intentions.

---

4. See, for instance, DARWALL 2006, GIBBARD 1990, MILL 1991, PORTMORE 2011, and SKORUPSKI 1999.

5. Admittedly, there's an even tighter connection between accountability and the failure to abide by one's *subjective* obligations. But this is not to say that there isn't a necessary connection between accountability and the failure to abide by one's objective obligations. Indeed, the latter is ensured by the former. For a subject's subjective obligations will coincide with her objective obligations whenever she knows all the relevant facts. So, just as one is necessarily accountable for failing to abide by one's subjective obligations absent some suitable nonepistemic excuse, one is necessarily accountable for failing to abide by one's objective obligations absent some suitable (epistemic or nonepistemic) excuse.

§2.2 The Necessity of Control

Following John Stuart Mill and others (e.g., DARWALL 2006, GIBBARD 1990, and SKORUPSKI 1999), I believe that a subject is obligated to refrain from φ-ing only if she would be accountable for φ-ing—at least, absent some suitable excuse. But, as I'll argue below, a subject can be accountable for φ-ing only if she had control over whether she was to φ. It follows, then, that obligations must be restricted to those over which their subjects exert control. And if obligations must be so restricted, then what's eligible for being obligatory— that is, our options—must also be so restricted.

Control is necessary for accountability, because to be accountable for φ-ing is to be appropriately held to account for it and, thus, to be liable to reward or sanction for it.[6] The reward or sanction needn't come from the law, society, or common opinion, but it must at least come from the approval or disapproval of one's own conscience (see MILL 1991, chap. 5). Thus, a subject is *accountable* for having φ-ed if and only if she is either blameworthy or praiseworthy for having φ-ed and is therefore the appropriate target of either retributive attitudes (such as guilt and indignation) or meritorious attitudes (such as pride and admiration) in virtue of having φ-ed.[7] And this, I'll stipulate, is just what I mean by the phrase "accountable for having φ-ed." Nevertheless, I need to explain what I mean by terms such as "pride," "guilt," and "appropriate."[8]

---

6. I've purposely used the word "accountable" as opposed to "responsible," as some philosophers hold both that there are several distinct types of responsibility and that only one type—namely, accountability—entails liability to reward or sanction. For instance, David Shoemaker (2015) argues that there are three distinct types: attributability, answerability, and accountability. See also Gary Watson (1996), who argues for two of these three. For criticisms of Shoemaker's view, see A. M. SMITH 2012. And note that, in general, a subject is *responsible* for having φ-ed if and only if she's the appropriate target of some normative assessment in virtue of her having φ-ed.

7. It would be appropriate for her to feel prideful for having φ-ed if and only if her φ-ing was something she ought to have done, and it would be appropriate for her to feel guilty for having φ-ed if and only if her φ-ing was something that she was obligated to have refrained from doing. Also, note that, as I've defined "accountability," no one can be accountable for a neutral event since it's never appropriate for one to feel prideful or guilty for having done something neutral. I do this solely for the sake of simplifying the discussion. If, instead, we want to allow that people can be accountable for neutral events, we can just tweak the right-hand side of my biconditional as follows: "φ is the sort of thing that she could be blameworthy or praiseworthy for provided it had either a positive or negative valence."

8. I'm going to focus on self-blame and self-praise (e.g., guilt and pride) as opposed to other-blame and other-praise (e.g., indignation and admiration) because only self-blame and self-praise are necessarily unpleasant and pleasant, respectively. For whereas being the target of self-blame (which involves feeling guilt) is necessarily unpleasant, being the target of other-blame is not. After all, one can be the target of other-blame while neither realizing it nor caring about it.

Like other emotions, pride and guilt have representational components in addition to their affective and motivational components. And it's an emotion's representational component that sets its appropriateness conditions, such that it's appropriate if and only if the thoughts (or representations) implicated by it are correct (or accurate).[9] The relevant sense of appropriateness, here, is not some domain-specific sense, such as that of being morally or legally appropriate. Rather, an emotion or attitude is appropriate in the relevant sense just in case the thoughts implicated by it are true. This is what Gideon Rosen (2015) calls the *alethic sense* of "appropriate," and I'll use the word "fitting" to mean "appropriate in the alethic sense" and the word "unfitting" to mean "inappropriate in the alethic sense."[10] In this sense, the fear of X is appropriate (i.e., fitting) if and only if X is dangerous, for the fear of X implicates the thought that X is dangerous.[11]

But what thought is constitutive of a subject's feeling pride (or guilt) for having φ-ed? As I see it, it's the thought that she deserves to experience the pleasantness (or unpleasantness) of this feeling in the recognition that she responded as she ought to have responded in φ-ing (or violated a legitimate demand in φ-ing). To illustrate, take guilt. Its affect is unpleasant, for if the feeling in question isn't unpleasant, it can't be guilt.[12] But guilt isn't just any

---

9. Perhaps, this is too quick. For it doesn't seem appropriate for a worm to fear a bird unless the worm is capable of forming the thought that this attitude implicates—that is, the thought that the bird is a danger to it. So I should probably qualify the above as follows: it's appropriate for a subject to form an attitude only if she has the option of forming this attitude as well as the thoughts implicated by this attitude. And, given my view of accountability above, this would mean that only those subjects with the capacity for feelings of pride and guilt can be accountable for their actions.

10. Thus, I'm not saying that pride and guilt are inappropriate whenever it would be immoral to have such attitudes. That would be to commit what Justin D'Arms and Dan Jacobson (2000) call the *moralistic fallacy*. After all, a reaction can be fitting even if morally inappropriate. For instance, laughter can be the fitting response to a funny joke even if that response would be morally inappropriate given that it's a cruel joke.

11. The idea that it would be appropriate/inappropriate in the alethic sense (i.e., fitting/unfitting) for a subject to φ is distinct from the idea that it would be fortunate/unfortunate that she φs. Consequently, we must allow that it could be fitting, say, to fear an animal even if this would be unfortunate given that the animal would then sense this fear and become even more dangerous as a result. Despite its being unfortunate to have this fear, it would, nevertheless, be fitting so long as it correctly represents its object as dangerous. In general, attitudes represent their objects as being a certain way and are, therefore, fitting to the extent that their representations are accurate. By contrast, an attitude is *fortunate* if and only if good consequences would result from one's having that attitude. For more on this distinction, see CHAPPELL 2012.

12. I'm not alone in thinking that guilt is essentially unpleasant. See, for instance, CARLSSON 2017 (p. 91), CLARKE 2016 (p. 122), MORRIS 1976 (p. 101), ROSEN 2015 (p. 67, n. 6), and WOLF 2011.

unpleasant feeling associated with certain motivational tendencies. To feel guilt, one must additionally have the thought that one deserves to feel bad given one's failure to live up to some legitimate demand.[13] Thus, a woman with Tourette's syndrome may feel bad for having involuntarily uttered some obscenity, but this feeling won't amount to guilt unless she experiences its unpleasantness as at least partially deserved. What's more, she could both feel bad about having involuntarily uttered this obscenity and experience the unpleasantness of this feeling as at least partially deserved and still not count as feeling guilt. For it will be guilt that she's feeling only if, in addition, it strikes her that she deserves this unpleasantness *in virtue* of having failed to live up to some legitimate demand.

Of course, none of this is to suggest that it's impossible to feel guilt unless one *believes* that one deserves to experience the unpleasantness of feeling bad about what one did in virtue of having violated some legitimate demand. Clearly, one can feel guilty without having this belief just as one can fear something without believing that it's dangerous. Although fearing something implicates the *thought* that it's dangerous, one needn't *believe* that it's dangerous in order to have this thought.[14] Having the thought that it's dangerous necessitates only experiencing it as dangerous. And to experience it as dangerous is just for it to strike one as dangerous in the same way that the lines in a Müller-Lyer illusion can strike one as unequal even if one believes that they're equal.[15] Likewise, to have the thought that one deserves to experience the unpleasantness of guilt in virtue of having failed to live up to some legitimate demand, one needn't believe this or be willing to assent to it. Rather, one need only have it strike one as being so.[16]

---

13. Here, I concur with Darwall and Mill: "Mill calls guilt a kind of 'internal sanction,' but it is important to appreciate that guilt is not merely painful, or the (painful) fear of further (external) sanctions (MILL 1991, chap. 3). It is the painful sense of having done wrong, having violated a legitimate demand that comes, not just from someone else, say God, but also that one implicitly makes of oneself, through blaming oneself in feeling guilt" (DARWALL 2013, p. 16).

14. Here, I follow CLARKE 2016 and ROSEN 2015 in distinguishing *thoughts* from *beliefs* such that having the latter, but not the former, necessitates assenting to the attitude's propositional content.

15. For more on this idea, see both CLARKE 2016 (pp. 122–123) and ROSEN 2015 (pp. 71–72).

16. Thus, my view is compatible with the possibility of experiencing recalcitrant guilt—that is, with the possibility of experiencing guilt while at the same time believing that one doesn't deserve to feel its associated unpleasant affect. My view, then, is a version of what D'Arms and Jacobson (2003) call *quasijudgmentalism*. And although D'Arms and Jacobson raise several interesting worries concerning quasijudgmentalism, I don't find any of them compelling. Unfortunately, I don't have the space here to address them all. But take this one. They worry

It's because the unpleasantness of guilt strikes us as being at least partially deserved that we experience it quite differently from the way we do, say, the unpleasantness of a headache. Unlike the unpleasantness of a headache, the unpleasantness of guilt strikes us as something that it would, in some respect, be morally problematic to get rid of. After all, to say that a subject *deserves X* is to say that, as a matter of justice and in virtue of her possessed characteristics or prior activities, she merits *X* in a certain sense. And, in the relevant sense of her "meriting X," the world in which she gets *X* while meriting *X* in this sense is, other things being equal, morally better than the world in which she gets *X* without meriting *X* in this sense.[17] Thus, taking a pill to alleviate one's appropriate guilt seems morally problematic in a way that taking a pill to alleviate one's headache does not. For it makes the world morally worse, other things being equal. And this difference isn't just due to the fact that guilt, but not a headache, can be fitting. For fear can be fitting and yet there seems to be nothing morally problematic about taking a pill to get rid of one's fitting fear—except, perhaps, when it would be instrumentally bad to do so. Getting rid of one's fitting fear doesn't make the world morally worse, other things being equal.

It's also important to note that the thought implicated by guilt is not the thought that the wrongdoer deserves to suffer generally.[18] Rather, the thought

---

that "the claim that emotions have constitutive thoughts seems incompatible with attributing them to animals and infants, who lack the requisite concepts" (p. 133). Unlike them, I don't find this worrisome. Indeed, although I think that animals and infants are capable of having the same affect, physiological changes, and motivational dispositions that humans typically have when they feel guilt, I doubt that they are capable of feeling guilt precisely because I doubt that they have the requisite concepts.

17. Thus, the sense in which I'm using the word "merits" is more restricted than its ordinary sense. For although, in ordinary usage, it would be felicitous to say that Southwest Airlines merits a five-star customer-approval rating given its exceptional customer satisfaction, this is not true in the restricted sense of the word that I'm employing here. For, in the sense that Southwest merits a five-star rating, it's not the case that the world in which Southwest gets this five-star rating while meriting it in this sense is, other things being equal, morally better than the world in which Southwest gets this five-star rating without meriting it in this sense. For if it's morally good for customer-approval ratings to reflect the level of customer satisfaction, this is only for instrumental reasons, and so, not other things being equal.

18. Many find this idea unacceptable. For instance, T. M. Scanlon rejects the idea that "it is good that people who have done wrong should suffer" (2013, p. 102). Likewise, R. Jay Wallace rejects the "problematic thought that wrongdoers positively deserve to suffer" (1994, p. 108). But rejecting this idea doesn't entail rejecting the idea that someone accountable for some wrongdoing deserves to suffer the unpleasantness of feeling guilt for having committed that wrongdoing. Indeed, Scanlon now accepts that wrongdoers deserve to feel guilt for their wrongdoing—see SCANLON 2008 (p. 188). So, even if we reject the idea that wrongdoers deserve to suffer generally, we shouldn't necessarily reject the idea that wrongdoers deserve

is only that (1) she deserves to suffer the specific unpleasant affect that's asso-ciated with feeling guilty, that (2) she deserves to suffer this unpleasantness only in the right way, at the right time, to the right extent, and with regard to its appropriate object (e.g., her failure to live up to some legitimate demand), and that (3) what's noninstrumentally good is, not her suffering per se, but her getting what she deserves (CLARKE 2016). To illustrate, suppose that my wife is accountable for having mistreated me. It would then be fitting for me to want her to feel guilty for having mistreated me, and to want this even if this would be of no instrumental value. Nevertheless, it would not be fitting for me to want her to feel lonely. Nor would it be fitting for me to want her to feel guiltier than she deserves to feel.[19] So, again, the idea is only that she deserves to suffer the unpleasantness of guilt and in the right way, at the right time, to the right extent, and with regard to its appropriate object: her failure to live up to some legitimate demand. Moreover, to claim that my wife deserves to feel guilty for her mistreatment of me implies only that it would, *in some re-spect*, be noninstrumentally good that she feels this way, not that her feeling this way would be *overall* good. Thus, the implication is only that the world in which she feels guilty for having accountably mistreated me is, other things being equal, noninstrumentally better than the world in which she likewise feels guilty for having nonaccountably mistreated me.[20]

---

to suffer the specific unpleasantness of feeling guilt for their wrongdoing—see, for instance, MCKENNA 2012 (chaps. 6–7).

19. Why think that she deserves to feel bad at all? Here's my argument: (P1) Given that she's accountable for having mistreated me, it's appropriate to want her to feel guilt for having mistreated me and to want her to have this experience even if her having this experience wouldn't be instrumentally valuable. (P2) If it's appropriate to want X even if X wouldn't be instrumentally valuable, then X must be noninstrumentally valuable. (C1) Thus, her feeling guilty for having mistreated me is noninstrumentally valuable. (P3) What most plausibly ac-counts for C1 is that she deserves to feel guilty for having mistreated me. (C2) Therefore, she deserves to feel guilty for having mistreated me. And, in defense of P3, I would add, first, that what explains the noninstrumental value of her feeling guilty for having mistreated me is not that her having this experience is itself noninstrumentally valuable. It isn't. After all, her having this experience wouldn't be noninstrumentally valuable if she weren't accountable for her mis-treatment of me. Second, the fact that it is *fitting* for her to feel guilty for having mistreated me is not what explains why her feeling guilty is noninstrumentally valuable. For, in general, there's nothing noninstrumentally valuable about having a fitting attitude. There's nothing, for instance, noninstrumentally valuable about fearing what's dangerous even though it is fit-ting to fear what's dangerous. Thus, it seems that what explains the fact that her feeling guilty is noninstrumentally valuable is both that she deserves to feel guilty and that it is, in general, noninstrumentally valuable that people get what they deserve.

20. If you think that there's nothing noninstrumentally good about her feeling guilty for having accountably mistreated me, then you would have to think (implausibly) that the world in which she feels guilty for having accountably mistreated me is, other things being

This, then, is a very minimal claim about desert; it claims only that feeling appropriate guilt is, other things being equal, less noninstrumentally worse than feeling inappropriate guilt.[21] And yet, even this rather minimal claim is quite explanatorily useful. First, it explains why there is something morally problematic about someone's taking a pill to alleviate her feeling guilt, whereas there is nothing morally problematic about someone's taking a pill to alleviate her feeling fear. Second, it explains why there is nothing morally problematic in our preferring the guilty feeling guilty to the innocent feeling guilty. Third, it explains the way in which feeling guilty for having φ-ed differs from other ways of feeling bad about having φ-ed (such as shame and embarrassment): only feeling guilty necessitates the thought that one deserves to feel this way. Fourth, it explains why there is nothing morally problematic in our expressing our resentment and indignation in the hopes of getting the guilty to feel guilty. And thus, it explains why we are appropriately angered and frustrated when the guilty respond to such expressions with only a sincere promise to do better next time, without any hint of guilt or remorse. And fifth, it explains why the sorts of excuses that exculpate us from blame (e.g., ignorance or a lack of control) are precisely those that diminish the degree to which we are deserving of the unpleasantness of feeling guilty.

So far, then, I've suggested that a subject is accountable for having φ-ed only if she is the appropriate object of the sorts of reactive attitudes that implicate the thought that she deserves to feel pride or guilt for having φ-ed. But before I move on to employ this claim in arguing that control is necessary for accountability, I should clarify that, although I have up until now focused mainly on feeling *moral* guilt for immoral *behavior*, I'm not exclusively concerned with either morality or behavior.[22] For we can appropriately feel bad about our imprudent choices, our fallaciously formed beliefs, and our

---

equal, no better than the world in which she likewise feels guilty for having nonaccountably mistreated me.

21. Note that my very minimal claim about desert is even more minimal than what others consider to be a relatively minimal claim about desert—see, for instance, Carlsson's claim that "if an agent deserves some harm, it will be noninstrumentally good that this harm occurs" (2017, p. 99). These others are committed to the view that the world in which my wife feels guilty for having accountably mistreated me is, other things being equal, better than the world in which she doesn't feel guilty for having accountably mistreated me. On this view, her feeling guilty is not just, *in some respect*, noninstrumentally good, but is, *overall*, noninstrumentally good. I'm not committed to this stronger claim.

22. So, to borrow a term from PEELS 2017, I'm interested in *normative responsibility*, where moral responsibility is but one type of normative responsibility.

aesthetically distasteful desires (SHOEMAKER 2015, p. 78). So, just as we can let others down, we can let ourselves down. Consequently, we may appropriately "beat ourselves up" for having been so stupid, foolish, or distasteful. After all, it's legitimate for us to demand of ourselves that we not be so stupid, foolish, or distasteful, so we can appropriately mentally kick ourselves for such things as swinging at a curve ball, laughing at a juvenile joke, and failing to anticipate an obvious objection to our argument. And it strikes us that, in some respect, we deserve to feel bad for having been so stupid, foolish, or distasteful. Consequently, even though we'll certainly lament our having been so stupid, foolish, or distasteful, we won't typically lament our having mentally kicked ourselves for having done so—and this is true even when we don't think that beating ourselves up in this way is instrumentally valuable. Like the feeling of moral guilt, then, feeling bad for having been stupid, foolish, or distasteful strikes us as at least partially deserved. So, just as someone can be accountable for her immoral behavior only if she is the appropriate object of the sorts of reactive attitudes that implicate the thought that she deserves to feel guilty for having so behaved, someone can be accountable for, say, her fallaciously formed belief only if she is the appropriate object of the sorts of reactive attitudes that implicate the thought that she deserves to feel bad for having been so stupid. Therefore, we should interpret my use of the word "guilt" broadly so as to cover not only *moral* guilt but also feeling bad for having been stupid, foolish, or distasteful—and the same follows for how we should interpret my use of the word "pride."[23]

At this point, I should note that the specific sort of pride that I have in mind—the sort that's the positive analogue of guilt—is not the general sort that one can appropriately take in even such things as one's natural talent or innate physical beauty. Rather, it's the specific sort that one can appropriately take only in something such as a good deed. And, to keep this specific sort of pride (which is the positive analogue of guilt) distinct from pride more generally, I'm going to call it *deontic pride*. Now, the positive analogue of pride

---

23. So, like Gunnar Björnsson (2017), I believe both that it can be appropriate to blame ourselves for such things as a poorly considered chess move, an ill-timed pass to a teammate, and a belief formed on the basis of insufficient evidence and that the sort of blame that's appropriate in such instances is not the characteristically moral type that implicates the thought, say, that the agent in question thereby demonstrated ill will. But unlike Björnsson, I believe that both moral and nonmoral blame have retributive elements, at least insofar as it strikes us that we deserve to beat ourselves up for having been so stupid, foolish, or distasteful. We feel that we deserve this, because we have let ourselves down, failing to meet the standards that we legitimately set for ourselves.

is shame. And the thought that's constitutive of being ashamed of X is the thought that X reveals that one is substandard in a way that could potentially result in a loss of honor, respect, or esteem. Analogously, then, the thought that's constitutive of being proud of X is the thought that X reveals that one is good or superior in a way that could potentially result in a gain of honor, respect, or esteem. Clearly, then, not just any sort of pride is the positive analogue of guilt. For although we can appropriately feel shame with respect to our natural talents and/or our innate physical characteristics, we can't appropriately feel guilt with respect such things. It seems, then, that the specific sort of pride that's the positive analogue of guilt (viz., *deontic pride*) is the sort that implicates the further thought that one is good or superior in that one deserves to experience the pleasantness of this feeling in virtue of having responded as one ought to have responded. So it's important to keep in mind that when I talk of pride in relation to accountability, I have deontic pride in mind.

I've argued, then, that a subject is accountable for having φ-ed only if she deserves to experience the pleasantness of feeling deontic pride or the unpleasantness of feeling guilty for having φ-ed. But, intuitively, no subject deserves to experience any feeling on account of her having φ-ed unless φ was under her control.[24] So we should think that a subject is accountable for having φ-ed only if φ was under her control. And to make things absolutely clear, I'll state the argument formally below.

(2.1) A subject is accountable for having φ-ed if and only if it's appropriate for her to feel deontic pride or guilt for having φ-ed. [Stipulation]

(2.2) It's appropriate for a subject to have a given feeling if and only if the thought that's constitutive of that feeling is true. [This is analytic given that "appropriate" is being used in the alethic sense throughout]

(2.3) The thought that's constitutive of a subject's feeling deontic pride for having φ-ed is the thought that she deserves to experience the pleasantness of this feeling in virtue of having done what she ought to have

---

24. I deny, then, what's known as *resultant moral luck* (see ZIMMERMAN 1987)—the idea that one's degree of accountability for φ-ing can be affected by the uncontrolled events that determine the results of one's φ-ing. For some compelling arguments against resultant moral luck, see KHOURY 2018. And for some experimental evidence suggesting that what most affects our judgments about an agent's degree of accountability for some act is not whether, by luck, the act had a bad result but whether we judge that the agent was unjustified in believing that her act had little chance of having that bad result, see YOUNG, NICHOLS, & SAXE 2010. See also KNEER & MACHERY 2019.

done in φ-ing, and the thought that's constitutive of her feeling guilty for having φ-ed is the thought that she deserves to experience the unpleasantness of this feeling in virtue of having violated a legitimate demand in φ-ing. [Assumption]

(2.4) Thus, a subject is accountable for having φ-ed only if she deserves to experience either the pleasantness of feeling deontic pride or the unpleasantness of feeling guilty in virtue of her having φ-ed. [From 2.1–2.3]

(2.5) A subject deserves to experience either the pleasantness of feeling deontic pride or the unpleasantness of feeling guilty in virtue of her having φ-ed only if φ was under her control. [Assumption]

(2.6) Therefore, a subject is accountable for having φ-ed only if φ was under her control. [From 2.4–2.5]

The only two assumptions here are 2.3 and 2.5, and I'll start by defending the latter. Premise 2.5 is quite intuitively plausible. It seems that no one deserves something in virtue of having φ-ed unless whether she was to φ was under her control. For if it wasn't under her control, then it was simply a matter of luck whether she was to φ. And no one deserves any reward (or sanction) in virtue of having had good (or bad) luck. So, unlike Susan Wolf (1980) and Dana Kay Nelkin (2011), I deny that there is an asymmetry between the conditions for being the appropriate object of praise (and specifically, for being the appropriate object of deontic pride) and the conditions for being the appropriate object of blame (and specifically, for being the appropriate object of guilt). As Watson (1996, p. 242) notes, such an asymmetry seems attractive only if we "shift between the perspectives of accountability and aretaic appraisal." So, admittedly, we think that it can be appropriate to admire someone for doing good even if she was unable to do otherwise. We may even admire the fact that she was so constituted as to find the alternative psychologically impossible. But if it was just a matter of luck that she happened to be so constituted, we wouldn't think that she deserves the reward of experiencing the pleasantness of pride. And even if Wolf and Nelkin have convincingly argued that it can be both fair and appropriate for others to praise those who are not deserving of any reward, they haven't given us any reason to think that a person can deserve the pleasantness of pride in virtue of φ-ing even when they didn't have the option of doing otherwise.[25]

---

25. Also, as Matthew Talbert (2016) points out, the sort of asymmetrical view that Wolf and Nelkin advocate seems quite unstable. If you think that a subject's having acted for good reasons and in a way that reflects well on her as a moral agent is sufficient for the appropriateness of

The only other assumption is 2.3. It claims that the thought that's constitutive of a subject's feeling pride (or guilt) for having φ-ed is the thought that she deserves to experience the pleasantness (or unpleasantness) of this feeling in the recognition that she responded as she ought to have responded in φ-ing (or violated a legitimate demand in φ-ing). There are several reasons to hold this view. First, it seems impossible to feel deontic pride (or guilt) without having this thought.[26] For instance, it seems that having this thought is (at least, in part) what differentiates feeling guilt for having φ-ed from other ways of feeling bad for having φ-ed (e.g., from feeling ashamed or embarrassed for having φ-ed). Although feeling ashamed or embarrassed for having φ-ed is, like feeling guilty, a way of feeling bad about having φ-ed, feeling guilty seems distinct from these two precisely because one can feel ashamed or embarrassed for having φ-ed without this striking one as being the way that one deserves to feel. And this in turn explains why it seems appropriate to feel ashamed or embarrassed, but not guilty, for things that weren't under one's control. For instance, it seems that it can be appropriate for people to be embarrassed about their innate physical features or ashamed of their child's behavior even if there was nothing that they could have done to change these. For, unlike the thought implicated by feeling guilt, the thoughts implicated by feelings of shame and embarrassment don't implicate the thought that one deserves to feel this way, and consequently, they don't presume that one had control over the intentional object of that feeling.

Another reason to hold that the thought constitutive of feeling guilty for having φ-ed is that one deserves to feel guilty for having φ-ed is that this view (call it *the desert view*) helps us to explain why, after a sufficient amount of self-reproach, it ceases to be appropriate to feel guilty any longer. For, on this

---

her feeling pride, then you should also think that a subject's having acted for bad reasons and in a way that reflects poorly on her as a moral agent is sufficient for the appropriateness of her feeling guilty.

26. When I say that the thought that one deserves to feel guilty for having failed to live up to some legitimate demand is constitutive of feeling guilty, I'm not suggesting that everyone who feels guilty can readily articulate this thought. They can have the thought even if they lack the words to articulate it. Thus, I depart with Rosen in that I deny that "an account of the thoughts implicit in [a feeling] must be framed in terms that everyone capable of [that feeling] understands" (2015, p. 75). For although I would agree that they must have the relevant concepts, I believe that someone can have the relevant concepts without understanding the terms that we would use to articulate them. For instance, a young child who has seen pictures of gryphons, lions, and eagles as well as pictures of their various detached parts could have the concept of a gryphon without being able to understand all or any of the terms used in the following articulation: a creature that has the torso, tail, and back legs of a lion and the head and wings of an eagle.

view, the relevant thought is that one deserves to suffer the unpleasantness of feeling guilty, and this thought ceases to be true after a sufficient amount of self-reproach has occurred. After all, one deserves to suffer only so much self-reproach for any given wrongdoing. So, after a sufficient amount of self-reproach has occurred, one will cease to deserve to feel guilt anymore. Consequently, it will cease to be appropriate for one to continue to feel guilty. So, where one has yet to suffer a sufficient amount of guilt, the thought constitutive of guilt—that is, the proposition "I deserve to suffer the unpleasantness of *this* feeling in virtue of having violated a legitimate demand"—will be true. But, where one has already suffered a sufficient amount of guilt, this thought will be false. Thus, the desert view explains why the appropriateness of one's feeling guilt depends (in part) on whether one has already suffered a sufficient amount of self-reproach.

To better understand these advantages for the desert view, it will be helpful to contrast it with the following three alternatives: (1) the quality-of-will view, according to which the thought implicated by guilt is that the agent's conduct manifests ill will; (2) the blameworthy view, according to which the thought implicated by guilt is that the agent is blameworthy; and (3) the wrongdoing view, according to which the thought implicated by guilt is that one has done wrong. I'll take each in turn.

Consider, first, the quality-of-will view. For one, it seems possible to feel guilty without having the thought that one has manifested ill will—that is, without it even seeming to one that one has acted out of ill will. For instance, a woman could feel guilty (although inappropriately so) for running over a boy who unexpectedly darted in front of her car without it seeming to her that her conduct manifested ill will. Perhaps, she realizes that it was physically impossible for her to have avoided running over the boy given the way that he unexpectedly darted in front of her car. Still, it could be guilt that she's feeling so long as her feeling bad about having run over the child strikes her as (at least, partially) deserved.[27]

---

27. In this case, it will likely strike her as if she deserves to feel guilty for killing the boy, but this is as much an illusion as a straight stick half immersed in water striking her as bent. Such illusions arise when the apparatus that we use for making such cognitions have been trained, or have evolved, under a range of contexts that differs significantly from the one in which the illusion presents itself. (I thank Mark Schroeder for reminding me of this.) In any case, it seems that if it's guilt that she's feeling, it must strike her both that she was under a legitimate demand not to kill the boy and that she deserves to experience the unpleasantness of guilt in virtue of having violated this demand. And the point, here, is only that it doesn't even have to strike her that she manifested some ill will in order for it to be guilt that she's feeling. Or so it seems to me.

For another, if the quality-of-will view were right about the thought that was constitutive of feeling guilt, there would be no reason to think that it would, after a sufficient amount of self-reproach, cease to be appropriate for one to feel guilty for having previously manifested ill will. For no matter how much one has already reproached oneself for that previous lapse, it will never cease to be true that one did manifest ill will. And so it will never cease to be appropriate to feel guilty for having done so. Yet, intuitively, it seems that, after a sufficient amount of self-reproach, one should cease to rebuke oneself any more.

Next, consider the blameworthy view. Here, too, it seems possible for someone to feel guilty without having the thought that one is blameworthy. For it seems that one needn't even have the concept of blameworthiness to feel guilty. And this makes sense of our thought that children can feel guilty even if they lack the concept of blameworthiness. This is because, as anyone with much experience with children knows, children have the concepts of merit, desert, and fairness, which is all the conceptual apparatus that, on the desert view, they need to feel guilty. Thus, it seems that what's needed to feel guilty is not the concept of blameworthiness, but the concept of merit, desert, or fairness.

And again, we see that, like the quality-of-will view, the blameworthy view has trouble explaining why, after a sufficient amount of self-reproach, it ceases to be appropriate to feel guilt anymore. For again, the relevant thought— which, in this case, is the thought that one was blameworthy for some past misdeed—never ceases to be true. And so we must on this view counterintuitively hold that no matter how much one has already reproached oneself for one's previous failure, it never ceases to be appropriate to continue to feel guilt for that failure.

Last, consider the wrongdoing view. Here, too, it seems that one can feel guilty for having φ-ed without thinking that one has done wrong in having φ-ed. To illustrate, imagine that Huck Finn (Mark Twain's famous fictional character) had, contrary to the actual story, turned his friend Jim over to the authorities for being a runaway slave. In such a case, it seems possible for Huck to feel guilty for having turned his friend in even if it doesn't strike him as wrong for him to have done so. This is because whereas guilt seems to track the violation of any legitimate demand (be it moral or nonmoral and be it overridden or not), moral wrongness seems to track only the violation of some non-overridden moral demand. So, even if, as Huck supposes, it wouldn't have been wrong for him to turn Jim in, he did violate a legitimate demand of friendship in turning him in. Thus, so long as it strikes him that he deserves to feel guilty for having turned Jim in, it is guilt that he's feeling.[28] So we should reject the wrongdoing view, for it wrongly assumes that we must have thoughts of having done wrong to feel guilty. What's more, we should reject the wrongdoing view, because, like the other two alternatives, it fails to account for the fact that after a sufficient amount of self-reproach, it ceases to be appropriate to feel guilt anymore. And it fails for the exact same reason that the other two failed: the thought in question is not one that ceases to be true after one has suffered a sufficient amount of self-reproach.[29]

Of course, even if, unlike me, you think that some of these other thoughts (e.g., the thought that one has done wrong) is constitutive of one's feeling guilt, this shouldn't cause you to reject my claim that the thought that one deserves to feel guilt is constitutive of feeling guilt. Rather, you should just amend my account and hold something like the following view: the thought constitutive of feeling guilt for having φ-ed is the thought that one deserves to suffer the unpleasantness of feeling guilt in the recognition that one has done wrong (or has done something blameworthy or has thereby manifested a poor quality of will). For my purposes, all that matters is that the idea that one deserves to suffer the unpleasantness of feeling guilt in virtue of having violated a legitimate demand is at least part of the thought (or one of the thoughts) that's constitutive of feeling guilt.

To sum up, then, we should accept that a subject can be accountable for only that which was under her control. For, according to the desert view, a subject can be accountable for having φ-ed only if she deserves to experience the relevant feeling (deontic pride or guilt) for having φ-ed. And no one, it seems, deserves to experience any feeling on account of one's φ-ing when φ wasn't under one's control. But, of course, some would argue that things are not as they seem. That is, some challenge the idea that subjects can be accountable only for that over which they exerted control, and they do so by appealing to Frankfurt-type cases, such as the following.[30]

---

28. Likewise, a mafioso could feel guilty for breaking the Mafia's Law of Omertà (a code of silence) without it seeming to him that it was morally wrong for him to have done so.

29. I'm assuming that on the wrongdoing view, what's implicated by one's feeling guilt for having φ-ed is the thought that it was all-in wrong for one to have φ-ed. If it were instead the thought that it was merely *pro tanto* wrong for one to have φ-ed, then it would, on this account, be appropriate for one to feel guilty for having broken a relatively unimportant promise so as to save a life. But this is inappropriate despite the fact that it's *pro tanto* wrong to break a promise.

30. I'm presuming that the relevant sort of control is what's known as *regulative control* as opposed to *guidance control*, the key difference being that you can have the latter, but not the former, with respect to φ even if not–φ-ing isn't an option. (For more on this distinction, see

The Sniper: Jones is a sniper who plans to shoot the mayor when she takes the podium at noon today. Black also wants the mayor dead and believes that Jones will decide on his own to pull the trigger, but he doesn't want to take any chances. So he implants a deterministic device in Jones's brain that will issue, at noon, in a decision to kill the mayor if Jones's own cognitive faculties aren't going to issue, at noon, in a decision to pull the trigger. Moreover, Jones will succeed in shooting the mayor if either his own cognitive faculties or Black's device issues in a decision to pull the trigger. As it happens, Jones's own cognitive faculties issue in a decision to pull the trigger, and, as a result, the mayor is shot dead. But neither Black's device nor its implantation played any causal role in the killing of the mayor. Things proceeded just as they would have had neither Black nor his device existed.

In this case, it certainly seems appropriate for Jones to feel guilty—or, at least, it seems that way so long as we are to imagine that Jones is a normal person with a normal history and thus, not someone who has, say, always lived under Black's influence. But even if it's clear that it's appropriate for Jones to feel guilty, it's not at all clear that we can legitimately hold him accountable for having killed the mayor. Indeed, there's good reason to think that we can't. After all, we're to assume that he didn't have the option of refraining from killing her. Indeed, what makes this a Frankfurt-type case is that he didn't have this option. But now, the nature of options is such that Jones was under an obligation to refrain from killing her only if this was an option for him, which it wasn't. For as I've previously stipulated, an option for a subject is just any member of the set such that, for any possible event φ, whether her φ-ing has a deontic status (e.g., that of being obligatory) depends on whether φ is a member of this set. And if it is a member, then what particular deontic status it has depends on how it compares to the other members in this set.[31] Thus,

---

FISCHER & RAVIZZA 1998.) Now, it's important to note that although I accept what's known as the principle of alternative possibilities (i.e., the view that a subject can be accountable for φ-ing only if she had the option of doing something other than φ), I do not accept the view that a subject can have the option of doing otherwise only if causal determinism is false. As we'll see in Chapter 3, I believe that having the option to do otherwise requires only rational control. And, as we'll see in the next chapter, it may well be that one can have rational control over φ-ing even if causal determinism is true.

31. Given this stipulation, there can be no question that "one is obligated to φ" implies "one has the option of φ-ing" even if there is some question whether "one is obligated to φ" implies "one can φ." For more on this, see PORTMORE FORTHCOMING.

given that he lacked the option to refrain from killing the mayor, he couldn't have been under any obligation to refrain from killing her. And if that's right, I don't see how we can think that Jones deserves to feel guilt for having killed her. Why would he deserve to suffer the unpleasantness of guilt for having done something permissible? Moreover, if he didn't have the option of doing anything other than kill the mayor, what could we have legitimately expected him to have done instead?[32]

So, given both the necessary connection between being blameworthy (or otherwise accountable) for having φ-ed and having had an obligation to refrain from φ-ing and the necessary connection between having had an obligation to refrain from φ-ing and having had the option to refrain from φ-ing, we should think that a subject can be blameworthy (or otherwise accountable) for having φ-ed only if she had the option to refrain from φ-ing. And since Jones didn't have the option to refrain from killing the mayor, he can't be blameworthy for having done so.

Here, then, is my second argument for control being necessary for accountability.[33]

(2.7) A subject is accountable for having φ-ed if and only if she is praise-worthy/blameworthy for having φ-ed. [Stipulation]

(2.8) A subject is praiseworthy/blameworthy for having φ-ed only if she ought to have φ-ed/was obligated to refrain from φ-ing.[34] [Assumption]

---

32. This is Widerker's "What-should-he-have-done defense" (called the "W-defense" for short) of the principle of alternative possibilities. See WIDERKER 2000.

33. This argument is inspired by those of COPP 1997A and WIDERKER 1991. One key difference is that whereas Copp and Widerker rely on the controversial principle that "ought" implies "can," I rely on the incontrovertible principle that both "ought" and "obligation" imply "option." This principle is incontrovertible, for I've defined an "option" such that only options are eligible for deontic status. The other key difference is that whereas they focus exclusively on blame, my argument is about accountability in general and, thus, concerns praise as well as blame.

34. Ishtiyaque Haji (1997) endorses a version of 2.8, which he calls "the Objective View of Blameworthiness." On this view, if a subject is blameworthy for φ-ing, then it must be that she had an obligation to refrain from φ-ing. And this view is presupposed by many others—see, for instance, COPP 1997A and PORTMORE 2011 (chap. 2). Also, note that for an act to be praiseworthy, it must have been something that one ought to have performed, not merely something that one was permitted to perform. By contrast, it can be that one ought to have done better without one's being blameworthy for not having done better. This is because an act is blameworthy only if it is contrary to what one was obligated to do. Thus, one can be blameworthy for not having given more to charity only if one was *obligated* to give more. That one *ought* to have given more is insufficient to make one blameworthy. Interestingly, given that it's a conceptual truth that "one is obligated to φ" implies "one has the option of φ-ing," Fischer

(2.9) A subject ought to have φ-ed/was obligated to refrain from φ-ing only if she had the option of φ-ing/refraining from φ-ing. [Analytic given my stipulative definition of "option"]

(2.10) A subject had the option of φ-ing/refraining from φ-ing only if whether she was to φ was under her control. [Assumption]

(2.11) Therefore, a subject is accountable for having φ-ed only if whether she was to φ was under her control. [From 2.7–2.10]

Of course, many would view *The Sniper* as a counterexample to 2.8.[35] They would claim that Jones is blameworthy for killing the mayor even though he had no obligation to refrain from doing so given his lack of the option to so refrain. But although it's clear that Jones is blameworthy, it's not clear that he is blameworthy for *killing the mayor* as opposed to for something else— perhaps, for doing something that entailed killing the mayor. And those who would deny 2.8 must assume that he is blameworthy for *killing the mayor*. Yet it's plausible to suppose that what he's instead blameworthy for is one or more of the following: (1) having formed the malicious desire to kill the mayor;[36] (2) having formed a willingness to do what he believes to be wrong; (3) having killed the mayor *on his own accord* or *for his own reasons* (NAYLOR 1984, ROBINSON 2012, and WEDGWOOD 2017); or (4) having exercised his rational capacities in a way that didn't trigger Black's device (WEDGWOOD

---

must bite the bullet and accept both that nothing anyone ever does is morally wrong and that, nevertheless, some people are morally blameworthy for doing what they were permitted to do—see FISCHER 2003 (esp. p. 249). Clearly, then, Fischer has a much higher tolerance for bullet-biting than I do.

35. Others take the following to be a counterexample to 2.8. Suppose that Arthur, a white supremacist, sneaks up behind an unsuspecting black man, named Bert, and clubs him over the head, knocking him unconscious. He does so out of a hatred for blacks. However, unbeknownst to Arthur, Bert was just about to shoot his ex-girlfriend Carla, who, we'll suppose, was completely innocent. As it turns out, Arthur's act saves an innocent life. Yet Arthur is clearly blameworthy. So this may seem to be a counterexample to 2.8. But it's a counterexample only if we think that Arthur was obligated to refrain from clubbing Bert. And we shouldn't think this. For if we thought this, we have to think (implausibly) that it would be appropriate for us to demand that he refrain from clubbing him, which it wouldn't be. Instead, we can rightly demand only that he not do so out of racial hatred. Thus, when we realize what Arthur was actually blameworthy for (i.e., his bad motive), we find that this is no counterexample to 2.8.

36. You may wonder, What if we were to imagine a variant on this case in which there was an additional device that would have caused Jones to form the desire kill the mayor had he not done so via his own cognitive faculties? In that case, I don't see how we could legitimately hold him accountable for forming this malicious desire. For in that case, he lacked the option of not forming this malicious desire. So I think that all we can hold him accountable for is his forming this malicious desire via his own cognitive faculties.

2017). I think that the only reason some may resist such alternatives is that they assume that Jones never had the relevant sort of control over any of 1–4 and so can't be accountable for any of them.[37] But, in §3.3, I'll argue that although Jones didn't have volitional control over any of 1–4, he did have the relevant sort of control—that is, rational control—over all of 1–4. And this, I think, will defuse whatever force such a Frankfurt-type case is meant to have. For, in that case, we can account for our intuition that Jones is deserving of blame without our having to reject our intuition that a subject can be accountable for having φ-ed only if she had an obligation to refrain from φ-ing.[38]

So far, I've argued that obligations have both a directive role and an inculpatory role. And I've argued that these are roles they can play only if their application is restricted to events over which their subjects exert control. For if obligations weren't so restricted, a subject could be obligated to φ without having any way to exert her control so as to φ and thereby avoid being accountable for not φ-ing. And since, by my stipulative definition, a subject's options are just those events that are eligible for being obligatory, it follows that her options must also be restricted to those events that are under her control. And thus, we must hold that one's having control over whether one φs is a necessary condition for one's having the option to φ.

Now, before I go on to argue that one's having control over whether one φs is also sufficient for one's having the option to φ, I want to address one last objection to the thought that it's necessary. The objection goes as follows. If I actually did φ, then I must have had the option to φ. But it's possible for me to φ without ever having had control over whether I was to φ. Thus, it's possible for me to have had the option to φ without φ's ever having been under my control.

The problem with this objection is that it mistakenly assumes that my having actually φ-ed establishes that I must have once had the option to φ. This assumption probably stems from the common practice of citing the fact that one has φ-ed as proof that one has (or, at least, had) the ability to φ. For instance, suppose that I'm about to tee off on the third hole of my favorite golf course when I turn to my golf partner and boastfully claim that I'm going to hit a hole-in-one. She may, of course, doubt my boastful claim and say: "You can't hit a hole-in-one." But suppose I reply: "Sure, I can. In

---

37. See, for instance, FISCHER 1994 (pp. 143–145).

38. So I would deny that the lesson of Frankfurt-type cases is that we should deny that control is necessary for accountability. Instead, I take the lesson to be that what we're directly accountable for is not our voluntary actions but how we exercise our rational capacities and whether we do so in a way that fails to trigger Black's device.

fact, I did so just last week." Now, even if it's often the case that the fact that one has φ-ed counts as evidence that one has or had the ability to φ, this is not always the case. In particular, it's not the case when it was just a fluke that one happened to have φ-ed.[39] Suppose, then, that I had tried to hit a hole-in-one on this hole hundreds of times in the past and just happened to luck out on my attempt last week. In that case, my claim that I can hit a hole-in-one rings false. Moreover, it seems that I didn't even have the option of hitting a hole-in-one on the occasion that I did so.

For me to have the ability or option to hit a hole-in-one, it must be up to me whether I do so. Yet it is never up to me whether I hit a hole-in-one. It is, of course, up to me whether I *try* to hit a hole-in-one, but since there are literally millions of different ways for me to try to hit a hole-in-one with only a very minute proportion of these resulting in my actually hitting a hole-in-one, whether I hit a hole-in-one is not up to me. Of course, I would admit that I had control over many aspects of my attempt to hit a hole-in-one, including over how much force, within some imprecise range, I exert in hitting the ball. But, unfortunately, to get a hole-in-one I must hit the ball within a much narrower range of forces than that. Suppose, for instance, that when I hit my hole-in-one last week, I hit the ball with precisely 14,756.09875 newtons of force. And suppose that, had the force with which I hit the ball been three hundred-thousandths of a newton more or less than that, I wouldn't have made a hole-in-one. In other words, assume that if the force with which I had hit the ball had been more than 14,756.09878 newtons or less than 14,756.09872 newtons, I wouldn't have made a hole-in-one. If that's right, then it was just a fluke that I happened to hit it within this narrow range, for the control that I exerted over how hard I would hit the ball was not nearly so precise. It seems, then, that I didn't have the option of hitting a hole-in-one even on the occasion that I happened to do so.

This explains why it would have been a mistake to think that I was obligated to hit a hole-in-one on that occasion as well as to have held me accountable had I failed to do so. If there had been something significant at stake with respect to my hitting a hole-in-one on that occasion, then I could have been obligated to *try* to hit a hole-in-one or even to hit it very hard, but I couldn't have been obligated to hit a hole-in-one or to hit the ball with between 14,756.09878 and 14,756.09872 newtons of force. And again, the explanation seems to be that whereas I had control over whether I was to try to

---

39. See SOUTHWOOD AND WIENS 2016.

hit a hole-in-one and over whether I was to hit the ball very hard, I didn't have control over either whether I would hit a hole-in-one or whether I would hit the ball with between 14,756.09878 and 14,756.09872 newtons of force. So we should deny that the fact that one has actually φ-ed establishes that one has (or even had) the option to φ. And this seems to support my contention that having the option to φ requires having control over whether one φs.

§2.3 The Sufficiency of Control

It seems that control over whether one φs is necessary for one's having the option to φ. But is it also sufficient? Intuitively, it seems to be. For if a subject has control over whether she φs, then it's up to her whether she φs, and that seems sufficient for her having the option to φ. For if it's up to her whether she φs, it seems that φ must have a deontic status and which deontic status it has is just a matter of how it compares to its alternatives.

Yet one may object that the following states a necessary condition for having the option to φ.

Tryism: For any event φ and any subject S, S has the option to φ only if she would φ if she were to try to φ.

According to tryism, I could have control over whether I am to φ, and yet, φ won't be an option for me if it's not the case that I would φ if I were to try to φ. Thus, tryism denies that my having control over whether I φ is sufficient for my having the option to φ.

Nevertheless, tryism is false. To see why, consider the following case.

Stupid Mistake: A genius named Albert took a math test and missed one of the easiest problems because he overthought things and consequently overlooked its simple solution.[40]

According to tryism, Albert didn't have the option of providing the correct answer to this easy problem. After all, it wasn't for a lack of trying that he

---

40. This is partly inspired by John Maier's example of a professional golfer who misses what should have been a gimme putt. Maier (2014) uses it to question whether its being the case that S would φ if she were to try to φ is necessary for S's having the option to φ. The example originates with AUSTIN 1956. My example, though, is also partly inspired by Michael Smith's example of someone blanking on the answer to a question—see his 2003.

failed to provide the correct answer. Rather, he tried to provide the correct answer and failed because he overthought things, consequently overlooking its obvious solution. So, if anything, he tried too hard. And given that he was going to try and fail, it was false that he would provide the correct answer if he were to try to do so. So tryism implies that providing the correct answer wasn't an option for him.

But that's implausible. Even Albert would admit that he could and should have gotten the correct answer to this easy problem. And we should too. For it seems that he had both the ability and the opportunity to provide the correct answer. In other words, it seems that he had control over whether he was to provide the correct answer, so it was up to him whether he would do so. The fact that he failed to exercise his control to good effect doesn't mean that it wasn't up to him. It just means that he messed up. Indeed, these sorts of stupid mistakes cause us the most frustration precisely because we think that we could and should have gotten things right. When we fail to come up with the correct solution to a problem and find out later that the solution was one that never would have occurred to us, we are not nearly as frustrated (if at all) as when we think that it would have occurred to us if only we had exercised our control differently. This suggests, then, that a subject's having control over whether she φs is not only necessary, but also sufficient, for her to have the option to φ. So, given all the arguments above, I think that we should accept that having control over whether one φs is both necessary and sufficient for one's having the option to φ.

§2.4 Conclusion

It seems that whereas any event—be it a seismic, cosmological, or meteorological event—can have an evaluative status, only certain types of events can have a deontic status. Indeed, everyone seems to agree that we must restrict the range of events for which subjects can be obligated to perform and can be accountable for failing to perform. Yet, if the only role that our obligations had to play was an evaluative one, this restriction would be misplaced. But it isn't misplaced precisely because obligations differ from mere evaluations in having two additional roles to play. One of these additional roles is a directive one. Obligations, unlike mere evaluations, must direct us to respond in certain ways, and for these directives to have any point at all, they must direct us to respond only in those ways that we have the option of responding. The other role that obligations play is an inculpatory one. For there is a conceptual connection between failing to abide by an obligation and being accountable for so failing—at least, absent some suitable excuse. And since it's inappropriate to hold subjects to account for events over which they lacked control, we must restrict a subject's options to those events over which she exerted the relevant sort of control.

But what counts as the relevant sort of control? I turn to this issue in Chapter 3.

Chapter 3

What's the Relevant Sort of Control?

I'VE ARGUED THAT our options include all and only those events over which we exert the relevant sort of control. In this chapter, I explain what I take the relevant sort of control to be.

The chapter has the following structure. In §3.1, I argue that the relevant sort of control must be complete as opposed to partial and synchronic as opposed to diachronic (i.e., the sort of control that we exercise at a moment in time rather than over a span of time). In §3.2, I argue that the relevant sort of control must be personal as opposed to subpersonal (i.e., the sort of control that makes our actions intelligible in terms of reasons and not just in terms of cause and effect). And in §3.3, I argue that the relevant sort of control is not the sort that we exert directly over our intentional acts by forming certain volitions but the sort that we exert directly over our reasons-responsive attitudes (e.g., our beliefs, desires, and intentions) by being both receptive and reactive to reasons—forming, revising, sustaining, and/or abandoning these attitudes in light of our awareness of facts (or what we take to be facts) that count for or against them.[1] In §3.4, I explain why we cannot plausibly account

---

1. The notion of a *reasons-responsive attitude* is, perhaps, the same as T. M. Scanlon's notion of a *judgment-sensitive attitude*, an attitude that is sensitive to the subject's judgments about reasons (1998, p. 20). But Scanlon's notion is, if not distinct, misleading, for we can respond to reasons without having any judgments about what our reasons are. "We respond to reasons when we are aware of facts that give us these reasons, and this awareness leads us [in the right way] to believe, or want, or do what these facts give us reasons to believe, or want, or do" (PARFIT 2011A, p. 493). Thus, we can respond to reasons while neither knowing that this is what we are doing nor having any judgments about our reasons (PARFIT 2011A, p. 461). Reasons-responsive attitudes include all and only those mental states that a rational subject will tend to have, or tend not to have, in response to reasons (or apparent reasons)—facts (or what are taken to be

for the responsibility that we have for our reasons-responsive attitudes by tracing that responsibility back to various voluntary acts. In §3.5, I explain why we shouldn't think that the relevant sort of control is voluntary control. And, in §3.6, I offer some concluding thoughts about options, control, and responsibility.

§3.1 Complete and Synchronic Control

In determining what the relevant sort of control is, we must address several issues. First, is the relevant sort of control complete or merely partial? Second, is it the sort of control that a subject exerts at a moment in time (i.e., *synchronic control*) or the sort that she exerts over a span of time (i.e., *diachronic control*)? Third, is it the sort of *personal control* that I exert over the contractions of my biceps when I flex them while looking at myself in the mirror or the sort of *subpersonal control* that I exert over the contractions of my cardiac muscles when their frequency increases in response to my increased anxiety? Fourth and last, is it the sort of *rational control* that we exert directly over our reasons-responsive attitudes or the sort of *volitional control* that we exert directly over our intentional actions? I'll take up these issues presently. In the remainder of this section, I'll argue that the relevant sort of control must be both complete and synchronic. Then, in the following two sections, I'll argue that it must be both personal and rational.

So let's start with whether the relevant sort of control needs to be complete. A subject's control over whether she φs is *complete* if and only if, holding everything else fixed, whether she φs just depends on how she exercises her control such that the objective probability that she'll φ will be 1 if she exercises her control in certain ways and will be 0 otherwise.[2] And let's say that a subject's control over whether she φs is merely *partial* if and only if, holding

---

facts) that count for or against the attitudes in question. So beliefs are clearly reasons-responsive attitudes, for a rational subject will, for instance, tend to believe that it will rain in response to her awareness of facts that constitute decisive reason for her believing this, such as the fact that a reliable weather service has predicted that it will rain. Although reasons-responsive attitudes include many mental states, they exclude feelings of hunger, nausea, tiredness, and dizziness, which are not responsive to reasons. Suppose, for instance, that I have too quickly consumed a good-sized meal and am still feeling hungry, as there has not yet been sufficient time for my brain to receive the relevant physiological signals from my stomach. Even if I am aware that I've eaten more than enough to be satiated, my hunger is not responsive to this awareness. Instead, it is responsive only to the physiological signals that supposedly take about twenty minutes to travel from my stomach to my brain.

2. For someone to have complete control over whether she φs is not for her φ-ing to depend only on what she controls. Indeed, whether someone φs is always going to depend on things outside her control. Nevertheless, one's control over φ-ing can be complete in the sense just

everything else fixed, how she exercises her control determines not whether she will φ, but only where between 0 and 1 the objective probability that she'll φ lies. Now, there are at least two problems with thinking that the sort of control that's relevant with respect to having the option of φ-ing needn't be complete. First, since all options are eligible for being obligatory, this thought implies that a subject could be accountable for φ-ing even if it were not entirely up to her whether she φs. To illustrate, suppose that I'm golfing and have a moderately difficult putt to make. And suppose that I'm sufficiently skilled that I can, by trying my hardest, make it quite likely that I'll make the putt. But assume that I cannot ensure that I'll make the putt, for although the control that I exert over my putting is almost sufficiently precise to ensure that I'll make the putt, it isn't quite that precise. Let's assume, then, that I'll make the putt only if I hit the ball with somewhere between 367.9 and 372.5 newtons of force, but that my control is such that I can determine only whether I hit the ball with *around* 370 newtons of force—"around" meaning, in this instance, plus or minus 3 newtons of force. Given such assumptions, it seems inappropriate to hold me accountable should I fail to make the putt—at least, it does if we assume that I tried my hardest and failed due only to the sheer bad luck of hitting the ball with 367.2 newtons of force instead of somewhere between 367.9 and 372.5 newtons of force. So the first problem is that if partial control is sufficient with respect to having an option, then people will be accountable for failures that are due to sheer bad luck, and yet it seems inappropriate to hold people accountable for events that are the result of sheer bad luck. That is, it seems inappropriate to think that people deserve to experience the unpleasantness of feeling guilty on account of their having been unlucky.[3]

---

defined. For instance, I had complete control over whether I was to type out this sentence—at least, I did assuming counterfactual determinism is true. For although I couldn't have typed out this sentence had the power gone out, the power (as it happens) was determined not to go out, and so whether I was to type out this sentence just depended on how I exerted my control. (*Counterfactual determinism* is the view both that, for any possible event *e*, the objective probability that *e* will occur is always either 0 or 1 and that there is some determinate fact as to what exactly the world would be like both if *e* were to occur and if *e* were not to occur. And the *objective probability* that some event will [or would] occur is the percentage of the time that it will [or would] occur under identical causal circumstances—circumstances where the causal laws and histories are the same.)

3. I deny, then, that the extent to which someone is deserving of the unpleasantness of feeling guilty can depend on luck. To illustrate, imagine two possible worlds. In one world, Ilhan drinks too much, gets behind the wheel of a car, and inadvertently swerves off the road and hits a trashcan, destroying it. In the other, Chrisoula drinks too much, gets behind the wheel of a car, and inadvertently swerves off the road and hits a boy, killing him. Assume, though, that the two worlds are otherwise identical. Thus, at all times prior to and including the moment where

The second problem is that if we hold that partial control is sufficient, then obligations won't be able to fulfill their directive role. Consider, again, the putting case. It seems pointless to direct me to make the putt as opposed to merely to try my hardest to make it. For whereas I can abide by the latter directive, I can't abide by the former directive. After all, what's up to me in this instance is whether I try my hardest, not whether I make the putt. Whether I make the putt depends both on how hard I try and on whether I luck out such that my trying hard results in my hitting it within the required narrow range of forces. So, given both the directive role and the inculpatory role of obligations, having an option requires complete, and not merely partial, control.

And, as I will show presently, these two roles also suggest that the relevant sort of control is synchronic as opposed to diachronic—that is, it's the kind of control that we exert at a given moment in time rather than over some span of time. But first, I need to explain why we need to talk about time at all. It's because, as many have observed, obligations are indexed to times.[4] Obligations are indexed to times because obligations apply only to options, which can vary over time. What was once an option may no longer be one. So, even if I once had an obligation to φ, I can't still have that obligation if φ-ing has ceased to be an option for me.

To illustrate, consider *The Letter*. Suppose that on Saturday evening, a traveling friend gives me a letter to mail for him on Monday morning, and I promise him (there and then) that I'll do so. Consequently, I have, as of

---

each swerves off the road, Ilhan and Chrisoula have the exact same mental states and make the exact same bodily movements. The only difference, then, lies with what rests besides the relevant portion of the road in the two worlds. I deny, then, that Chrisoula is more deserving of suffering the unpleasantness of feeling guilty than Ilhan is. And I don't find this counterintuitive. But I know that some will. To help assuage those who do, let me make a couple of points. First, we can deny that the degree to which Ilhan and Chrisoula are accountable differs while affirming that what they are accountable for differs (see ZIMMERMAN 2002). That is, we can say that, whereas Ilhan is accountable for driving negligently and thereby destroying a trashcan, Chrisoula is accountable for driving negligently and thereby killing a boy. Second, we can deny that their degrees of accountability differ without denying that, in virtue of killing the boy, Chrisoula incurs obligations that Ilhan doesn't incur, such as an obligation to make reparations to the boy's family. So I admit that what obligations one incurs can depend on luck; I just deny that whether, or how much, one deserves to suffer the unpleasantness of feeling guilty can depend on luck. Thus, I deny what's known as *resultant moral luck* (see ZIMMERMAN 1987)—the idea that one's degree of accountability for φ-ing could be affected by the uncontrolled events (which are entirely outside of one's control) that determine what results from one's φ-ing. For citations of some literature supporting my stance on resultant moral luck, see note 24 of Chapter 2. '

4. See, for instance, FELDMAN 1986, GOLDMAN 1976, and CURRAN 1995.

that moment, an obligation to mail the letter come Monday morning. And this fact explains why I have the further obligation, as of Saturday evening, to find a safe place to store the letter until Monday. Nevertheless, suppose that I neglect to store it in a safe place and a housemate inadvertently grabs it along with some other papers on Sunday evening, using it and those other papers as kindling to start the logs in the fireplace. It seems that as of that moment on Sunday evening, I cease having the option of mailing the letter. For the letter ceases to exist as of that moment. And since, as of that moment, I do not have the option of mailing the nonexistent letter, I do not, as of that moment, have an obligation to do so. And this means that no one can, as of that moment, legitimately expect me to mail that (nonexistent) letter come Monday morning. Of course, even so, I'm not blameless for failing to mail the letter. For I had, from Saturday evening until Sunday evening, an obligation to mail it: an obligation that I failed to fulfill and without having had a suitable excuse for so failing. Moreover, I had the obligation, from Saturday evening until Sunday evening, to store it in a safe place, which I also failed to fulfill and, again, without any suitable excuse.

Of course, subjects not only lose options, but also acquire new ones. To illustrate, consider *Island Rescue*. Suppose that a child on a nearby island needs rescue. To rescue this child named Niko, I must first swim from the mainland to his island. But the waters between them are shark-infested, and so there's no way for me to attempt his rescue without swimming in shark-infested waters and thereby risking my life. As of time t_1, then, I don't have the option of attempting Niko's rescue without risking my own life. But suppose that, at time t_2, I go ahead and risk my life by swimming to the island, luckily making it past the sharks. Having arrived safely at time t_4, I now have the option of attempting his rescue without risking my own life, for assume that there's a boat on his island that I can use to get us back safely to the mainland. Now that my options have changed, so too have my obligations changed. Although I didn't have, as of t_1, an obligation to attempt his rescue, I do now (at t_4) given that I can now do so without jeopardizing my own welfare. Thus, we find that our obligations change as our options expand and contract. Consequently, we must index both options and obligations to times.

If you're having trouble making sense of time-indexed options and obligations, then think of them as I do: as properties that are possessed by the given subject at a given time. Thus, the phrase "Doug was, on Saturday evening, obligated to mail the letter Monday morning" just means "Doug had on Saturday evening the property of being obligated to mail the letter Monday morning." Likewise, the phrase "Mailing the letter Monday morning was, on

Saturday evening, an option for Doug" just means "Doug had on Saturday evening the property of having the option of mailing the letter Monday morning." Call the first sort of property a deontic property and the latter, an option property. Clearly, people's option properties can change over time. And, given this and the opting-for-the-best view, it follows that so can their deontic properties.

Since options are, as I've argued, a function of our control, we must index our control to times as well. Thus, we must ask, At what time or times must a subject possess control over whether she will φ at some later time t' for her to have, as of the present time t, the option of φ-ing at t'? Clearly, it's not enough for her to have exerted control sometime prior to t. Saturday evening, I had control over whether I would mail the letter on Monday morning, but that doesn't mean that I had, as of Sunday evening, the option of mailing the letter that had been destroyed in the fireplace. It seems, then, that the most natural answer to this question is that, to have, as of t, the option of φ-ing at t', a subject must be able to exert—or, at least, start exerting—control over this at t. And thus, we have the following two contenders.

The Synchronic View: A subject has at t the option of φ-ing at t' if and only if whether she will φ at t' depends (in the right way) merely on how she exerts her control at t.[5]

The Diachronic View: A subject has at t the option of φ-ing at t' if and only if whether she will φ at t' depends (in the right way) on how she exerts her control from t onward.

We should, I believe, reject the diachronic view. To understand why, consider the following popular version of the diachronic view.

---

5. We are, to the extent possible, to hold everything else (such as the external circumstances) fixed. So the idea is that if we hold (to the extent possible) everything else fixed and the subject will φ at t' if she exerts her control at t in one way but not if she exerts her control at t in some other way, then whether she φs at t' depends merely on how she exerts her control at t. To illustrate, imagine that one way for her to exert her control at t is for her to form at t the intention to φ at t' and that another way for her to exert her control at t is for her to refrain from forming at t the intention to φ at t'. And assume that whether she'll φ at t' just depends on whether she forms or refrains from forming at t the intention to φ at t'. This would, then, be a case of her having at t synchronic control over whether she φs at t'—at least, it would so long as we're to assume that the formation of this intention would cause her to φ at t' via some nondeviant causal process.

Schedulism: A subject has at t the option of φ-ing at t' if and only if whether she will φ at t' depends (in the right way) on her having certain intentions from t onward—that is, on her having a certain schedule of intentions from t onward.[6]

On this view, a subject needn't be able to ensure that she will φ at t' simply by exerting the control that she has at t. To illustrate, suppose that no matter how I exert the control that I have at this moment, I'm not going to get up and exercise when the alarm wakes me at 5:00 AM tomorrow. Indeed, no matter which acts and attitudes I form and perform now, I'm not going to get up and exercise when the alarm wakes me at 5:00 AM tomorrow but will instead hit the snooze button several times in a row. Still, on schedulism, I have now the option of getting up and exercising at 5:00 AM so long as that's what I would in fact do if I were to form the intention to do so when I'm woken up by the alarm at 5:00 AM. The fact that no matter what I intend now to do later, I won't form the intention to get up and exercise when the alarm wakes me is, on schedulism, irrelevant. But this seems to be a mistake. In order for my getting up and exercising at 5:00 AM tomorrow to be, as of the present, an option for me (and not just something that I will have the option of doing at 5:00 AM tomorrow), I must have, as of the present, control over whether I will get up and exercise at 5:00 AM tomorrow. But if I'm not going to get up and exercise at 5:00 AM tomorrow no matter what my present actions and attitudes are, then it seems that I don't now have control over whether I'll get up and exercise at 5:00 AM tomorrow. After all, to have control now over what I'll do at 5:00 AM tomorrow is to have the present ability to determine what I'll do then—or, if not that, then at least the present ability to affect the likelihood that I'll do certain things then. But in this case, I have, at present, no way to affect even the likelihood that I'll get up and exercise at 5:00 AM tomorrow, or so we're assuming. Indeed, we're assuming that regardless of which acts and attitudes I form and perform at present (and, thus, regardless of how I currently exercise my rational capacities), there is absolutely no chance that I'll get up and exercise at 5:00 AM tomorrow.[7]

---

6. This is adapted from my definition of *personally possible*—see my 2011 (p. 166). And this in turn was adapted from Jacob Ross's definition of a *performable option*—see his 2012 (p. 81). Proponents of this sort of view include Fred Feldman (1986), Travis Timmerman (2015A), and Michael J. Zimmerman (1996).

7. Admittedly, if I set the alarm this evening, I will, when the alarm goes off, have control at that point over whether I'll get up and exercise. After all, I will at that point be able to determine

To better understand just how counterintuitive schedulism's implications are, consider the following case.

> *Curing Cancer:* A seven-year-old boy named Saru is playing with a computer keyboard. Millions of lives depend on his writing and sending an email to the director of the National Institutes of Health that explains how to cure cancer in such a way that the director will have to take it seriously and implement it.[8]

Schedulism implausibly implies that Saru has the option of curing cancer (or, more accurately, the option of effecting a cure for cancer). After all, to do so, he need only write and send a certain email message, which in turn just involves his making a certain series of keystrokes. And Saru would make each keystroke in this series if he were to form the right intentions at the right times. To illustrate, suppose that such an email would start with: "The cure for cancer is . . ." Now, if at t_1 Saru were to intend to hit Shift + T, he would do so at t_2, thereby typing an uppercase T. And, having done that, he would have the capacity to form at t_3 the intention to hit the H key. Moreover, if he were to form this intention at t_3, he would then hit the H key at t_4, thereby typing a lowercase H. And similar assumptions apply for all the remaining keystrokes in the series. Thus, schedulism implies that Saru has, as of t_0, the option of curing cancer. And since the relevant considerations favor Saru's doing so, it seems that the proponent of schedulism must insist that Saru is obligated to cure cancer. Or, if she objects to this description of the act, she must, at least, insist that Saru is obligated to make the specific series of keystrokes that will result in cancer's being cured.

This, of course, is absurd. Saru does not now control whether he will make this specific series of keystrokes. For, as we'll plausibly assume, Saru will not

---

that I'll exercise by jumping out of bed. For let's suppose that if I jump right out of bed when the alarm goes off, I'll exercise, but if I hit the snooze button, I won't. But I'm concerned with whether I have the option now (this evening) of exercising tomorrow morning, not whether I will have the option of doing so tomorrow morning. And I'm claiming that if I'm not going to exercise tomorrow morning no matter what acts and attitudes I form and perform this evening, then I don't have control this evening over whether I'm going to exercise tomorrow morning. And if I don't have control now over whether I'm going to exercise tomorrow morning, then I don't now have the option of exercising tomorrow morning.

8. This example is modeled after a similar one given in WILAND 2005. And it should be noted that I'm assuming that a seven-year-old can be a moral agent. Thus, I'm assuming that Saru would, in right circumstances, be morally obligated to hit a certain key on the keyboard that he's playing with.

make this series of keystrokes no matter what he does now or intends now to do later. Even if he does happen to hit Shift + T at t_2, he wouldn't, as it happens, follow up by making each of the other 50,000 or so specific keystrokes that are required to complete the task of writing and sending such an email (or so I'll stipulate). And even if Saru were to intend to type out (or to try to type out) the cure for cancer, he would, in fact, fail to do so (or so I'll stipulate). And although God could perhaps form the complex intention to make the entire series of specific keystrokes required, Saru does not have the capacity to cognize such a complex intention. Thus, Saru has no way at t_0 to effect his typing out such an email. No present attitude or action that he has the capacity to form or perform would result in his curing cancer. Thus, he does not now control whether he cures cancer. So the problem with schedulism is that it counterintuitively implies that Saru has, at present, the option of curing cancer (or, at least, the option of making the series of keystrokes that will result in cancer's being cured) even though he does not now control whether he performs this option.

Of course, you may think that Saru should at least make the first couple of keystrokes: that is, Shift + T. For even if Saru doesn't have the capacity to form the complex intention to make the entire series of specific keystrokes required to cure cancer, he has, we'll assume, the capacity to form the much simpler intention to hit the Shift-key and T-key simultaneously. But I don't see why he (objectively) ought to do this unless his doing so would increase the objective probability of his typing out the entire cure for cancer, such that the prospect of his hitting Shift + T is better than that of his performing any alternative option. So let me just stipulate that, in this case, counterfactual determinism is true and the objective probability of his curing cancer conditional on his hitting Shift + T is zero. Thus, the prospect of his playing with his dolls would be better than that of his hitting Shift + T. Yet, even in this case, schedulism implies that Saru has the option of curing cancer and will be obligated to do so unless there is some sufficiently good alternative available to him. And this just seems absurd.

Of course, schedulism isn't the only version of the diachronic view that has proponents. Consider, for instance, the following precisified version of Berislav Marušić's diachronic view.[9]

---

9. He holds that, "in general, when something is entirely up to us, there is no gap between φ-ing and continuing to try to φ. Of course, that does not mean that there is no difference between trying to φ and φ-ing; it's just that if one fails to φ, one did not try hard enough or long enough" (MARUŠIĆ 2015, p. 19).

Continualism: A subject has at *t* the option of φ-ing at *t'* if and only if whether she will φ at *t'* depends (in the right way) on her continually trying, from *t* onward, to φ at *t'*.[10]

This view can, perhaps, avoid the implication that Saru is obligated to cure cancer, for it's stipulated that he would fail to do so even if he were to continually try to do so.[11] But the view has counterintuitive implications in other cases, such as the following.

Severing Toes: Unless I use solid platinum bolt cutters to sever all ten of my toes, one per minute from 5:01 AM to 5:10 AM tomorrow morning, my wife will have both of her arms cut off from just above her elbows. Unfortunately, if I were to experience the pain of using bolt cutters to sever a toe at 5:01 AM, I would, then, stop trying to sever my other toes and end up severing only one toe. Last, the truth of the above does not depend on which acts and attitudes I form and perform prior to 5:01 AM. Thus, even if I were to resolve now to continue trying to sever all my toes after severing the first toe, I would change my mind upon experiencing that pain and decide not to try to sever any more toes. Now, since I don't have any solid platinum bolt cutters, I can't save my wife's arms without purchasing them, and they are very expensive given that they are solid platinum. Indeed, they're so expensive that purchasing them would require all the money that we have saved. So, if I purchase them, we won't be able to afford to buy any prosthetics. Last, I know all the above. See Table 3.1.

---

10. Marušić recognizes that this will need to be revised in order to deal with some of the standard worries associated with conditional analyses of ability. But my objections to it will not turn on whether it's suitably revised in this way. Last, I should note that Marušić considers this view to be only a helpful heuristic, and not a metaphysical analysis. See MARUŠIĆ 2015 (pp. 167–168). Nevertheless, it will be useful to consider where this sort of view goes wrong even if it is not officially endorsed by anyone.

11. Of course, this depends on how we describe what it is that Saru is trying to do. Although it's clear that Saru would not cure cancer even if he were to continually try to type out the cure for cancer, perhaps he would cure cancer if he were to continually try to type out the following: "The cure for cancer is . . ." (and let's imagine that the ellipses are filled in with the remaining 50,000 or so keystrokes). If the relevant description is the latter, then continualism, like schedulism, implausibly implies that Saru has the option of typing out those 50,000 or so specific keystrokes.

Table 3.1 My Present Options in *Severing Toes*

Option	Outcome	Ranking
Purchase bolt cutters today and sever only one toe tomorrow	I lose a toe, my wife loses both arms, and we can't afford prosthetics	Worst event
Purchase bolt cutters today and sever no toes tomorrow	I lose no toes, my wife loses both arms, and we can't afford prosthetics	3rd best event
Purchase no bolt cutters today and sever no toes tomorrow	I lose no toes, my wife loses both arms, and we buy prosthetics for my wife	2nd best event
Option?	**Outcome**	**Ranking**
Purchase bolt cutters today and sever all ten toes tomorrow	I lose ten toes and my wife loses neither arm	Best event

Given these stipulations, it follows that I cannot, by exerting what control I have at present, see to it that I will do tomorrow morning all that I must do to save my wife's arms. Of course, there are things that I can do now that will ensure that I will at least be able to use solid platinum bolt cutters to sever one of my toes at 5:01 AM tomorrow. I could, for instance, set the alarm now to make sure that I'll be awake then. And I could purchase solid platinum bolt cutters. But even having done these things, there will be zero chance of my doing tomorrow all that I need to do to save my wife's arms. For after experiencing the pain of severing the first toe, I'm going to decide not even to try to sever any more toes. So what's the point of my purchasing these expensive bolt cutters if doing so won't increase the probability that I'll achieve my goal of saving my wife's arms?

Nevertheless, according to continualism, I have, as of the present, the option of doing tomorrow all that I must do to save my wife's arms. For if I were (from here on) to continue to try to save my wife's arms, I would succeed in doing so. Indeed, if I were to fail to save my wife arms, it could only be because, as Marušić would put it, I "did not try hard enough or long enough." For the fact that I wouldn't keep trying if I were to experience the pain of losing the first toe doesn't change the fact that, if I were to keep trying (and assume that I could keep trying even after severing the first toe), I would succeed in saving my wife's arms. Thus, continualism implies that I have, as of the present, the option of doing tomorrow morning all that I need to do to save her arms. But, given the stipulations of the case, this seems false. This doesn't seem to be an option that I have at present.

We've seen, then, that both versions of the diachronic view have counter-intuitive implications. But perhaps there is some version of the diachronic view that avoids these specific implications. I won't take a stand on this, for it seems to me that there are deeper problems with the diachronic view, and these have nothing do with the particularities of any version of it.

One problem is that the diachronic view implies that a subject can have, as of t, an option and, thus, an obligation to φ at t' even if it would be pointless or counterproductive for her to include the thought that she will fulfill this obligation in her planning at t. To illustrate, consider, again, *Severing Toes*, and ask whether I should plan on using platinum bolt cutters to sever all ten of my toes. If so, I should probably include in my present plans the intention to go purchase some platinum bolt cutters. But this seems pointless. This would lead only to my severing one of my toes, but it wouldn't lead to my severing all ten of my toes. After all, it's stipulated that I would not go on to sever a second toe after severing the first and that this is true regardless of how I exert my control at present. So it seems to me that I shouldn't plan on severing all ten of my toes, and, consequently, shouldn't plan on buying platinum bolt cutters. Indeed, it seems that I should plan instead on my wife's losing her arms. So rather than planning on purchasing platinum bolt cutters, I should plan instead on purchasing prosthetic arms for her. And if I shouldn't include in my planning at t the thought that I'll be severing all ten of my toes, then what's the point of ascribing to me at t the property of being obligated to sever all ten of my toes? How is this obligation supposed to fulfill its directive role when it seems that I should just exclude the possibility of my abiding by its directives in my present planning? And this problem generalizes, because, in general, the diachronic view is committed to the view that I can have, as of t, an option and, thus, an obligation to φ at t' even if there is no way for me to exercise the control that I possess at t to determine (or increase the likelihood) that I will φ at t'. And this is why I and others (see, e.g., GOLDMAN 1978) think, in accordance with the synchronic view, that a subject can't have, as of t, the property of being obligated to φ at t' if her planning at t on fulfilling this obligation would be pointless and, perhaps, even counterproductive.

It's not just pointless (and possibly counterproductive) to plan on fulfilling the kinds of obligations that the diachronic view supposes that we have. What's worse, it can be impermissible to make such plans. This is because, as discussed in Chapter 1, it's impermissible to be such that the propositional contents of one's beliefs and intentions are logically inconsistent. To illustrate, suppose that I know that I won't sever more than one toe. Since the propositional content of this belief is logically inconsistent with the propositional content of an intention (or plan) to sever my ten toes, it is, then, impermissible for me to plan on severing my ten toes unless I change my belief. So, if the diachronic view were correct in holding that I have, as of t, an obligation to sever my ten toes, I would be in a real bind. For there's no getting around the fact that I must either (1) refrain from planning on severing my ten toes (which, let's assume, would lead me to refrain from purchasing platinum bolt cutters) or (2) plan on severing my ten toes. If I do the former, I will ensure that I violate the obligation that I supposedly now have to sever all ten toes using platinum bolt cutters, for this will lead to my refraining from purchasing such bolt cutters. And if I do the latter, I will thereby violate the obligation that I now have not to be such that the propositional contents of my beliefs and intentions are logically inconsistent. Thus, I'll have jointly unsatisfiable obligations despite having done nothing wrong to end up in such a predicament.

So the problem with the diachronic view is that it implies that I can now have an obligation to φ even if I know that I won't φ and won't φ regardless of how I now exert my control. For instance, in *Severing Toes*, the diachronic view implies that I have, as of now, an obligation to sever a second toe even though I know that I won't sever a second toe no matter how I now exert my control. And we can see that this implication is implausible via the following *reductio ad absurdum* argument.

(3.1) I am, as of today, obligated to sever a second toe at 5:02 AM tomorrow morning.[12] [Assumption for *reductio*]

(3.2) If I am, as of today, obligated to sever a second toe at 5:02 AM tomorrow morning, then I am, as of today, obligated to intend today to sever a

12. In his 2015A, Travis Timmerman argues that the synchronic view yields counterintuitive implications in a case that's relevantly similar to *Severing Toes*. The case, called *Selfish Sid*, involves a man named Sid who cannot exert his control today so as to ensure that he rescues three people tomorrow, but he can exert his control today so as to ensure that he'll have the necessary means of rescuing the three tomorrow—that is, he can exert his control today such that he'll then have the opportunity to exert his control tomorrow so as to ensure that he rescues the three then. But he assumes that Sid is, as of today, obligated to rescue the three tomorrow despite the fact that an analogue of 3.5 is true in his case. Thus, my response to Timmerman is just to give the analogue of this *reductio ad absurdum* argument against his claim that Sid is, as of today, obligated to rescue the three people tomorrow.

second toe at 5:02 AM tomorrow morning. [From the fact that all practical obligations are intention-guiding—see §1.2]¹³

(3.3) Thus, I am, as of today, obligated to intend today to sever a second toe
at 5:02 AM tomorrow morning. [From 3.1–3.2]

(3.4) The propositional content of my intention to sever a second toe at
5:02 AM tomorrow morning is <I will sever a second toe at 5:02 AM
tomorrow morning>. [Stipulation]

(3.5) I am, as of today, obligated to believe today that I won't sever a second
toe at 5:02 AM tomorrow morning. [From the fact that I know both
that I won't sever a second toe at 5:02 AM tomorrow morning and that
I wouldn't do so even if I were to intend now to do so]¹⁴

(3.6) The propositional content of my belief that I won't sever a second toe
at 5:02 AM tomorrow morning is <it is not the case that I will sever a
second toe at 5:02 AM tomorrow morning>. [Stipulation]

(3.7) Thus, I am, as of today, obligated to have beliefs and intentions whose
propositional contents are logically inconsistent. [From 3.3–3.6]

(3.8) It is not the case that I am, as of today, obligated to have beliefs and
intentions whose propositional contents are logically inconsistent.
[From the consistency requirement on beliefs and intentions—see §1.2]

(3.9) It is both the case and not the case that I am, as of today, obligated to
have beliefs and intentions whose propositional contents are logically
inconsistent. [From 3.7–3.8]

(3.10) Therefore, it is not the case that I am, as of today, obligated to sever a
second toe at 5:02 AM tomorrow morning. [From 3.1–3.9 by *reductio ad
absurdum*]

What's most controversial about the above argument is, I believe, premise
3.5. Indeed, I suspect that Marušić would deny it. I suspect that Marušić
would claim that, given continualism, it is, as of today, up to me whether
I sever a second toe at 5:02 AM tomorrow morning. And since this is both

---

13. Strictly speaking, the consequent should read "I am, as of today, obligated to intend today
to do something that entails severing a second toe at 5:02 AM tomorrow morning." But I think
that we can safely ignore this complication for present purposes.

14. Someone might think that if whether you'll φ just depends on whether you now intend
to φ, then you can't now know whether you'll φ except by knowing whether you now intend
to φ—and, thus, you can't know whether you'll φ simply by having the sort of evidence that
someone else might use in predicting that you will or will not φ. But, importantly, whether
I sever a second toe does not depend on whether I now intend to do so. Indeed, it's stipulated
that I won't regardless of what I now intend to do.

up to me and something that, according to him, I ought to do, I ought to decide today to sever a second toe at 5:02 AM tomorrow morning and, consequently, believe that I will do so. In other words, Marušić (2015) holds that sometimes I ought to believe that I will do what I ought to do even when it's false that I will do what I ought to do—and this can be so even when my evidence strongly favors the proposition that I won't do what I ought to do. Thus, Marušić believes that sometimes a subject ought to believe that p even though p is, as her evidence suggests, false.

Now, although I think that we should, contrary to Marušić, accept 3.5, I concede that Marušić is right that sometimes, a subject ought to believe that p even though p is, as her evidence suggests, false. Here's such a case. It's a variant on the above case in which my knowing today that I won't sever a second toe tomorrow depends on my not intending today to sever a second toe tomorrow. Assume that, in this variant, I would sever all ten of my toes tomorrow if only I were to form now the intention to do so. But assume that I won't form this intention now simply because I am currently being unreasonably selfish. Moreover, assume that I currently have the capacity to form this intention and would do so if I were now to respond appropriately to my reasons. In this case, as in the original, I know that I won't sever a second toe at 5:02 AM tomorrow morning. But, in this case, I know that I won't sever a second toe at 5:02 AM tomorrow morning only in virtue of my not now forming the intention to sever a second toe at 5:02 AM tomorrow morning. For if I were to form at present the intention to sever a second toe at 5:02 AM tomorrow morning, I would thereby come to know instead that I will sever a second toe at 5:02 AM tomorrow morning.

In this case, then, it would be a mistake to think that I shouldn't plan/intend today on severing all ten toes tomorrow given that I believe that I won't sever all ten toes tomorrow and shouldn't form an intention that's inconsistent with that belief. This would be a mistake, because, in this case, whether I should believe that I won't sever all ten toes tomorrow just depends on whether I currently plan/intend on severing all ten toes tomorrow. Thus, this sort of reasoning amounts to the worst kind of circular reasoning. I would be reasoning that I shouldn't now form the intention to φ because I believe that I won't φ, when the only reason that I believe that I won't φ is because I'm not now forming the intention to φ. More concisely, then, I would be reasoning that I shouldn't now form the intention to do so because I don't now have any intention to do so. But this sort of reasoning just misunderstands the nature of my obligation for having consistent beliefs and intentions. From this obligation and the fact that I believe that I won't sever my ten toes, I cannot infer that I ought not to form the intention to sever my ten toes. For this is an obligation that I can fulfill in either of two ways: (1) by not forming the intention to sever my ten toes and, consequently, maintaining my belief that I won't sever my ten toes, or (2) by forming the intention to sever my ten toes and, consequently, coming to believe instead that I will.[15] And it seems that the best (if not the only) way to fulfill such an obligation in this kind of case is by my forming the intention to sever my ten toes and thereby come to believe that I will.[16]

But although Marušić is right about its sometimes being the case that a subject ought to believe that *p* even though *p* is, as her evidence suggests, false, he's wrong to reject 3.5. Given that, in *Severing Toes* (the original case), my knowing that I won't sever a second toe at 5:02 AM tomorrow morning doesn't depend on my not intending to do so, this is not the sort of case where I ought to believe that I will φ even though I know that I won't φ. For, in *Severing Toes*, I can't satisfy the obligation that I have not to be someone who both intends to sever a second toe at 5:02 AM tomorrow morning and believes that I will not do so by both forming the intention to sever a second toe at 5:02 AM to-morrow morning and believing that I will do so. For, in this case, I should not believe that I will sever a second toe at 5:02 AM tomorrow morning even if that's what I now intend to do. After all, it's stipulated that I will not sever a second toe at 5:02 AM tomorrow morning even if that's what I now intend to do. And this means that the only way for me to fulfill this obligation is to both refrain from intending to sever a second toe at 5:02 AM tomorrow morning and believe that I won't do so. Thus, accepting the diachronic view forces us to hold that knowing the truth about what one will do regardless of what one intends to do is incompatible with one's having jointly satisfiable obligations. For, in *Severing Toes*, I will, according to the diachronic view, have an obligation to sever a second toe at 5:02 AM tomorrow morning despite having an

---

15. Thus, this conditional obligation should be given the following wide-scope interpreta-tion: (WS) I'm obligated to <either cease intending to sever my ten toes or cease believing that I will not sever my ten toes>. It should not, then, be given the following narrow-scope interpretation: (NS) If I believe that I will not sever my ten toes, then I'm obligated to <cease intending to sever my ten toes>.

16. Of course, you may wonder: Should I really revise my belief even if my current evidence suggests that my belief is true? For, perhaps, your current evidence suggests that you have no intention of severing your toes, that you will not likely revise your intention, and that you won't sever your toes unless you so intend. Still, I think that you should revise your belief given that you should revise your intention. For more on the issue of what you should believe you'll do when what you'll do is up to you, see MARUŠIĆ 2015.

obligation not to be such that the propositional contents of my beliefs and intentions are logically inconsistent. And these two obligations are jointly unsatisfiable. And since such jointly unsatisfiable obligations are implausible, I think that we should reject the diachronic view and accept the synchronic view instead.

§3.2 Personal Control versus Subpersonal Control

Another issue concerns whether the sort of control that's relevant with respect to having the option to φ is personal or subpersonal.[17] I'll argue that it's personal. But first consider the following two examples to see how the two differ.

Balancing (an instance of subpersonal control): Imagine that I'm standing on a tree stump when someone accidentally bumps into me from behind, unexpectedly shifting my center of gravity forward and knocking me off balance. Consequently, I automatically and without deliberation make numerous adjustments to my posture and limbs to regain my balance. That is, in response to the stimuli received by my senses (including those of my visual, vestibular, and somatosensory systems), my brainstem transmits impulses via my motor-neurons to the muscles that control the movements of my eyes, head, neck, trunk, legs, and arms, the result being that I take a small quick step forward, throw my arms backward, and bend backward at the hips, knees, and ankles so as to shift my center of gravity backward and regain my balance.

Driving (an instance of personal control): Imagine that I'm driving home from work on mental autopilot, thinking about the revisions that I need to make to Chapter 2. That is, assume that I'm manifesting what's known as automaticity, whereby the conscious and unconscious aspects of the mind concentrate on different things. Thus, automatically and without deliberation, I make numerous adjustments to the car's controls so as to make my way home safely. I press down and ease up on the accelerator depending on what's needed to keep my vehicle within the flow of traffic. I brake whenever the vehicle in front of me brakes and also whenever I come to a stop sign or stoplight. I adjust the steering wheel to keep my vehicle inside its lane. I make all the appropriate twists, turns, and lane changes, using my turn signal as

17. I thank Philip Pettit for encouraging me to consider this issue.

appropriate. I even swerve to avoid a pothole. Yet, when I arrive home, I can't even remember driving across town or making all the turns that I must have made. I recall only my thoughts on what revisions I need to make to Chapter 2.

What makes the former subpersonal and the latter personal is that in *Driving*, my adjustments to the car's controls are intelligible to me in a way that in *Balancing*, my adjustments to my posture and limbs are not. Of course, both are intelligible in terms of cause and effect, but only my adjustments to the car's controls are intelligible in terms of reasons and my capacity for responding to them. And, as Joseph Raz explains, it is this sort of rational intelligibility that's crucial to our understanding of ourselves and to our sense of control over our own lives.

> Reason makes us intelligible to ourselves. Through it we direct our lives, we are in control. Sometimes this means acting, or choosing, etc., in light of reason, sometimes it means no more than forming beliefs or emotions where they are reasonable, where their formation and persistence is under the control of our rationality, even though there is no self-awareness or decision. . . . When [an] emotion, or desire, etc., is incomprehensible because of its incomprehensible object (an urge to lick the wall) or strength (why can I not resist the desire for heroin as I can the desire for chocolate, simply by resolving not to do what I know is bad for me?), we lose the ability to understand ourselves and to control our life. (RAZ 2000, p. 20)

This is why we are inclined to view my driving as something I do qua rational subject, whereas we are inclined to view my maintaining my balance by automatically adjusting my posture in response to some unexpected physical perturbation to be something that I do only qua biological organism. But, note that it's not the automaticity that's making the difference here. The adjustments that I make while driving on mental autopilot are just as automatic as those that I make to keep my balance. The relevant difference is that in *Driving* but not *Balancing*, my automatic responses are responses to reasons and not merely responses to impulses received by the brainstem. And thus, they issue, in *Driving*, from me *the person*, whereas they issue, in *Balancing*, from a subpersonal, proprioceptive system. After all, the former reflects my values and my assessments of what counts as a reason. I swerve to avoid the pothole, because I value keeping my car free of damage and believe that hitting the pothole could damage my car, so I see the presence of a pothole as a reason to swerve around it. But I don't swerve to avoid the leaf lying in the road, because I don't value keeping the leaf from damage, so I don't take the presence of a leaf in the road as a reason to swerve.

In *Balancing*, my values, beliefs, and assessments of reasons don't play a role in my responses. When I throw my arms backward, I don't do so because I value keeping my balance and believe that throwing my arms back in a certain way will help to keep my balance. I would have thrown my arms backward even if I had valued losing my balance or regaining it without throwing my arms backward. It's much like when, as a boy, I played "Made you blink!" with my friends. We would each try to keep from blinking while the other quickly thrust his or her fingers toward our eyes. Most times, I would lose. I would blink despite valuing not blinking and believing that the fact that fingers were being thrust toward my eyes constituted, in this context, a decisive reason for me to refrain from blinking. After all, I wanted to show my friends just how unflinchingly tough I was. But it can be very difficult, if not impossible, to control such automatic and subpersonal reactions. The same is true of the way my arms get thrown backward when I'm unexpectedly thrown off balance. It is something that happens to me rather than something that I, qua rational subject, do in response to my situation.

Thus, when I talk about doings, I'm talking about the things that one does in response to reasons, such as touching one's nose, thinking of potential problems for one's view, and forming the belief that it's raining as a result of feeling raindrops on one's head. And this contrasts with things that I do qua biological organism, such as fainting, digesting, and perspiring. Although these are things that I do in some sense, they are not things that I, qua rational subject, do. For they are not things that I do in response to reasons and are, thus, intelligible only in terms of cause and effect.

And note that it's not just that in *Driving* my reactions are caused by mental states whereas in *Balancing* they're caused by electrical impulses that travel from my inner ear to my brainstem and finally out to my muscles. The mere fact that a reaction of mine is caused by one of my mental states is not enough to make it intelligible to me in the way that my reason-guided responses are. To illustrate, consider the following example from Nomy Arpaly.

> Suppose the thought of meeting my one o'clock class fills me with dismay.
> If any sensible form of materialism is true, then in some way or another

both my thought of meeting the class and my dismay are, or are realized by, physical states: brain states. One neural state—my thought of the class—causes another neural state—my dismay. (ARPALY 2006, p. 46)

But now there are two further possibilities. One possibility is that the content of the thought of meeting my one o'clock class is relevant in causing my dismay in that I take the fact that I'm going to have to lecture in front of a large crowd of unenthusiastic first-year students as constituting a reason for my feeling dismay given that I find this sort of activity unpleasant and disheartening. And, on this possibility, I will find my dismay perfectly intelligible. But another possibility is that I don't take the fact that I'm going to meet my one o'clock class as a reason for me to feel dismay given that I enjoy the challenge of trying to get new students interested in philosophy. And in that case, I will find my dismay unintelligible in the relevant sense. Of course, I may be able to understand it in terms of cause and effect. Suppose, for instance, that I've been told that I have a brain tumor that is resulting in random thoughts (or their corresponding brain states) causing each other. But this kind of intelligibility is at the subpersonal level. It's at the level of cause and effect rather than at the level of rational intelligibility.[18]

Thus, my responses in *Driving* are rationally intelligible not merely because they are caused by mental states, but because they are caused by mental states whose contents consist in the awareness of facts that I take to be reasons for them. Had these responses been caused simply by impulses from my brain that are indifferent to whether I take the facts that I'm aware of as reasons for these responses, I would find these responses rationally unintelligible. And this is how the case of *Driving* differs from that of *Balancing*. Even when driving on mental autopilot, my responses are still responsive to my awareness of facts that I take to be reasons for or against various possible responses. And this is why I swerve to miss the pothole but not to miss the leaf. In neither case do I deliberate and consciously decide whether to swerve, but in each case, I am responding to my awareness of facts that I take to constitute or not constitute reasons for swerving. Thus, I find my responses in *Driving*, even though automatic and subconscious, rationally intelligible in a way that I don't find my responses in *Balancing* to be. And, importantly, this accounts for why I can be accountable for my responses in *Driving* but not for my responses in *Balancing*. For instance, I can be accountable for swerving or not

_____

18. For more on the personal/subpersonal distinction and its history, see DRAYSON 2014.

swerving to avoid something in the road in *Driving*, but I cannot be account-able for bending or failing to bend at some joint in *Balancing*. And, given this, I suggest that the relevant sort of control with respect to our options and obligations must be a kind of personal control as opposed to any kind of subpersonal control.

§3.3 Rational Control versus Volitional Control

Even if we accept my claim that a subject's having at t complete and personal control over whether she φs at t' is both necessary and sufficient for φ-ing at t' to be an option for her at t, we still need to know what the relevant type of complete and personal control is. I turn now to this issue. As I see it, there are two main contenders: volitional control and rational control.[19] I'll explain each in turn.

Volitional control is the sort of control that we exert directly over our in-tentional actions (such as intentionally using one's arms to rotate the car's steering wheel) and indirectly over those things that we manipulate via such actions (such as the turning of the car that one's driving). A subject who has direct *volitional control* over whether she φs (1) can φ at will and, thus, can φ simply by trying, intending, or otherwise willing to φ; (2) can φ for whatever reason she takes to be sufficient for φ-ing and, thus, can φ to win a bet or to please her partner; and (3) can—at least, typically—choose when to φ and, thus, can choose whether to φ now or later.[20] Thus, to have direct volitional control over whether one φs is, in essence, to be able to φ at will and thus, for whatever reason one takes to be sufficient for φ-ing. More precisely, though, I offer the following as a tentative gloss on the idea.

> **Volitional Control:** For any event φ, a subject has at time t direct vo-litional control over whether she φs at some later time t' if and only if she has at t the capacity to form the intention to φ at t' and to do so for whatever reason she takes to be sufficient for φ-ing at t', and whether she φs at t' depends (and in the right way) on whether and how she exercises this capacity at t—specifically, on whether she exercises it so as to form at t the intention to φ at t'.

---

19. I'll consider a third contender—namely, voluntary control—in §3.5 below.

20. See McHugh 2012, 2014, and 2017.

I offer this gloss, not as something that I'm committed to in all its details but only as an approximation that will be sufficient for our purposes. Thus, volitional control just is whatever sort of control we exercise directly over our intentional actions and indirectly over those things that we manipulate via such actions, and this holds regardless of whether I have gotten all the details exactly right.

Even with only this rough and ready account to work with, though, it's clear that we don't typically (if ever) exert direct volitional control over our reasons-responsive attitudes. For the sort of control that I have, say, over whether I believe that Aristotle went for a swim on his thirtieth birthday is clearly distinct from the sort of control that I have, say, over whether I perform an intentional act, such as that of scratching my nose. I can do the latter but not the former at will. And, given this, I can do the latter but not the former to win a bet or for any other reason that I take to be sufficient for doing so. And whereas I can choose if and when to scratch my nose, I cannot choose when, or whether, to believe that Aristotle went for a swim on his thirtieth birthday.[21]

The fact that we don't typically exert volitional control over our reasons-responsive attitudes along with the common intuition that people can both be obligated to form certain reasons-responsive attitudes and be accountable should they fail to do so has led several philosophers to conclude that the sort of control that's relevant to determining our obligations and responsibilities is not volitional control, but *rational control*. By "rational control," I just mean whatever sort of control we exert directly over our reasons-responsive attitudes and indirectly over those things we influence via such attitudes (such as our intentional actions). We exercise direct control over our reasons-responsive attitudes by being both receptive and reactive to reasons—forming, revising, sustaining, and/or abandoning these attitudes in light of our awareness of facts (or what we take to be facts) that count for or against them.[22]

---

21. For a further defense of the claim that we don't typically exert volitional control over our reasons-responsive attitudes as well as a response to those who have argued to the contrary, see McHugh 2012, 2014, and 2017.

22. The term "rational control" comes from McKenna 2012, A. M. Smith 2005, and A. M. Smith 2015. Others use a different term for the sort of control that we exert directly over our reasons-responsive attitudes. For instance, Pamela Hieronymi (2006) uses the term "evaluative control," Conor McHugh (2017) uses the term "attitudinal control," and Ralph Wedgwood (2017) uses the term "deliberative control." And each of these philosophers has a slightly different idea about what exactly this sort of control amounts to. But the important thing is that they all agree that there's a kind of control that we exert directly over our reasons-responsive attitudes.

So, whereas having volitional control over φ is just to have the relevant volitional capacities such that whether one φs just depends on whether and how one exercises those capacities (and, thus, on whether one exercises them so as to form or not form the intention to φ), having rational control over φ is just to have the relevant rational capacities such that whether one φs just depends on whether and how one exercises these capacities (thus, on whether one exercises them so as to respond appropriately or inappropriately to one's reasons). But what does this sort of rational control amount to more precisely? Here, then, is a tentative gloss on the idea.

Rational Control: For any event φ, a subject has at time t direct rational control over whether she φs at some later time t' if and only if she has at t the relevant rational capacities and whether she φs at t' depends (and in the right way) on whether and how she exercises these capacities at t.

Rational Capacities: A subject has at time t the relevant rational capacities with respect to whether she φs at some later time t' if and only if she is inherently so structured that, under a suitably wide range of counterfactual conditions, she would recognize the considerations that count for and against her φ-ing at t' and either φ or refrain from φ-ing at t' depending on which response those considerations make appropriate.[23]

To illustrate, recall the case *Stupid Mistake*, where a genius named Albert fails to come up with the correct solution to an easy problem on his math test

Some may question whether control that doesn't involve the exercise of one's volitions counts as genuine control, but to my mind, this just begs the question. For, in ordinary English, to exercise control over something is just to manage, regulate, or influence it. Consequently, it's perfectly felicitous to talk of our heart rate being controlled by our autonomic nervous system, of our engine's air-fuel ratio being controlled by its carburetor, and of our office's temperature being controlled by the thermostat. Yet none of these involve volitions. Now we should, as I've argued above, think that the relevant sort of control must be personal control as opposed to subpersonal. But rational control is clearly a kind of personal control even when it doesn't involve one's volitions. Moreover, it seems that personal control is the sort of control that underlies our judgments of accountability. For whereas we would deny that people deserve praise or blame for anything that's not under their personal control (e.g., for fainting, digesting, and perspiring), we would accept that people deserve praise and blame for anything that they do in response to reasons, such as touching their noses, thinking of a potential objection to their view, and forming a belief in response to the evidence.

23. This account of rational capacities is inspired by Michael Smith's account—see his 2003.

because he overthinks things and consequently overlooks its simple solution. In this case, Albert had direct rational control over whether he would provide the correct solution to the problem, so he had the option of providing the correct solution. After all, he was, we'll assume, inherently so structured that he would have come up with the correct solution in a suitably wide range of counterfactual conditions (i.e., possible worlds).

What sorts of worlds will this suitably wide range of possible worlds include? Well, incompatibilists will argue that these worlds must include ones in which Albert comes up with the correct solution to the problem even though the causal laws and histories of these worlds are identical to those of the actual world.[24] But it could, to the contrary, be enough that these worlds include worlds in which Albert comes up with the correct solution to the problem only because the casual history of this world differs slightly from that of the actual one. Perhaps, it's enough that there's some slight difference in Albert's environment in this world that triggers him to remember how important it is not to overthink things. I won't take a stand on this issue, for I'm concerned to argue only that options require rational control. That is, I'm concerned to argue only that whether or not a subject has rational control at t over whether she'll φ at t' just depends on whether certain subjunctive conditionals are true of her at t. Whether the relevant subjunctive conditionals include ones with causally identical antecedents, whether such conditionals are true, how we are to assess their truth, and whether we can do so in an interest-neutral way are difficult questions that need not concern us here.

In any case, it will be helpful to contrast *Stupid Mistake* with the case in which a two-year-old child fails to provide the correct solution to the same problem. In this case, we should deny that the two-year-old had the option of providing the correct solution. For even though the math problem is a relatively easy one for a math genius, we can plausibly assume that in no nearby possible world in which we hold fixed the way this child's underdeveloped brain is structured will the child provide the correct solution to the problem. For, in the case of the two-year-old child, there will be no nearby possible

---

24. Indeed, some incompatibilists may want to claim that the sort of control that's required for accountability is incompatible with determinism and that, therefore, what I'm calling "rational control" will be of the right sort only if we understand the phrase "suitably wide range of possible worlds" to include worlds in which the agent acts differently even though the causal laws and histories of these worlds are identical to those in the actual world. But I'll remain neutral on such issues.

world in which we, say, simply vary the environment so as to trigger different memories and the child comes up with the correct solution.

Of course, we may wonder, To what degree and in what ways may a compatibilist plausibly vary the causal history or laws while holding the brain's structure fixed? Again, I'll remain neutral on such issues. For the only points that I'm trying to make here are that (1) there seems to be a perfectly ordinary sense in which Albert could have come up with the correct answer but the two-year-old couldn't, and that (2) appealing to the presence or absence of rational control can help us explain this difference quite nicely in terms of the inherent differences in the rational capacities of the two subjects. Whereas the two-year-old failed to come up with the correct answer because he lacked the rational capacities needed to come up with it, Albert failed to come up with it despite having the requisite capacities because he failed to exercise those capacities to good effect (M. SMITH 2003). Thus, I'm suggesting that the way to determine whether a subject had the option of doing other than what she actually did is to look first at whether she had the relevant rational capacities, where she had the relevant rational capacities just in case, abstracting away from all but the relevant aspects of her brain's structure, she would have succeeded in doing otherwise in the relevant nearby possible worlds. And if she did have those capacities, to look second at whether what explains her failure to do otherwise was her failure to exercise those capacities to good effect (perhaps because she forgot something important and nothing in her environment triggered her memory) or something else entirely (perhaps because some evil neuroscientist manipulated her brain).[25]

This, of course, is just a sketch of what rational control amounts to, but the important thing to realize is that this sort of control is distinct from volitional control. Thus, we really do have the following two distinct accounts of what our options are.

Volitionalism: For any event φ, a subject has at time t the option of φ-ing at some later time t' if and only if she has at t volitional control over whether she will φ at t'.

---

25. Here, I follow M. SMITH 2003. And note that exercising our rational capacities isn't something we do by deciding to exercise them. Rather, we exercise them simply by responding (or failing to respond) to reasons—that is, by our awareness of facts that constitute reasons for us to φ interacting with these capacities and thereby causing (or failing to cause) us to φ.

Rationalism: For any event φ, a subject has at time *t* the option of φ-ing at a later time *t'* if and only if she has at *t* rational control over whether she will φ at *t'*.

Of these two views (and I see no plausible third alternative),[26] I think that rationalism is the clear winner. I think this because it's reasonable to expect that a theory about what our options consist in should, other things being equal, be able to vindicate the bulk of our intuitions about what sorts of possible events a subject can be obligated to perform and accountable for failing to perform. And, as I'll show presently, rationalism does a much better job of this than volitionalism does. Indeed, there are at least six kinds of events where it is rationalism, and not volitionalism, that vindicates our intuition that this event is, or is not, of the sort that a subject can be obligated to perform and accountable for failing to perform.

§3.3.1 Formations of attitudes

Volitionalism forces us to deny that people can be obligated to form, revise, sustain, or abandon their reasons-responsive attitudes except when they have volitional control over whether they do. But intuitively, it seems that people often have such obligations even when they don't exert volitional control over such attitudes. We think, for instance, that parents are obligated to want what's best for their children, that agents are obligated to intend to do what they take to be the necessary means to their ends, and that those who believe that the Earth is no more than a few thousand years old are obligated to abandon this belief in light of the overwhelming scientific evidence to the contrary. But wanting, intending, and believing are not typically, if ever, under our volitional control. If I don't want what's best for my daughter because, say, I'm envious of her greater success, I can't just will myself to want what's best for her. If I am to form this desire at all, it will not be by intending or otherwise willing myself to do so but by responding to the reasons that I have for doing so. But responding to reasons is not something that I do at

---

26. It may seem that I'm overlooking a plausible alternative—namely, *voluntarism*. Voluntarism holds that, for any event φ, a subject has at time *t* the option of φ-ing at some later time *t'* if and only if she has at *t* voluntary control over whether she φs at *t'*, where a subject has *voluntary control* over whether she φs at *t'* if and only if she has both volitional control over whether she φs at *t'* and rational control over whether she forms the volition to φ at *t'*. I address this view in §3.5.

will. It is rather something I do nonvoluntarily as when I come to believe that it's raining as a result of seeing and/or feeling raindrops.

To illustrate just how plausible it is to suppose that subjects can have obligations to form reasons-responsive attitudes even when these formations are not under their volitional control, let's consider a couple of examples. First, consider an example that's loosely based on one of van Inwagen's (1978). Suppose that Shyam saw a crime in progress but didn't even try to call the police. And let's suppose that unbeknownst to him, he couldn't have called the police even if he had tried, because, unbeknownst to him, his cellphone was recently stolen by a pickpocket and there were no landlines available to him. Even so, it seems appropriate for us to have various reactive attitudes toward Shyam. Nevertheless, it's hard to see how we can blame him for not calling the police given that he wasn't able to do so. It seems, then, that what we should blame him for is his failing to form the intention to call the police. And yet, forming this intention is not something that he could have done at will. It's something that he could have done only by responding appropriately to the reasons that he had for forming the intention to call the police.[27]

To take another example, consider someone who fails to lower her credence in a proposition after becoming aware of new evidence that counts significantly against its truth. Or consider someone who comes to believe a proposition based on insufficient evidence. It seems that so long as these two have the relevant rational capacities such that they could have formed the appropriate credences, they are the appropriate object of various reactive attitudes—at least, insofar as their failure to properly exercise these capacities is what explains their failure to form the appropriate credences. Thus, it would be appropriate for them to feel bad (e.g., for them to feel foolish) for having formed such inappropriate credences. Yet, it's not as if they voluntarily chose to form these inappropriate credences. The fault lies not with their

---

27. Consider the toxin puzzle (KAVKA 1983). I will receive a million dollars tomorrow morning if and only if, at midnight tonight, I intend to drink some toxin tomorrow afternoon. Drinking the toxin will not kill me, but it will make me terribly ill for several days. Whether I receive the million dollars tomorrow morning depends only on what I intend to do at midnight tonight, not on whether I drink the toxin tomorrow afternoon. Realizing this, I'm unable to intend at midnight tonight to drink the toxin tomorrow afternoon. For I see no reason to drink the toxin. I know that, come tomorrow afternoon, I'll either have the million dollars or I won't. And in neither case will I have any reason to drink the toxin. So I have decisive reason not to drink the toxin. Given this, I'm unable to form the intention to drink the toxin. And this shows that forming an intention is not typically something that I can do at will—that is, by forming the intention to form that intention.

volitions but with their failure to respond appropriately to their evidence by nonvoluntarily forming the appropriate credences.

Rationalism can vindicate our intuition that we have such obligations, for whether rational subjects respond appropriately to their evidence by forming the appropriate credences is under their rational control even if not under their volitional control.

§3.3.2 Mixed acts

Volitionalism not only fails to vindicate our intuition that people are accountable for their nonvoluntary belief formations, but it also fails to vindicate our intuition that people are accountable for failing to perform certain types of acts that have a nonvoluntary component. Note, then, that many of the acts that we are obligated to perform and accountable for failing to perform are *mixed acts*—acts that have both a voluntary component and a nonvoluntary component.[28] Such acts include acting in good faith, offering a sincere apology, expressing one's gratitude, and diverting a trolley onto to the side track with the intention of saving the five on the main track.[29] To perform such acts, we must have certain reasons-responsive attitudes. For instance, we can't act in good faith without having the intention to follow through on our part of the bargain. We can't offer a sincere apology without feeling contrite. We can't *express* our gratitude without feeling grateful. And we can't divert a trolley with the intention of having one effect and not another without intending to have the one but not the other. So, whereas we may have volitional control over whether we say the words "I'm sorry" or "Thank you," we don't have volitional control over whether we offer a sincere apology or express our gratitude. For we don't have volitional control over whether we feel contrite or grateful, which is essential to our performing such mixed acts. The

---

28. Alex King (2014) is, as far as I know, the first to point out that we often presume that we ought to perform such mixed acts even though we cannot perform them at will. I'm indebted to her 2014 for many of the ideas presented in this paragraph.

29. One type of mixed act is what Ralph Wedgwood (2011) calls *thick act-types*: act-types that incorporate specific intentions. Examples include "diverting the trolley in order to kill the person on the side track" and "diverting the trolley in order to save the five people on the main track." And, as Wedgwood points out, we must be able to prescribe such mixed acts (and not merely the physical acts of flipping or not flipping a switch) if we are to give a plausible account of the Doctrine of Double Effect. So, if Wedgwood is right about this, and I'm right in thinking that such mixed acts essentially include a nonvoluntary component, we would have to abandon hope of giving a plausible account of the Doctrine of Double Effect if we were to endorse volitionalism.

volitionalist must, therefore, deny that we have the option of performing such mixed acts (at least, where we don't already have the relevant attitudes) and also deny both that we can be obligated to perform such acts and that we can legitimately be held accountable when we fail to do so.

It seems that we can also be prohibited from performing certain mixed acts. For instance, it seems impermissible both to refuse to rent to someone because of her race and to put a child up for adoption because of the money that one would get in return.[30] And although whether we refuse to rent to someone or refuse to put a child up for adoption is something that we have volitional control over, we don't have volitional control over our motivations. Thus, it seems that the volitionalist must deny that we can be prohibited from having certain motives as well as prohibited from performing the mixed acts that stem from such motives.

Being unable to account for the fact that some mixed acts are obligatory and that others are prohibited seems like a substantial cost for accepting volitionalism. Fortunately, rationalism doesn't come at such a price. Since we have rational control, for instance, over both whether we utter the words "I'm sorry" and over whether we feel contrite, the rationalist holds that we have the option of performing such mixed acts and thus, can be obligated or prohibited from performing them and accountable for either performing or failing to perform them. And intuitively, we do find people accountable for, say, failing to offer a sincere apology and instead merely parroting the words "I'm sorry." Likewise, we find people accountable for, say, refusing to rent to someone because of her race instead of refusing to rent to her because of her poor credit history. Moreover, we hold such people accountable even when we know that they didn't have volitional control over the relevant attitudes.

§3.3.3 Automatic, unthinking acts

Many of our actions are automatic, unthinking acts. I automatically and unthinkingly raise my hands to block an errant Frisbee heading for my nose. And when a child unexpectedly darts in front of my car, I automatically and unthinkingly slam on the brakes. These actions seem no more voluntary than do the formation of the beliefs about the objects to which they are reactions. As Mattias Steup (2001) has pointed out, in each case I respond as I do for good reasons, but in none of these cases do I have any choice in the matter. I could

---

30. I borrow these examples from SVERDLIK 2011.

no more have voluntarily chosen not to slam on the brakes than I could have voluntarily chosen not to believe that the child had just darted in front of my car. Yet, in each case, it seems that you can rightly hold me accountable for my automatic responses. I can, for instance, be praiseworthy for slamming on the brakes or blameworthy for failing to do so.

So it seems that we can be accountable for such automatic responses. We're accountable for them, for they, just as much as our deliberate acts, reflect both our take on what our reasons are and our degree of responsiveness to them. Thus, when I slam on the brakes, this can indicate both that I take facts about the safety of children to be reason-providing and that I have exercised my rational capacities appropriately. And if it does indicate this, I can be praiseworthy as a consequence. Of course, some may want to argue that what I am most directly praiseworthy for is caring appropriately for the child's safety. But contrary to what the volitionalist must claim, I see no reason to think that what I'm ultimately responsible for must be some intentional act, such as the one that led me to care about the child's safety. For that doesn't seem to fit the phenomenology. If, for instance, I had failed to apply the brakes when the child darted in front of my car, you wouldn't think that I must ultimately be blameworthy for having refrained from performing some act that would have led to my caring about the child's safety. Rather, you would blame me for not responding appropriately to the obvious reasons that I had for caring about the child's safety.

§3.3.4 Acts stemming from volitions that weren't under the subject's rational control

It's possible for a subject to have volitional control over her actions even if she lacks rational control over her volitions. Perhaps, this is true of many non-human animals. To illustrate, let's imagine that pigeons have the capacity to form intentions and that where they roost just depends on where they intend to roost. But let's assume that they don't have rational control over their intentions. Let's assume, then, that their intentions stem, not from the exercise of any rational capacity, but from some subpersonal system—perhaps, instinct.

On these assumptions, pigeons would have volitional control, but not rational control, over where they roost. And, of course, whether these assumptions are, in fact, correct is irrelevant. What's important for my purposes is only that if these assumptions were true, we wouldn't think that pigeons could be obligated to refrain from roosting in certain places or accountable for roosting in such places. After all, it's implausible to suppose (even given these assumptions) that the pigeons that roost on my roof deserve to feel guilt for roosting there given that they're incapable of recognizing or responding to the moral reason that they have for intending to roost elsewhere—the one that's constituted by the fact that I would get a better night's sleep if they were to roost elsewhere.[31] Thus, volitional control doesn't seem to be the sort of control that's necessary for obligations and accountability. For, as I argued in §3.2, the relevant sort of control has to be personal—that is, the sort of control that makes our responses rationally intelligible to us. But volitional control amounts to a kind of personal control only when it proceeds via volitions that are under one's rational control. That is, volitional control amounts to a kind of personal control just when it is equivalent to rational control. But, as the case of the pigeons illustrates, a subject can have volitional control over whether she φs (e.g., over whether she roosts on my roof) without having rational control over whether she intends to φ. And where a subject lacks this sort of personal control over whether she φs, it seems mistaken to think that it would be appropriate for her to feel guilt for having φ-ed.

Now, if we can't hold subjects accountable for actions that were under their volitional control except when they had rational control over the volitions that produced them, then we should accept rationalism as opposed to volitionalism. For rationalism rightly holds that although we're often accountable for the acts over which we exerted volitional control, we're accountable for them just when we had rational control over the volitions that produced them. Thus, rationalism, not volitionalism, vindicates our intuitions about when we are accountable for our actions.

§3.3.5 Acts that manifested a poor quality of will and were expressive of one's deep self but were not under one's rational control

Some, following Peter Strawson, hold both that "reactive attitudes . . . are essentially reactions to the quality of others' wills towards us, as manifested in

---

31. To respond appropriately to this moral reason, the pigeons would have to be aware of the fact that I would get a better night's sleep if they were to roost elsewhere, and this awareness would then need to be what, via their rational capacities, nondeviantly causes them to roost elsewhere. Furthermore, if they are to be accountable for failing to respond appropriately to these moral reasons, they'll need to have the capacity for feel guilty for failing to do so. See note 9 of Chapter 2.

their behaviour" (2008, p. 15) and that, consequently, these attitudes are appropriate to the extent that they accurately represent their objects as having a poor quality of will—a will that, perhaps, also reflects their true or deep self. But, as Gary Watson (2004, p. 228) has pointed out, there is an important challenge to such a view. A psychopath can act cruelly and in a way that both expresses her true self and manifests her ill will toward others, yet she won't be the appropriate object of reactive attitudes (such as guilt, indignation, and resentment) if she lacked the relevant sort of control over both her nature and the quality of her will. So it seems that the appropriateness of our reactive attitudes toward a given individual is not simply a function of the quality of that individual's will and nature but is also a function of whether she had the relevant sort of control over these two.

To illustrate, consider *The Psychopath:* the case of a ten-year-old psychopath named Mariko who was born with a genetic predisposition for psychopathic behavior—a disposition that was then triggered by years of abuse in which she was locked up by herself in a tiny room only to be removed occasionally to be physically and sexually abused. And let's assume that Mariko does terrible things to the doctors who are now trying to help her. Moreover, assume that these actions reflect the ill will that she bears toward them and are expressive of her true nature. Even so, it doesn't seem that Mariko deserves to suffer the unpleasantness of feeling guilt for her cruel behavior given that she lacked the relevant sort of control over the formation of her malicious will and her cruel nature. For it seems that we hold people accountable for their behavior—even behavior that both manifests a malicious will and expresses a cruel nature—only when we think that they had the relevant sort of control over their malicious will and their cruel nature. And it seems that Mariko didn't have the relevant sort of control (i.e., rational control) over these. For, as I'm assuming, psychopaths such as Mariko lack the capacity to recognize and respond appropriately to the moral reasons that they have for behaving morally.[32] And if they don't have the relevant rational capacities (in this case, the capacity to recognize and respond to moral reasons), then rationalism holds that they don't have the option of behaving morally. So rationalism,

---

32. I'm making things out to be simpler than they are. After all, psychopathy comes in degrees. So certain people with moderate psychopathic tendencies may have the limited or diminished capacity to recognize and respond to at least some moral reasons. But the true nature of psychopathy is unimportant for my purposes. Let me just stipulate, then, that I'll use the term "psychopath" to refer only to those who altogether lack the capacity to recognize and respond appropriately to moral reasons.

not volitionalism, accounts for the fact that we don't take psychopaths like Mariko to be accountable for their immoral behavior even if it manifests their ill wills and cruel natures.

§3.3.6 Lapses

Intuitively, it seems that we can be directly accountable for our lapses—that is, for our failures to respond in certain ways. To say that I can be *directly* accountable for such failures is to say that I can be accountable for them without being accountable for anything else—without being accountable, say, for some act or omission that led to this failure. It seems, for instance, that I can be directly accountable for the following sorts of lapses: failing to notice that my wife's upset, forgetting my daughter's birthday, and not being happy to hear of my friend's success. But it seems impossible to account for this on volitionalism. After all, whether I forget my daughter's birthday is not under my volitional control. I don't forget by intending to forget. Nor do I remember by intending to remember—at least, not typically. If I remember, it's most likely because it occurs to me quite nonvoluntarily. Likewise, if I forget, it's most likely because it just failed to occur to me. Of course, the volitionalist can hold me accountable for not choosing to do things that might have ensured that I would realize that it's my daughter's birthday. Thus, the volitionalist can hold me accountable for, say, not bothering to tie a string around my finger. Yet this seems insufficient. For it seems reasonable for my daughter to expect me to remember her birthday without having to tie a string around my finger. Thus, she would be right to think that I should remember because I have good reason to remember and not because I'm curious why I tied a string around my finger. Thus, it seems that she can legitimately hold me accountable for not remembering and not just for failing to do something like tying a string around my finger.

Now, rationalism has no trouble in accounting for our intuition that I can be directly accountable for forgetting my daughter's birthday and not just for having failed to tie a string around my finger. For suppose that I do forget. It seems that despite forgetting, I was aware or had access to both the fact that it was such-and-such a date and the fact that such-and-such a date is my daughter's birthday. Moreover, I'm assuming that my rational capacities were such that, in the various nearby possible worlds in which I exercise these capacities properly, I put two and two together and remember her birthday. And, thus, my daughter would be right to blame me for forgetting her birthday, as my forgetting clearly indicates that I did not properly exercise my rational capacities. After all, we're supposing that, had I properly exercised my rational capacities, I would have remembered.[33]

§3.4 Volitional Control and the Trouble with Insisting on Always Tracing Back to Some Intentional Act

Volitionalists—those who think that volitional control is necessary for accountability—are likely to respond to the previous section by arguing that they can accommodate our intuition that a subject can be accountable for an event that wasn't under her direct volitional control by tracing that event's causal history back to some event over which she did exert direct volitional control. For instance, the volitionalist can accommodate our intuition that I'm accountable for forgetting my daughter's birthday by tracing its cause back to my intentionally choosing not to tie a string around my finger. And the volitionalist may hope to employ the same strategy to accommodate our intuitions in all the above cases, including cases in which we have the intuition that a subject is accountable for forming reasons-responsive attitudes over which she didn't exert direct volitional control. There are, however, three problems with this strategy: (1) it won't always work, (2) even when it does work it forces us to accept a counterintuitive view about what we're ultimately accountable for, and (3) it's unmotivated in the case of reasons-responsive attitudes given that such attitudes are themselves responsive to reasons. I'll take each in turn.

To see that the tracing strategy won't always work, consider *Earth's Age:* a well-educated woman of normal intellect named Chen believes, as she was brought up to believe, that the Earth is no more than a few thousand years old. But, being well educated, Chen is aware of all the scientific evidence to the contrary. What's more, she possesses the relevant rational capacities for recognizing and responding appropriately to the reasons that such evidence

---

33. Others, such as Matthew Talbert (2017), hold that my forgetting my daughter's birthday is blameworthy only if it reveals that I don't appropriately care about her or our relationship. But this is to deny that I can be directly accountable for forgetting her birthday, as this is to hold that I'm accountable for forgetting her birthday only in virtue of being accountable for failing to care appropriately for her or our relationship. So this seems only to kick the problem down the road. For now, we'll need to account for what sort of control I had over whether I was to care appropriately for her and our relationship. And presumably, the relevant sort of control will have to be rational control, as I don't have volitional control over my cares. So why not just think that I can be directly accountable for forgetting her birthday given that this was itself under my rational control?

provides. Given this, she seems accountable for not having responded appropriately to her reasons—that is, for not having abandoned her ill-founded belief. Yet she couldn't have abandoned her belief at will; for abandoning it in response to the decisive reasons that she had for doing so was not something over which she exerted volitional control. Consequently, the volitionalist must trace the source of her accountability back to something over which she did exert volitional control. That is, the volitionalist must trace it back to her having failed to perform some intentional act that would have caused her to abandon that belief (A. M. SMITH 2015).

But this strategy won't work if we assume, as I will, that the only intentional act that would have caused her to abandon the belief was one that she was required to refrain from performing. Assume, then, that given her penchant for conspiracy theories, the only intentional act that would have caused her to abandon this belief was her reading a book by some quack claiming that the Bible was written and propagated by the CIA for the purposes of controlling the masses. And assume that she's required to refrain from reading such books both because they contain a lot of dangerous misinformation that she's liable to believe and because she promised her mother that she would not read such books. Here, then, is a case where Chen should have responded appropriately to her reasons and abandoned her belief, and yet the volitionalist can't even claim that there was something that she ought to have done intentionally to have caused this. For in this case, the only intentional act that would have caused this was one that she was required to refrain from performing. So the tracing strategy fails in this case.

Of course, the tracing strategy will work in other cases, such as *Earth's Age 2*—a case that's exactly like the original except that in this case, Chen could have caused herself to abandon her belief by permissibly and intentionally choosing to surround herself by clear-thinking friends who would have persuaded her to abandon her belief. The problem, though, is that this strategy forces us to accept an implausible view about what she's ultimately accountable for. According to this strategy, what Chen is ultimately accountable for is her failure to perform the acts that would have resulted in her being surrounded with clear-thinking friends. She would not, then, be accountable for her failure to respond appropriately to her evidence except insofar as her failure to perform these acts led to this failure. Thus, the norm that she would ultimately be accountable for violating is not the epistemic norm requiring her to believe in accordance with her evidence but the practical norm requiring her to act in accordance with her practical reasons. But intuitively, it seems that what she's ultimately accountable for is violating an epistemic norm. And this is why, when we interact with people like Chen, we exhort them to respond to their epistemic reasons for abandoning their ill-founded beliefs, not to their practical reasons for doing what would cause them to abandon those beliefs. That is, we appeal to their epistemic reasons, not to their practical reasons.

These are not the only problems with the volitionist's attempt to trace our accountability for our reasons-responsive attitudes back to something over which we exerted direct volitional control. What's perhaps most troubling about this strategy is that it's unmotivated. The motivation for our employing a tracing strategy always lies with our having the intuition that a subject is accountable for something that wasn't itself responsive to reasons. Thus, it's only because the something in question isn't itself responsive to reasons that we feel the need to trace the source of the subject's accountability back to something that was. To illustrate, consider *The Drunk Driver:* a drunk driver inadvertently hits a pedestrian due to her blurred vision and impaired motor skills. Here, there's a motive for tracing, because it seems that she can't be directly accountable for failing to apply the brakes sooner given that she was incapacitated and, consequently, incapable of recognizing and/or responding appropriately to the reasons that she had for doing so. Therefore, we feel the need to trace back the source of her accountability to something that was responsive to her reasons—something such as her decision to start drinking without first arranging for a designated driver.[34] And, here, it does make sense to insist that she should have recognized and responded appropriately to the reasons that she had for doing so (A. M. SMITH 2015), because, unlike in the case of the reasons for braking sooner, she was capable of recognizing and responding appropriately to these reasons.

Note then that the motivation for tracing in *The Drunk Driver* is completely lacking in any case in which the event in question is itself responsive to reasons. In any such case, there's no need to trace the source of the subject's accountability back to some event that was responsive to reasons. For in any such case, the event in question is itself responsive to reasons. So the volitionalist's strategy of tracing the source of our accountability for our

---

34. Note that it wouldn't be sufficient to trace back the source of her accountability merely to something that was under her volitional control. For we wouldn't think her accountable for having hit the pedestrian in virtue of her having intentionally chosen to start drinking without having first arranged for a designated driver unless we thought that she was capable of recognizing and responding appropriately to the reasons she had for doing so.

reasons-responsive attitudes to some event over which we exerted direct volitional control is unmotivated.

In sum, we've seen that the volitionalist cannot provide a plausible explanation either for the fact that a subject can be accountable for events over
which she did not exert direct volitional control (e.g., someone's forming a
belief on the basis of insufficient evidence) or for the fact that a subject is not
always accountable for events over which she did exert direct volitional control (e.g., the pigeon's intentionally roosting on my roof).

§3.5 What about Voluntary Control?

It may seem that I've been overlooking a plausible alternative to both rationalism and volitionalism: namely, *voluntarism*. Voluntarism is a hybrid. It
holds that for any event φ, a subject has at time *t* the option of φ-ing at some
later time *t′* if and only if she has at *t* both rational control over whether she
forms the volition to φ at *t′* and volitional control over whether she φs at *t′*
in that she'll φ at *t′* just in case she forms the volition to do so. This view accounts for the intuition specified in §3.3.4—the intuition that a subject can
be accountable for an action that was under her volitional control only if she
had rational control over the volitions that produced them. Thus, it accounts
for the fact that a pigeon won't be accountable for roosting on my roof simply
because it had volitional control over whether it was to do so. For it to be accountable for such behavior, the relevant volitions must have been under the
pigeon's rational control.

Given its ability to accommodate such intuitions, voluntarism is more
plausible than volitionalism. Nevertheless, it faces at least two significant
problems. First, like volitionalism, it insists that a subject's having volitional
control over an event is a necessary condition for its being an option for her
and, thus, for its being something that she could be obligated to perform and
accountable for failing to perform. Consequently, voluntarism fails to vindicate our intuition that a subject can be accountable for events over which she
does not exert volitional control—events such as forgetting a birthday, failing
to offer a sincere apology, and forming a belief on the basis of insufficient
evidence.

Second, voluntarism cannot adequately explain why we must have rational control over our volitions in order to be accountable for the actions
that they produce. After all, it denies that we're accountable for the volitions
over which we exert rational control given that we lack volitional control (and
thus, voluntary control) over such attitudes. And it provides no explanation

as to how we become accountable for our actions in virtue of their being produced by volitions that we're not accountable for. Thus, we're left to wonder: Why would our having rational control over the volitions that produce our actions matter as to whether we're accountable for those actions if we're not even accountable for those volitions in virtue of our having rational control over them?

By contrast, rationalism offers a plausible explanation for why we must have rational control over our volitions in order to be accountable for the actions that they produce. For it's only by exerting rational control over the volitions that produce our actions that we can exert rational control over them. Thus, we need volitional control over our actions, because this is the only way for us to exert rational control over our actions, and, according to rationalism, it's rational control that matters for accountability. In other words, we must exert volitonal control over our actions in order to exert rational control over them, because our actions are sensitive to our reasons only insofar as the volitions that produce them are sensitive to our reasons. Here's how Conor McHugh puts it.

> While voluntary control is a requirement for responsibility for bodily action, this is because of features particular to bodily action, and not because of the requirements for responsibility in general. Our actions respond to reasons, when they do, through the will—through voluntary control. How else could they do it? After all, full-blown actions just are those bits of conduct that get done through the will. To perform such an action is to execute an intention; to act for a reason is to execute an intention held for that reason. (2017, p. 2,758)

So we should favor rationalism over voluntarism for two reasons. For one, rationalism, unlike voluntarism, can account for our intuition that a subject can be accountable for events that were not under her voluntary control. For another, it provides a much more plausible account of why we must have rational control over our volitions in order to be accountable for the actions that they produce.

§3.6 Conclusion

Intuitively, it seems that we can be accountable for events that were not under our volitional control—events such as forgetting one's anniversary, failing to offer a sincere apology, and forming a belief on the basis of insufficient evidence. And this leaves us with three options: (O1) reject these intuitions, (O2) deny that control is a necessary condition for accountability, or (O3) accept that the sort of control that's necessary for accountability is not volitional control but the sort of control that we exert over such nonvoluntary events.

O1 should, I believe, be a last resort. And O2 is, as we learned in Chapter 2, an unattractive option. This leaves us with O3. I've proposed that the relevant sort of control is not volitional control or voluntary control, but rational control, which is the sort of control that we exert directly over our reasons-responsive attitudes and indirectly over those things that we manipulate via our reasons-responsive attitudes. Only by taking option O3 can we adequately vindicate our intuitions concerning what sorts of events are of the kind that a subject can be obligated to perform and accountable for failing to perform. And if I'm right about rational control being the relevant sort of control, then this means that our options include all and only those things over which we exert rational control. And this means that our options include such nonvoluntary events as lapses, the formations of attitudes, and the performances of mixed and unthinking acts. What's more, it means that not all of the acts that are under our volitional control are options, since not all such acts are under our rational control.

In Chapter 4, I'll argue that it's not all options but only a proper subset of our options that should be assessed in terms of their own goodness. Specifically, I'll argue for a view called *maximalism*. And in Chapter 5, I'll explain how the account of our options that I've argued for in this chapter (viz., rationalism) has significant implications regarding the plausibility of maximalism. I'll show that by adopting this account, maximalism can avoid the sorts of objections that have typically been leveled against it. Furthermore, I'll show how combining maximalism with rationalism has other benefits, such as enabling us to account for how a moral theory can be morally harmonious such that the agents who satisfy it, whoever and however numerous they may be, are guaranteed to produce the morally best world that they could (in some relevant sense) together produce.

CHAPTER 4

Which Options Have Their Deontic Statuses in Virtue of Their Own Goodness?

I'VE ARGUED THAT we should accept the following fairly uncontroversial view.

> **The Opting-for-the-Best View (short version):** For any subject S and any member φ of a certain subset of S's options, S ought to φ if and only if φ is the best member of this subset in terms of whatever ultimately matters.[1]

As already noted, this view leaves a lot unspecified. One thing that it leaves unspecified is what the relevant subset is and, thus, whether the variable 'φ' is to range over all of S's options or only a proper subset of her options. In this chapter, I'll argue that we should not let 'φ' range over all of her options, for this leads to what is known as the *problem of act versions*.[2] I'll argue that

---

1. Remember that I leave implicit the relevant grounding clauses. For instance, I leave implicit that if a subject ought to φ, this is in virtue of the fact that φ is the best member of the relevant subset of her options. Also, recall that the relevant deontic statuses are the objective ones, which are a function of what her options are, how they relate to each other, what ultimately matters, and how they compare in terms of whatever ultimately matters. Thus, this view holds that a subject objectively ought to perform what is, in fact, the best member of the relevant subset of her options.

2. It has long been acknowledged that the problem of act versions is a problem for act-consequentialism—see, for instance, BERGSTRÖM 1966 and CASTAÑEDA 1968. But what hasn't been appreciated is that it is, as I argue below, as much a problem for other versions of the opting-for-the-best view, including deontological versions such as Rossian pluralism (W. D. ROSS 1930).

we should instead hold that 'φ' ranges over only what I'll call her *maximal options*.

§4.1 Omnism (All Options) and the Problem of Act Versions

To accept the version of the opting-for-the-best view that holds that the variable 'φ' ranges over all of a subject's options is to accept the following.

> **Omnism:** For any subject S and any option of hers φ: (OUGHT) S ought to φ if and only if φ is her best option, (PERMI) S is permitted to φ if and only if φ is one of her sufficiently good options, and (SUPER) S's φ-ing is supererogatory if and only if there is some alternative option ψ such that (a) she is both permitted to φ and permitted to ψ and (b) her φ-ing is better than her ψ-ing.[3]

I call this *omnism*, because it holds that 'φ' ranges over *all* of a subject's options, and *omnis* is Latin for "all."

We should, I believe, reject omnism. As I explained briefly in Chapter 1, it leads to the problem of act versions. I'll now spell out the problem more carefully. The problem is that omnism is incompatible with the conjunction of two very plausible propositions. The first of these two is that an option can inherit its deontic status from the options that entail it.[4] More carefully stated, the proposition is that the property of being what ought to be done is closed under performance entailment. Its official statement is as follows.

---

3. Here too I leave implicit the relevant grounding clauses. And again, the relevant deontic statuses are the objective ones.

4. Recall that an option's *deontic status* is one or more of the following: wrong, optional, obligatory, permissible, supererogatory, that which ought to be done, etc. By contrast, an option's *evaluative status* is one or more of the following: good, bad, better, worse, best, worst, sufficiently good, insufficiently good, and so on. And note that, for any subject S and any two of her options φ and ψ, φ is a *better option* than ψ only if φ is better than ψ in terms of whatever ultimately matters. Thus, if the only thing that S should ultimately care about is how much aggregate happiness there is, then her φ-ing is better than her ψ-ing only if her φ-ing would produce more aggregate happiness than her ψ-ing would.

Deontic inheritance: For any subject S and any two of her options φ and ψ, if S ought to φ and S's φ-ing entails S's ψ-ing, then S ought to ψ.[5]

The entailment, here, is not *logical* entailment but *performance* entailment. To say that the performance of one option entails the performance of another is just to say that there isn't the option of performing the one without performing the other. More precisely, for any subject S and any two of her options φ and ψ, S's φ-ing *entails* S's ψ-ing if and only if S doesn't have the option of φ-ing without ψ-ing. And, to save words, I'll sometimes talk of one option entailing another, but I'll just be using this as shorthand for talk of the *performance* of one option entailing the *performance* of another. In any case, such instances of performance entailment are ubiquitous. Kissing passionately entails kissing. Driving under 55 mph entails driving under 100 mph. Marrying your sister entails marrying your female sibling. Charging a laptop entails using a charger. Typing the word "the" entails typing the letter T. And stretching at t_1 and then going for a run at t_2 entails going for a run at t_2.

So deontic inheritance just says that if you ought to φ but don't have the option of φ-ing without ψ-ing, then you ought to ψ as well. And we need this claim to provide a systematic justification for a great many seemingly valid inferences of the following general form: (P1) S ought to φ. (P2) S's φ-ing entails S's ψ-ing. Therefore, (C) S ought to ψ. We find many instances of this general form in our everyday reasoning, because there are many ways for φ-ing to entail ψ-ing, including all the following: (1) φ-ing is the same as ψ-ing, (2) ψ-ing is a necessary means to φ-ing, (3) ψ-ing (e.g., *x*-ing) consists in performing a proper subset of the set of options of which φ-ing (e.g., both *x*-ing and *y*-ing) consists, and (4) φ-ing is a more specific instance of ψ-ing. So, corresponding to these four ways for φ-ing to entail ψ-ing, we have four different subtypes of the above general form. I'll illustrate each in turn. First, suppose that I ought to marry your female sibling. Given that my marrying your female sibling is the same as my marrying your sister, it seems that we can infer that I ought to marry your sister. Second, suppose that I ought to charge my laptop. Given that my using a charger is a necessary means to charging my

---

5. I think that the following two other propositions are also plausible: (*obligation inheritance*) for any subject S and any two of her options φ and ψ, if S obligated to φ and S's φ-ing entails S's ψ-ing, then S obligated to ψ, and (*permission inheritance*) for any subject S and any two of her options φ and ψ, if S permitted to φ and S's φ-ing entails S's ψ-ing, then S permitted to ψ. But see CARIANI 2013 for some worries about such inheritance principles, many of which I address below.

laptop, it seems that we can infer that I ought to use a charger. Third, suppose that I ought to both exercise and eat healthily. Given that my exercising is a proper subset of my both exercising and eating healthily, it seems that we can infer that I ought to exercise. Fourth and finally, suppose that I ought to kiss my partner passionately. Given that my kissing her passionately is a more specific instance of my kissing her, it seems that we can infer that I ought to kiss her.[6] In order both to accept the validity of these four different subtypes and to give a unified and systematic account of their validity in terms of the above general form, we must accept deontic inheritance.[7]

So I think that we should accept that an option can inherit its deontic status (or, at least, the specific status of being something that ought to be performed) from the options that entail it. But I think that we should deny that an option inherits its evaluative status from the options that entail it. That is, we should deny that the property of being best is closed under performance entailment. So the second plausible proposition that we should accept is the following.

Evaluative noninheritance: It is not the case that, for any subject S and any two of her options φ and ψ, if φ is S's best option and S's φ-ing entails S's ψ-ing, then ψ is also S's best option.[8]

---

6. We can't infer that I'm permitted to kiss her nonpassionately, but we can infer that I ought to kiss her.

7. Some philosophers reject the validity of the above general form—see, most notably, JACKSON & PARGETTER 1986. Nevertheless, even Jackson now accepts the validity of some inferences of this form. Specifically, he claims that, from the fact that he ought to raise both his left arm and his right arm at t, we can infer that he ought to raise his left arm at t—see JACKSON 2014 (pp. 645–646). But I see no reason for thinking that only when φ-ing does not consist in performing two options at distinct times is this type of inference valid—that is, valid only when φ-ing consists in something like raising both his left arm and his right arm at t as opposed to something like raising both his left arm at t and his right arm t' (t' being later than t). Admittedly, Jackson thinks that the case of Professor Procrastinate provides such a reason, but, as I'll show in Chapter 5, it does not.

8. You may think that if two options are distinct, they couldn't possibly both be the subject's best option. But, in fact, they could, because distinct options needn't be alternative options. Recall that whereas two options, φ and ψ, are *alternative options* if and only if <φ-ing and ψ-ing> is not an option, they are *distinct options* if and only if it is not the case that each entails the other. To illustrate, then, let 'φ' stand for "kissing my partner passionately" and let 'ψ' stand for "kissing her." In that case, φ and ψ are distinct options since kissing her does not entail kissing her passionately. But φ and ψ are not alternatives, for I have the option of <kissing her and kissing her passionately>. Moreover, the two distinct options—<kissing her> and <kissing her passionately>—could both be my best option. For an option is best just in case it is both sufficiently good and better than all *its* alternatives, and each of φ and ψ could both be sufficiently good and better than all *its* alternatives given that each has different alternatives. For instance,

Table 4.1 Doc's Options in *The Injection*

Option	Outcome	Ranking
Inject Pat with a proper dose	Both live happily ever after	Best
Refrain from injecting Pat	Pat suffers; Doc loses her license	2nd best
Inject Pat with an improper dose	Pat dies; Doc goes to prison	Worst
Inject Pat	Pat dies; Doc goes to prison	Worst

To see why we should accept this proposition, consider the following case.

The Injection: Doc's patient, Pat, needs an injection of drug D, and the sooner he gets it, the better. Doc has the following four options: (1) inject him with D, (2) inject him with a proper dose of D, (3) inject him with an improper dose of D, and (4) refrain from injecting him with D. The worst thing would be for Doc to inject him with an improper dose of D. That would kill Pat and result in Doc's going to prison. It would be better not to inject him with D at all; in which case, Doc would lose her medical license but stay out of prison, while Pat would suffer for a few more days before going to another doctor who would then inject him with a proper dose of D. What would be best, though, is Doc's injecting Pat with a proper dose of D. In that case, everyone would live happily ever after. But, as a matter of fact, if Doc were to inject Pat with D, she would inject him with an improper dose of D. This is not because of coercion or outside interference or anything like that, but because Doc is about to form the intention to kill Pat, for she mistakenly believes that Pat belongs to a certain race, one toward which she harbors murderous hatred. And assume that Doc has the capacity to form the intention to perform any one of her four options and will perform whichever one she intends to perform. See Table 4.1.

Assume that I haven't left out any important details. Given that and the above description, it seems that Doc's best option is to inject Pat with a

---

it could be both that kissing her is better than not kissing her and that kissing her passionately is better than not kissing her passionately.

proper dose of D. Doing so is both sufficiently good and better than either of its two alternatives (i.e., refraining from injecting him with D and injecting him with an improper dose of D) in terms of everything that could possibly be what ultimately matters. It's better in terms of the production of happiness for others. It's better in terms of the production of happiness for Doc. It's better in terms of the production of overall happiness. It's better in terms of expected utility. And it's better in terms of fidelity, given that Doc's doing anything else would entail her violating both her Hippocratic Oath as well as her contractual obligation to provide her patient with the standard of care. It's better in terms of respect for autonomy given that Pat has, we'll assume, autonomously requested to receive the standard of care and would never consent to being killed. It's better in terms of justice given that Doc has no right to kill Pat and certainly has no right to kill someone based on the person's actual or perceived race. It's even better in terms of desire satisfaction given that Doc has no desire to hurt anyone of Pat's actual race. Moreover, Doc's injecting him with a proper dose of D seems to be better than the alternatives in terms of every other possibly relevant consideration. It seems, therefore, to be Doc's best option.

But although Doc's injecting Pat with a proper dose of D is her best option, it entails another (distinct) option that is not Doc's best option: that of injecting Pat with D. Injecting him with D is not Doc's best option, for refraining from injecting him with D is a better alternative.[9] Her refraining from injecting him with D is a better alternative, because she's going to inject him with an improper dose of D if she injects him with D. Thus, her injecting him with D would result in his dying and her going to prison, whereas her refraining from injecting him with D would result merely in his suffering a bit longer and her losing her medical license. And such results are, I'll assume, at least one of the things that ultimately matters. Thus, Doc's injecting Pat with D is not her best option even though it is entailed by her best option. And this implies evaluative noninheritance.

Now, I've just assumed that Doc's injecting Pat with D is not her best option. I've done so because it seems to me that what ultimately matters in this sort of case is that things go as well as possible and that, therefore, what would make her injecting him with D her best option is its having better consequences than any of its alternatives would—that is, its having

---

9. It doesn't seem to be a sufficiently good option either.

optimific consequences.[10] But, as a matter of fact, it doesn't have optimific consequences, for her refraining from injecting him with D is an alternative with better consequences. Nevertheless, someone might, to the contrary, suggest that what would make her injecting him with D best is not whether her doing so would itself have optimific consequences, but whether her doing so is entailed by an option with optimific consequences. And her doing so is entailed by an option with optimific consequences. For her injecting him with a proper dose of D has optimific consequences and entails injecting him with D. So, whereas I've been assuming that whether Doc's injecting Pat with D is best depends on whether *its* consequences are optimific, someone might suggest that it depends instead on whether it is entailed by an option with optimific consequences.

But I think that we should reject this suggestion. It presupposes an implausible view about what ultimately matters. Although it is intuitive to think that we should ultimately be concerned with whether things go as well as possible, it is counterintuitive to suppose that we should *ultimately* be concerned with whether people perform options that are entailed by options that have optimific consequences. Recall that to say that something ultimately matters is to say that it matters for its own sake and, thus, not for the sake of its being instrumental with respect to something else that matters. For instance, utilitarians hold that what ultimately matters is utility, for they hold that utility matters for its own sake. By contrast, a divine command theorist who holds that God commands her to maximize utility holds that what ultimately matters is that she not disobey God. On her view, then, whether her acts maximize utility matters only derivatively, because her maximizing utility is instrumental to what ultimately matters—namely, her not disobeying God. And this distinction between what ultimately matters and what derivatively matters is important because whereas it's plausible to suppose that performing options that are entailed by options with optimific consequences *derivatively* matters (in that performing such options is necessary for producing optimific consequences), it is implausible to suppose that performing options that are

---

10. Whereas an option's consequences are *optimal* if and only if there is no alternative option whose consequences are better than it, an option's consequences are *optimific* if and only if its consequences are better than that of any alternative option. And note that the consequences of a subject's φ-ing is what would be the case if she were to φ, where what would be the case if she were to φ depends on what she would, in fact, simultaneously and subsequently do if she were to φ.

entailed by options with optimific consequences *ultimately* matters and, thus, matters for its own sake.

Moreover, if someone thought that we should ultimately be concerned with performing options that are entailed (i.e., singly entailed) by options with optimific consequences, I would want to know why she thinks this rather than that we should ultimately be concerned with performing options that are *doubly* entailed by options with optimific consequences—that is, options that are entailed by options that are in turn entailed by options with optimific consequences. And I would want to know why she thinks this rather than that we should ultimately be concerned with performing options that are triply, quadruply, or quintuply entailed by options with optimific consequences. For I see no principled reason for our ultimate concern to lie with one rather than the other. Of course, she could retort that *all* of them ultimately matter. That is, she could claim that we should ultimately be concerned not only with whether an option is singly entailed by an option with optimific consequences but also with whether it is doubly, triply, quadruply, or quintuply entailed by such an option. But why should we be concerned with all of them rather than just one of them? And why should we be concerned with any of them but for the sake of making things as good as possible?

In any case, this all leads me to conclude that, although we should ultimately be concerned with things going as well as possible, we should be only *derivatively* concerned with performing options that are singly, doubly, triply, quadruply, or quintuply entailed by options with optimific consequences— that is, we should be concerned with performing such options only because we don't have the option of making things go as well as possible without performing them. For every option with optimific consequences is singly, doubly, triply, quadruply, and quintuply entailed by *itself*, which is an option with optimific consequences. So I think that we should deny the suggestion that Doc's injecting Pat with D is best in virtue of its being entailed by an option with optimific consequences and, thus, accept my argument for evaluative noninheritance.

It's important to understand why evaluative noninheritance holds. It holds both because an option that entails another can have different alternatives than it has and because whether an option is best in terms of what ultimately matters can depend on whether there is some alternative that promotes a given end to a greater extent than it does. For this means that an option, φ, can be better than all *its* alternatives in terms of promoting a given end even though the option that it entails, namely, ψ, isn't better than all *its* (distinct set of) alternatives in terms of promoting that end. For instance, Doc's injecting Pat with a proper dose of D entails injecting him with D, but these two options have different sets of alternatives. Whereas Doc's injecting him with an improper dose of D is an alternative to injecting him with a proper dose of D, it is not an alternative to injecting him with D. And this explains why one compares better to its alternatives than the other does to its (distinct set of) alternatives.

There is no better alternative to injecting him with a proper dose of D, as this would result in the best outcome, the one in which everyone lives happily ever after. But there is a better alternative to injecting him with D: namely, refraining from injecting him with D. For whereas injecting him with D would result in the worst outcome (the one in which he dies and she goes to prison), the alternative of refraining from injecting him with D would result in the second-best outcome (the one in which he suffers a bit longer but lives and she loses her medical license but stays out of prison). And the reason that injecting him with D can result in injecting him with an improper dose of D whereas injecting him with a proper dose of D cannot is because injecting him with an improper dose of D is an alternative to injecting him with a proper dose of D but not an alternative to injecting him with D. Thus, so long as we accept that there are certain ends (such as making things go as well as possible) that we should, other things being equal, promote, evaluative noninheritance will hold given that an option that entails another can have different alternatives than it does.

But now if we accept both deontic inheritance and evaluative noninheritance, as I've argued that we should, we must reject omnism, for the three together entail a contradiction. This is because evaluative noninheritance implies that there is some case such as *The Injection* in which the given subject's best option is to ϕ and her ϕ-ing entails her ψ-ing and, yet, her ψ-ing is not her best option. So accepting evaluative noninheritance commits us, for instance, to accepting premise 4.1 below, and this premise, together with omnism and deontic inheritance, entails a contradiction. Here's the proof.

(4.1) Doc's best option is to inject Pat with a proper dose of D and doing so entails injecting him with D, and yet her injecting him with D is not her best option. [That there must be some example with this structure follows from evaluative noninheritance]

(4.2) For any subject S and any option of hers φ, S ought to φ if and only if φ is her best option. [From omnism]

(4.3) Thus, Doc ought to inject Pat with a proper dose of D. [From 4.1–4.2]

(4.4) Doc's injecting Pat with a proper dose of D entails injecting him with D. [From 4.1]

(4.5) For any subject S and any two events φ and ψ, if S ought to φ and S's φ-ing entails S's ψ-ing, then S ought to ψ. [Deontic inheritance]

(4.6) Thus, Doc ought to inject Pat with D. [From 4.3–4.5]

(4.7) Doc's injecting Pat with D is not her best option. [From 4.1]

(4.8) Thus, it is not the case that Doc ought to inject Pat with D. [From 4.2 and 4.7]

(4.9) Therefore, it is both the case and not the case that Doc ought to inject Pat with D. [From 4.6 and 4.8][11]

This argument shows that we must reject at least one of omnism, deontic inheritance, and evaluative noninheritance. And, thus, it shows that if both deontic inheritance and evaluative noninheritance are, as I've argued, true, then omnism is false. But, of course, one person's *modus ponens* is another's *modus tollens*. So the reader may wonder why we shouldn't instead argue that since omnism is true, either deontic inheritance or evaluative noninheritance is false. But although I see very good reasons both for accepting deontic inheritance (i.e., it allows us to accept the validity of the above four subtypes of inference and to give a unified and systematic account of their validity)[12] and for

---

11. Technically, this shows only that we must reject omnism's OUGHT. But I could have just as easily shown that we must reject omnism's PERMI. For all the premises in this argument would be just as plausible if I had substituted "is permitted" for "ought" and "one of Doc's sufficiently good options" for "Doc's best option" throughout. And, in that case, the revised argument would refute omnism's PERMI. This is why I mentioned in note 9 that Doc's injecting Pat with D isn't even a sufficiently good option. Of course, this still leaves omnism's SUPER unrefuted. But I will argue against it in §4.4 below.

12. Another reason to accept deontic inheritance is that it follows from what we might call *reasons inheritance* and some additional assumptions. See KIESEWETTER 2015 and KIESEWETTER 2018 for the details. But here's a brief sketch of the argument: (1) S ought to φ, and S's φ-ing entails S's ψ-ing (assumption for conditional proof). (2) S ought to φ if and only if S has most reason to φ (assumption). Thus, (3) S has most reason to φ (from 1 and 2). (4) If S has *x* reason to φ (where '*x*' stands for some word such as "a," "some," "most," "decisive," "sufficient," etc.) and S doesn't have the option of φ-ing without ψ-ing, then S has *x* reason to ψ (reasons inheritance). (5) If S's φ-ing entails S's ψ-ing, then S doesn't have the option of φ-ing without ψ-ing (analytic). Therefore, (6) S has most reason to ψ (from 1, 3, 4, and 5). Therefore, (7) S ought to ψ (from 2 and 6). Therefore, (8) if S ought to φ and S's φ-ing entails S's ψ-ing, then S ought to ψ (from 1–7 by conditional proof).

accepting evaluative noninheritance (i.e., it allows us to accept the plausible view that whether an option is singly, doubly, or triply entailed by an option that promotes those ends matters only derivatively—that is, only in virtue of promoting those ends that themselves matter), I don't see any reason nearly as good for accepting omnism. Admittedly, many philosophers have tended to just assume that all options are to be assessed directly in terms of their own goodness. For instance, many utilitarians have assumed that their view should be formulated as the following version of omnism: for any subject S and any option of hers φ, S ought to φ if and only if φ is optimific in terms of the production of aggregate utility. But the mere fact that many philosophers have presupposed it isn't a good reason to accept it. It seems, then, that the only good reason for accepting omnism is the idea that it constitutes a more unified account of the deontic statuses of our options in that it holds that we are to assess the deontic statuses of all, and not merely some, our options in terms of their own goodness.[13] But this reason doesn't seem nearly as strong as the reason that we have to accept evaluative noninheritance: that it is implausible to suppose that whether an option is singly, doubly, or triply entailed by an option that promotes certain ends matters regardless of whether those ends themselves matter.

Of course, if we deny omnism, we must hold that some options have their deontic statuses in virtue of their being entailed by options that promote certain ends, and not in virtue of their themselves promoting those ends. So we might wonder why this isn't just as bad as what I've just argued is bad: holding that some options have their evaluative statuses in virtue of their being entailed by options that promote certain ends. To see why it isn't, note that whereas our holding that an option has the evaluative status of being best commits us to the view that the properties in virtue of which it has this evaluative status are properties with which we should ultimately be concerned, our holding that an option has the deontic status of being that which ought to be done doesn't. The latter commits us only to the view that the properties in virtue of which it has this deontic status are properties in virtue of which the agent (if relevantly informed) ought to intend to perform it. And whereas

---

13. Some may suggest that our intuitions in cases such as Frank Jackson's case of Professor Procrastinate is another good reason to accept omnism, but, as I'll argue in Chapter 5, omnism's implications in this case are in fact counterintuitive. Also, see BROWN 2018 for why we should think that what explains the deontic statuses of maximal options is not what explains the deontic statuses of nonmaximal options: maximal options are special in that every option is reducible to a maximal option.

it is quite counterintuitive to think that a subject ought ultimately to be concerned with whether an option is entailed by an option that promotes certain ends, it is not at all counterintuitive to think that a subject ought to intend to perform an option that promotes those ends. After all, the fact that a subject can't promote those ends unless she performs a given option seems like a perfectly good reason for her to intend to perform that option. And if promoting those ends entails performing that option, then she can't promote those ends unless she performs that option. So it seems that denying omnism isn't nearly as unattractive (if unattractive at all) as denying evaluative noninheritance. And given this and the fact that denying deontic inheritance is also quite unattractive, we should, I believe, reject omnism.[14]

Now, if we reject omnism and its position that we are to evaluate all options in terms of their own goodness, we are left with only two alternatives: evaluate only some options in terms of their own goodness or evaluate no option in terms of its own goodness. I'll consider each in turn over the next two sections.

§4.2 Nonnullusism (Only Some Options)

According to nonnullusism (*nonnullus* meaning "not none" or "some" in Latin), only some options are to have their deontic statuses assessed in terms of their own goodness. But, of course, proponents of this view will need to say which ones these are. Of course, given deontic inheritance, some options will inherit their deontic status from the options that entail them. So these will be assessed, not in terms of their own goodness, but in terms of the goodness of the options that entail them. But lest we end up in a vicious regress, some options must be assessed in terms of their own goodness. And there are only two plausible candidates for which options these could be: (1) options that are entailed only by themselves—that is, options that are not entailed by any distinct option, and (2) options that are entailed only by evaluatively equivalent options (those being options that are identical in terms of whatever ultimately matters)—that is, options that are not entailed by any *evaluatively*

---

14. Nevertheless, if you think that it's better to reject evaluative noninheritance, we'll accept all the same deontic verdicts. For instance, we'll both accept that Doc should inject Pat with D. It's just that whereas I'll say that this is because her doing so, although not itself best, is entailed by what's best, you'll say that this is because her doing so is itself best. So we'll accept different evaluative verdicts but the same deontic verdicts. Moreover, we'll both accept deontic inheritance.

distinct option. Call the former *maximally specific options* and the latter *maximally evaluatively specific options*.

Maximally specific options are plausible candidates for needing to be assessed in terms of their own goodness, because they are not entailed by any other option and so couldn't possibly be assessed in terms of the goodness of the nonexistent, distinct options that entail them. But there's a worry about maximally specific options: they may not exist. For, perhaps, there is no limit to how specific an option can get.[15] And if that's right, then no matter how specific an option is, there will always be some more specific option that entails it.[16] Nevertheless, further specificity can sometimes be evaluatively irrelevant and, hence, deontically irrelevant (see BROWN 2018). To illustrate, suppose that utility is the only thing that ultimately matters and that I will maximize utility if and only if I think of an integer greater than 10. In that case, my thinking of an integer greater than 11 will be evaluatively equivalent to my thinking of an integer greater than 10, for these two options are identical in terms of what ultimately matters: utility. Likewise, my thinking of an integer greater than 12 will be evaluatively equivalent to my thinking of an integer greater than 11. So, in this case, my thinking of an integer greater than 10, my thinking of an integer greater than 11, my thinking of an integer greater than 12, and so on are all maximally evaluatively specific options—options that are entailed only by evaluatively equivalent options such that each is no better or worse than the others. And since these other options are identical to them in terms of their goodness, we can just assess each of them in terms of their own goodness. What's more, since any maximally specific option will

---

15. In fact, I think that there is a limit to how specific an option can get for a subject of limited abilities. For, as I argued, in Chapter 2, an option must be something over which the subject exerts control and the control that human beings possess is limited in a way that the descriptive power of language is not. For instance, even if I have the option of spinning a wheel as well as the option of spinning it either gently or with all my might, I need not have the option of spinning it with precisely 15.88351 N ('N' standing for "newtons") of force. For I may lack control over precisely how many newtons of force with which I spin the wheel. This example is adapted from HARE 2011.

16. Of course, the fact that an option can always be described in more and more specific ways may be due to the nature of our language and not to the nature of our options themselves. To borrow an analogy from BROWN 2018, note that "it is impossible for us to write down the decimal expansion of π, because π is infinite and we are finite. We can write down each of a sequence of decimal expansions—3, 3.1, 3.14, . . .—each one a more accurate approximation of π than the previous. But we will never reach one that cannot be further refined by appending another digit at the end. This surely is no reason to doubt that π exists." Likewise, the fact that we can always give a more specific description of an option should be no reason to doubt that maximally specific options exist.

necessarily also be a maximally evaluatively specific option (given that an option is always evaluatively equivalent to itself), we can collapse the above two plausible candidates for options that are to be assessed in terms of their own goodness into the second of the two: maximally evaluatively specific options. And, to save words, I'll hereafter refer to maximally evaluatively specific options simply as *maximal options*. To sum up, then, it seems that, given deontic inheritance, we should hold that nonmaximal options (i.e., options that are entailed by some evaluatively distinct option) should be assessed in terms of the evaluatively distinct options that entail them and that maximal options (i.e., options that are not entailed by any evaluatively distinct option) are to be assessed in terms of their own goodness.

When we identify the options that are and are not to assessed in terms of their own goodness as maximal and nonmaximal options, respectively, the resulting view is what I call *maximalism*. More precisely, it is as follows.

> **Maximalism**: (OUGHT) For any maximal option M, a subject ought to M if and only if M is her best maximal option. And, for any nonmaximal option N, S ought to N if and only if N is entailed by a maximal option that she ought to perform. (PERMI) For any maximal option M, a subject is permitted to M if and only if M is one of her sufficiently good maximal options. And for any nonmaximal option N, she is permitted to N if and only if N is entailed by a permissible maximal option.[17]

On maximalism's OUGHT, if I ought to do something, it's because it is either itself my best maximal option or entailed by my best maximal option. And, on maximalism's PERMI, if I'm permitted to do something, it's because it is either itself one of my sufficiently good maximal options or entailed by one of my sufficiently good maximal options.

In what follows, I will first address a worry concerning how maximalism has just been formulated. Second, I'll explain how maximalism solves the problem of act versions. And third, I'll explain why we should favor this

---

17. Again, I leave implicit the relevant grounding clauses. And, as always, the relevant deontic statuses are the objective ones. Also, note that this is incomplete, as I haven't given the conditions for an option's being supererogatory. I'll do that in §4.4 below. Last, note that although maximalism is similar to the view known as *possibilism* (see, e.g., JACKSON & PARGETTER 1986), the two views are distinct, and I'll have more to say about how maximalism and possibilism differ in Chapter 5.

solution to that of an alternative view, the view that we are to evaluate no option in terms of its own goodness (viz., nullusism). I'll do the first two in the remainder of this section and the third in the next section (§4.3). Then, in §4.4, I'll complete the above formulation by adding to it the conditions for an option's being supererogatory.

I'll start with the worry. It is that maximalism, as formulated above, is incompatible with the assumption that a subject must always have at least one permissible alternative available to her.[18] To see why it's incompatible with this assumption, suppose that there is no limit to how large an integer I can think of and that, for whatever integer I think of, God will give me and my loved ones precisely those many days in heaven, and will give us no days in heaven if I fail to think of any integer.[19] Further suppose that an option is sufficiently good only if there is no alternative to it that would result in more days in heaven for us.[20] In that case, I will act impermissibly no matter what I do, or fail to do. For I must perform either of the following two alternatives: (1) think of some integer or (2) refrain from thinking of any integer. And both are impermissible. My refraining from thinking of any integer is impermissible, because no sufficiently good maximal option entails my refraining from thinking of any integer. After all, for any maximal option that entails my refraining from thinking of any integer, there is an alternative that would result in more days in heaven for us: the one that is otherwise relevantly identical but for the fact that I think of some integer. And thinking of some integer is also impermissible, because, no matter what integer I think of (and call that number 'n'), no

---

18. The general assumption that, for any set of norms, a subject must have at least one alternative that is permitted by those norms is clearly false—see VALLENTYNE 1992 (p. 118). But it could be, as some claim, that certain sets of norms (say, the norms of morality) are such that their very nature ensures that a subject must have at least one alternative that is permitted by those norms. For instance, we might think that since no one deserves to suffer the unpleasantness of feeling guilty in virtue of having φ-ed unless she could have done otherwise and thereby avoided being liable to such internal sanction, there must always be some permissible alternative—that is, an alternative that she can perform without being liable to such internal sanction.

19. For some more realistic instances in which a subject has no best option, see some of Warren Quinn's everyday examples in his 1990. And, for my take on such cases, see my MANUSCRIPT.

20. One may take the lesson to be that it is implausible to suppose that an option can be sufficiently good only if there is no alternative to it that would result in more days in heaven for us. That's fair enough. But my point is only that some will object to maximalism as formulated above because it allows for a possibility that they believe to be impossible: a situation in which a subject has no permissible alternative available to her. And to assess what's possible on a given theory we can combine it with other claims that, although implausible, are compatible with the theory.

sufficiently good maximal option entails my thinking of n. After all, for any maximal option that entails my thinking of some integer n, there is an alternative that would result in more days in heaven for us: the one that is otherwise relevantly identical but for the fact that I think of an integer greater than n. Thus, as formulated above, maximalism is incompatible with the assumption that a subject must always have at least one permissible alternative available to her.[21]

This is, perhaps, problematic. But if it is, there's an easy fix. We need only replace maximalism's PERMI with something like the following: "(PERMI*) For any (maximal or nonmaximal) option φ, a subject is permitted to φ if and only if φ is either a (sufficiently good) member of an infinite set of ever-better options or is entailed by a sufficiently good maximal option."[22] Moreover, anyone who insists that I must have at least one permissible option in the case just described must concede that being a (sufficiently good) member of an infinite set of ever-better options makes an alternative permissible. So they can't object that this revision is ad hoc. And, if we do make this revision, maximalism ensures that a subject will always have at least one permissible alternative. For instance, my thinking of the integer 998 in the case just described would be permissible even though the alternative of thinking of the integer 999 would result in more days in heaven for us. It would be permissible simply because it is a (sufficiently good) member of an infinite set of ever-better options. In any case, I will remain neutral regarding whether we should make this revision, for none of the claims that I'll make in this book hinges on this.

With this worry out of the way, I can now explain how maximalism solves the problem of act versions—the problem of having to deny one of omnism, deontic inheritance, and evaluative noninheritance. It does so by denying omnism and holding that we should assess Doc's injecting Pat with D (and any other nonmaximal option), not in terms of its own goodness, but rather in terms of the goodness of the maximal options that entail it. Thus, maximalism implies that Doc ought to inject Pat with D even though this is not her best option. It implies this, because all her best maximal options entail injecting

---

21. Thanks to Brad Armendt, William Kilborn, and Ángel Pinillos for pressing me on this.

22. If we want to make it permissible to think of any relatively high positive integer but not to think of just any positive integer, then we should remove the parentheses around "(sufficiently good)." If, by contrast, we want to make it permissible to think of any positive integer, then we should just delete "(sufficiently good)" altogether. Another way to handle cases in which none of the agent's options are ranked best or even tied for best is to adopt what Eric Swanson (2014) calls *ordering supervaluationism*.

him with a proper dose of D and injecting him with a proper dose of D entails injecting him with D. So, unlike omnism, maximalism doesn't run afoul of the conjunction of deontic inheritance and evaluative noninheritance. For, unlike omnism, it doesn't hold that Doc ought to perform all and only those options that are best. Consequently, it doesn't hold that Doc ought to inject Pat with a proper dose of D but ought not to inject him with D. Instead, maximalism holds that Doc ought to perform all and only those nonmaximal options that are entailed by her best maximal option. Thus, it holds that Doc ought both to inject him with a proper dose of D and to inject him with D.

§4.3 Nullusism (No Option)

I've argued that to solve the problem of act versions, we should reject omnism and replace it with a view that implies, as maximalism does, that Doc ought to inject Pat with D even though this is not her best option—that is, even though it is not better than all of its alternatives. Now, maximalism isn't the only view that solves the problem of act versions in this way. There is at least one other way of arriving at the verdict that Doc is permitted to inject Pat with D even though this is not her best option. We could, for instance, adopt the view that we are to assess no option in terms of its own goodness and are instead to assess all options in terms of the goodness of the options that entail them. Because this view holds that no option has its deontic status simply in virtue of its own goodness and because *nullus* is Latin for "none," I call this view *nullusism*. It is as follows.

> **Nullusism:** For any subject S and any option of hers φ: (OUGHT) S ought to φ if and only if φ is entailed by her best maximal option and (PERMI) S is permitted to φ if and only if φ is entailed by one of her sufficiently good maximal options.[23]

Nullusism yields the exact same verdicts that maximalism does regarding both which options are permissible and which options ought to be performed. But although they yield the same verdicts, they differ as to what makes a maximal option have one of these deontic statuses. To illustrate, let's simply focus on the OUGHT-clauses of both maximalism and nullusism, because what I'll

---

23. Again, I leave implicit the relevant grounding clauses. And, as always, the relevant deontic statuses are the objective ones. Again, I'll wait until §4.4 to add to it the conditions for an option's being supererogatory.

say about them applies equally to the PERMI-clauses, *mutatis mutandis*. And let's suppose both that Doc's best maximal option is M_b and that M_b-ing entails injecting Pat with a proper dose of D. Given this, both maximalism's OUGHT and nullusism's OUGHT imply that Doc ought to perform the nonmaximal option of injecting Pat with D, and they agree that this is in virtue of the fact that Doc's best maximal option (viz., M_b) entails her doing so. What's more, both maximalism's OUGHT and nullusism's OUGHT imply that Doc ought to perform the maximal option of M_b-ing. But in this case, they disagree about what grounds this deontic verdict. Whereas maximalism's OUGHT holds that Doc ought to M_b in virtue of the fact that M_b is best, nullusism's OUGHT holds that Doc ought to M_b in virtue of the fact that M_b is entailed by her best maximal option—namely, M_b. So, whereas maximalism's OUGHT assesses maximal options directly in terms of their own goodness, nullusism's OUGHT does so only indirectly, assessing maximal options in terms the goodness of the maximal options that entail them.

Admirably, nullusism's OUGHT avoids the problem of act versions. For, like maximalism's OUGHT, it holds that Doc ought to inject Pat with D despite this not being her best option. The problem, though, is that the nullusist is committed to rejecting the most plausible and straightforward explanation for why she ought to perform M_b. Rather than simply claiming, as maximalism does, that she ought to perform M_b *in virtue of its being her best maximal option*, the nullusist claims that she ought to perform M_b *in virtue of its being entailed by her best maximal option*—namely, M_b. In other words, it claims that she ought to perform M_b in virtue of its being entailed by itself. And this seems like an implausible account of what makes M_b the maximal option that she ought to perform. Whether M_b is best seems relevant to whether she ought to perform it. But whether M_b is entailed by itself doesn't seem at all relevant to whether she ought to perform it. After all, it's not as if performing M_b is instrumental in performing M_b. M_b just is M_b. What's more, the fact that M_b is singly entailed by her best maximal option seems no more relevant to whether she ought to perform M_b than does whether M_b is doubly, triply, or quadruply entailed by her best maximal option. Thus, it seems arbitrary for nullusism to take being singly entailed by her best maximal option as opposed to doubly, triply, or quadruply entailed by her best maximal option as the relevant fundamental ought-making feature of maximal options. So the nullusist solves the problem of act versions at the cost of adopting an arbitrary and implausible view about what makes certain maximal options the ones that ought to be performed. I think that we should reject nullusism's OUGHT.

And since the same sort of case can be made against nullusism's PERMI, we should reject it as well.

So far, I've argued that omnism should be rejected given that it is subject to the problem of act versions. And I've argued that although both maximalism and nullusism avoid the problem of act versions, we should favor maximalism over nullusism since it offers a much more plausible and straightforward account of what makes a maximal option one that ought to be performed. Thus, I conclude that of these three, we should adopt maximalism. This, however, may seem premature since we have yet to consider each view's account of supererogation. And if either omnism or nullusism offered a far superior account of supererogation, it may be that we shouldn't adopt maximalism after all. In the next section, I'll argue that maximalism's account of supererogation is, in fact, superior to those of its two rivals.

§4.4 Supererogation and the Latitude Problem

The term "supererogatory" is a technical term that one can use however one wants. But I'll use it such that an act counts as supererogatory if and only if, in performing it, the agent exceeds what's minimally required of her. As such, my use of the term coincides with such colloquial expressions as "going the extra mile," "doing more than one has to," and "going (above and) beyond the call of duty."[24]

In this section, I'll consider three competing accounts of supererogation so conceived: omnism's, nullusism's, and maximalism's. And to simplify the discussion, I'll focus solely on their accounts of *moral* supererogation (i.e., M-SUPER), although what I say about these three accounts of moral supererogation applies, *mutatis mutandis*, to their accounts of other kinds of

---

24. On this conception of supererogation, a *morally* supererogatory act morally exceeds the demands of *morality* by being morally better than what's minimally required by morality. Likewise, a *rationally* supererogatory act rationally exceeds the demands of *rationality* by being rationally better than what's minimally required by rationality. Thus, reading through the entire menu to select the best entrée when all that rationality requires is that you read through enough of it to select the first good enough entrée that you come across is rationally supererogatory if it is rationally better for you to read through the entire menu to select the best entrée. But others conceive of supererogation differently. For instance, Dale Dorsey (2013A and 2016) holds that a *morally* supererogatory act morally exceeds the demands of *rationality* by being morally better than what's minimally required by rationality. Clearly, then, Dorsey and I are talking about different concepts even though we are using the same technical term to refer to them. And, of course, there's nothing wrong with using a technical term in whatever way one chooses. But see ARCHER 2016B and PORTMORE 2017B for some criticisms of Dorsey's view.

supererogation—for example, *rational* supererogation. And I'll argue that maximalism's account is the most plausible of the three.

To start, let's consider why I think that nullusism's account is a nonstarter. It's account of moral supererogation is as follows.

> **Nullusism's M-SUPER:** For any subject S and any option of hers φ, S's φ-ing is morally supererogatory if and only if φ is entailed by some maximal option M_x with an alternative maximal option M_y such that (a) she is both morally permitted to M_x and morally permitted to M_y, and (b) her M_x-ing is morally better than her M_y-ing.

One problem with this view is that it offers an implausible account of why supererogatory maximal options are supererogatory. Nullusism's M-SUPER holds that if performing a maximal option—say, M_s—is supererogatory, this is in virtue of the fact that it's entailed by a maximal option that is morally better than some permissible alternative maximal option. But it seems much more plausible to suppose that M_s is supererogatory simply in virtue of the fact that it is itself morally better than some permissible alternative maximal option. After all, the notion of being morally supererogatory is the notion of exceeding what's minimally morally required, not that of being entailed by an option that exceeds what's minimally morally required.

But although this problem alone seems fatal, the view also has counterintuitive implications. To illustrate, consider the following two examples.

> *The Miser:* Morality requires one to dedicate at least 20 percent of one's surplus time and resources (i.e., that portion of one's time and resources exceeding what's needed to ensure that one is sufficiently happy and virtuous) to promoting the happiness of others over the course of one's adult life. However, Mr. Scrooge fell well short of this required minimum. He lived from 1920 to 1995, and in all that time, he did only one rather trivial thing to help others. On Christmas eve 1938, he picked up a lost five-dollar bill off the ground and placed it in a Salvation Army donation bucket as he entered a store. This five-dollar donation amounted to less than 0.01 percent of his lifetime surplus income. Moreover, had he not done this, he would have ended up never having done anything for anyone, because he let himself get even more miserly as time went on.
>
> *The Visit:* Morality requires us to keep our promises. And Carlos promised his grandmother that he would visit her at least twice during

the week of her hospitalization. Yet he ended up visiting her only once: on Tuesday. Moreover, had he not visited her then, he would not have visited her at all, for he let things pile up such that he only got busier as the week progressed (although he never got so busy that he was unable to visit his grandmother).

Nullusism's M-SUPER counterintuitively implies both that Mr. Scrooge performs a morally supererogatory act in donating the five-dollar bill that he found and that Carlos performs a morally supererogatory act in visiting his grandmother in the hospital on Tuesday.[25] Nullusism's M-SUPER implies that Mr. Scrooge's act is supererogatory because it is entailed by the maximal option in which he dedicates over 20 percent of his surplus time and resources to promoting the happiness of others by performing many charitable acts, including this one, over the course of his adult life. And nullusism's M-SUPER implies that Carlos's act is morally supererogatory because it is entailed by the maximal option in which he visits his grandmother on Tuesday, Wednesday, and Thursday. Yet neither Mr. Scrooge's act nor Carlos's act exceeds what is minimally morally required of them. Indeed, both agents end up falling well short of what is minimally morally required of them. For Mr. Scrooge doesn't come anywhere close to meeting (let alone exceeding) his moral duty to dedicate at least 20 percent of his surplus time and resources to promoting the happiness of others. Likewise, Carlos falls well short of meeting his moral duty to visit his grandmother at least twice during the week of her hospitalization. Thus, nullusism's account of moral supererogation (nullusism's M-SUPER) is simply a nonstarter.

Omnism's account of moral supererogation is not, I believe, a nonstarter. But, as I explain below, it suffers from a significant problem of its own, one that maximalism's account avoids. Omnism's account of moral supererogation is as follows.

Omnism's M-SUPER: For any subject S and any option of hers φ, S's φ-ing is morally supererogatory if and only if there is some alternative option ψ such that (a) she is both morally permitted to φ and morally permitted to ψ and (b) her φ-ing is morally better than her ψ-ing.

---

25. I would allow that such acts could be called *superperfecterogatory*—a term coined by Sinnott-Armstrong (2005), where a subject's φ-ing is superperfecterogatory if and only if, in φ-ing, she goes beyond the call of perfect duty—a *perfect duty* being a duty that doesn't derive from a duty to adopt a certain set of ends. But such acts are not supererogatory, for, in performing them, these subjects do not go beyond what's minimally required by morality given that morality includes both perfect and imperfect duties.

The problem with omnism–M-SUPER (and I call it *the latitude problem*) is that it has counterintuitive implications in cases in which the duty to be exceeded is one that allows for significant latitude in how to comply with it.[26] Such is the case with the relevant duties in the above two examples. In both cases, the agent has significant latitude in how to comply with the relevant duty. In *The Miser*, the relevant duty is the imperfect duty of beneficence. This duty requires one "to make the happiness of others a serious, major, continually relevant, life-shaping end" (Hill 2002, p. 206) and, derivatively, to live one's life in one of the many ways that's consistent with having done so.[27] Thus, it requires one to act throughout one's adult life so as to exhibit a sufficient propensity to promote the happiness of others—sufficient, that is, to count as having adopted the happiness of others as "a serious, major, continually relevant, life-shaping end." For having such a propensity is constitutive of having adopted the happiness of others as such an end. Thus, if someone with the abilities and opportunities that are typical of those living in the First World did little or nothing to promote the happiness of others, this would show that she had not truly adopted the happiness of others as such an end (HILL 2002, p. 204).

But being that this is an imperfect duty, it gives one a lot of leeway as to how and when to promote this end. For having a propensity to promote the happiness of others does not necessitate that one takes advantage of every favorable opportunity to do so. It requires only that one does so to some sufficient extent.[28] Thus, Mr. Scrooge was not obligated to donate that five-dollar bill to charity on Christmas eve 1938. He was permitted to spend it instead on himself. After all, he was only eighteen years old at the time, and there were to be plenty of future opportunities for him to promote the happiness of others. That said, donating the money to charity was better than

---

26. This sort of problem was first introduced by MELLEMA 1991.

27. Note, then, that those without any surplus resources (i.e., those without any resources beyond what's needed to ensure that they are sufficiently happy and virtuous) can comply with the imperfect duty of beneficence. For, even without such resources, they can make the happiness of others a serious, major, continually relevant, life-shaping end. It's just that, given their lack of resources, there are ways for them to live their lives consistent with their having adopted this end that don't involve them ever doing anything to help others. Thus, I take a life-shaping end to be one that would shape one's life in significant ways under certain circumstances, not one that would shape one's life in significant ways regardless of one's circumstances.

28. Perhaps it also requires us to take advantage of certain golden opportunities—that is, opportunities that are especially favorable and not likely to arise again. For more on this, see NOGGLE 2009.

spending it on himself. In doing so, he did more good than he could have ever done by spending it on himself. Still, he was permitted to forego this opportunity to promote the happiness of others and to choose instead to do so to a greater extent in the future. So, in donating that five-dollar bill, Mr. Scrooge performed a morally optional act that was morally better than the morally permissible alternative of spending that five-dollar bill on himself. Thus, on omnism's M-SUPER, his donating that five-dollar bill counts as supererogatory.

Next, consider *The Visit*. Here, the relevant duty was for Carlos to visit his grandmother at least twice during the week. And this duty allowed for significant latitude in how he was to comply with it. For instance, he wasn't required to visit his grandmother on any particular day that week. He was just required to visit her at least twice.[29] Thus, he was not obligated to visit her when he did—that is, on Tuesday. For he could have fulfilled his duty by visiting her on, say, Wednesday and Thursday, Thursday and Friday, or Monday and Friday. Nevertheless, it was good that he visited her on Tuesday. For it was morally better for him to visit her on Tuesday than for him not to do so. After all, had he not visited her on Tuesday, he would have ended up not visiting her at all. So, in visiting his grandmother on Tuesday, Carlos performed a morally optional act that was better than the morally permissible alternative of not visiting her on that day. So omnism's M-SUPER implies that his visiting his grandmother that Tuesday was supererogatory.

But, as we saw above, such verdicts are implausible. Neither Mr. Scrooge nor Carlos went beyond what was minimally required of them in performing these acts. The problem lies with the fact that an agent can easily meet both condition-a and condition-b of omnism's M-SUPER without exceeding what's minimally required of her. Take the duty of beneficence. Since it is almost always better to act beneficently than to act self-interestedly on a given occasion, and since this imperfect duty almost never requires one to act beneficently

---

29. We may wonder whether this too is best understood as an imperfect duty—a duty to adopt a certain end and, derivatively, to live one's life in one of the many ways that's consistent with having done so. Perhaps, then, it is best understood as the duty to adopt visiting his grandmother at least twice during the week as one of his ends and, derivatively, to live his life in one of the many ways that's consistent with his having done so. The problem with this, though, is that it's possible that his other ends could take precedence over this end in a way that would allow him to count as having adopted this end even though he failed to visit his grandmother at least twice during the week. Thus, if we think that it would take more than just more pressing incompatible ends to excuse him from failing to fulfill his promise to visit his grandmother at least twice during the week, we should not take this duty to be an imperfect duty.

on any specific occasion, an agent can often meet both condition-a and condition-b on a given occasion without exceeding the minimum required by the duty of beneficence. For instance, Mr. Scrooge was able to meet these two conditions in donating that five-dollar bill without ever coming anywhere close to meeting the required minimum of dedicating at least 20 percent of his surplus time and resources to promoting the happiness of others.

So, if we're going to avoid the latitude problem, we'll need to adopt an account that, unlike omnism's M-SUPER, acknowledges that one can meet or exceed the call of such a duty only by performing a certain series of actions over time. Moreover, we'll need to adopt an account that acknowledges that for such a series of actions to count as supererogatory, it must more than just partially or minimally fulfill the relevant duty. Thus, we'll need to adopt maximalism's account of supererogation. And its account of moral supererogation is as follows.

> **Maximalism's M-SUPER:** For any subject S and any maximal option M_x, a subject's M_x-ing is morally supererogatory if and only if there is an alternative maximal option M_y such that (a) she is both morally permitted to M_x and morally permitted to M_y, and (b) her M_x-ing is morally better than her M_y-ing. And for any subject S and any nonmaximal option N_x, her N_x-ing is morally supererogatory if and only if both (a) in N_x-ing, she does not merely minimally or merely partially satisfy some necessary condition for performing a morally permissible maximal option and (b) there is an alternative nonmaximal option N_y such that (i) she is both morally permitted to N_x and morally permitted to N_y, and (ii) her N_x-ing is morally better than her N_y-ing.

When it comes to maximal options, the maximalist account and the omnist account converge on the same verdicts. The two diverge only when it comes to nonmaximal options. To illustrate, take Carlos's nonmaximal option of visiting his grandmother on Tuesday. Whereas omnism's M-SUPER holds that this option is supererogatory given that performing it was better than performing the permissible alternative of not visiting her that day, maximalism's M-SUPER holds that this was not supererogatory given that in performing this option, he merely partially satisfies a necessary condition for performing a maximal option that entails his visiting her at least twice that week. Let me explain.

In φ-ing, a subject *merely partially satisfies* some necessary condition for performing a permissible maximal option if and only if her φ-ing is a proper subset of some set of actions by which she merely minimally satisfies that condition. And in φ-ing, she *merely minimally satisfies* such a condition if and only if, although her φ-ing satisfies the condition, her φ-ing is no better than her performing any alternative that would satisfy the condition. Now, in order for Carlos to have performed a permissible maximal option, he needed to have visited his grandmother at least twice during the week. And he had several ways of merely minimally satisfying this condition: (W1) visiting her on Monday and Tuesday, (W2) visiting her on Tuesday and Wednesday, (W3) visiting her on Monday and Wednesday, (W4) visiting her on Wednesday and Thursday, etc. These were all ways for him to merely minimally satisfy the condition, for they each would have satisfied the condition and none were morally better than the others. This means that his visiting his grandmother on Tuesday counted only as partially satisfying the condition that he visit her at least twice during the week. For, in visiting her on Tuesday, he performed only a proper subset of a set of acts that would merely minimally satisfy the condition, such as the set consisting of his visiting her on only Tuesday and Wednesday.

To exceed what was minimally required of him, Carlos needed to have done something better than just visiting her twice that week—for example, he needed to visit her three or more times. Thus, on maximalism's M-SUPER, visiting her only on Tuesday did not count as supererogatory, but his visiting her on Tuesday, Wednesday, and Thursday would have. The latter would have counted as morally supererogatory, because Carlos was morally permitted both to (N_1) visit her on Tuesday, Wednesday, and Thursday and to (N_2) visit her on only Tuesday and Wednesday, and N_1 is morally better than to N_2.

It seems that, unlike omnism's M-SUPER, maximalism's M-SUPER is immune to the latitude problem. And maximalism's M-SUPER has plausible implications in cases such as *The Visit*, where the duty to be exceeded is one that allows for significant latitude in how to comply with it. And, as we saw, nullusism's account of moral supererogation was a nonstarter. So, of these three accounts of moral supererogation, maximalism offers the most plausible one. And since maximalism also offered more plausible accounts of permissible acts and acts that ought to be performed, we should favor maximalism over both omnism and nullusism.

§4.5 Supererogation Inheritance and Evaluative Inheritance

Having considered cases such as *The Miser* and *The Visit*, we find that we should reject the following view.

> **Supererogation inheritance:** For any subject S and any two of her options φ and ψ, if S's φ-ing is supererogatory and S's φ-ing entails S's ψ-ing, then S's ψ-ing is also supererogatory.

Consider, for instance, *The Visit*. Carlos's visiting his grandmother on Tuesday, Wednesday, and Thursday is supererogatory and entails his visiting her on Tuesday. But, as we've just seen and contrary to what supererogation inheritance implies, Carlos's visiting her on Tuesday is not supererogatory. So supererogation inheritance is false.

Interestingly, this gives us another reason to accept evaluative noninheritance, as I earlier argued we should. For it gives us reason to reject its logical contradictory—that is, the following.

> **Evaluative inheritance:** For any subject S and any two of her options φ and ψ, if φ is S's best option and S's φ-ing entails S's ψ-ing, then ψ is also S's best option.

To see this, let's stipulate that Carlos's visiting his grandmother on Tuesday, Wednesday, and Thursday is best. For assume that these would be the best days to visit her. And assume that, although she would prefer that he visits more than twice, she also prefers that he not visit more than three times. Now, if evaluative inheritance were true, it would follow from this and the fact that visiting her on Tuesday, Wednesday, and Thursday entails visiting her on Tuesday that Carlos's visiting her on Tuesday is also best. And since visiting her on Tuesday, Wednesday, and Thursday is supererogatory, it must be better than some permissible alternative. But then anything just as good as visiting her on Tuesday, Wednesday, and Thursday would also have to be better than that permissible alternative and, thus, supererogatory. And, of course, if visiting her on Tuesday is tied for best with visiting her on Tuesday, Wednesday, and Thursday, then it must be that his visiting her on Tuesday is also supererogatory. But, of course, visiting her on Tuesday is not supererogatory.

Thus, evaluative inheritance forces us to accept supererogation inheritance, which is clearly false.[30] So we should reject evaluative inheritance and accept its logical contradictory: evaluative noninheritance. So here, we have yet another argument for evaluative noninheritance. And, as we've seen, accepting evaluative noninheritance in conjunction with deontic inheritance leads us to reject omnism. This and the fact that nullusism is, as I've argued, untenable leaves us with only nonnullusism.

§4.6 Three Objections to Maximalism

At this point, readers may wonder whether they must accept maximalism even if I'm right about our needing to accept nonnullusism. After all, maximalism isn't the only possible version of nonnullusism. We could, for instance, distinguish between *minimally specific options* (i.e., options that do not entail any distinct option—e.g., the option of doing something, which entails only itself) and *non–minimally-specific options* (options that do entail some distinct option—for example, the option of running, which entails doing something) and then adopt the following alternative version of nonnullusism.[31]

> **Minimalism:** (OUGHT) For any minimally specific option m, a subject ought to m if and only if m is her best minimally specific option. And, for any nonminimally specific option n, she ought to n if and only if n-ing entails performing a minimally specific option that she ought to perform. (PERMI) For any minimally specific option m, a subject is permitted to m if and only if m is one of her sufficiently good minimally specific options. And, for any nonminimally

---

30. I thank G. Shyam Nair for suggesting this to me.

31. As discussed above, there may be situations in which a subject with options has no maximally specific options—for there may be no limit to how specific options can get. And this is why I formulated maximalism in terms of *maximal options* (i.e., options that are maximally *evaluatively* specific in that they are entailed by no evaluatively distinct option) as opposed to *maximally specific options* (i.e., options that are simply maximally specific in that they are entailed by no distinct option). But since there can be no situations in which a subject with options has no minimally specific option given that a subject with options will always have the option of doing something (i.e., the option of performing some option), there is no need to resort to formulating minimalism in terms of options that are minimally *evaluatively* specific as opposed to just simply minimally specific.

specific option n, she is permitted to n if and only if n-ing entails performing a minimally specific option that's permissible.[32]

However, this view is a nonstarter. On this view, if doing something is permissible, then doing anything is permissible. To illustrate, suppose that the only thing that ultimately matters is how much aggregate happiness there is and that, therefore, what ultimately matters with respect to one's options is that one maximizes aggregate happiness. And assume that if I were to do something, I would feed my daughter a nutritious meal, for this is, in fact, what I'm intending to do. Last, assume that my feeding her a nutritious meal would maximize aggregate happiness. Given these assumptions and minimalism, it follows that I'm permitted to do something, for I'm permitted to feed my daughter a nutritious meal and this, of course, constitutes doing something. But now, consider that there are many other things that I could do besides feed my daughter a nutritious meal. I could, among other things, kill her pet turtle, set her room ablaze, or feed her shards of glass. And note that each of these entails my doing something. Moreover, as we've just seen, my doing something is a minimally specific option that would maximize aggregate happiness. Thus, according to minimalism, I'm permitted to kill my daughter's pet turtle, set her room ablaze, and feed her shards of glass, for each of these entails my doing something, which, we've established, is a permissible minimally specific option. But it's absurd to think that I'm permitted to do any of these things. An option is not permissible simply in virtue of its entailing doing something, even if it's permissible to do something.[33] We should, therefore, reject minimalism.

Nevertheless, there could be some other version of nonnullusism that I have yet to consider that's preferable to maximalism. I can't dismiss this possibility. But I am at a loss as to what this alternative might be. In any case, much of what I say in the remainder of this book will support my contention that maximalism

---

32. Again, I leave implicit the relevant grounding clauses. And, as always, the relevant deontic and evaluative notions are the objective ones. Last, given that this view is, as we'll soon see, a nonstarter, I haven't bothered specifying its account of supererogation.

33. This problem lies specifically with minimalism's view about what determines the deontic statuses of non–minimally specific options, but minimalism's view about what determines the deontic statuses of minimally specific options is also problematic. Suppose that if I were to do something, I would do something that is not sufficiently good. In that case, minimalism implies that it is not the case that I'm permitted to do something, for this is a minimally specific option that is not sufficiently good. But it's implausible to suppose that I'm not permitted to do something (and, so, not permitted to do even what's best) just because, if I were to do something, I would do something that is not sufficiently good.

is the most plausible version of nonnullusism. For, as I will show, maximalism solves many problems. Moreover, I'll show that none of the objections that have typically been leveled against it survive scrutiny. In total, I'll consider seven objections. The first three will be considered below, the second three will be considered in the first section of Chapter 5, and the last will be considered in Chapter 6. The second three are, I'll argue, not objections to maximalism per se, but objections to maximalism when applied to certain implausible views about what our options are, views that I've already argued against. But I'll wait to address these objections until Chapter 5, since that's where I show, more generally, that it's best to combine maximalism with a rationalist view about what our options are. And the last objection that I'll consider concerns reasons for action, which is the focus of Chapter 6. So I'll wait until then to address it. But the first three objections can be addressed presently.

§4.6.1 Ross's paradox

Some people will reject maximalism on the grounds that it implies deontic inheritance, which in turn gives rise to what's known as "Ross's paradox" (A. ROSS 1941). To illustrate the putative paradox, consider the following example.

> *The Letter:* Ignacio promised Jorge that he would mail an important letter for him. It would be best if he were to do as promised and mail the letter. And it would be very bad if he were instead to burn the letter. Indeed, there is no reason whatsoever for Ignacio to burn the letter and numerous reasons for him not to do so.

This example gives rise to a paradox insofar as the following four jointly incompatible propositions all seem compelling.[34]

(4.10) Ignacio ought to mail the letter.

(4.11) For any subject S and any two of her options φ and ψ, if S ought to φ and S's φ-ing entails S's ψ-ing, then S ought to ψ. [Deontic inheritance]

(4.12) Ignacio's mailing the letter entails his either mailing it or burning it.

(4.13) It is not the case that Ignacio ought to either mail it or burn it.

---

34. For other similar formulations and solutions to the paradox, see CASTAÑEDA 1981 and WEDGWOOD 2007 (p. 115).

Admittedly, I don't see how we can reject 4.12; it just follows from the definition of "entails" and the fact that Ignacio doesn't have the option of mailing the letter while neither mailing it nor burning it. Nor do I see how we can reject 4.10. People ought to keep their promises at least in situations, like this one, in which their doing so would be best. And I can't reject 4.11 (i.e., deontic inheritance) given my commitment to maximalism, for maximalism implies deontic inheritance. Thus, it should be no surprise that I think that we should reject 4.13.

Admittedly, it would be infelicitous to assert 4.13 while knowing that Ignacio ought not to burn the letter. But we can easily explain this without supposing that the reason for this is that the assertion is false. The explanation is that such an assertion would violate Grice's maxim of quantity, which holds that it's infelicitous to make a less informative assertion when one is in a position to make a more informative assertion that would clearly be useful in the conversational context.[35]

Of course, some are not going to be satisfied with its merely being infelicitous to assert 4.13 in certain circumstances. They'll insist that 4.13 is false.[36] I think that what drives them to think that 4.13 is false is that it unacceptably yields the false conclusion that Ignacio has a reason to burn the letter when combined with the following two assumptions: (A1) one can fulfill an obligation to either φ or ψ in either of two ways: (i) by φ-ing or (ii) by ψ-ing, and (A2) the fact that one could fulfill an obligation by ψ-ing is itself a reason for one to ψ. And if I'm right about this being what drives people to reject obligations such as 4.13, then the extent to which Ross's paradox should trouble us is in strict proportion to how compelled we should feel to endorse both A1 and A2. And I don't feel compelled to endorse either, let alone both. I'm happy to say that, in a case in which only one of φ and ψ is permissible, the only way to fulfill an obligation to either φ or ψ is to perform the permissible one. And I'm also happy to say, contrary to DARWALL 2010, that the mere fact that one's ψ-ing would fulfill an obligation is not itself a reason for one to ψ— and, thus, to hold that the only reasons for one to ψ are those that account for one's being obligated to ψ. So I don't think that we should reject maximalism on account of its giving rise to Ross's "paradox."

---

35. Wedgwood (2007, p. 115) makes the same point.

36. See, for instance, KIESEWETTER 2017 (p. 51) and CARIANI 2013.

§4.6.2 *The arbitrariness objection*

Consider the following example from Chapter 1.

> *Arm Raising:* "Wonderful things will happen if I raise both my arms at some given time *t*. OK things will happen if I raise neither arm at *t*, and also if I raise my right arm but not my left arm at *t*. Dreadful things will happen if I raise my left arm but not my right arm at *t*. If I raise my left arm at *t*, I will not raise my right arm at *t*. I am completely free to raise or not to raise either [or neither or both] of my arms at *t*" (JACKSON 2014, p. 645). Everything else is equal.

Given that everything else is equal and that wonderful things will happen if I raise both of my arms at *t*, we can assume that my best maximal option will be one in which I raise both of my arms at *t*. And given this and the fact that my performing a maximal option in which I raise both of my arms at *t* entails my raising my left arm at *t*, maximalism implies that I ought to raise my left arm at *t*. Thus, maximalism holds that I ought to raise my left arm at *t*, because my doing so is entailed by my performing my best maximal option: the one in which I raise both of my arms at *t*. But someone might object that I could have just as well argued that I ought to refrain from raising my left arm at *t* because my doing so is entailed by my performing my worst maximal option: the one in which I raise only my left arm at *t*. And the objection would continue as follows. In itself, the fact that my raising my left arm at *t* is entailed by both my best maximal option and my worst maximal option shows nothing. For although the fact that it's entailed by my best maximal option supports the contention that I ought to raise my left arm at *t*, the fact that it's entailed by my worst maximal option supports (and just as strongly) the contention that I ought to refrain from raising my left arm at *t*. So it's just arbitrary to focus on the one fact as opposed to the other. Instead, we must look for some reason to break the tie. And the fact that I would not raise my right arm at *t* if I were to raise my left arm at *t* is a tie-breaking reason for me to refrain from raising my left arm at *t*.[37]

In response, I would argue that although the fact that I would not raise my right arm at *t* if I were to raise my left arm at *t* is a reason for me to refrain from raising my left arm at *t* if either (1) I lack the option of raising both of my arms at *t* or (2) I ought to refrain from raising my right arm at *t*, this is no reason (let alone a tie-breaking one) for me to refrain from raising my left arm at *t* if

---

37. This objection is pressed in JACKSON & PARGETTER 1986 (p. 237).

neither of these obtains. And, in the case at hand, neither of these obtains.[38] Of course, the objector can still claim that it is arbitrary for the maximalist to focus on the fact that that my raising my left arm at t is entailed by my best maximal option as opposed to the fact that' my doing so is entailed by my worst maximal option. But the objector would be mistaken, for there is a perfectly good reason to focus on the fact that my doing so is entailed by my best maximal option and not on the fact that my doing so is entailed by my worst maximal option: that reason being that I ought to take the necessary means to achieving the ends that I ought to adopt and that I ought to adopt as my end performing my best maximal option but not performing my worst maximal option. Since I ought to adopt as an end performing my best maximal option but not performing my worst maximal option, the fact that I don't have the option of performing my best maximal option without raising my left arm at t is relevant in a way that the fact I don't have the option of performing my worst option without raising my left arm at t isn't.[39] And even some of those who initially pressed this arbitrariness objection now admit as much.[40] So I don't consider this a serious objection.

§4.6.3 The implausible grounds objection

Above, I argued that nullusism provides an implausible account of why a subject is permitted to perform a sufficiently good maximal option: it's because

---

38. In other words, I accept that we can detach an unconditional obligation for me to refrain from raising my left arm at t from both (1) a conditional obligation for me to refrain from raising my left arm at t if I'm going to refrain from raising my right arm at t and either (2) the fact that I'm necessarily going to refrain from raising my right arm at t or (3) the fact that I ought to refrain from raising my right arm at t, but I deny that we can detach this unconditional obligation from both this conditional obligation and (4) the fact that I'm going to refrain from raising my right arm at t. That is, I accept both restricted factual detachment and deontic detachment, but deny factual detachment. For more on this and on why we should reject factual detachment, see McNamara 2014 and especially its supplement entitled "A Bit More on Chisholm's Paradox."

39. Of course, I ought to adopt refraining from performing my worst maximal option as an end, but I can achieve this end without refraining from raising my left arm at t. I can just raise both my arms at t and thereby achieve both the end of performing my best maximal option and the end of refraining from performing my worst maximal option. By contrast, if I refrain from raising my left arm at t, the most that I can achieve is the single end of not performing my worst maximal option. So, although I could achieve all the ends that I ought to adopt if I were to raise my left arm at t, I couldn't do so if I were to refrain from raising my left arm at t.

40. See Jackson 2014 (p. 645), where he writes: "I once worried about this [referring to the asymmetry in appealing to the fact that my raising my left arm at t is entailed by my best option but not to the fact that my raising my left arm at t is entailed by my worst option], but now I think that a general commitment to doing what's best out of what's available at the time in question justifies the asymmetry."

it is entailed by one of her sufficiently good maximal options and not simply because it is itself sufficiently good. But now, one may worry that maximalism similarly provides an implausible account of why a subject is permitted to perform a sufficiently good nonmaximal option: it's because it is entailed by one of her sufficiently good maximal options and not simply because it is itself sufficiently good.[41] Let's consider the objection more carefully.

According to maximalism, if a subject is permitted to perform a nonmaximal option N, this is in virtue of the fact that her N-ing is entailed by one of her sufficiently good maximal options. But it may seem that the explanation for why she is permitted to N lies simply with the fact that her N-ing is itself sufficiently good. To illustrate, suppose that I'm getting ready for bed and that, under the circumstances, it is permissible for me to brush my teeth as part of my preparations. Indeed, let's assume that brushing my teeth would have optimal consequences in the circumstances. Furthermore, let's assume that an option is sufficiently good if and only if it has optimal consequences. Now, the explanation for my being permitted to brush my teeth in these circumstances may seem to lie simply with the fact that my doing so would itself have optimal consequences and not with the fact that it is entailed by a maximal option that would have optimal consequences. So, it may seem that, contrary to maximalism, maximal options have nothing to do with the explanation for why I'm permitted to brush my teeth.

Yet, if I'm permitted to brush my teeth, it must be in virtue of my being permitted to perform some specific instance of teeth-brushing. After all, if my circumstances were different such that the only brush available to me was a wire-bristled one, I wouldn't be permitted to brush my teeth. For brushing my teeth with such a brush would cause more damage to my teeth than not brushing would. And if my circumstances were such that there was no permissible way for me to follow up with brushing my teeth, I wouldn't be permitted to brush my teeth. Suppose, for instance, that there was an evil demon who would kill me and my family if I were to brush my teeth without following up by drinking a glass of orange juice immediately afterward. In that case, I would not be permitted to brush my teeth. For it would be bad to brush my teeth and then drink a glass of orange juice immediately afterward. The combination of brushing and then immediately drinking something acidic would cause more damage to my teeth's enamel than not brushing at all. And it would be even worse to brush my teeth and not follow up by drinking the

---

41. Thanks to G. Shyam Nair for pressing me on this.

orange juice immediately afterward, for that would result in the evil demon's killing me and my family.

So, it seems that if I'm permitted to brush my teeth, it must be because I'm permitted to perform some option that entails brushing my teeth (e.g., the option of brushing my teeth with a soft-bristled toothbrush in the dentist-recommended fashion and then following up by going straight to bed without eating or drinking anything). And, in turn, if I'm permitted to perform this option, it must be because I'm permitted to perform some option that entails performing this option—and so on and so forth, until we reach a maximal option that has optimal consequences. And we have to continue until we reach a maximal option, because nonmaximal options, unlike maximal options, are entailed by options that are evaluatively distinct. So we haven't reached the point of maximal evaluative specificity until we've reached a maximal option. It seems to me, then, that, upon reflection, we should be happy to think that the explanation for why I'm permitted to brush my teeth has everything to do with its being entailed by a maximal option that is sufficiently good.

To further illustrate the plausibility of maximalism's explanatory component, consider the following case.

Two Drugs: Dr. Singh is deliberating at t_0 about what drugs, if any, to give her patient, Prasad, at t_2. In fact, there are exactly two drugs available to her: A and B. If she gives Prasad both A and B at t_2, using her right hand to inject him with A and her left hand to inject him with B, he'll be cured of his painful, but nonfatal, medical condition. If she gives him just one of A and B at t_2, he'll die immediately. And if she gives him neither A nor B at t_2, he'll be rendered incurable, having, then, to live the rest of his life with this painful medical condition. And although this would be quite bad, it would not be as bad as his dying immediately. Now, as a matter fact, Dr. Singh is going to form at t_1 the intention to kill him by giving him just one of A and B at t_2. Moreover, she's going to follow through with this intention. For, as it turns out, she has a grudge against Prasad. Given that she's going to form, and then follow through with, the intention to give him just one of A and B at t_2, the following two subjunctive conditionals are true: (SC_1) if she were to give him A at t_2, she would not give him B at t_2 and (SC_2) if she were to give him B at t_2, she would not give him A at t_2. Nevertheless, if she were to respond appropriately to the decisive reason that she has for curing him and thereby come instead to form at t_1 the intention to cure him by giving him both A and B at t_2,

Table 4.2 Dr. Singh's Options in *Two Drugs*

Option	Outcome	Ranking
Give both A and B at t_2	Both live happily ever after	Best
Give neither A nor B at t_2	Prasad lives in pain; Singh loses her license	2nd best
Give just one of A and B at t_2	Prasad dies; Singh goes to prison	Worst
Give A at t_2	Prasad dies; Singh goes to prison	Worst
Give B at t_2	Prasad dies; Singh goes to prison	Worst

she would follow through with that intention and everyone would, as a result, live happily ever after. Last, assume that Dr. Singh will lose her medical license if she fails to cure him and will go to prison if she kills him. See Table 4.2.

It seems that Dr. Singh is both permitted to give Prasad A at t_2 and permitted to give him B at t_2. After all, she's permitted (indeed, obligated) to give him both A and B at t_2, and this both entails giving him A at t_2 and entails giving him B at t_2. But the explanation for why each of these acts is permissible has nothing to do with the facts about each. For instance, the explanation has nothing to do with the consequences of each of these acts. For, given the truth of SC_1, injecting him with A at t_2 would have terrible consequences. And, given the truth of SC_2, injecting him with B at t_2 would also have terrible consequences. And it can't be that what explains the permissibility of each of these acts is that each would have terrible consequences. Instead, the explanation for why Dr. Singh is both permitted to give him A at t_2 and permitted to give him B at t_2 must lie with the fact that she's permitted to do something that entails doing each of these—something that would have good consequences. After all, she is permitted to give Prasad both A and B at t_2, and this both entails giving him A at t_2 and entails giving him B at t_2. Taking this further, it would seem that the explanation for why she is permitted to give Prasad both A and B at t_2 is that she is permitted to perform some option that entails doing this, such as injecting him with these two drugs using sterile needles—and so on and so forth, until we reach some maximal option that is sufficiently good.

So, although it may seem strange at first to think that the explanation for its being permissible to perform some nonmaximal option lies with the fact that it is entailed by the performance of a maximal option that is sufficiently good, these cases illustrate that, on reflection, this is indeed what we should think. We should think, for instance, that it is permissible for Dr. Singh to inject Prasad with A at t_2, not because doing so would itself be sufficiently good (it wouldn't be), but because it is entailed by a maximal option that is sufficiently good—the one in which she injects Prasad with both A and B at t_2. Moreover, we often cite this kind of explanation for why a subject is permitted to do something. Why is the veterinarian permitted to forcibly restrain my dog despite the fact that this causes my dog distress: because she doesn't have the option of safely performing the recommended skin biopsy without doing so. In other words, all her best maximal options entail her forcibly restraining my dog and performing a skin biopsy. And all these options entail her forcibly restraining my dog, which is what explains why she is permitted to do so. So, even if we don't typically cite maximal options as the reason a subject is permitted to do something, we often cite evaluatively distinct options that entail doing this something when explaining why we're permitted to do so. It's just that we don't continue to do so until we reach an appropriate maximal option given various conversational assumptions. But if we were to discard those conversational assumptions, we would need to continue to do so until we reached an appropriate maximal option.

§4.7 The Implications of Maximalism

I've argued that we should reject omnism and accept maximalism instead. Moreover, I've shown that maximalism offers a plausible solution to the problem of act versions, is immune to the latitude problem, and does not fall victim to either the arbitrariness objection or the implausible explanation objection. By contrast, the alternative views—omnism, nullusism, and minimalism—all suffer from insurmountable problems.

If I'm right in thinking that we should accept maximalism instead of omnism, then many philosophers need to change the way they formulate moral theories, for they tend to formulate them as versions of omnism.[42] That is, they tend to use the following schema in formulating a moral theory: For any subject S and any option of hers φ, S's φ-ing is right (or wrong) if and only if S's φ-ing is F, where 'F' stands for whatever they take the relevant right-making (or wrong-making) feature of options to be. As proof, I offer the following

---

42. As far as I know, the only exceptions are the theories defended in BROWN 2018, FELDMAN 1986, GOLDMAN 1978, GOMBERG 1989, PORTMORE 2011, PORTMORE 2013, and ZIMMERMAN 1996, which are all versions of maximalism.

paradigmatic examples of philosophers formulating moral theories. Walter Sinnott-Armstrong (2015) says: "*Act consequentialism* is the claim that an act is morally right if and only if that act maximizes the good." Brad Hooker (2015) says: "Rule-consequentialism claims that an act is morally wrong if and only if it is forbidden by rules justified by their consequences." T. M. Scanlon formulates his contractualist theory as follows: "An act is right if and only if it can be justified to others" (1998, p. 189). Rosalind Hursthouse formulates virtue theory as follows: "An act is right if it is what a virtuous agent would do in the circumstances" (1991, p. 225). And Mark Timmons states the universal law formulation of Kant's moral theory as follows: "An action A is wrong if and only if one cannot universalize the maxim of commission associated with A" (2013, p. 222).

All these theories are, as formulated, versions of omnism. And if, as I've argued, omnism is false, then they're all false. Of course, having to reject all the many versions of omnism that have been offered in the literature doesn't mean that all is lost. We just need to reformulate these theories. These theories specify what they take to ultimately matter, and, for all that I've said, they may have correctly done so. They just make the mistake of assuming that we can assess all options in terms of what ultimately matters when we should assess only maximal options in terms of what ultimately matters. The lesson, then, is that Kantians, contractualists, consequentialists, and others need to reformulate their theories on the model of maximalism, inserting what they take to be the fundamental right-making feature of options for "sufficiently good" in the above formulation of maximalism. Still, it's important for these theorists to do so. Otherwise, as I've shown, their theories will suffer either from the problem of act versions or from the problem of giving an implausible account of what makes permissible maximal options permissible. So they may have figured out what makes a maximal option sufficiently good, but, if I'm right, they've misunderstood which options are to be evaluated directly in terms of their own goodness and which are instead to be evaluated in terms of the goodness of the options that entail them.

CHAPTER 5

Rationalist Maximalism

I'VE ARGUED THAT we should accept both rationalism and maximalism. Rationalism holds that our current options consist in all and only those events over which we presently exert rational control. And maximalism holds that the only options that have their deontic status in virtue of their own goodness are maximal options. When we combine these two, we get *rationalist maximalism*.

In this chapter, I argue that there are reasons to accept rationalist maximalism apart from the reasons that I've already given for accepting each of its two components. First, it avoids the sorts of objections to which other versions of maximalism are susceptible. Second, it provides us with a plausible alternative to both actualism and possibilism—two problematic views about the extent to which a subject's future free choices can affect what she ought to do presently. And, third, it is uniquely well situated to accommodate the idea that a moral theory ought to be morally harmonious—that is, ought to be such that the agents who satisfy it, whoever and however numerous they may be, are guaranteed to produce the morally best world that they could (in the relevant sense) together produce.[1]

---

1. This is not to assume that the correct moral theory must be agent-neutral. For the morally best world that some group could together produce needn't be the world in which, say, they produce the most aggregate utility that they could together produce. It could instead be the world in which none of them violate any agent-centered constraints. Or it could be the world in which they produce the most aggregate utility that they could together produce without any of them violating any agent-centered constraints. Nor does this assume that the correct moral theory *requires* each of us to do what would be morally best, because, as I'll use the term "satisfy," satisfying a moral theory entails doing everything that it directs one to do—that is, it entails doing everything that it says that one ought to do, where this includes everything that one is required to do as well as any other acts that are morally best, including supererogatory acts. Thus, the idea that the correct moral theory must be morally harmonious is compatible

Table 5.1 Possible Events in *Teeing Off*

Event	Outcome
Alejandro refuses to tee off	Evil demon does nothing
Alejandro tees off and doesn't slice the ball	Evil demon gives everyone a tiny reward
Alejandro tees off and slices the ball	Evil demon kills everyone

§5.1 Three More Objections to Maximalism

In Chapter 4, I considered three objections to maximalism, but I saved four others for later. One of these will be addressed in Chapter 6, but the other three will be addressed here. These three are not objections to maximalism per se, but are rather objections to maximalism combined with various nonrationalist views about what our options are. Consequently, we can avoid these objections by combining maximalism with rationalism, as I'll explain below.

§5.1.1 The "did φ"-implies-"had the option to φ" objection

Some may worry that maximalism has counterintuitive implications in the following sort of case.

> *Teeing Off:* Alejandro is playing golf and is preparing to tee off on the second hole when an evil demon presents him with the following dilemma. If he quits the game, refusing to tee off, the evil demon will do nothing. But if he tees off and slices the ball, the evil demon will kill everyone. And if he tees off and doesn't slice the ball, the evil demon will give everyone a tiny reward. See Table 5.1. Although Alejandro can easily control whether he tees off, he doesn't, when teeing off, have control over whether he avoids slicing the ball. For even when he recognizes that it would be best for him to tee off without slicing the ball and so tries his hardest not to slice it, there is still an objective

---

with the idea that the correct moral theory may have agent-centered options as well as agent-centered constraints.

probability of 0.5 that he'll slice the ball.[2] That said, he can ensure that he slices the ball by trying to slice it. He just can't ensure that he doesn't slice it. Last, let's assume that he chooses to tee off, tries not to slice it, and, by sheer luck, succeeds in not slicing it. Consequently, everyone receives a tiny reward.

If we were to accept tryism from Chapter 3 (which implies that a subject had the option of φ-ing if and only if she either tried to φ and succeeded or didn't try to φ but would have succeeded had she tried), we would have to accept that Alejandro had all the following options: (Opt_I) teeing off; (Opt_{II}) not teeing off; (Opt_{III}) teeing off and slicing the ball; and (Opt_{IV}) teeing off and not slicing the ball. And it seems both that Opt_I (i.e., teeing off) was objectively impermissible and that Opt_{IV} (i.e., teeing off and not slicing the ball) was objectively permissible. Opt_I seems objectively impermissible given how objectively risky it was. For, in teeing off, Alejandro took a 50 percent objective chance of everyone's being killed for only a 50 percent objective chance of everyone's receiving a tiny reward. And Opt_{IV} (i.e., teeing off and not slicing the ball) seems objectively permissible given that it's better than each of its alternatives. Indeed, Opt_{IV} was guaranteed to bring about the best possible outcome. But now, if all this is right, then maximalism is false. For maximalism implies that if Opt_{IV} is objectively permissible, then Opt_I must be as well. After all, his performing Opt_{IV} entails his performing Opt_I—that is, his <teeing off and not slicing> entails his <teeing off>.[3]

But if we accept rationalism, we can and should deny that from the fact that Alejandro did perform Opt_{IV}, it follows that his performing Opt_{IV} was an option for him. For, according to rationalism, his performing Opt_{IV} was an option for him only if he had rational control over whether he was to tee off without slicing the ball. And it just doesn't follow from the fact that he did tee off without slicing the ball that he had rational control over whether he was to do so. For although he had rational control over whether he was to *try* not to slice it, he didn't have rational control over whether he was to try in a way

2. The *objective probability* that some event will (or would) occur is just the percentage of the time that it will (or would) occur under identical causal circumstances—circumstances in which the causal laws and histories are exactly the same. It's important that the relevant probabilities are objective, because, unless I explicitly state otherwise, the deontic statuses that I'm discussing are always the objective ones, which don't depend on the evidential probabilities of certain events occurring.

3. Thanks to Campbell Brown for pressing me on this.

that would succeed. Indeed, it's stipulated that even if he exercises his rational capacities appropriately and tries not to slice the ball, he'll end up slicing it 50 percent of time. Thus, he didn't have rational control over whether he was to avoid slicing the ball, and it was just a fluke that, on this particular occasion, he happened to avoid doing so.[4]

So, if we accept rationalism as opposed to tryism, we'll deny that Alejandro ever had Opt_{IV}.[5] Thus, we'll deny that *Teeing Off* presents a problem for maximalism. On rationalist maximalism, we'll hold, contrary to tryism, that Alejandro's options were (Opt_I) teeing off, (Opt_{II}) not teeing off, (Opt_V) teeing off while trying to slice the ball, and (Opt_{VI}) teeing off while trying not to slice the ball. For these were the only events that were under his rational control. And although Opt_{VI} entails Opt_I, this is not a problem for maximalism, for neither of these is objectively permissible. They're both too objectively risky. So *Teeing Off* doesn't constitute a counterexample to rationalist maximalism even if it does constitute one to tryist maximalism.[6]

§5.1.2 Gustafsson's objection

Another recent objection to maximalism comes from Johan Gustafsson.[7] He argues that maximalism has counterintuitive implications in the following sort of case.

> *Newcomb's Nonproblem:* At t_0, you are offered a chance to participate in a nonpuzzling version of Newcomb's problem, which involves two

---

4. Recall from Chapter 3 that rational control is a type of complete control, where a subject's control over whether she φs is complete if and only if, holding everything else fixed, whether she φs just depends on how she exercises her control such that the objective probability that she'll φ will be 1 if she exercises her control in certain ways and will be 0 otherwise.

5. Since Alejandro didn't have volitional control over whether he was to avoid slicing the ball either, we needn't adopt rationalism in particular in order to avoid this problem. Nevertheless, by adopting rationalism (or any other suitable alternative to tryism), we can avoid this potential problem for maximalism.

6. Tryist maximalism combines maximalism (i.e., the view that the only options that are to be assessed in terms of their own goodness are maximal options) with tryism (i.e., the view that a subject's current options include all and only those events that she would perform provided she were to continually try to perform them).

7. See his 2014. I've revised his case so that even those who deny that there are pragmatic reasons for forming intentions (thus, denying that the fact that intending to φ, which is distinct from φ-ing, would have good consequences is a reason to intend to φ) will still accept Gustafsson's conclusions about which intentions the agent should form.

boxes: one transparent and one opaque. At t_1, you must choose whether to participate. If you agree at t_1 to participate, you must take at t_3 either just the transparent box or both boxes. And, as you are told, you must take possession of (and responsibility for) the contents of whatever box or boxes you take, whether those contents be good or bad. Thus, if you take both boxes, and the opaque box happens to contain a writ of debt for \$1,000,000, you will be responsible for paying that debt. Now, as you can see, the transparent box contains \$1,000. But the contents of the opaque box are a complete mystery to you—that is, until t_2, which is when you are given the following additional information: the opaque box contains either \$1 or \$1,000,001. It contains \$1 if you formed at t_1 the intention to take both boxes. Otherwise, it contains \$1,000,001.

Even if you end up choosing at t_1 to participate and end up taking both boxes at t_3, there are two possibilities concerning what transpired, each with a very different outcome:

(Poss$_1$)   At t_1, you chose to participate. At t_3, you took both boxes. But you did not form the intention to take both boxes until t_2, which is when you learned that there was nothing bad in the opaque box. Consequently, you ended up with \$1,001,001.

(Poss$_2$)   At t_1, you chose to participate. And you formed at t_1 the intention to take both boxes even though you did not, at that time, have any idea what was in the opaque box. At t_3, you took both boxes. You ended up with only \$1,001.

Clearly, if Poss$_2$ is actualized, you have failed in some way. For, as Gustafsson notes, it was up to you at t_0 which of Poss$_1$ and Poss$_2$ would be actualized. And if Poss$_2$ is actualized, then you ended up with a million fewer dollars. Of course, from the mere fact that you ended up with less money, it doesn't follow that you failed in some way. But the thought is that you ended up with less money than you *should* have ended up with, which does imply that you failed in some way. More specifically, the thought is that you should not have formed at t_1 the intention to take both boxes. That was irrational given that, for all you knew at the time, the opaque box contained a writ of debt for \$1,000,000 or more. Moreover, had you not irrationally formed this intention at t_1, you would have actualized Poss$_1$, ending up with an additional million dollars. Thus, as Gustafsson claims, it seems that a plausible theory will require you to actualize $Poss_1$ as opposed to $Poss_2$. The problem with maximalism, Gustafsson believes, is that maximalism cannot do this. But while it's true that some versions of maximalism (e.g., volitionalist maximalism) cannot do this, there is a plausible version of maximalism that can—namely, rationalist maximalism.

On volitionalist maximalism, only that which is under your volitional control counts as an option for you.[8] Thus, your only options are $(O1)$ choose at t_1 to participate and take both boxes at t_3, $(O2)$ choose at t_1 to participate and take only the transparent box at t_3, and $(O3)$ choose at t_1 not to participate. Volitionalist maximalism takes these to be your only options, because, on volitionalism, only that which is under your volitional control counts as an option, and your forming or refraining from forming an intention is not something that's under your volitional control. So the best that volitionalist maximalism can do is to require you to perform $O1$. However, your performing $O1$ doesn't necessitate your actualizing $Poss_1$ as opposed to $Poss_2$. Thus, there is no way for such versions of maximalism to require you to actualize $Poss_1$ as opposed to $Poss_2$.

Fortunately, there is no reason for us to combine maximalism with volitionalism. We should, I've argued, combine it with rationalism instead, where our options include forming reasons-responsive attitudes in addition to performing intentional acts. Thus, we should think that our maximal options will include both voluntary acts as well as the formations of reasons-responsive attitudes. And this means that the relevant options are $(O2)$ choose at t_1 to participate and take only the transparent box at t_3; $(O3)$ choose at t_1 not to participate; $(O4)$ choose at t_1 to participate while simultaneously forming the intention to take both boxes and then take both boxes at t_3; and $(O5)$ choose at t_1 to participate while not forming at t_1 the intention to take both boxes, learn at t_2 that there's nothing bad in the opaque box and, consequently, form at t_2 the intention to take both boxes, and take both boxes at t_3.[9] Since rationalist maximalism allows that $O5$ is an option, and since your performing $O5$ necessitates your actualizing $Poss_1$, rationalist maximalism

---

8. Volitionalist maximalism combines maximalism (i.e., the view that the only options that are to be assessed in terms of their own goodness are maximal options) with volitionalism (i.e., the view that a subject's current options include all and only those events over which she currently exerts volitional control).

9. It may seem strange to think that a sequence that involves my forming at t_2 the intention to take both boxes could constitute an option for me now at t_0. Do I really have at t_0 the option of forming an intention at t_2? In fact, I do. For whether I form this intention at t_2 depends on whether, and how, I exercise my rational control at t_0. For if I fail to exercise my rational control appropriately at t_0, I'll irrationally form at t_1 the intention to take both boxes, and if I form this intention at t_1, I won't form it at t_2.

can require you to actualize Poss$_1$ by requiring you to perform O5. Thus, maximalism can avoid Gustafsson's objection by adopting rationalism.[10] It's just that Gustafsson wrongly assumed that maximalism must be combined with volitionalism.

§5.1.3 The Professor Procrastinate objection

Perhaps, the most significant objection to maximalism is that it is alleged to have counterintuitive implications in cases such as *Professor Procrastinate*:

> Professor Procrastinate receives an invitation to review a book. He is the best person to do the review, has the time, and so on. The best thing that can happen is that he says yes and then writes the review when the book arrives. However, suppose it is further the case that were Procrastinate to say yes, he would not in fact get around to writing the review. Not because of incapacity or outside interference or anything like that, but because he would keep on putting the task off.... Moreover, we may suppose, [his saying yes and never writing the review] is the worst that can happen. It would lead to the book's not being reviewed at all. (JACKSON & PARGETTER 1986, p. 235) [See Table 5.2.]

Employing this sort of case, critics offer the following argument against maximalism. They argue that since Professor Procrastinate isn't the victim of either incapacity or outside interference, we should accept that he has the option to accept and write. Moreover, we should accept that he's permitted to accept and write, for it's stipulated that this is the best thing that he could do. Yet, if maximalism were true, we must infer from the permissibility of

---

10. See BYKVIST 2002 for another objection to maximalism, and see BROWN 2018 and GUSTAFSSON 2014 (pp. 587–588) for some discussion. As with the objections discussed in the body of this chapter, Bykvist's objection relies on an implausible account of what our options are. For his objection to even get off the ground, he must presume that a subject has, as of t, the option of φ-ing at t' only if she can form at t the intention to φ at t'. On this view, I don't now have the option of forming tomorrow the belief that there are two sticks of butter in my fridge (assume that tomorrow there will be exactly two sticks of butter in my fridge) even though I can now form the intention to look inside my fridge tomorrow and would form this belief if I were to do so. On Bykvist's view, I don't now have the option of forming this belief tomorrow, because I cannot now form the intention to form this belief. For I'm a rational person, and a rational person cannot form the belief to φ when she knows that φ is not something that she can intentionally do.

Table 5.2 Procrastinate's Options in *Professor Procrastinate*

Option	Outcome	Ranking
Accept	Book is never reviewed	Worst
Don't accept	Book is reviewed by the 2nd best person	2nd best
Accept and then write	Book is reviewed by the best person	Best
Accept and then don't write	Book is never reviewed	Worst

his accepting and writing that he's permitted to accept, for his accepting and writing entails his accepting. Yet, intuitively, it seems wrong for him to accept given that he wouldn't write if he were to accept. So the critics conclude that we should reject maximalism.

More formally, the argument goes as follows.[11]

(5.1) Maximalism is true. [Assumption for conditional proof]

(5.2) Thus, for any subject S, any time t, and any nonmaximal option N, S's N-ing is, as of t, permissible if and only if there is, as of t, a permissible maximal option that entails S's N-ing. [From 5.1 and the definition of "maximalism"]

(5.3) Thus, if Professor Procrastinate has, as of the present, the permissible nonmaximal option of accepting and then writing, then there is, as of the present, a permissible maximal option that entails his accepting and then writing. [From 5.2]

(5.4) Professor Procrastinate has, as of the present, the permissible nonmaximal option of accepting and then writing. [Assumption]

(5.5) Thus, there is, as of the present, a permissible maximal option that entails Professor Procrastinate's accepting and then writing. [From 5.3–5.4]

(5.6) Performing a permissible maximal option that entails accepting and then writing entails accepting. [Analytic]

(5.7) Thus, Professor Procrastinate's accepting is, as of the present, permissible. [From 5.2 and 5.5–5.6]

(5.8) Thus, if maximalism is true, Professor Procrastinate's accepting is, as of the present, permissible. [From 5.1–5.7 by conditional proof]

---

11. See, for instance, CARIANI 2013, JACKSON & PARGETTER 1986, and SNEDEGAR 2014.

(5.9) It is not the case that Professor Procrastinate's accepting is, as of the present, permissible. [Assumption]

(5.10) Therefore, it is not the case that maximalism is true. [From 5.8–5.9]

Such critics find 5.9 intuitively obvious. They claim that Professor Procrastinate is not, as of the present, permitted to accept the invitation given that he would not write the review if he were to accept.

Of course, not everyone finds 5.9 intuitively compelling, but that's the argument that many critics give. I suspect that a lot of the disagreement about 5.9 stems from the fact that such cases (e.g., *Professor Procrastinate*) are underdescribed. And once we take note of the two ways in which the missing details might be spelled out, we see that we should reject either 5.4 or 5.9. Here's my argument.

(5.11) Professor Procrastinate's tendency to procrastinate is, as of the present, either (a) *repressible* or (b) *irrepressible*—that is, either (a) he will accept and then write provided that he, at present, appropriately exercises his rational capacities and resolves not to procrastinate, or (b) it is not the case that he will accept and then write provided that he, at present, appropriately exercises his rational capacities and resolves not to procrastinate.[12] [From the law of excluded middle and the facts of the case]

(5.12) If Professor Procrastinate's tendency to procrastinate is, as of the present, repressible, then we should reject 5.9. After all, if Professor Procrastinate's tendency to procrastinate is, as of the present, repressible, then he can ensure that he accepts and then writes simply by presently exercising his rational capacities appropriately, thereby resolving not to procrastinate. [Assumption]

---

12. I'm assuming, as Jackson and Pargetter seem to, that Professor Procrastinate's world is one in which counterfactual determinism is true. Thus, I take it to be a stipulation of the case that there is a fact about whether Procrastinate would write if he were to accept, and not just some objective probability between 0 and 1 that he would write if he were to accept. Also, note that a *resolution* to φ consists in both a first-order intention to φ and a second-order intention not to let that first-order intention be deflected by anticipated future temptation to do otherwise—see HOLTON 2009 (pp. 11–12). Thus, if I resolve now to exercise tomorrow morning, then I not only intend now to exercise tomorrow morning, but I also presently anticipate being tempted tomorrow morning to sleep in and, consequently, intend now to resist that temptation by, say, jumping out of bed as soon as the alarm goes off and, thus, before I even have a chance to try to rationalize my sleeping in.

(5.13) If Professor Procrastinate's tendency to procrastinate is, as of the present, irrepressible, then we should reject 5.4. After all, if Professor Procrastinate's tendency to procrastinate is, as of the present, irrepressible, then he doesn't, at present, have the option of accepting and then writing—and if this isn't even an option, then it can't be a permissible nonmaximal option. [From rationalism, which holds that the relevant sort of control is synchronic control—see Chapter 3]

(5.14) Therefore, we should reject either 5.4 or 5.9. [From 5.11–5.13]

Note that it's unclear from Jackson and Pargetter's description of *Professor Procrastinate* whether Professor Procrastinate's tendency to procrastinate is, as of the present, repressible or irrepressible. For all that they say, it could be that Professor Procrastinate is aware of his tendency to procrastinate and that, when it's really important to him that he doesn't procrastinate, he resolves presently not to give in to the anticipated future temptation to procrastinate. And it may even be, as we'll indeed suppose, that his making this resolution now would be sufficient to ensure that he won't procrastinate later on. And, in that case, his tendency to procrastinate is entirely repressible, for he will write the review if he responds appropriately to his reasons by resolving now, as he accepts the invitation, to write the review as soon as the book arrives in the mail. So one possibility for why he wouldn't write if he were to accept is that he's not going to respond appropriately to his reasons by resolving to write the review as soon as the book arrives. And, in that case, my clear intuition is that Professor Procrastinate is not only permitted, but obligated, to accept. For he's obligated to respond appropriately to his reasons, accepting the invitation while also resolving to write the review as soon as the book arrives. In which case, he will accept and then write the review. So it seems that we should reject 5.9 if his tendency to procrastinate is repressible.[13]

---

13. Another possibility is that he has made the following prior arrangement with a colleague: if he copies this colleague on an email in which he accepts an invitation to do something, he thereby bets this colleague ten thousand dollars that he will do that thing. Further suppose that, given such high stakes, Professor Procrastinate would write the review if he were to copy this colleague on an email in which he accepts the journal's invitation to write the book review. And this is compatible with Jackson and Pargetter's description of the case, for it may be that Professor Procrastinate doesn't want to make this bet and so wouldn't copy this colleague on such an email even if he were to choose to accept. And, in that case, it would still be that were Professor Procrastinate to accept, he would not write the review. But, in such a case, I have the intuition that Professor Procrastinate should accept the invitation (that is, I do not find 5.9 plausible). For he should accept by an email in which he copies this colleague and should, therefore, accept. Even Frank Jackson (2014, pp. 645–646) now rejects 5.9 in cases where doing one's best does not consist in performing two options at distinct times, and such is the case

Table 5.3 Procrastinate's Options in *The Irrepressible Professor Procrastinate*

Option	Outcome	Ranking
Accept	Book is never reviewed	Worst
Don't accept	Book is reviewed by the 2nd best person	Best
Accept and then don't write	Book is never reviewed	Worst

Of course, it could instead be that Professor Procrastinate's tendency to procrastinate is, as of the present, irrepressible. And, in that case, his later self is going to choose to procrastinate when the book arrives, and this holds regardless of how he presently exercises his rational capacities. And, in that case, I think that we just have to accept that he has no more control at present over whether his future self will write the review than I have over whether the next US Congress will amend the constitution so as to prohibit the private ownership of firearms. And if that's how we're supposed to imagine things, then although we should readily accept that Professor Procrastinate is not permitted to accept (and so, concede that 5.9 is true), we should deny that he has, as of the present, the option of accepting and writing—and, thus, deny 5.4.[14] And in that case Professor Procrastinate's options are not as they were depicted in Table 5.2 but as they are depicted in Table 5.3. For if he doesn't, as of the present, have rational control over whether he will write the review when the book arrives, in what sense does he have, at present, the option of writing when the book arrives? For him to have the option now of φ-ing in

---

here, where Professor Procrastinate's doing his best consists in his hitting send on an email accepting the invitation with his colleague copied.

14. Not everyone agrees. Jean-Paul Vessel has argued that the sort of view that I advocate is implausible in that it "implies that morality is radically more demanding for the virtuous than it is for the vicious" (see his 2016, p. 164). For instance, rational maximalism implies that, unlike the irrepressible Procrastinate, the repressible Procrastinate is obligated to accept and then write. Yet, the only difference between the two is that repressible Procrastinate lacks the vice of having an irrepressible tendency to procrastinate. But I don't find it implausible to suppose that having such a vice could account for one's not having certain obligations that others without that vice have. After all, it could be that possessing a vice entails having fewer options than those without that vice have. Regardless, this implication seems less implausible than the implication of Vessel's own view, which is that the irrepressible Procrastinate ought, as of the present, to accept even though this will result in the worst possible outcome regardless of how he now responds to his reasons.

the future is for him to have rational control over whether he φs in the future. But if Professor Procrastinate's tendency to procrastinate is irrepressible, he doesn't, at present, have rational control over whether he will write when the book arrives. So I think that we should deny 5.4 if his tendency to procrastinate is irrepressible. Indeed, if we accept rationalism, as I've argued we should, we must deny 5.4. So, even if there are some versions of maximalism that fall victim to the Professor Procrastinate objection, rationalist maximalism isn't one of them.

§5.2 The Actualism-Possibilism Debate versus the Omnism-Maximalism Debate

At this point, the reader may wonder how what I've just said about maximalism and the case of *Professor Procrastinate* fits in with the debate between actualism and possibilism in ethics. After all, discussions of cases such as *Professor Procrastinate* typically arise in the context of the actualism-possibilism debate. So, in this section, I'll explain how the actualism-possibilism debate differs from the omnism-maximalism debate.

The actualism-possibilism debate concerns cases that have the following three features: (F1) Each of the following is something that the given subject, S, could possibly do: (a) φ, (b) φ well, (c) φ poorly, and (d) refrain from φ-ing—where, for all x, x is, as of t, something that S *could possibly perform at t'* if and only if there exists a schedule of available intentions from t onwards such that, if S's intentions were to follow this schedule, S would x at t' (t being earlier than t'). (F2) Her φ-ing well is the best thing that she could possibly do, her refraining from φ-ing is second best, and her φ-ing poorly is the worst thing that she could possibly do. And, (F3) as a matter of fact, she would φ poorly if she were to φ.[15] And the debate between actualists and possibilists concerns whether or not S ought to φ. Whereas actualists hold that she ought to refrain from φ-ing given that she *would actually* φ poorly if she were to φ, possibilists claim that, because she *could possibly* φ well if, and only if, she were to φ, she ought to φ.

---

15. As is standard in the actualism-possibilism literature, I'm assuming that there is a fact about whether she would φ poorly if she were to φ, and not just some objective probability between o and 1 that she would φ poorly if she were to φ.

Table 5.4 Gifre's Options and Some of His Nonoptions in *Cookies*

Option	Outcome	Ranking
Eat all the cookies—i.e., eat a cookie and then finish the rest of the bag	Sick to his stomach	Worst option; worst event
Eat a cookie	Sick to his stomach	Worst option; worst event
Refrain from eating a cookie—i.e., eat no cookies	Unsatisfied	Best option; 2nd best event
Nonoptional Events that He Could Possibly Perform	**Outcome**	**Ranking**
Eat just one cookie—i.e., eat a cookie and then put the bag away	Satisfied	Not an option; best event

To illustrate, consider the following case.

Cookies: If Gifre were to eat some cookies, he would continue eating one after another until he finishes the whole bag and is sick to his stomach. But if, after eating just one cookie, he were to decide to stop and put the bag away, he would then stop after having eaten just one cookie, which is what would be best. Second best would be his refraining from eating any cookies. And worst of all would be his eating all the cookies. The problem is that although he would stop eating after having eaten just one cookie if he were to decide then (that is, after having eaten the first cookie) to stop and put the bag away, he is in fact going to decide, after tasting how delicious they are, to continue eating them. And this unfortunate decision will lead to his eating all of them and becoming sick to his stomach. Moreover, there's nothing that Gifre can do now to change the fact that he would continue eating the whole bag if he were to eat some cookies. Thus, even if he were, say, to resolve now to put the bag of cookies away after eating just one, he would change his mind after eating the one and, so, continue eating the whole bag.[16] See Table 5.4.

---

16. Thus, his tendency to continue eating the whole bag after eating one cookie is presently irrepressible.

We can make this case fit the above schema simply by substituting 'Gifre' for 'S,' 'eating a cookie' for 'φ-ing,' 'eating just one cookie' for 'φ-ing well,' and 'eating all the cookies' for 'φ-ing poorly.' And, thus, whereas actualists hold that Gifre ought to refrain from eating a cookie given that he would actually eat all the cookies if he were to eat a cookie, possibilists hold that, because he could possibly eat just one cookie if, and only if, he were to eat a cookie, he ought to eat a cookie. More generally, actualists and possibilists disagree on which of the following two views to accept.

> **Actualism:** For any subject S and any act φ that she could possibly perform, S ought to φ if and only if there is no alternative act that she could possibly perform, ψ, such that what would actually happen if she were to ψ is at least as good as what would actually happen if she were to φ.[17]

> **Possibilism (also known as schedulist maximalism):** For any subject S and any maximal act MA_x that she could possibly perform, S ought to MA_x if and only if there is no alternative maximal act that she could possibly perform, MA_y, such that what would actually happen if she were to MA_y is at least as good as what would actually happen if she were to MA_x. And for any subject S and any nonmaximal act NA that she could possibly perform, S ought to NA if and only if there is an MA_x that she ought to perform that entails her NA-ing.[18]

Both of these views are problematic. The main problem with actualism is that it forces us to deny the following plausible principle.[19]

---

17. As noted in Chapter 1, when I talk about the deontic status of an option (e.g., that it is obligatory, permissible, or that which ought to be done), this status is meant to be intention-guiding, where the claim that a subject ought (or is obligated or is permitted) to φ is intention-guiding if and only if it implies that she ought (or is obligated or is permitted) to intend to do something that entails φ-ing. And this means that dual obligations hybridism (which is discussed in TIMMERMAN & COHEN 2016 and which holds that there are two types of obligations only one of which is meant to be intention-guiding) is a version of actualism despite the fact that it endorses an analogue of possibilism for non–intention-guiding obligations, which I take to be a kind of oxymoron.

18. Again, as is standard in the actualism-possibilism literature, I'm assuming that there is a fact about what would happen if she were to perform a given act. I'm also assuming that we are to understand what would happen if she were to perform a given act broadly so as to include everything that would be the case if she were to do so.

19. For other problems with actualism, see, for instance, ZIMMERMAN 2017 and COHEN & TIMMERMAN 2016 (which is distinct from TIMMERMAN & COHEN 2016).

Deontic Inheritance: For any subject S and any two of her options φ and ψ, if S ought to φ and S's φ-ing entails S's ψ-ing, then S ought to ψ.

To illustrate, consider that, in *Cookies*, actualism implies that Gifre ought to eat just one cookie, both because this is something that he could possibly perform and because what would actually happen if he were to eat just one cookie (i.e., his enjoying one cookie, becoming satisfied, and not getting sick) is better than what would actually happen if he were to perform any alternative that he could possibly perform (i.e., either his enjoying no cookies and being left unsatisfied or his eating the whole bag and becoming very sick).[20] But actualism also implies that Gifre ought to refrain from eating a cookie. For what would actually happen if he were to eat a cookie (i.e., his eating the whole bag and becoming very sick) is worse than what would actually happen if he were to refrain from eating a cookie (i.e., his enjoying no cookies and being left unsatisfied). But, of course, eating just one cookie entails eating a cookie, as it's impossible to eat just one cookie without eating a cookie. Thus, actualism forces us to deny deontic inheritance.

Possibilism, by contrast, allows us to accept deontic inheritance, for it implies not only that Gifre ought to eat just one cookie, but also that he ought to eat a cookie. Indeed, it holds that he ought to perform a maximal act that entails eating just one cookie and, consequently, ought to eat a cookie given that performing such a maximal act entails doing so. And yet, this implication creates a problem for possibilism. For, contrary to possibilism, it's intuitive to think that Gifre ought to refrain from eating a cookie given both that he would eat the whole bag and become sick if he were to do so and that he is powerless at present to change this fact. Thus, it seems that, contrary to possibilism, whether an agent ought to φ sometimes depends on facts about what would actually happen if she were to φ.[21]

---

20. Note that, on both actualism and possibilism, the relevant acts are all and only those that the agent in question could possibly perform, and this holds even though, on what I've argued is the most plausible account of our options (viz., rationalism), some acts that an agent could possibly perform are not even options. Thus, actualism implies that Gifre ought to eat just one cookie even though this is not an option for him—at least, not according to rationalism.

21. My view is that whether a subject ought to φ depends on the fact that <she would φ poorly if she were to φ> just in case she is powerless at present to change this fact. Thus, if she could now resolve not to φ poorly and thereby make it the case that she wouldn't φ poorly if she were to φ, then whether she ought to φ doesn't depend on the fact that she would φ poorly if she were to φ. For this, then, is a fact only because she's not going to respond appropriately to her reasons and resolve not to act poorly.

We find, then, that if, on the one hand, we accept actualism, we must counterintuitively deny deontic inheritance. And if, on the other hand, we accept possibilism, we must counterintuitively deny that whether an agent ought to φ sometimes depends on facts about what would actually happen if she were to φ. Fortunately, this isn't a dilemma, for actualism and possibilism are not logical contradictories. So we can reject both. Of course, some have thought that we must accept either actualism or possibilism, but they have come to this erroneous conclusion only because they have wrongly equated actualism and possibilism with the following two contradictory positions.

> **Omnism:** Every action has its deontic status in virtue of its own goodness. Thus, for any subject S and any option of hers φ, the deontic status of S's φ-ing depends on how φ's goodness compares to that of its alternatives.

> **Maximalism:** Not every action has its deontic status in virtue of its own goodness. Specifically, for any subject S and any maximal option of hers M, the deontic status of S's M-ing depends on how M's goodness compares to that of its alternatives. But for any subject S and any nonmaximal option of hers N, the deontic status of S's N-ing depends on how the goodness of the maximal options that entail her N-ing compare to that of the maximal options that don't entail her N-ing.

Admittedly, if we hold that a subject always has the option of doing whatever she could possibly do (which is to accept schedulism), then actualism will be equivalent to omnism and possibilism will be equivalent to maximalism. And, in that case, we must accept either actualism or possibilism. But if we deny that a subject always has the option of doing whatever she could possibly do, we can accept maximalism while denying both actualism and possibilism. Let me explain.

Recall that, for all x, x is, as of t, something that S could possibly perform at t' if and only if there exists a schedule of available intentions from t onward such that, if S's intentions were to follow this schedule, S would x at t'. Thus, in *Cookies*, eating just one cookie counts as something that Gifre could possibly do even though it is not something that he has, as of the present, the option of doing—at least, not on the version of rationalism that I defended in Chapter 3. Eating just one cookie counts as something he could possibly do, because if he were to intend to eat a cookie, he would eat a cookie. Moreover, having eaten just that one cookie, he would then not eat any more if he were then to intend to put the bag of cookies away. Neither the fact that he wouldn't form this intention after tasting how delicious they are nor the fact that he doesn't, as of the present, have the option of putting the bag away after having eaten just one cookie is relevant to whether his eating just one cookie counts as something that he could possibly do. But if we accept rationalist maximalism, then what's relevant is not whether his eating just one cookie counts as something he could possibly do, but whether he has, as of the present, the option of eating just one cookie. And, given the stipulation that he wouldn't stop at just one cookie even if he were to resolve now to put the bag of cookies away after eating just one, it follows that he doesn't have, as of the present, the option of eating just one cookie—at least, not on rationalism. See Table 5.4.

If we accept rationalist maximalism, we'll deny that that Gifre ought to eat just one cookie, because we'll deny that he has the option of eating just one cookie. So we'll deny actualism. Thus, if we accept rationalist maximalism, we can avoid actualism's counterintuitive implication that deontic inheritance is false. What's more, we can avoid possibilism's counterintuitive implication that Gifre ought to eat a cookie. For if we accept rationalist maximalism, we'll agree with the actualist that Gifre ought to refrain from eating a cookie. We'll hold that he ought to refrain from eating a cookie because the best maximal option that he currently has is one that entails his refraining from eating a cookie. Thus, one key advantage of rationalist maximalism is that it allows us to avoid the counterintuitive implications of both actualism and possibilism.

Rationalist maximalism, therefore, provides us with a plausible intermediate position between actualism and possibilism. Unlike actualism, rationalist maximalism holds that if the given subject's tendency to act poorly is presently repressible, then she's required to repress that tendency by resolving now not to give into that temptation later on, thereby ensuring that she will instead act well. Thus, if Professor Procrastinate's tendency to procrastinate is repressible, he should accept. For he should accept while resolving to write the review as soon as the book arrives, thereby ensuring that he won't later give in to the temptation to procrastinate and will instead get to work on the review as soon as the book arrives. Thus, unlike actualism, rationalist maximalism endorses deontic inheritance, holding that the repressible Professor Procrastinate ought to accept and write and, therefore, ought to accept. See Table 5.2.

And, unlike possibilism, rationalist maximalism holds that if the given subject's tendency to act poorly is presently irrepressible, then she ought now to do what's necessary to avoid later encountering that presently irrepressible temptation. Thus, if Professor Procrastinate's tendency to procrastinate is presently irrepressible such that he can't now prevent himself from giving into the temptation later on, then he ought now to avoid later encountering that temptation by declining the invitation. See Table 5.3. And so, unlike possibilism, rationalist maximalism allows that whether an agent ought to φ sometimes depends on facts about what would actually happen if she were to φ. It's just that, unlike actualism, rationalist maximalism holds that such facts are relevant only when the agent is presently powerless to change those facts. For where the tendency to act poorly is repressible, it's a fact that she would act poorly if she were to φ only because she isn't going to respond appropriately to her reasons and resolve not to give in to that temptation. For if she were at present to respond appropriately to her reasons and so resolve, it wouldn't be a fact that she would act poorly if she were to φ.

§5.3 The Principle of Moral Harmony and the Problem of Overdetermination

I've argued that rationalist maximalism is superior to other versions of maximalism in that it avoids the objections that plague these others. But rationalist maximalism is not just the most plausible version of maximalism; it's plausible in its own right. For one, it provides us with a plausible alternative to both actualism and possibilism. For another, its moral version is, I'll argue, uniquely well situated to accommodate the *principle of moral harmony*. This principle holds that the correct moral theory must be such that the agents who satisfy it, whoever and however numerous they may be, are guaranteed to produce the morally best world that they could (in the relevant sense) together produce. In other words, it holds that, if each member of some set of individuals does exactly what the correct moral theory says that it would be morally best for each of them to do, they must, as a result, produce the morally best world that they could together produce.

The principle has, in one form or another, been endorsed by several philosophers.[22] But before we can figure out what exact form it should take

---

22. Proponents include BAIER 1958, CASTAÑEDA 1974, PARFIT 1984 (p. 94), PINKERT 2015, REGAN 1980, and ZIMMERMAN 1996. Admittedly, not all philosophers accept the principle. Critics include FELDMAN 1980 and KIERLAND 2006. Also, anyone who thinks that the correct moral theory need only specify what we owe to each other would likely be a critic. But although what we owe to each other is clearly an important part of morality, it seems that there is more to it than that. And this principle helps to identify what more there is.

	Slice does his part	Slice golfs
Patch does his part	Their patient lives, which is the best world that they could together produce.	Their patient dies in agony, which is the worst world that they could together produce.
Patch golfs	Their patient dies in agony, which is the worst world that they could together produce.	Their patient dies painlessly, which is the 2nd best world that they could together produce.

FIGURE 5.1   Slice and Patch Go Golfing

and, in particular, what the relevant sense of "could" is, we need to understand the general motivation for it. The motivation for it stems from our intuition that there has been some moral mistake (that is, some failure to follow morality's directives) in the following sort of case, which I borrow, with some modification, from David Estlund (2017, p. 53).[23]

> *Slice and Patch Go Golfing:* Unless a patient's tumor is removed very soon, she'll die (though not painfully). Immediate surgery and stitching by the only two available doctors, Dr. Slice and Dr. Patch, is the one thing that will save her. Dr. Slice is the only one who can perform the surgery, and Dr. Patch is the only one who can perform the stitching. If there is surgery without stitching, the patient's death will be physically agonizing. And if there is stitching without surgery, her death will be physically agonizing. It would even be cruel for one of them to show up at the hospital knowing that the other won't, for this would only needlessly get the patient's hopes up, making her death psychologically agonizing. See Figure 5.1. Unfortunately, neither Slice nor Patch is willing to do his part in saving the patient. That is, neither has the conditional intention to do his part to save the patient on the condition that he knows that his doing his part would be best. (And, hereafter, I'll refer to this complex conditional intention simply as "the

23. The case is essentially just a more concrete version of Donald Regan's case of Whiff and Poof—see his 1980.

conditional intention to do his part.") Indeed, each plans to go golfing regardless of what anyone else does or intends to do. Moreover, each is powerless to affect what anyone else does or intends to do. Also, neither can form (nor keep from forming) an intention at will. Each can do so only by nonvoluntarily responding (appropriately or inappropriately) to his reasons. Last, each knows all the above. Predictably, then, the patient dies (though not painfully) while Slice and Patch each enjoy a pleasant round of golf with their colleagues, thereby fostering the moral good of collegiality among themselves.[24]

As Estlund (2017, p. 53) points out, "Many of us respond to this case with the intuition that there is some moral violation here, but the puzzle is to find an agent who has committed it." Certainly, a common response to the patient's being allowed to die while her two doctors go golfing is moral outrage. But to vindicate this response we need to identify some moral failure and someone who is guilty of it. Let's call this *the problem of overdetermination* since it arises as a result of the patient's death being overdetermined by the fact that each doctor is going to omit doing his part to save the patient regardless of what the other plans on doing.[25]

---

24. One nice thing about this case as compared to the sorts of cases of overdetermination that are typically discussed in the literature is that, in this case, the person whose diminution in well-being was overdetermined did not have her autonomy violated. Contrast this case, then, with the following typical sort of case from the literature: two people (say, Pekka and Puanani) each lethally shoot at another (say, Lamar) and at the exact same time such that neither of their individual acts makes any difference to Lamar's well-being—for his death at that moment is thereby overdetermined. In shooting Lamar, Pekka and Puanani each violated Lamar's bodily autonomy by interfering with his body without his consent. And it seems wrong for them to have violated his bodily autonomy even though this made no difference to his well-being. So, in such cases, it's not at all puzzling why each of their acts was wrong. But in *Slice and Patch Go Golfing*, it's much more difficult to account for where the moral failure lies given that each doctor benefited the patient in not showing up and neither violated her autonomy in not showing up.

25. One putative solution involves claiming that there is a group agent who has violated its obligation to save the patient. This is sometimes called "the group agency solution to the overdetermination problem"—see, for instance, KILLOREN & WILLIAMS 2013. But I find it implausible to suppose that the set <Slice, Patch> constitutes a group agent, especially when we assume, as I will, that these two can't communicate with each other beforehand, and have no contractual arrangement or obligation to work together on this or any other patient. Assume, then, that they are just two freelance doctors each of whom happens to know both that (1) the patient will die unless each shows up to do his part and that (2) each lacks the conditional intention to do his part. In any case, the set <Slice, Patch> doesn't meet the plausible conditions for group agency that have been set out in PETTIT & LIST 2011. And Killoren and Williams admit as much but argue that we need to broaden our metaphysical account of agency so as to account for our intuitive moral judgments in cases such as *Slice and Patch Go Golfing*. But,

Unfortunately, there doesn't seem to be any easy solution to this problem. For it seems that each doctor performed all the voluntary acts that he ought to have performed as well as refrained from performing all the voluntary acts that he ought to have refrained from performing. For instance, it seems that Dr. Slice was right to refrain from showing up at the hospital given that he knew both that Dr. Patch wasn't going to show up and that he was powerless to change this. Likewise, it seems that Dr. Patch was right to refrain from showing up and for the same reason. Indeed, if either of them had shown up, this would have only made things morally worse by making their patient's death psychologically agonizing. What's more, it seems that each was right to enjoy a pleasant round of golf with his colleagues given that this was a morally good way for them to foster collegiality. And I'll just stipulate that there was no morally better way of fostering collegiality and also no other moral value besides collegiality that they could have promoted instead.

Of course, both failed to form the conditional intention to do his part. But this failure wasn't the failure to perform some voluntary act. For although one can perform the mental act of imagining an elephant in a pink tutu simply by intending to do so, neither Slice nor Patch can form a conditional intention by intending to form it. They can no more do that than I can form the belief that Aristotle went for a swim on his thirtieth birthday by intending to form it. For I've stipulated that neither Slice nor Patch has volitional control over his intentions. Slice and Patch do, however, have rational control over their intentions. So, if one of them were to respond appropriately to the fact that it would be a worthy choice for him do his part in any situation in which doing so would be best, he would, thereby, nonvoluntarily form the conditional intention to do his part on the condition that he knows that doing so would be best. He would thereby nonvoluntarily form this conditional intention in response to his reasons just as you have nonvoluntarily formed the belief that I'm the author of this book in response to your reasons.

But even if the moral failure doesn't lie with a failure to perform or refrain from performing any voluntary act, it seems that there must have been some moral failure in this case. After all, the set consisting of Slice and Patch could have brought about the world in which their patient lives. For if Slice had shown up at the hospital and performed the surgery and Patch had shown up at the hospital and stitched up the patient afterward, she would have lived.

---

as I show below, we can adequately account for our intuitive moral judgments in such cases without broadening our metaphysical account of agency.

And the world in which their patient lives is morally better than the actual one in which she dies. So how could it be that each did everything that he morally ought to have done and, as a result, they ended up together producing a morally worse world that they could have otherwise produced? Of course, to even pose this rhetorical question is to presuppose that the satisfaction of a moral theory by some group must guarantee that they produce the morally best world that they could (in the relevant sense) together produce. For as I'm using the term "satisfy," satisfying a moral theory entails doing everything that it directs one to do as well as everything it demands that one does. That is, it entails doing everything that it says that one ought to do, where this includes everything that one is required to do as well as any other acts that are morally best, including any that are supererogatory. It seems, then, that if we are to accommodate the intuition that there has been a moral failure in this case (that is, some failure to abide by morality's directives), we must accept the principle of moral harmony. And, perhaps, we should formulate the principle as follows.

> **The Principle of Schedulist Moral Harmony (SMH):** A moral theory is correct if and only if the agents who satisfy it, whoever and however numerous they may be, are guaranteed to produce the morally best world that they could together produce by their following a certain schedule of intention-formations whereby each of them forms (or doesn't form) certain intentions at certain times.[26]

However plausible the principle of moral harmony is, SMH is an implausible formulation of it. For if SMH were true, no moral theory could be correct. Donald Regan proved this back in 1980 in his excellent book

---

26. This is based on Donald Regan's definition of "adaptability": "A theory T is adaptable if and only if the agents who satisfy T, whoever and however numerous they may be, are guaranteed to produce the best consequences possible as a group, given the behavior of everyone else" (1980, p. 6). The difference is that whereas Regan is concerned only with consequentialist moral theories, I'm concerned with moral theories in general. Thus, the morally best world could, if, say, Kantianism is correct, be the world in which the group commits the fewest and/or least significant violations possible of the categorical imperative as opposed to the world in which the group produces the best consequences possible. Now, unfortunately, Regan never defines what it means for it to be possible for a group to produce something, but, given his examples, it seems that the idea is that something counts as being possible for a group to produce if that something would be produced so long as each member of that group were to form (or not form) certain intentions at certain times.

Utilitarianism and Co-operation.[27] Let me explain his reasoning. First, Regan showed that no moral theory that is exclusively act-oriented can satisfy SMH, where a theory is *exclusively act-oriented* if and only if it directs us only to perform and to refrain from performing certain voluntary acts.[28] For recall that in *Slice and Patch Go Golfing*, neither Slice nor Patch performed any voluntary act that they ought not to have performed and both refrained from performing every voluntary act that they ought to have refrained from performing. For each was right to refrain from showing up at the hospital given that this would have only made things worse for their patient. And each was right to go golfing given that this fostered collegiality, which I've stipulated is the morally best thing that each could have done given the other's unwillingness to cooperate. Thus, if we are to claim that there has been some moral failure in this case, the failure must lie, not with what they did (or didn't) voluntarily do, but with something else: such as their failure to nonvoluntarily form a conditional intention to do one's part in response to the reasons one had for forming this attitude. And this means that the only way for a moral theory to pass SMH is for it to require that agents not only perform certain voluntary acts, but also nonvoluntarily form certain attitudes.[29]

Second, Regan showed that any moral theory that is not exclusively act-oriented will violate SMH. For any moral theory that's not exclusively act-oriented must require "something more" of agents than just the performance (or nonperformance) of certain voluntary acts. And, as Regan notes, "There is always the possibility that there will be a mad telepath . . . who will blow up Macy's [or half of the planet] in response to that 'something more'" (1980, p. 181). And, of course, a world in which half of the planet is blown up is not going to be the morally best world that Slice and Patch could together produce by each of them forming (or not forming) certain intentions at certain times. For they could just not form the conditional intention do one's part, in which case billions of lives would be spared. And it's better that one patient dies painlessly than that billions die in a horrible explosion. (Assume that the other half

27. He proved that no theory can be "adaptable" (see note 26) unless we ignore the direct consequences of applying that theory's decision procedure. See his 1980 (chap. 10).

28. This is not Regan's definition, for he provides no definition—see 1980 (p. 109). But I believe that this definition captures (at least, sufficiently well for our purposes) the notion that he had in mind.

29. I'll just stipulate that, in this case, there is no voluntary act available to them that would cause them to form this conditional intention. So the only way for them to form the relevant conditional intention is by non-voluntarily responding to the decisive reasons that they have for doing so.

of the planet would be unaffected by the explosion and that the patient resides on the would-be-unaffected half of the planet.) So, consider a revised version of *Slice and Patch Go Golfing*, which I'll call *The Mad Telepath*. In this case, everything is the same as in the original but for the addition of a mad telepath who will blow up half the planet if either Slice or Patch forms the conditional intention to do his part in saving the patient—conditional, you'll recall, on his knowing that doing so would be best. So, unlike *Slice and Patch Go Golfing*, if either or both of Slice and Patch were to form the conditional intention to do his part, they would thereby prevent themselves from producing the morally best world that they could together produce by each of them forming (or not forming) certain intentions at certain times. See Figure 5.2.

To illustrate the problem with SMH, note that for Slice and Patch to save their patient they must perform the set of voluntary acts consisting in Slice's showing up at the hospital and performing the surgery and Patch's showing up at the hospital and stitching up the patient afterward. Call this set of voluntary acts 'SET.' And consider the following two theories. The first is an exclusively act-oriented theory (call it 'ACTS-ONLY') that holds that an agent's only moral directive is to voluntarily perform her portion of SET if and only if the other agent has fitting attitudes, including the conditional intention to do his part. The second theory, by contrast, is not exclusively act-oriented. Call it 'MORE-THAN-ACTS,' because its directives include more than just

	Slice responds appropriately and forms the conditional intention	Slice responds inappropriately and doesn't form the conditional intention
Patch responds appropriately and forms the conditional intention	Their patient lives, but the other half of the planet is destroyed.	Their patient dies painlessly, and the other half of planet is destroyed.
Patch responds inappropriately and doesn't form the conditional intention	Their patient dies painlessly, and the other half of planet is destroyed.	Their patient dies painlessly, and the other half of planet is saved.

FIGURE 5.2 *The Mad Telepath*

directives to perform and to refrain from performing certain voluntary acts. Specifically, it holds that an agent is under exactly two moral directives: (1) an obligation to voluntarily perform her portion of SET if and only if the other agent has fitting attitudes, and (2) an obligation to nonvoluntarily form fitting attitudes, including the conditional intention to do one's part.

Now, before I get to the problems associated with each of these theories, it's important to note that what makes an attitude that has X as its intentional object fitting is that it accurately represents X. Thus, given that beliefs represent their intentional objects as being true, the belief that p is fitting if and only if p is true. Likewise, given that intentions represent their intentional objects as being choiceworthy, the intention to φ is fitting if and only if φ is choiceworthy. And, similarly, the conditional intention to <φ if p> is fitting if and only if φ-ing is choiceworthy in any situation in which p is the case. For the conditional intention to <φ if p> represents φ-ing as being choiceworthy in any situation in which p is the case. Thus, what makes it fitting for, say, Slice (and I could say the same for Patch) to form the conditional intention to do his part so long as he knows that his doing so would be best is that doing his part is choiceworthy in any situation in which he knows that doing his part would be best. Thus, it is fitting for Slice to conditionally intend to do his part even though a mad telepath is going to destroy half of the planet if he forms this intention. For although the mad telepath's threat makes it instrumentally bad (and, thus, unfortunate) for him to form this intention, it doesn't change the fact that it is choiceworthy for him to do his part in any situation in which his doing so would be best. After all, it's just analytic that doing what's best is choiceworthy. And note that it's crucial to make the obligation to perform one's portion of SET conditional on one's having *fitting attitudes* (attitudes that it would be appropriate to form) as opposed to *fortunate attitudes* (attitudes that it would be good to form); otherwise, there would, in *Slice and Patch Go Golfing*, be no obligation for Slice to form the conditional intention to do his part. After all, no good will come from his forming this intention given that Patch is going golfing regardless. Thus, a theory must require an agent like Slice to form all fitting attitudes if it's going to satisfy SMH in cases such as *Slice and Patch Go Golfing*. And recall that, as I've just stipulated, neither Slice nor Patch can form (or keep from forming) this conditional intention by willing themselves to do so. They can do so only nonvoluntarily: by responding appropriately or inappropriately to their reasons.

Having explained this, I can now point to the problems associated with each of ACTS-ONLY and MORE-THAN-ACTS. The problem with ACTS-ONLY (a problem that other exclusively act-oriented theories share) is that it implies that, in *Slice and Patch Go Golfing*, neither Slice nor Patch fails to satisfy any moral directive. For ACTS-ONLY directs them only to perform certain voluntary acts, and, as I noted above, they both performed the voluntary acts that they ought to have performed. Thus, ACTS-ONLY does not satisfy SMH. For, as *Slice and Patch Go Golfing* illustrates, Slice and Patch can each comply with ACTS-ONLY and yet fail to bring about the morally best world that that they could together bring about by each of them forming (or not forming) certain intentions at certain times.

Admittedly, MORE-THAN-ACTS avoids this problem. To satisfy this theory, Slice and Patch must each form certain fitting attitudes—specifically, each must form the conditional intention to do his part. Moreover, each must perform his portion of SET if the other forms this intention, which the other must form if he is to satisfy MORE-THAN-ACTS. But, unfortunately, MORE-THAN-ACTS has its own problem (one that it shares with other theories that are not exclusively act-oriented). It implies that, in *The Mad Telepath*, Slice and Patch are each required to form an attitude (specifically, the conditional intention to do his part) that would result in the mad telepath's blowing up half of the planet. And the world in which the mad telepath blows up half of the planet is far from the morally best world that they could together bring about by each of them forming (or not forming) certain intentions at certain times. Together they could bring about the world in which only their patient dies if they were each to fail to form the conditional intention to do his part. Indeed, as a matter of fact, each does fail to form the conditional intention to do his part, for each fails to respond appropriately to his reasons. So MORE-THAN-ACTS also fails to satisfy SMH.

We see, then, that there is no way for a moral theory to satisfy SMH. A moral theory will either have to be exclusively act-oriented or not. If, on the one hand, it is exclusively act-oriented, then there will be instances, such as in *Slice and Patch Go Golfing*, where a group of agents who all satisfy the theory fail to bring about the morally best world that they could together bring about by their each forming (or not forming) certain intentions at certain times. If, on the other hand, a moral theory is not exclusively act-oriented, then there will be instances, such as in *The Mad Telepath*, where a group of agents who all satisfy the theory fail to bring about the morally best world that they could bring about by each forming (or not forming) certain intentions at certain times. So, either way, there will be instances in which the moral theory is satisfied by everyone in the group and yet the group fails to bring about the morally best world that they could together bring about by each of them forming (or not forming) certain intentions at certain times.

For there is no way for a moral theory to require agents to have certain fitting attitudes (such as the conditional intention to do one's part) so as to get the right answer in *Slice and Patch Go Golfing* while also requiring them not to have those same attitudes so as to get the right answer in *The Mad Telepath*.

Clearly, then, SMH is too strict a formulation of the principle of moral harmony. I think that SMH goes wrong in insisting that a moral theory must be such that if, in *The Mad Telepath*, either Slice or Patch forms the conditional intention to do his part, he must thereby commit a moral failure given that this results in the mad telepath's destroying half the planet. This, I believe, is a mistake, because neither Slice nor Patch has any way to keep from forming this attitude except by responding inappropriately to his reasons. Take Slice. He can't just keep from forming this attitude via an exercise of his volitional control. For, as I've stipulated, he lacks volitional control over such attitudes. Consequently, he cannot form or keep from forming this attitude for whatever reason he takes to be sufficient reason for doing so. And so, even if he takes the fact that his forming this intention would lead to the destruction of half the planet as sufficient reason for him to keep from forming this attitude, he cannot keep from forming this attitude for this reason.

So Slice and Patch can keep from forming the conditional intention to do their parts only by responding inappropriately to their reasons.[30] But I don't think that morality can require one to respond inappropriately to one's reasons. That is, I don't think that morality can require one either to form attitudes for which one lacks sufficient reason or to keep from forming attitudes for which one has decisive reason.[31] To see why, consider the following example.

---

30. I believe (somewhat controversially) that the fact that Slice's forming the conditional intention to do his part would have undesirable consequences is not a reason for Slice to keep from forming this intention. I believe rather that only facts about the desirability of one's φ-ing under certain conditions count as reasons for one to form (or to keep from forming) the conditional intention to φ under those conditions. Facts about the desirability (or undesirability) of a subject's forming a given intention give her reason to want to form that intention and to act so as to cause herself to form that intention, but they don't give her any reason to form (or to keep from forming) that intention; they're just the wrong kind of "reason" for that. For more on this, see WAY 2012. In any case, even those who disagree with me on this issue should not object to the arguments above, for I've stipulated that neither Slice nor Patch is able to form or to keep from forming an intention in response to his awareness of the fact that having that intention would be desirable or undesirable. So, even if such facts could count as reasons for others, they can't count as reasons for Slice or Patch—at least, not given the response constraint that I argued for in chapters 1 and 2.

31. As I'll use the terms, S has *decisive reason* to φ if and only if S's reasons are such as to make S obligated to φ, and S has *sufficient reason* to φ if and only if S's reasons are such as to make S permitted to φ.

Hating and Saving Rocks: Unless I both hate actor and former wrestler Dwayne Johnson (The Rock) because of his Samoan ancestry and intend to kill him with my bare hands in a fair fight, an evil demon will destroy the third rock from the sun (that is, the planet Earth).

Note that the fact that Dwayne Johnson is of Samoan ancestry is no reason to hate him. And I can't just voluntarily hate him for the fact that he is of Samoan ancestry. I cannot even hate him for the fact that my hating him would save the planet. Given that I don't have volitional control over whether I hate him, I cannot hate him for whatever "reason" I take to be sufficient reason for hating him. I can hate him only for the reason that I think him despicable or otherwise deserving of hatred—that is, only because I think that it is fitting for me to hate him. The problem is that I don't think that he's despicable. Certainly, neither the fact that he is of Samoan ancestry nor the fact that an evil demon will destroy our planet if I don't hate him makes him despicable. So, I can't hate him—at least, not insofar as I respond appropriately to my reasons.[32] What's more, I can't form the intention to kill him with my bare hands in a fair fight insofar as I respond appropriately to my reasons. For I know that I cannot take him in a fair fight given his massive physique and superior fighting abilities.[33] Moreover, even if I could, I would not intend to kill him, for I have no good reason to kill him and have many good reasons not to. And so, if I respond appropriately to my reasons, I will not intend to kill him with my bare hands in a fair fight. Thus, responding appropriately to my reasons precludes me from forming the attitudes that I must form in order to prevent the destruction of our planet.

Now, it would be very strange to think that morality could require me to respond inappropriately to my reasons given that what makes me the sort of subject to whom moral obligations and responsibilities apply is that I'm the

---

32. Again, I believe (somewhat controversially) that the relevant reasons for forming an attitude are only *fittingness reasons* (i.e., reasons having to do with the fittingness of that attitude) and not *pragmatic reasons* (i.e., the so-called reasons that supposedly stem from the instrumental value in forming that attitude). Thus, I respond appropriately to my reasons by forming fitting attitudes, not by forming attitudes that are instrumentally valuable. Again, see WAY 2012 for more on this issue. But if you disagree with me here, let me just inform you that I, personally, am unable to respond to so-called pragmatic reasons for forming an attitude. Therefore, such pragmatic considerations cannot count as reasons for *me* to form an attitude—at least, not given the response restraint.

33. I'm assuming that I cannot rationally intend to φ while knowing that I will not φ given the consistency requirement on beliefs and intentions.

sort of subject who's capable of responding appropriately to my reasons—that is, a rational agent. And it seems nonsensical for some moral requirement to apply to me because I have the capacity to respond appropriately to my reasons if I can fulfill that requirement only by failing to respond appropriately to my reasons. That is, it seems nonsensical to think that the very capacity in virtue of which I'm obligated to φ is the one that, if exercised flawlessly, leads me not to φ.[34] Such would be the nature of a moral requirement for me either to hate Johnson because of his Samoan ancestry or to intend to kill him with my bare hands in a fair fight.

What I'm suggesting is that although two important reasons for thinking that a subject couldn't be obligated to φ are that (1) she doesn't have the option of φ-ing or that (2) φ-ing is incompatible with her performing an even better option, we should not think that these are the only two. Another reason to think that a subject couldn't be obligated to φ is that there's no way for her to φ except by responding inappropriately to her reasons. For it just doesn't make sense to suppose that the norms that apply to a subject in virtue of her having the capacity to respond appropriately to her reasons could require (or even direct) her to respond inappropriately to her reasons. So, although Slice, in *The Mad Telepath*, has the option of responding inappropriately to his reasons so as to keep from forming the conditional intention to do his part, and even though this would be a substantially better alternative to his forming the intention, he can't be obligated to keep from forming the intention given that he has decisive reason to do so. Thus, it seems a mistake to think, as SMH supposes, that morality could legitimately direct both Slice and Patch to respond inappropriately to their reasons and, thereby, keep from forming the conditional intention to do their parts.

Now, if this is right, the principle of moral harmony should not insist that the correct moral theory guarantees that we produce the morally best world that we could together produce by each of us forming (or not forming) certain intentions at certain times. It should, instead, insist only that the correct moral theory guarantees that we produce the morally best world that we could together produce by each of us responding appropriately to our reasons. For, as we just established, no legitimate norm could direct a subject to respond inappropriately to her reasons. Thus, it seems that, contrary to SMH, we should formulate the principle of moral harmony as follows.

---

34. For a further defense of this idea, see both my MANUSCRIPT and my 2011 (pp. 38–51).

The Principle of Rationalist Moral Harmony (RMH): A moral theory is correct if and only if the agents who satisfy it, whoever and however numerous they may be, are guaranteed to produce the morally best world that they could together produce by each of them, at present, responding appropriately to their reasons.[35]

RMH allows us to account for our intuition that there must have been some moral failure in *Slice and Patch Go Golfing*. The moral failure lies with the fact that Slice and Patch each failed to form the conditional intention to do his part.[36] For it seems that they were both morally required to form

---

35. My formulation of the principle of moral harmony is distinct from those that have been proposed by Pinkert (2015), Regan (1980), and Zimmerman (1996). I don't have space here to explain why I reject each of these alternative proposals, but see KIERLAND 2006 and FORCEHIMES & SEMRAU 2015 for criticisms of each of these proposals. Now, Kierland would reject my proposal as well on the grounds that it violates the principle that "ought" implies "can." But it violates this principle only if we assume that the relevant sense of "can" is to be analyzed in terms of voluntary control as opposed to rational control, contrary to what I've argued for in Chapter 3. And Forcehimes and Semrau would probably question the need to appeal to the principle of moral harmony at all and suggest that we would do better to locate Slice's and Patch's moral failures with whatever past voluntary acts of theirs that led them to have such unfitting attitudes. But see Chapter 3 for why I think that this sort of tracing strategy is implausible.

I should note, though, that the solution that rationalist maximalism provides to the overdetermination problem is somewhat similar to that provided by Michael J. Zimmerman in his 1996. The main difference is that Zimmerman rejects the idea that the solution involves requiring subjects to form (nonvoluntarily) a willingness to cooperate on the grounds that this would violate the principle that "ought" implies "can." But I've argued that what's important is that requiring subjects to form the conditional intention to cooperate doesn't violate the principle that "obligation" implies "option" given a rationalist account of our options.

36. This is what Estlund (FORTHCOMING) calls the "conditional intention proposal." I first started working on this proposal long before Estlund sent me his forthcoming manuscript in June of 2017. Indeed, I published my first attempt at spelling out this proposal in the 2016 online-first version of PORTMORE 2018. Nevertheless, as noted in Estlund's manuscript, the proposal originates with Sean Aas and Derek Bowman, two students in his Spring 2012 graduate seminar. Estlund (FORTHCOMING) rejects this proposal on the grounds that it faces the following dilemma. Slice's (as well as Patch's) failure to form the relevant conditional intention occurred either at or before noon—noon being the "moment at which the patient is denied vital help." If, on the one hand, this failure occurred at noon, then there's no accounting for the "special value . . . in any of the individuals forming this virtuous conditional intention, beyond the value that such a motivational state would have possessed whether there were any patient in need or not." For Estlund thinks that Slice could have formed any number of other conditional intentions at earlier times that would have also been sufficient to ensure that he plays his part in any situation in which Patch is willing to play his. If, on the other hand, his failure occurred before noon, then it seems that "nothing went particularly wrong at noon." And, therefore, there's no accounting for our "reaction that the patient is wronged by what happens at noon." Unsurprisingly, I'm not convinced that there's much of a dilemma here. I admit that

this intention. And if they had both formed this intention, they would have each been such that the other was required to do his part in saving the patient. Thus, abiding by a moral theory that passes RMH ensures that Slice and Patch produce, in *Slice and Patch Go Golfing*, the morally best world that they could together bring about by each of them, at present, responding appropriately to their reasons: that is, the world in which they save their patient.

But RMH does not imply that abiding by the correct moral theory ensures that Slice and Patch prevent, in *The Mad Telepath*, the destruction of half the planet. Abiding by a moral theory that passes RMH ensures only that Slice and Patch produce the morally best world that they could together produce by each of them, at present, responding appropriately to their reasons. And for them, at present, to respond appropriately to their reasons, they must each now form the conditional intention to do his part (or so I'm assuming). So, unfortunately, the morally best world that's compatible with their responding appropriately to their reasons is, in *The Mad Telepath*, the world in which the mad telepath destroys half of the planet. But this is no reason to reject RMH. After all, we should not expect the correct moral theory to ensure that no disaster ever befalls us as a result of our responding appropriately to our reasons. For no matter what attitudes our reasons require us to form, the mad telepath can always punish us for forming those attitudes in accordance with reason.[37] Moreover, we should think that the correct moral theory will never require us to respond inappropriately to our reasons given that our being appropriately reasons-responsive is what subjects us to moral obligations and responsibilities in the first place. So we should expect only rationalist moral harmony from the correct moral theory.

According to RMH, a moral theory is correct if and only if the agents who satisfy it, whoever and however numerous they may be, are guaranteed to produce the morally best world that is compatible with each of them, at present, responding appropriately to their reasons. And the only sort of theory that

---

there were many times before noon such that, had Slice and Patch both responded appropriately to their reasons at that time so as to each form the relevant conditional intention, the patient would not have been denied vital help at noon. But I'm not sure why I should think that something went particularly wrong at noon or why, if something did, I can't cite one or more of the occasions in which Slice and Patch failed to respond appropriately to their reasons prior to noon in accounting for what went particularly wrong at noon. In any case, I certainly find my proposal (even if it is burdened by this dilemma) more plausible than Estlund's own. For his proposal insists that there can be "wrongs without culprits," which I find very implausible.

37. Unlike those who favor one-boxing in Newcomb's problem, I don't believe that being disposed to respond appropriately to one's reasons must necessarily pay off.

can do this in a plausible way is one that, like rationalist maximalism, holds that the permissibility of some particular act depends on whether it is part of some permissible whole that includes both the performance of certain voluntary acts and the formation of certain reasons-responsive attitudes. Indeed, the only sort of theory that can satisfy RMH in a plausible way is some version of rationalist maximalism that implies that a maximal option is morally best if and only if it includes all and only those attitudes that are fitting and includes all and only those acts that would, if the agent were to have all and only fitting attitudes, produce the morally best world.[38]

Let me explain. Only those theories that endorse rationalism will satisfy RMH. To satisfy RMH, a theory must require not only that agents perform certain voluntary acts (such as showing up at the hospital), but also that they nonvoluntarily form certain attitudes (such as the conditional intention to do one's part). This was the lesson of *Slice and Patch Go Golfing*, a case that shows that no exclusively act-oriented theory will satisfy RMH. And the only way for a theory to require agents to not only voluntarily perform certain acts but also to nonvoluntarily form certain attitudes is to embrace rationalism's idea that the sort of control that's relevant to what an agent's obligations and responsibilities are is rational control. For this is the only sort of control that we have over both our acts and our attitudes.[39]

For another, only those theories that endorse maximalism will satisfy RMH in a plausible way. For unless a theory adopts maximalism, it's going to generate conflicting obligations: that is, both an obligation to refrain from φ-ing and an obligation to jointly φ and ψ. And this is to deny joint satisfiability, which I've argued we should accept—see §1.2. To illustrate how conflicting obligations will arise unless we accept maximalism, consider the case

---

38. If we interpret rationalist maximalism as a theory about only *moral* permissibility and hold that a maximal option is sufficiently morally good if and only if it includes all and only those attitudes that are fitting and includes all and only those acts that would, if the agent were to have all and only fitting attitudes, actualize a sufficiently morally good world, then rationalist maximalism will entail that a maximal option is morally permissible only if it includes all those attitudes that are fitting. This may seem problematic since, in many instances, the fittingness of an attitude will have nothing to do with morality. For instance, the fitting response to the perception of a bright flash of lightning is often the belief that one will hear a loud clap of thunder in the near future. Nevertheless, there wouldn't necessarily be anything morally impermissible about a maximal option that failed to include this fitting attitude. I suggest, then, that we may need to interpret rationalist maximalism as a theory about when a maximal option is *both rationally and* morally permissible.

39. Thus, only a rationalist view can accommodate RMH. And this is another reason for us to accept rationalism, one that wasn't mentioned in Chapter 3.

called *Only Slice Goes Golfing*. In this case, Patch conditionally intends to do his part. So he'll show up at the hospital and stitch up the patient if he knows that Slice likewise intends. Nevertheless, Patch knows that Slice doesn't conditionally intend to do his part and, in fact, intends to go golfing regardless of what he thinks Patch might do. Consequently, Patch waits at a nearby café, standing ready to show up at the hospital should Slice change his mind. And now let's compare a version of maximalism that is not exclusively act-oriented with a version of nonmaximalism that is not exclusively act-oriented. Call these two "FA-versions," because they both require agents to have fitting attitudes (hence, "FA").

> **FA-Maximalism:** (1) For any subject S and any maximal option M, S's M-ing is permissible if and only if S's M-ing includes all and only those attitudes that are fitting and includes all and only those acts that would, if the agent were to have all and only fitting attitudes, produce a sufficiently morally good world. And, (2) for any subject S and any nonmaximal option N (which could be any nonmaximal set of acts and/or attitudes), S's N-ing is permissible if and only if there is a permissible maximal option that entails N-ing.
>
> **FA-Nonmaximalism:** (1) For any subject S and any attitude α, S is permitted to form α if and only if it would be fitting for S to form α. And, (2) for any subject S and any act φ, S is permitted to φ if and only if S's φ-ing would, given the S's actual (fitting or unfitting) attitudes, produce a sufficiently morally good world.

On FA-maximalism, Slice is obligated both to form the conditional intention to do his part and to show up at the hospital and perform the surgery. This is because Slice's only permissible maximal options are ones in which he forms the conditional intention to do his part, shows up at the hospital, and performs the surgery. For recall that Patch has already formed the conditional intention to do his part. And since Slice's <forming the conditional intention to do his part, showing up at the hospital, and performing the surgery> entails his <showing up at the hospital and performing the surgery>, he's obligated to <show up at the hospital and perform the surgery>. So there are no conflicting obligations here. But, on FA-nonmaximalism, there are. FA-nonmaximalism, like FA-maximalism, implies that Slice is obligated to <form the conditional intention to do his part, show up at the hospital, and perform the surgery>. But, unlike FA-maximalism, FA-nonmaximalism also implies that Slice is obligated to refrain from showing up at the hospital. Given that Slice hasn't formed the conditional intention to do his part, Patch isn't going to show up at the hospital. And given that Patch isn't going to show up at the hospital, it would be better if Slice didn't show up either. So, on FA-nonmaximalism, we get conflicting obligations. Slice is obligated to form and perform the set consisting of his forming the conditional intention to do his part, showing up at the hospital, and performing the surgery. Yet, he's obligated to refrain from showing up at the hospital.[40]

Thus, it seems that rationalist maximalism is uniquely well suited to accommodate the idea that the correct moral theory must be reasonably morally harmonious.[41] A theory must accept rationalism so as not to be exclusively act-oriented and thus accommodate RMH. And it must endorse maximalism to avoid conflicting obligations. Thus, insofar as we think that a moral theory must both be morally harmonious and avoid conflicting obligations, we have reason to think that the correct moral theory is some version of rationalist maximalism.

---

40. Admittedly, not everyone (e.g., JACKSON & PARGETTER 1986) finds such conflicting obligations (e.g., an obligation to not-ϕ as well as an obligation to $<\phi\&\psi>$) problematic, but see §1.2, COHEN & TIMMERMAN 2016 (pp. 11–12), KIESEWETTER 2015 (pp. 929–934), and PORTMORE 2011 (pp. 181–183) for why we should deny that there can be such conflicting obligations. The worry about them is not, as Jackson and Pargetter presume, that such conflicting obligations entail that their subjects have no way of fulfilling all their obligations. For, as Jackson and Pargetter rightly explain, that's false. They can fulfill all their obligations by jointly ϕ-ing and ψ-ing, in which case there will cease to be any obligation to not-ϕ. The worry, though, is that such conflicting obligations are problematic when it comes to planning what to do, since it would be irrational to plan both on not-ϕ-ing and on jointly ϕ-ing and ψ-ing.

41. Rationalist maximalism also has the benefit of avoiding Fred Feldman's objection to the principle of moral harmony. Feldman asks us to imagine "that, a group of adults has taken a group of children out to do some ice skating. The adults have assured the children and their parents that, in case of accident, they will do everything in their power to protect the children. . . . A lone child is skating in the middle, equidistant from the adults. Suddenly, the ice breaks, and the child falls through. There is no time for consultation or deliberation. Someone must quickly save the child. However, since the ice is very thin, it would be disastrous for more than one of the adults to venture near the place where the child broke through. For if two or more were to go out, they would all fall in and all would be in profound trouble. In fact, let us suppose, no one goes to the aid of the child" (1980, pp. 171–172). Feldman believes that each adult was morally obligated to quickly head out to the hole in the ice to rescue the child. But, of course, if each adult did this, disaster would ensue. Thus, Feldman concludes that the principle of moral harmony is false. But if we accept rationalist maximalism, we should say that the relevant moral obligation was not merely to head out to the hole in the ice to rescue the child, but to do so while intending to stop abruptly should there be any indication that others are heading out toward the hole as well. And it is not the case that if each adult satisfied this moral requirement, disaster would ensue.

§5.4 Rationalist Maximalism

Rationalist maximalism is, I've argued, the most plausible version of maximalism. For, as I've argued, rationalism is the most plausible account of our options, and so the one that we should combine with maximalism. And I've done more than just argue that rationalist maximalism is the most plausible version of a certain class of theories (viz., maximalist theories). I've also argued that, insofar as we think that a moral theory must both be morally harmonious and avoid conflicting obligations, we have reason to think that the correct moral theory must be a version of rationalist maximalism. Furthermore, I've argued that we have additional reason to find rationalist maximalism plausible in that it allows us to avoid the problems associated with both actualism and possibilism.

In Chapter 6, I'll turn to the issue of how, given maximalism, we should think that reasons function to determine the deontic statuses of our acts and attitudes.

CHAPTER 6

Maximalism and the Ought-Most-Reason View

IN CHAPTER 4, I argued that only maximal options have their deontic statuses in virtue of their own goodness. Thus, if aggregate happiness is the only thing that ultimately matters, then the deontic status of a maximal option depends solely on how much aggregate happiness it would produce in comparison to how much each of its alternatives would produce. But things are different for nonmaximal options. The deontic status of a nonmaximal option depends instead on the deontic statuses of the maximal options that entail it. For instance, a nonmaximal option is permissible if and only if there is some permissible maximal option that entails it. And I've called this view *maximalism*. But for reasons that will soon become apparent, I'll now refer to it as *maximalism about statuses*.

In previous parts of the book (specifically, both §4.6 and §5.1), I explained how the proponent of maximalism about statuses can rebut six potential objections. But I have one last objection to consider: maximalism about statuses forces us to deny either that we ought to do whatever we have most reason to do or that how much reason there is to perform a given option is directly proportional to how good that option is in terms of whatever ultimately matters. In other words, the following three views are jointly incompatible.

The Ought-Most-Reason View: For any subject S and any option of hers φ, S ought to φ if and only if S has most reason to φ—that is, if and only if S has more reason to φ than to perform any alternative option.[1]

---

1. I borrow the name for this view from SNEDEGAR 2016 (p. 185). Advocates include Kolodny (2005, p. 510), Robertson (2008, p. 263), Schroeder (2007, p. 130), and Snedegar (2016, p. 185).

Omnism about Reasons (incomplete): For any subject S and any option of hers φ, S has most reason to φ if and only if φ is S's best option.

Maximalism about Statuses (incomplete): For any subject S and any nonmaximal option of hers N, S ought to N if and only if N is entailed by her best maximal option.

To illustrate how accepting both maximalism about statuses and omnism about reasons forces us to deny the ought-most-reason view, assume (merely for the purposes of illustration) that aggregate happiness is the only thing that ultimately matters and recall the case entitled *Professor Procrastinate* from Chapter 5.

> Professor Procrastinate receives an invitation to review a book. He is the best person to do the review, has the time, and so on. The best thing that can happen is that he says yes, and then writes the review when the book arrives. However, suppose it is further the case that were Procrastinate to say yes, he would not in fact get around to writing the review. Not because of incapacity or outside interference or anything like that, but because he would keep on putting the task off.... Moreover, we may suppose, [his saying yes and never writing the review] is the worst that can happen. It would lead to the book not being reviewed at all. (JACKSON & PARGETTER 1986, p. 235)

Given the assumption that aggregate happiness is the only thing that ultimately matters, omnism about reasons implies that a subject has most reason to perform all and only those options that are optimific in terms of the production of aggregate happiness. Professor Procrastinate's accepting the invitation is not optimific in terms of the production of aggregate happiness, for his declining (i.e., not accepting) the invitation is an alternative that would produce more aggregate happiness—see Table 6.1. So, according to omnism about reasons, Professor Procrastinate does not have most reason to accept the invitation. And, given both this and the ought-most-reason view,

---

Of course, some philosophers may reject it. Perhaps, Dancy does (see his 2004). But I'm not sure, because Dancy seems to conflate what a subject ought to do with what a subject is obligated to do, and one can accept the ought-most-reason view while denying that a subject is obligated to φ if and only if she has most reason to φ.

Table 6.1 Procrastinate's Options in *Professor Procrastinate*

Option	Outcome	Ranking
Accept	Book is never reviewed	Worst
Don't accept	Book is reviewed by the 2nd best person	2nd best
Accept and then write	Book is reviewed by the best person	Best
Accept and then don't write	Book is never reviewed	Worst

it follows that it is not the case that he ought to accept the invitation. Yet, according to maximalism about statuses, accepting the invitation *is* what he ought to do—at least, assuming, as we will here, that his tendency to procrastinate is presently repressible.[2] On maximalism about statuses, whether he ought to accept the invitation depends not on whether his doing so would be optimific in terms of the production of aggregate happiness but on whether there is a maximal option that's optimific in terms of the production of aggregate happiness that entails his accepting the invitation. And there is. The maximal option that's optimific in terms of the production of aggregate happiness entails his both accepting the invitation and writing the review, which in turn entails his accepting the invitation. So, if we accept maximalism about statuses, we must hold that Professor Procrastinate ought to accept the invitation. And this contradicts the conclusion that we arrived at via both omnism about reasons and the ought-most-reason view. Thus, we cannot accept the ought-most-reason view if we accept both omnism about reasons and maximalism about statuses.

This may seem like a huge problem for maximalism about statuses, for it's tough to deny the ought-most-reason view. Consider, first, that it's quite intuitive. If I ought to perform a given option, it seems that this option must rank higher than all its alternatives in terms of the considerations that are relevant to determining what I ought to do—that is, in terms of the reasons for and against it and its alternatives. Second, consider that although many who

---

2. Recall that a subject is presently repressible with respect to her tendency to φ if and only if it is not the case that she will φ regardless of how she now responds to her reasons. Thus, you're to assume that if Professor Procrastinate were, at present, to respond appropriately to his reasons and resolve now to write the book review as soon as the book arrives, he would in fact start working on the book review as soon as it arrives and finish shortly afterward. It's just that he's not going to respond appropriately to his reasons and form this resolution despite his having rational control over whether he does so or not.

come to accept the ought-most-reason view do so on the basis of accepting the *reasons-first view* (that is, the view that the notion of a reason has some sort of conceptual, metaphysical, or grounding priority over all other normative notions), even those who reject the reasons-first view should be happy to endorse it. For they can accept it so long as they deny that the right-hand side of its bi-conditional has the relevant sort of priority over the left-hand side.[3] And consider, third, that although accepting the ought-most-reason view commits us to a kind of maximization, it's not the sort of maximization that satisficers and others object to. After all, one can accept the ought-most-reason view and deny the controversial view that a subject is obligated to φ if and only if she has most reason to φ. For although a subject ought always to do what she is obligated to do, she is not always obligated to do what she ought to do. It may be, for instance, that I ought to send my mother some flowers for Mother's Day, but, even so, the most I'm obligated to do is to send her a card—or so we'll suppose.[4]

It's important to note, then, that maximalism about statuses forces us to reject the ought-most-reason view only if we combine it with omnism about reasons. And I'll argue that we should reject omnism about reasons and

---

3. Thus, those who, like Broome (2004), reject the reasons-first view can nevertheless accept the ought-most-reason view.

4. Thus, those who, like Gert (2004) and Dancy (2004), reject the idea that we're always obligated to do what we have most reason to do can still accept the ought-most-reason view—at least, they can given the way that I'm understanding things. As I understand things, a subject has *most reason* to φ if and only if she has more reason to φ than to perform any alternative option. And a subject has *more reason* to φ than to ψ if and only if the set of all the reasons that she has to φ has greater combined favoring strength than the set of all the reasons that she has to ψ. And, last, one reason, R1, has more *favoring strength* than another, R2, if and only if both (1) R1 would make it the case that one ought to do anything that R2 would make it the case that one ought to do and (2) R1 would make it the case that one ought to do some things that R2 would not make it the case that one ought to do. Thus, as I understand things, reasons with only justifying strength have no favoring strength, but both reasons with enticing strength and reasons with requiring strength do. And this means that both Gert and Dancy can accept the ought-most-reason view. And if you're not familiar with these three types of strength, their definitions are as follows. One reason, R1, has more *enticing strength* than another, R2, if and only if both (1) R1 would make it noncompulsorily attractive to do anything that R2 would make it noncompulsorily attractive to do and (2) R1 would make it noncompulsorily attractive to do some things that R2 would not make it noncompulsorily attractive to do. One reason, R1, has more *requiring strength* than another, R2, if and only if both (1) R1 would make it impermissible to do anything that R2 would make it impermissible to do and (2) R1 would make it impermissible do some things that R2 would not make it impermissible to do (GERT 2003, pp. 15–16). And one reason, R1, has more *justifying strength* than another, R2, if and only if both (1) R1 would make it permissible to do anything that R2 would make it permissible to do and (2) R1 would make it permissible do some things that R2 would not make it permissible to do (GERT 2003, pp. 15–16).

should instead accept maximalism about reasons. What's more, we can accept the ought-most-reason view while accepting maximalism about both reasons and statuses. Thus, the fact that the view that I've argued for in the preceding chapters—namely, rationalist maximalism (about statuses)—is incompatible with our accepting both the ought-most-reason view and omnism about reasons is not a problem for it. We should just reject omnism about reasons and accept maximalism about reasons instead. There are, as I'll show, at least three good reasons to reject omnism about reasons (§6.2–§6.4), at least one good reason to accept maximalism about reasons (§6.5), and no good reason to reject maximalism about reasons (§6.6). But first, let me explain these two views more thoroughly.

§6.1 Omnism and Maximalism about Reasons

Maximalism about reasons holds that what grounds the fact that there is most reason to perform a given option is either that it is itself best in terms of what ultimately matters or that it is entailed by some maximal option that's best in terms of what ultimately matters. Which it is depends on what type of option it is. More specifically, it depends on whether it is either a maximal option or a nonmaximal option. And recall that a maximal option is any option that is entailed only by evaluatively equivalent options and that a nonmaximal option is any option that isn't a maximal option.

More precisely, the view is as follows, where 'T' stands for some adjective referring to some type of normative domain—for example, "moral," "rational," "prudential," etc.

Maximalism about Reasons:
- (A-REASON) For any subject S and any maximal option of hers M, S has a reason to M if and only if there is something good (or something T-ly good) about S's M-ing. And, for any subject S and any nonmaximal option of hers N, S has a reason (or a T reason) to N if and only if there is a maximal option M_x such that S has a reason (or a T reason) to M_x and S's M_x-ing entails S's N-ing.
- (MOST-REASON) For any subject S and any maximal option of hers M, S has most reason (or most T reason) to M if and only if M is better (or T-ly better) than every alternative maximal option. And, for any subject S and any nonmaximal option of hers N, S has most reason (or most T reason) to N if and only if there is a maximal option M_x such

that S has most reason (or most T reason) to M_x and S's M_x-ing entails S's N-ing.[5]

In contrast to maximalism about reasons, omnism about reasons holds that whenever there is most reason to perform a given option—be it a maximal or a nonmaximal option—this is grounded in the fact that it is best in terms of whatever ultimately matters. More precisely, the view is as follows.

Omnism about Reasons:
- (**A-REASON**) For any subject S and any option of hers φ, S has a reason (or a T reason) to φ if and only if there is something good (or T-ly good) about S's φ-ing.
- (**MOST-REASON**) For any subject S and any option of hers φ, S has most reason (or most T reason) to φ if and only if φ is better (or T-ly better) than every alternative option.

Both views agree on what grounds the reasons for performing maximal options: how good they are in terms of whatever ultimately matters. But they disagree on what grounds the reasons for performing nonmaximal options. Whereas omnism about reasons holds that what grounds the reasons for performing nonmaximal options is their own goodness, maximalism about reasons holds that it's the goodness of the maximal options that entail them. It's this difference that presents three significant problems for omnism, or so I'll argue in §6.2–§6.4 below.

§6.2 The Inheritance Problem for Omnism

The first problem for omnism about reasons is that it is susceptible to the reasons analogue of the problem of act versions. The problem, in brief, is that omnism about reasons is committed to a view that's incompatible with two views that are very difficult to deny. (One of these views is *reasons inheritance*, which is why I call this the *inheritance problem*.) To illustrate, let's divide the reasons that are relevant to determining whether S ought to φ into two types: (1) the consequentialist reasons that concern how the goodness of φ's consequences compares to that of each of its alternatives and (2) the

---

5. Both here and in my formulations below, I leave implicit that the right-hand sides of these bi-conditionals have grounding priority. Thus, we are to assume that, when the left-hand side of one of these bi-conditionals holds, it holds in virtue of the fact that the right-hand side holds.

nonconsequentialist reasons that concern everything else that's relevant to determining whether a subject ought to φ.[6]

Now, consider the following three claims.

OMNISM ABOUT MOST CONSEQUENTIALIST REASON: For any subject S and any option of hers φ, S has most consequentialist reason to φ if and only if S's φ-ing would have optimific consequences—that is, if and only if the consequences of S's φ-ing would be better than that of any alternative option.[7]

REASONS INHERITANCE: For any subject S and any two of her options φ and ψ, if S has a T (or most T) reason to φ and S's φ-ing entails S's ψ-ing, then S has a T (or most T) reason to ψ.

OPTIMIFIC NONINHERITANCE: It is not the case that, for any subject S and any two of her options φ and ψ, if S's φ-ing would have optimific consequences and S's φ-ing entails S's ψ-ing, then S's ψ-ing would have optimific consequences.

Unsurprisingly, the omnist is committed to OMNISM ABOUT MOST CONSEQUENTIALIST REASON. After all, the omnist holds that for any subject S and any option of hers φ, S has most T reason to φ if and only if φ is S's T-ly best option. And since 'T' can stand for "consequentialist," the omnist must hold that for any subject S and any option of hers φ, S has most consequentialist reason to φ if and only if φ is S's consequentially best option. And what makes φ S's consequentially best option is that S's φ-ing would have optimific consequences. Thus, the omnist must accept OMNISM ABOUT MOST CONSEQUENTIALIST REASON.

But this creates a problem for the omnist, because if OMNISM ABOUT MOST CONSEQUENTIALIST REASON is true, then either REASONS INHERITANCE or OPTIMIFIC NONINHERITANCE is false. This is because the three views together entail a logical contradiction. Here's the proof.

---

6. What makes this consequentialist is that it holds that the reasons for performing an act are grounded in the desirability of its outcome.

7. Note, then, that I draw a distinction between optimal consequences and optimific consequences. The consequences of an option are *optimal* if and only if there is no alternative that has better consequences. By contrast, the consequences of an option are *optimific* if and only if its consequences are better than that of every alternative.

(6.1) There exists a subject S_1 and with options x and y such that S_1's x-ing would have optimific consequences, S_1's x-ing entails S_1's y-ing, but S_1's y-ing wouldn't have optimific consequences. [From OPTIMIFIC NONINHERITANCE]

(6.2) For any subject S and any of option of hers φ, S has most consequentialist reason to φ if and only if S's φ-ing would have optimific consequences. [OMNISM ABOUT MOST CONSEQUENTIALIST REASON]

(6.3) Thus, S_1 has most consequentialist reason to x. [From 6.1–6.2]

(6.4) S_1's x-ing entails S_1's y-ing. [From 6.1]

(6.5) For any subject S and any two of her options φ and ψ, if S has most consequentialist reason to φ and S's φ-ing entails S's ψ-ing, then S has most consequentialist reason to ψ. [From REASONS INHERITANCE]

(6.6) Thus, S_1 has most consequentialist reason to y. [From 6.3–6.5]

(6.7) It is not the case that S_1's y-ing would have optimific consequences. [From 6.1]

(6.8) Thus, it is not the case that S_1 has most consequentialist reason to y. [From 6.2 and 6.7]

(6.9) Therefore, it both is and is not the case that S_1 has most consequentialist reason to y. [From 6.6 and 6.8]

This is a problem for the omnist about reasons, because it's very difficult to deny either REASONS INHERITANCE or OPTIMIFIC NONINHERITANCE. Take REASONS INHERITANCE. It seems that we need REASONS INHERITANCE to account for the validity of the following seemingly valid inference form: (1) S has a (or most T) reason to φ. (2) S's φ-ing entails S's ψ-ing. Therefore, (3) S has a (or most T) reason to ψ. We need this to be a valid inference form so as to provide a unified and systematic account of the validity of its great many instances, all of which are relied upon in our everyday practical reasoning. And there are many such instances of this form, for there are many ways for φ-ing to entail ψ-ing, including all of the following: (a) φ-ing is logically equivalent to ψ-ing, (b) ψ-ing is a necessary means to φ-ing, (c) ψ-ing is a proper subset of the set of acts of which φ-ing consists, and (d) φ-ing is a specific instance of ψ-ing.

I'll illustrate each in turn. First, suppose that I have a moral reason to refrain from marrying my sister. Given that refraining from marrying my sister is logically equivalent to refraining from marrying my female sibling, it seems that we can infer that I have a moral reason to refrain from marrying my female sibling. Second, suppose that I have a most prudential reason to charge my laptop. Given that using a charger is a necessary means to charging my laptop, it seems that we can infer that I have most prudential reason to use a charger. Third, suppose that I have an instrumental reason to walk and chew gum. Given that my walking is a proper subset of my walking and chewing gum, it seems that we can infer that I have an instrumental reason to walk. Fourth and finally, suppose that I have most amorous reason to kiss my partner passionately. Given that my kissing her passionately is a specific instance of my kissing her, it seems that we can infer that I have most amorous reason to kiss her.[8]

Such inferences are, I believe, everyday occurrences, and they all seem to presume REASONS INHERITANCE. And, other things being equal, a unified and systematic account of the validity of these sorts of inferences is more plausible than one that isn't. So, for this reason, we should accept REASONS INHERITANCE and the unified and systematic account that it provides.[9]

Now, regarding OPTIMIFIC NONINHERITANCE, we need only consider the following example from Chapter 4 to see that it's true.

The Injection: Doc's patient, Pat, needs an injection of drug D, and the sooner he gets it, the better. Doc has the following four options: (1) inject him with D, (2) inject him with a proper dose of D, (3) inject him with an improper dose of D, and (4) refrain from injecting him with D. The worst thing would be for Doc to inject him with an improper dose of D. That would kill Pat and result in Doc's going to prison. It would be better not to inject him with D at all; in which case, Doc would lose her medical license but stay out of prison, while Pat would suffer for a few more days before going to another doctor who would then inject him with a proper dose of D. What would be best, though, is Doc's injecting Pat with a proper dose of D. In that case, everyone

---

8. We can't infer that I have most amorous reason to kiss her *non*-passionately, but we can infer that I have most amorous reason to kiss her. Yet someone may object: (P1) One specific instance of kissing my partner is kissing her nonpassionately. And (P2) if I have most amorous reason to kiss her, and kissing her nonpassionately is a specific instance of kissing her, then I must have most amorous reason to kiss her nonpassionately. But (P3) I don't have most amorous reason to kiss her nonpassionately, for this will, let's assume, have disastrous consequences for our relationship. Therefore, (C) I don't have most amorous reason to kiss her, as reasons inheritance implies. But we should reject P2. If this doesn't seem obvious to you, see NAIR 2016 for an explanation.

9. For a further defense of reasons inheritance (at least when it comes to instrumental reasons), see KIESEWETTER 2015.

would live happily ever after. Now, as a matter of fact, if Doc were to inject Pat with D, she would inject him with an improper dose of D. This is not because of coercion or outside interference or anything like that, but because Doc is about to form the intention to kill Pat, for she mistakenly believes that Pat belongs to a certain race, one toward which she harbors murderous hatred. And assume that Doc has the capacity to form the intention to perform any one of her four options and will perform whichever one she intends to perform. See Table 6.2.

Clearly, Doc's injecting Pat with a proper dose of D would have optimific consequences. It would, after all, cure Pat of his painful medical condition, and curing him would have better consequences than any alternative would—the alternatives being killing him (by injecting him with an improper dose of D) and having him suffer a few more days (by refraining from injecting him). But, interestingly, Doc's injecting Pat with D would not have optimific consequences. For there's an alternative—that is, her refraining from injecting him with D—that would have better consequences. After all, it's stipulated that (1) what would happen if she were to inject him with D is that Pat dies, that (2) what would happen if she were to refrain from injecting him with D is that Pat would suffer a few more days before going to see a different doctor, and that (3) it is better that Pat suffer a few more days than that he dies. Thus, her injecting him with D would not have optimific consequences. Yet, her injecting him with a proper dose of D entails injecting him with D. So *The Injection* establishes OPTIMIFIC NONINHERITANCE: it is not the case that for any subject S and any two of her options φ and ψ, if S's φ-ing would have optimific consequences and S's φ-ing entails S's ψ-ing, then S's ψ-ing would have optimific consequences. For *The Injection* establishes that there exists a subject, namely, Doc, who has both the option of injecting him with a proper dose of D and the option of injecting him with D such that injecting him

Table 6.2 Doc's Options in *The Injection*

Option	Outcome	Ranking
Inject Pat with a proper dose	Both live happily ever after	Best
Refrain from injecting Pat	Pat suffers; Doc loses her license	2nd best
Inject Pat with an improper dose	Pat dies; Doc goes to prison	Worst
Inject Pat	Pat dies; Doc goes to prison	Worst

with a proper dose of D would have optimific consequences, injecting him with a proper dose of D entails injecting him with D, but injecting him with D wouldn't have optimific consequences.

So, the omnist about reasons must either deny that *The Injection* is a coherent case or reject the idea that there is a unified and systematic account of the validity of the sorts of inferences that REASONS INHERITANCE validates.[10] Both are tough pills to swallow. It would be better, then, to deny OMNISM ABOUT MOST CONSEQUENTIALIST REASON, which we can, and must, do if we accept maximalism about reasons. For if we accept maximalism about reasons, we must replace OMNISM ABOUT MOST CONSEQUENTIALIST REASON with the following.

> **MAXIMALISM ABOUT MOST CONSEQUENTIALIST REASON**: For any subject S and any maximal option of hers M, S has most consequentialist reason to M if and only if S's M-ing would have optimific consequences. And, for any subject S and any nonmaximal option of hers N, S has most consequentialist reason to N if and only if there is a maximal option M_x such that S has most consequentialist reason to M_x and S's M_x-ing entails S's N-ing.

The problem with OMNISM ABOUT MOST CONSEQUENTIALIST REASON is that it implies both that Doc has most consequentialist reason to inject Pat with a proper dose of D and that she lacks most consequentialist reason to inject him with D. This, in conjunction with REASONS

---

10. More generally, the problem with omnism about reasons is that it assesses whether a subject S has most reason to ψ in terms of whether ψ is itself best and so regardless of whether or not there is some best maximal option that entails ψ-ing. This creates a problem because it seems that (1) whether S has most reason to φ (or ψ) depends on whether it's better than its alternatives, (2) φ-ing can entail ψ-ing even though each has different alternatives, and (3) "has most reason" is closed under performance entailment such that, if S has most reason to φ and φ-ing entails ψ-ing, then S has most reason to ψ. Thus, it seems that although Doc has most reason to inject Pat with a proper dose of D given that there is no better alternative, she does not have most reason to inject him with D given that refraining from injecting him with D is a better alternative. And yet Doc's injecting him with a proper dose of D entails injecting him with D. The problem arises because although injecting him with a proper dose of D entails injecting him with D, the two have different alternatives. Injecting him with an improper dose of D is an alternative to injecting him with a proper dose of D, but it's not an alternative to injecting him with D. And this means that, although injecting him with a proper dose of D could not result in injecting him with an improper dose of D, injecting him with D could result in injecting him with an improper dose of D (as, indeed, it does in this case). And this is why injecting him with D is not one of Doc's best options despite the fact that it is entailed by one of her optimal maximal options—namely, the one that entails injecting him with a proper dose of D.

INHERITANCE and the fact that the former entails the latter, generates a contradiction—see the argument above. But MAXIMALISM ABOUT MOST CONSEQUENTIALIST REASON avoids implying a contradiction, because MAXIMALISM ABOUT MOST CONSEQUENTIALIST REASON implies that Doc has most consequentialist reason not only to inject Pat with a proper dose of D, but also to inject him with D, and this despite the fact that injecting him with D would not itself have optimific consequences. For, on MAXIMALISM ABOUT MOST CONSEQUENTIALIST REASON, whether she has most consequentialist reason to inject him with D depends not on whether it would itself have optimific consequences but on whether it is entailed by a maximal option that would have optimific consequences. And it is entailed by a maximal option that would have optimific consequences, because only those maximal options that entail her injecting him with a proper dose of D would have optimific consequences, and any such maximal option entails her injecting him with D.

So, one reason to favor maximalism about reasons is that, in contrast to omnism about reasons, it is compatible with both REASONS INHERITANCE and OPTIMIFIC NONINHERITANCE. But this isn't the only reason to favor maximalism about reasons. There are, as I'll show in the following two sections, two other problems with omnism about reasons.

§6.3 The Intuition Problem for Omnism

So far, I've specified both omnism's and maximalism's views about when there is *a reason* as well as about when there is *most reason* to perform an option. But that's not enough. For suppose that a subject has both a reason to φ and a reason to ψ, but has neither most reason to φ nor most reason to ψ. We may need to know, then, whether there is more reason to φ than to ψ or vice versa. Thus, we need to supplement the above with the following.

> **Omnism about Reasons (continued . . .):** (MORE-REASON) For any subject S and any two of her options φ and ψ, S has more reason (or more T reason) to φ than to ψ if and only if φ is better (or T-ly better) than ψ.
>
> **Maximalism about Reasons (continued . . .):** (MORE-REASON) For any subject S and any two of her maximal options M_x and M_y, S has more reason (or more T reason) to M_x than to M_y if and only if M_x

is better (or T-ly better) than M_y. And, for any subject S and any two of her nonmaximal options N_x and N_y, S has more reason (or more T reason) to N_x than to N_y if and only if the best maximal option that entails her N_x-ing is better (or T-ly better) than the best maximal option that entails her N_y-ing.[11]

Having made these additions, I can now present what I'll call *the intuition problem* for omnism about reasons—the problem being that this view is incompatible with our considered moral intuitions. To illustrate the problem, I'll first need to explain some terminology. A *morally requiring reason* is a reason that has some morally requiring strength, where one reason, R1, has more morally requiring strength than another, R2, if and only if both (1) R1 would make it morally impermissible to do anything that R2 would make it morally impermissible to do and (2) R1 would make it morally impermissible to do some things that R2 would not make it morally impermissible to do. To illustrate, the reason that I have to save two people (and call it 'R_{2p}') has more morally requiring strength than the reason that I have to save just one person (and call it 'R_{1p}'). After all, it seems that R_{2p} would make it morally impermissible to do anything that R_{1p} would make it morally impermissible to do. For instance, just as R_{1p} would make it morally impermissible to refuse to wade into a shallow pond so would R_{2p}. For if it would be impermissible to refuse to wade into a shallow pond to save just one, then it would also be impermissible to refuse to wade into it to save two. Moreover, it seems that R_{2p} would make it morally impermissible to do some things that R_{1p} would not make it morally impermissible to do. For instance, although R_{2p} would make it impermissible to save only Barry when the alternative supported by R_{2p} is to

---

11. Consider *Knees and Elbows*, where we're to assume that (1) M_e and M_k are two maximal options of mine that are tied for best, that (2) M_e entails my bending both my elbows but neither of my knees at t, that (3) M_k entails my bending both my knees but neither of my elbows at t, that (4) disastrous things would happen if I were to either bend my left elbow without bending my right elbow or bend my left knee without bending my right knee, that (5) I wouldn't, as a matter fact, bend my right elbow if I were to bend my left elbow, but that (6) I would, as a matter of fact, bend my right knee if I were to bend my left knee. According to maximalism's MORE-REASON I have no more reason to bend my left knee at t than I do to bend my left elbow at t despite the fact that my bending my left elbow at t would, unlike my bending my left knee at t, result in disaster. Some may, then, view this as a clear counterexample to maximalism's MORE-REASON. I don't. Since I could just as easily bring about the best outcome by bending my left elbow (as well as my right elbow) at t as by bending my left knee (as well as my right knee) at t, I find it plausible to think that I have just as much reason to do one as the other. But I thank Travis Timmerman for urging me to consider this sort of case.

save both Agnes and Alberto, R_{1p} wouldn't make it impermissible to save only Barry when the alternative supported by R_{1p} is to save only Chantal.

With this terminology in hand, consider the following claim.

> **LIVES TRUMP CLEAN HANDS**: One has more morally requiring reason to save twenty specific distant strangers from death than to refrain from threatening someone. In other words, it takes more to morally justify letting twenty specific distant strangers die than it does to morally justify threatening someone.

I'll argue that the problem with omnism about reasons is that it forces us to accept LIVES TRUMP CLEAN HANDS in order to accommodate one of our considered moral intuitions, and yet accepting LIVES TRUMP CLEAN HANDS forces us to deny a different considered moral intuition. Thus, omnism about reasons forces us to reject one or another of our considered moral intuitions. By contrast, maximalism about reasons doesn't force us to accept LIVES TRUMP CLEAN HANDS. Thus, we can accommodate all of our considered moral intuitions so long as we accept maximalism, as opposed to omnism, about reasons.

As I'll explain below, accepting LIVES TRUMP CLEAN HANDS forces us to reject one of our considered moral intuitions. We should, therefore, reject it if we can. But, unfortunately, the omnist about reasons must accept it in order to accommodate one of our other considered moral intuitions. To illustrate, consider the following case.

> *Roy:* Roy knows that Terry has just inherited a substantial amount of money from a wealthy relative. Were Roy to use threats to coerce Terry into giving the money to charity, that donation would, then, save twenty specific distant strangers from death. If, however, Roy doesn't threaten Terry at t, Terry is going to use the money instead to buy himself a new car, and those twenty specific strangers that would have otherwise been saved will instead die. Everything else, though, is equal. We are, then, to assume that Roy would avoid punishment even if he were to threaten Terry.[12]

---

12. This case is closely modeled after the case of Stan from DORSEY 2013A (p. 366).

It seems that, on any moral theory that hopes to accommodate our considered moral intuitions, there will be some number of people such that it would be morally better to threaten someone in order to save at least that many specific distant strangers from death than to refrain from doing so and let them all die. Moreover, it seems that, on any such theory, that number will be less than twenty—at least, it will so long as we assume that the threat in question is sufficiently mild (perhaps, the threat only to shun or shove someone). So, even though there will certainly be moral theories that include an agent-centered constraint against threatening someone, it seems that, in order to accommodate our considered moral intuitions, such theories must hold that this constraint has a threshold such that it will be considered morally better to threaten that someone so as to save twenty specific distant strangers from death than to refrain from doing so and let them all die. In other words, if a moral theory wants to accommodate our considered moral intuitions, it will need to accommodate the following intuition.

> **THREAT BETTER THAN NO THREAT**: Other things being equal, it would be morally better for Roy to threaten Terry so as to save the twenty specific strangers than for him to refrain from doing so and let them all die.

But when THREAT BETTER THAN NO THREAT is conjoined with omnism's MORE-REASON, we get LIVES TRUMP CLEAN HANDS. Thus, the omnist who wants to accommodate THREAT BETTER THAN NO THREAT must accept LIVES TRUMP CLEAN HANDS. And this creates a problem for the omnist, because in accepting LIVES TRUMP CLEAN HANDS, she is forced to deny at least one of the following three considered moral intuitions.

> **SELF-INTEREST TRUMPS LIVES**: The self-interested reason that one has to buy a new car for oneself morally justifies acting contrary to the morally requiring reason that one has to save twenty specific distant strangers from death. In other words, one is morally justified in buying a new car for oneself even if one could instead donate that money to charity and thereby save twenty specific distant strangers from death.
>
> **MORE REASON JUSTIFIES NO LESS**: For any subject S and any two of her options φ and ψ, if S has more morally requiring reason to φ than to ψ, then whatever reason would morally justify her acting contrary to the morally requiring reason that she has to φ would also morally

justify her acting contrary to the morally requiring reason that she has to ψ. In other words, the moral justifying strength of a morally requiring reason is at least as great as its moral requiring strength.

SELF-INTEREST DOESN'T TRUMP CLEAN HANDS: It is not the case that the self-interested reason that one has to buy a new car for oneself morally justifies acting contrary to the morally requiring reason one has to refrain from threatening someone. In other words, one isn't morally justified in threatening someone just so one will be able to buy a new car for oneself.

These three are jointly incompatible with LIVES TRUMP CLEAN HANDS. For LIVES TRUMP CLEAN HANDS together with both SELF-INTEREST TRUMPS LIVES and MORE REASON JUSTIFIES NO LESS entail the negation of SELF-INTEREST DOESN'T TRUMP CLEAN HANDS. And this is a problem for the omnist, because it's difficult to deny any of the above three considered moral intuitions.[13]

Take SELF-INTEREST TRUMPS LIVES, first. To deny SELF-INTEREST TRUMPS LIVES is to accept that morality is extremely demanding—at least, assuming, as many philosophers believe, that one could easily save the lives of twenty specific distant strangers by donating many thousands of dollars (e.g., the cost of a new car) to certain charities.[14] It's one thing to hold that we have an imperfect duty of beneficence that requires each of us "to make the happiness of others a serious, major, continually relevant, life-shaping end" (HILL 2002, p. 206) and, thus, to act throughout our adult lives so as to exhibit a sufficient propensity to promote this end—perhaps, by dedicating

---

13. This problem draws inspiration from discussions of similar problems in ARCHER 2016A, DORSEY 2013A, KAGAN 1989, and KAMM 1985. Now, some philosophers (such as Archer and Kamm) view this as a problem involving intransitivity given that something along the lines of SELF-INTEREST TRUMPS LIVES, LIVES TRUMP CLEAN HANDS, and SELF-INTEREST DOESN'T TRUMP CLEAN HANDS would show that the relevant trumping relation is intransitive. However, I find it easier to present the problem along the lines that Dorsey does, where the problem is presented as being one simply involving how to accommodate our considered moral intuitions. Nonetheless, I believe that my solution would work just as well in solving the problem if presented as one involving intransitivity.

14. See, for instance, SINGER 2009 and UNGER 1996. Note that we may not be able to identify which specific ten strangers we saved by making a specific donation (that is, a donation of a specific amount that was transferred in a specific way at a specific time to a specific organization), but nevertheless there must be some specific people who were saved as a result of our donation, for if all the same people would have lived whether or not we had made the donation, our donation did not save anyone.

at least 20 percent of our surplus time and resources to doing so.[15] But it's quite another to hold that we are required to act so as to sacrifice our time and resources on each and every occasion in which it would, other things being equal, be morally better to do so. For such a theory would require us to dedicate far more than just 20 percent of our surplus time and resources to promoting the happiness of others. And that would be extremely demanding, leaving us with little to no time or resources to further our own projects and interests. And our considered moral intuition is that morality isn't so demanding.[16] To illustrate, consider the following case.

> *Gus:* Gus finds himself the recipient of an inheritance from a wealthy relative. This inheritance will allow Gus to buy a new car, which Gus desires to do, and which will allow Gus to see much more of his significant other, who lives in a distant town. Alternatively, Gus could donate this specific resource (that is, this inheritance) to charity when he receives it at *t*, which would save twenty specific distant strangers from death. Assume that everything else is equal.[17]

Our considered moral intuition is that Gus is not obligated to perform this specific charitable act. Common-sense morality may hold that Gus is obligated to dedicate substantial portions of his surplus time and resources to helping others, but it would not hold that he is required to do so on every occasion in which it would, other things being equal, be morally better if he were to do so. In other words, even if he's obligated to dedicate substantial portions of his time and resources to saving distant strangers, he's not obligated (given that the duty of beneficence is an imperfect one) to save the twenty specific strangers that he could save by donating this specific resource to charity. Thus, he's permitted to use his inheritance to buy a new car for himself and to fulfill his imperfect duty of beneficence by performing other charitable acts on other occasions. So, unless the omnist about reasons wants to accept a counterintuitively demanding moral theory, she'll need to endorse SELF-INTEREST TRUMPS LIVES.

---

15. For more on this, see NOGGLE 2009. And note that our *surplus time and resources* is whatever time and resources we have in excess of what's necessary to ensure a sufficient degree of our own happiness and moral virtue.

16. For a further defense of this claim, see PORTMORE 2011 (chap. 2). See also TIMMERMAN 2015B.

17. This case is closely modeled after the case of Gus from DORSEY 2013A (p. 365).

MORE REASON JUSTIFIES NO LESS is, I believe, even more difficult to deny. If some reason can morally justify acting contrary to the morally requiring reason that one has to φ, which is stronger than the morally requiring reason that one has to ψ, then wouldn't it also be able to morally justify acting contrary to the weaker morally requiring reason that one has to ψ? Suppose, for instance, that you would be morally justified in punching both Kian and Kendra to save a million lives. In other words, suppose that the reason that you have to do what's necessary to save a million lives morally justifies your acting contrary to the morally requiring reason that you have to refrain from punching both Kian and Kendra. And further suppose that the morally requiring reason that you have to refrain from punching just Kian is weaker than the morally requiring reason that you have to refrain from punching both Kian and Kendra. Given these assumptions and MORE REASON JUSTIFIES NO LESS, it follows that the reason that you have to do what's necessary to save a million lives would also morally justify your acting contrary to the morally requiring reason that you have to refrain from punching just Kian. What's more, this result seems to generalize. If the morally requiring reason that you have to refrain from merely slapping Kian is weaker than the morally requiring reason that you have to refrain from punching him, then the reason that you have to do what's necessary to save a million lives would morally justify acting contrary to the morally requiring reason that you have to refrain from merely slapping Kian.

What's more, MORE REASON JUSTIFIES NO LESS seems to be analytically true. For the moral requiring strength of a morally requiring reason is just a measure of how difficult it is to morally justify acting contrary to it. So, in what sense would the morally requiring reason that one has to refrain from allowing ten specific distant strangers to die have more moral requiring strength than the morally requiring reason that one has to refrain from threatening someone if it is less difficult to morally justify acting against the former than it is the latter? Thus, it seems that a morally requiring reason must have at least as much moral justifying strength as it has moral requiring strength. So, even if a moral reason can have more moral justifying strength than it has moral requiring strength, it must have at least as much moral justifying strength as it has moral requiring strength.

This leaves us with SELF-INTEREST DOESN'T TRUMP CLEAN HANDS, which is also difficult to deny. To deny it is to accept that morality is fairly egoistic and, thus, counterintuitively permissive. On this view, morality would permit one to threaten someone merely for the sake of furthering one's own personal projects and interests. To illustrate, consider the following case.

"*Stan:* Stan knows that Jerry has just inherited a substantial amount of money from a wealthy relative. Were Stan to intimidate Jerry into giving him the money as a result of [threatening] Jerry . . . this would be a prudential benefit to Stan, given that this would allow him to buy a new car, from which he will derive pleasure, and which will allow Stan to see much more of his significant other, who lives in a distant town." Everything else, though, is equal. Thus, we are to assume that Stan would avoid punishment even if he were to threaten Jerry. (DORSEY 2013A, p. 366)

But our considered moral intuition is that Stan would not be permitted to threaten Jerry just so that he could use the money thereby obtained to buy himself a new car, not even if it's a fairly mild threat. Thus, the omnist has a problem—an intuition problem. Since MORE REASON JUSTIFIES NO LESS seems to be true simply in virtue of what it means for one morally requiring reason to be stronger than another and since her omnism about reasons commits her to LIVES TRUMP CLEAN HANDS given THREAT BETTER THAN NO THREAT, she must deny at least one of THREAT BETTER THAN NO THREAT, SELF-INTEREST TRUMPS LIVES, and SELF-INTEREST DOESN'T TRUMP CLEAN HANDS. And regardless of which she rejects, she'll be forced to reject one or more of our considered moral intuitions. If she rejects THREAT BETTER THAN NO THREAT, she must counterintuitively deny that it would, other things being equal, be morally better if Roy were to threaten Terry so as to save the twenty distant strangers than if he were to refrain from threatening him and let them all die.[18] If she rejects SELF-INTEREST TRUMPS LIVES, she'll have to hold that morality is counterintuitively demanding, requiring Gus to donate his inheritance to charity as well as to make sacrifices on each and every other occasion in which it would be morally better, other things being equal, for her to do so. And if she rejects SELF-INTEREST DOESN'T TRUMP CLEAN HANDS, she would have to hold that morality is counterintuitively permissive, allowing Stan to threaten Jerry just so that he can further his own prudential interests. Of course, many moral

---

18. This is counterintuitive for we are assuming that everything else is equal. Thus, we are assuming that Roy will, in fact, save the same number of people in the future whether or not he saves these ten specific strangers at present. Even so, there are maximal options open to Roy in which he doesn't save these twenty at present but compensates for this by saving twenty additional strangers in the future. So even if we are to assume that Roy won't perform this maximal option, we should not lose sight of the fact that it is a genuine option for him.

theorists are ultimately willing to accept such counterintuitive implications. But my point is only that there are substantial costs associated with omnism about reasons, and thus, the omnist owes us some account of what unique and sufficient advantage her view has that makes these costs worth bearing. Since I fail to see any such advantage, I suggest that we reject omnism about reasons.

Fortunately, if we accept maximalism's MORE-REASON, we don't have this problem. We can deny LIVES TRUMP CLEAN HANDS and, importantly, we can do so without denying THREAT BETTER THAN NO THREAT—that is, without denying that, other things being equal, it would be morally better for Roy to threaten Terry so as to save the twenty specific strangers than for him to refrain from doing so and let them all die. Thus, the important difference between maximalism and omnism about reasons is that whereas both can deny LIVES TRUMP CLEAN HANDS, only maximalism can do so while endorsing THREAT BETTER THAN NO THREAT. For, on maximalism's MORE-REASON, we don't look at whether Roy's threatening Terry is morally better than Roy's refraining from doing so. Rather, we look at whether the morally best maximal option that entails his threatening Terry is morally better than the morally best maximal option that entails his refraining from doing so. And, as I'll now argue, it isn't. We should then conclude that maximalism's MORE-REASON implies that Roy does not have more moral reason to threaten Terry than to refrain from doing so even though the former is better than the latter. So, if we accept maximalism, we can deny LIVES TRUMP CLEAN HANDS without denying THREAT BETTER THAN NO THREAT.

To see that the morally best maximal option that entails Roy's threatening Terry isn't morally better than the morally best maximal option that entails his refraining from doing so, note first the rather obvious point that a maximal option that entails Roy's saving a total of n distant strangers without threatening anyone is, other things being equal, morally better than any maximal option that entails Roy's saving a total of n distant strangers by threatening Terry. After all, it's morally bad to threaten someone, so if Roy is going to save a total of n distant strangers regardless, it would, other things being equal, be morally better for him to do so without threatening anyone. For if Roy is going to save a total of n distant strangers in the end, it doesn't matter, morally speaking, whether he saves these specific twenty distant strangers on this occasion—at least, not other things being equal. But it is, other things being equal, morally better for him to save a total of n distant strangers without threatening anyone than by threatening someone.

Second, note that it is, other things being equal, morally better for Roy to perform the morally best maximal option that entails his saving a total of n distant strangers without threatening anyone than to perform the morally best maximal option that entails his saving a total of $n+20$ distant strangers by threatening Terry. For I'll just stipulate that n stands for the morally optimal number of distant strangers that Roy currently has the option of saving over time.[19] Why think that there is such a morally optimal number? That is, why not think that it would always be morally better for Roy to save more distant strangers? The reason is that the morally optimal maximal options will, over time, strike an appropriate balance between using more of one's limited time and resources to save more distant strangers and using more of one's limited time and resources to promote various other moral goals, such as justice, self-improvement, and the improvement of one's family. Thus, the morally optimal maximal options available to Roy will not be the ones in which Roy dedicates all of his time and resources to saving more than n distant strangers at the expense of neglecting other important moral ends, such as justice, self-improvement, and the improvement of his family. After all, we could all save more distant strangers if we were to disregard justice, our families, and our own self-improvement. We could, for instance, all save many more distant strangers by robbing the rich and donating the spoils to charity. But that's not what's morally best, or so I'll assume. It seems, then, that the morally best maximal option that entails Roy's saving no more than n distant strangers over the time period in which his current options unfold is morally better than any maximal option that entails Roy's saving a total of $n+20$ distant strangers by threatening Terry. And remember that n is significantly less than the number of distant strangers that he could save over that same time period if he were to disregard all other moral goals.

Admittedly, then, Roy could save more than n strangers if he were to neglect other moral goals. But it would not be morally better for him to do so. After all, to exceed n is, we're assuming, to fail to strike an appropriate balance between the goal of saving more distant strangers and the goal of doing more to promote various other moral ends, such as that of not unjustly threatening anyone. Moreover, if Roy were to insist on saving $n+20$ strangers, the morally best way for him to do so would not be by setting aside the moral end of respecting justice (by, say, threatening Terry), but by instead setting aside either

---

19. And let me just stipulate that Roy's situation is such that he has, at present, the option of saving a total of n distant strangers in the future without ever threatening anyone.

some prudential goal (such as the goal of living in greater material comfort) or some less important moral goal (such as the goal of self-improvement). It seems, then, that if Roy were to insist on saving $n+20$ strangers, it would be better for him to do so by using less of his time and resources on either his self-improvement or his other projects than by obtaining additional resources by threatening Terry.[20]

If all this is correct, we should think, for one, that the morally best maximal option that entails Roy's saving a total of n distant strangers without threatening anyone—and thus, without saving the twenty specific strangers that would be saved by his threatening Terry—is morally better than any maximal option that entails Roy's saving a total of n distant strangers by threatening Terry. And, for another, we should think that the morally best maximal option that entails Roy's saving only n distant strangers is going to be morally better than any maximal option that entails Roy's saving $n+20$ distant strangers by threatening Terry. And given this and maximalism's MORE-REASON, we should conclude that Roy doesn't have more morally requiring reason to threaten Terry than to refrain from doing so despite the fact that it would be morally better, other things being equal, if he did. So we should deny LIVES TRUMP CLEAN HANDS—or, at least, we should so long as we adopt maximalism's MORE-REASON as opposed to omnism's MORE-REASON.

§6.4 The All or Nothing Problem for Omnism

The last problem for omnism about reasons that I'll be considering is known as *the all or nothing problem*.[21] The problem arises with respect to the following sort of case.

---

20. In the case of *Roy*, we are to assume that everything else will be the same regardless of whether or not he threatens Terry. Thus, we are to assume that Roy will, in the future, dedicate the same amount of time and resources to each moral and prudential goal that he has regardless of whether he threatens Terry and saves these twenty at present. And this is why the omnist is committed to the view that Roy has more moral reason to threaten Terry than to refrain from doing so. After all, we should accept THREAT BETTER THAN NO THREAT. It's fortunate, then, that on maximalism, we don't look at how things would be if he were, at present, to act this way or that way. Instead, we look at how things would be if he were to perform this or that optimal maximal option. And we derive his reasons for performing this or that action at present from his reasons for performing this or that optimal maximal option.

21. See HORTON 2017. I use the same label for the problem that Horton does, but I set up the problem differently. The problem has, under various guises, received a flurry of attention recently—see, for instance, McMAHAN 2018, PUMMER 2016, and RULLI 2016. I thank Jonathan Quong for pressing me to think about whether maximalism might provide a solution to this problem.

Burning Building I: Two tiny babies—baby Ángel and baby Nestor—are trapped inside a burning building. Monima is the only one who can save them. To save one or both of them, she must enter through the unlocked front door, which is ablaze. And, unfortunately, doing so would be extremely costly to her; she would thereby suffer extremely painful, and eventually fatal, burns. But once inside the building, she can carry one, both, or neither of the two babies to safety out the back door and at no additional cost to herself. The babies are so tiny that she can easily carry one under each arm. But there's no going back in; the doors shut and lock automatically. Assume that she knows all the above. And most important, assume that everything else is equal. Thus, assume that she'll do the same amount of good on future occasions regardless of how much good she does on this occasion.[22]

It seems that Monima is morally obligated to do either all that she can do to help or nothing at all to help—hence, its name: *the all or nothing problem.* It's considered a problem, because it's unclear why Monima would be prohibited from saving one child if she's permitted to save no child. For why would she be morally prohibited from doing something that would be morally better than something else that she's morally permitted to do? To understand the problem better, consider the following five jointly incompatible claims.

(6.10) Monima's saving neither baby is morally permissible.[23]

(6.11) Monima's saving only baby Ángel is morally impermissible.

(6.12) For any subject S and any two of her alternative options φ and ψ, if S's φ-ing is morally permissible but S's ψ-ing is morally impermissible, then S has more moral reason to φ than to ψ.[24]

(6.13) Monima's saving only baby Ángel is morally better than her saving neither baby—remember that we're assuming that, in this case, everything else is equal.

---

22. This is loosely based on a case from KAGAN 1989 (p. 16).

23. Specifically, it's permissible for Monima to refrain from entering the burning building and, as a result, save neither baby. But of course, it's not permissible for her to save neither baby by entering the building and then walking out the back door without either baby. But to say that Monima is permitted to save neither baby is just to say that there is some instance of the saving-neither-baby type that she's permitted to perform.

24. I'm assuming, here, that a subject counts as having more moral reason to φ than to ψ even if she has no positive reason to φ but just has less moral reason to refrain from φ-ing than to refrain from ψ-ing.

(6.14) For any subject S and any two of her alternative options φ and ψ, if S's ψ-ing is morally better than S's φ-ing, then S has more moral reason to ψ than to φ. (From omnism about reasons)

These five claims are jointly incompatible because, whereas 6.10–6.12 entail that Monima has more moral reason to save neither baby than to save only baby Ángel, 6.13–6.14 entail that she has more moral reason to save only baby Ángel than to save neither baby. So we must reject at least one of these five claims. But which one?

Of course, some philosophers (e.g., act-utilitarians) are not averse to accepting counterintuitive moral verdicts about particular cases. They may, then, be content with rejecting either 6.10 or 6.11. But I think that rejecting our considered moral intuitions about particular cases should be a last resort. So I suggest that we look elsewhere. But we shouldn't, I think, look to 6.12. For I don't see how we can reject 6.12 if we are to accept the increasingly popular view that the deontic status of an action is to be explained by the reasons for and against it and its alternatives.[25] And I, for one, don't want to reject this plausible view, as it has proved extremely fruitful in normative theorizing. This leaves us with rejecting either 6.13 or 6.14. But I don't see how we can reject 6.13. For, in *Burning Building I*, it's clear that it would, other things being equal, be morally better for Monima to save only baby Ángel than for her to save neither baby. And it's stipulated that everything else is equal. Even so, several people have suggested to me that Monima's saving only baby Ángel and thereby manifesting her ill will toward baby Nestor is not morally better than her saving neither baby and manifesting no ill will. And, of course, I agree. But the question is not whether saving only baby Ángel while manifesting ill will toward baby Nestor is morally better than saving neither baby while manifesting no ill will. Rather, the question is whether Monima's saving only baby Ángel is morally better than her saving neither baby, where it's stipulated that everything else is equal. So, in evaluating these two scenarios, we're to assume that the motive is the same. We should be comparing something like the following two scenarios: (1) Monima wants baby Nestor to die, so she stays outside pretending to be too scared to enter the burning building, and (2) Monima wants baby Nestor to die, so she goes inside and rescues only baby Ángel, pretending afterward

---

25. There are too many advocates to list here, but see both NAIR 2016 and LORD & MAGUIRE 2016 for an explanation of the view's rightful popularity.

that she was so scared once she got into the burning building that she just completely forgot what she was there for and just accidentally scooped up the only baby she happened to bump into: namely, baby Ángel. And if that's right, it certainly seems to me that the second scenario is morally better than the first.[26] Monima is a horrible person on both scenarios, but it is, nevertheless, morally better when a horrible person saves a life than when she doesn't. So I think that we must accept 6.13, and this leaves us with rejecting 6.14 as our only remaining option.

Of course, it may seem unfair for me to argue against 6.14 in virtue of the intuitiveness of the other four. After all, couldn't I have just as easily argued against any of the other five by appealing to the intuitiveness of the other four? I don't think so. For it seems to me that 6.14 is not nearly as difficult to deny as the other four are. Indeed, if we accept maximalism about reasons, as I've argued we should, we must reject 6.14. On maximalism's MORE-REASON, whether there is more moral reason for Monima to save only baby Ángel than for her to save neither baby depends not on whether her saving only baby Ángel is morally better than her saving neither baby (as it does on omnism's MORE-REASON) but on whether the morally best maximal option that entails her saving only baby Ángel is morally better than the morally best maximal option that entails her saving neither baby. And, as I'll argue presently, it isn't.

The morally best maximal option that entails Monima's saving only baby Ángel seems to be the one in which, after carrying baby Ángel to safety, she refuses any life-prolonging medical treatment and accepts only palliative care so as to make her imminent death as quick and painless as possible. By contrast, the morally best maximal option that entails her saving neither baby is the one in which she refuses to enter the building so that she can continue

---

26. Tina Rulli has rightly suggested to me that one could argue that there's something agent-relatively morally bad about being someone who had the opportunity to save the greater number at no additional cost but saved the lesser number instead. And, given this, it could be that from Monima's position, her saving only one is, contrary to 6.13, morally worse than her refraining from entering the building and saving none, for by not entering the building, she avoids being someone who had the opportunity to save the greater number at no additional cost but saved the lesser number instead. But I find it hard to believe that this specific agent-relative moral badness could outweigh the agent-neutral moral goodness of saving a child who would otherwise die. Indeed, I find scenario 2 in which Monima saves only baby Ángel out of a desire to see baby Nestor die to be morally better than scenario 1 in which Monima saves neither out of the very same desire. The fact that it's only in scenario 2 that Monima turns out to be someone who had the opportunity to save the greater number at no additional cost but saved the lesser number instead doesn't seem to make enough of a moral difference to outweigh the moral goodness of saving baby Ángel.

living and make use of the options that this extra life affords her to do even more good in the long run. Of course, given the assumption that everything else of moral significance is equal, we're to assume that, as a matter of fact, the amount of good that she would subsequently produce if she were to save neither baby is the same as the amount of good that she would subsequently produce if she were to save only baby Ángel—that is, zero. And this is why her saving only baby Ángel is, in fact, morally better than her saving neither baby. But just because she *would*, as a matter of fact, subsequently produce zero good if she were to save neither baby doesn't mean that she doesn't have the option of subsequently producing a lot of good. Indeed, she does have this option. She *could* do a lot more good if she doesn't enter the burning building. For if she doesn't enter the burning building, she will have many potentially productive years of life ahead of her and, consequently, the present option of doing a great deal of good in the future. Thus, the morally best maximal option that entails her saving neither baby is the one in which she refuses to enter the building and resolves to take every option that this extra life will afford her to do good, and this maximal option would be far morally better than the morally best maximal option that entails her saving only baby Ángel—the one where she dies soon after, doing zero subsequent good. It follows, then, that, on maximalism's MORE-REASON, Monima does not have more moral reason to save only baby Ángel than to save neither baby. Thus, we can solve the all or nothing problem by rejecting 6.14 and substituting maximalism's MORE-REASON for omnism's MORE-REASON, which implies that whether Monima has more moral reason to perform one nonmaximal option (e.g., saving neither) than another (e.g., saving only one) depends, not on how good each of these nonmaximal options is, but on how good the optimal maximal options that entail them are. And when we look at that (see Table 6.3), we find that Monima has more moral reason to save neither than to save only one.

Admittedly, this solution won't work when it comes to the following variant on the above case.

> *Burning Building II:* This case is exactly like *Burning Building I*, except that in this case it's not Monima, but Massimo, who is the only one who can save the babies. And Massimo, unlike Monima, is wearing fire-retardant clothing. Consequently, he can enter the burning building without suffering fatal burns. His burns will be severe enough to cause him a lot of pain and permanent disfigurement. But they won't limit his options for doing good in the future.

Table 6.3 Some of Monima's Options in *Burning Building I*

Nonmaximal Options	Reasons Ranking on Maximalism	Evaluative Ranking
N_1: Save neither (entailed by M_1 and M_4)	Most moral reason	Worst
N_2: Save only one (entailed by M_2)	Least moral reason	2nd best
N_3: Save both (entailed by M_3)	2nd most moral reason	Best
Optimal Maximal Options that Entail these Nonmaximal Options	**Reasons Ranking on Maximalism**	**Evaluative Ranking**
M_1: Save neither, live, and act altruistically afterward so as to save more than two	Most moral reason	Best
M_2: Save only one and die afterward	3rd most moral reason	3rd best
M_3: Save both and die afterward	2nd most moral reason	2nd best
M_4: Save neither, live, and do zero good subsequently	Least moral reason	Worst

Unlike Monima, Massimo can do just as much good on future occasions regardless of how much good he does on this occasion. So we must rank Massimo's options differently—see Table 6.4. But although the solution in this case won't be exactly the same as the one in the previous case, it will still rely on rejecting 6.14. For once we substitute maximalism's MORE-REASON for omnism's MORE-REASON, as I've argued we should, we must reject 6.14. So we'll hold that whether Massimo has more moral reason to perform one nonmaximal option (e.g., saving neither) than another (e.g., saving only one) depends, not on how good each of these nonmaximal options is, but on how good the optimal maximal options that entail them are. And when we look at that (again, see Table 6.4), we find that Massimo has more moral reason to save neither than to save only one.

Note that none of the optimal maximal options that entail his saving only one of the two babies is as morally good as the best maximal option that entails his saving neither. The reason for this is that whereas there are suffi-ciently morally good maximal options in which he saves neither baby (i.e., ones in which he saves neither out of a concern for his self-interest), there are no sufficiently morally good maximal options in which he saves only one of the two babies. This is because maximal options are maximally evaluatively

Table 6.4 Massimo's Options and Nonoptions in *Burning Building II*

Nonmaximal Options	Reasons Ranking on Maximalism	Evaluative Ranking
N_1: Save neither (entailed by M_1)	2nd most moral reason	Worst
N_2: Save only one (entailed by M_2 and M_4)	Least moral reason	2nd best
N_3: Save both (entailed by M_3)	Most moral reason	Best
Optimal Maximal Options that Entail these Nonmaximal Options	**Reasons Ranking on Maximalism**	**Evaluative Ranking**
M_1: Save neither out of self-interest and act altruistically afterward	2nd most moral reason	2nd best option; 3rd best event
M_2: Save only one out of callousness and act altruistically afterward	Least moral reason	Worst option; worst event
M_3: Save both out of altruism and act altruistically afterward	Most moral reason	Best option; 2nd best event
Nonoptional Event	**Reasons Ranking on Maximalism**	**Evaluative Ranking**
M_4: Accidentally save one out of altruism	Nonapplicable	Not an option; best event

specific and so must specify any morally relevant motives. In other words, maximal options will include both acts and attitudes, so we must assess their moral goodness in terms of both. And whereas there are sufficiently morally good attitudes that could move Massimo to save neither baby (e.g., a desire to live free of terrible pain and permanent disfigurement), there is no sufficiently morally good attitude that could move Massimo to save only one of the two babies. For Massimo to be so moved, he would need some motivational attitude such as a desire to save fewer lives, other things being equal. And no such motivational attitude is sufficiently morally good to be morally permissible.[27] Such an attitude would reflect unacceptable callousness toward the other baby. Thus, whereas Massimo will have sufficiently good

---

27. Note that this is compatible with holding that the nonmaximal option in which Massimo saves only one is morally better than the nonmaximal option in which he says neither. This is because nonmaximal options are not maximally evaluatively specific and so, they needn't specify what the relevant motive was. When comparing such nonmaximal options, we have no choice but to abstract away from the specifics and consider everything else to be equal.

maximal options in which he saves neither baby, he won't have any sufficiently good maximal options in which he saves only one baby. Therefore,
the optimal (and sufficiently good) maximal options in which he saves neither are going to be morally better than the insufficiently good maximal
options in which he saves only one.

Of course, what would be even better than his being moved to save neither out of a desire to live free of terrible pain is his entering the building out
of a desire to save both but then accidentally ending up saving only one. But
this isn't an option for him. No one has the option of doing something by
accident (for no one has direct rational control over whether they do something by accident).[28] So Massimo will have no maximal option in which he
accidentally saves only one despite being motivated to save the two. And this
means that all his maximal options in which he saves only one will be insufficiently good (for they will all involve unacceptable callousness), whereas some
of his maximal options in which he saves neither will be sufficiently good
(for some will involve an acceptable degree of partiality concerning his own
interests).[29] And, of course, a sufficiently good option is better than any insufficiently good option. Therefore, there is, on maximalism's MORE-REASON,
more moral reason for Massimo to save neither than for him to save only one
despite the fact that his saving only one is, other things being equal, morally
better than his saving neither.

So it seems that the solution to the all or nothing problem lies with
rejecting 6.14, and this holds regardless of which version of the burning
building case we're worried about. Still, there is another sort of case from the
literature that may seem relevantly different from the burning building cases.
In the burning building cases, the choice of whether to incur a large cost (by,
say, running into the burning building) is separable from the choice of how
much, if any, help to provide once that cost is borne. But in other sorts of

---

28. At best, someone might have the option of doing something that would increase the
chances that she'll do something by accident. But I'll just stipulate that Massimo has no such
option.

29. There are, of course, maximal options that entail his saving neither baby that are not sufficiently good, such as the one in which he goes into the burning building and saves a trash bin
instead of either baby out of a callous disregard for human life. This maximal option would
not be sufficiently good for it too would entail his forming or maintaining some inappropriate
motivational attitude, such as a preference for saving a trash bin as opposed to two lives. But
on maximalism, we look only to the optimal maximal options, and the best maximal option
that entails his saving neither baby is the one in which he forms or maintains what seems to be
the appropriate preference for safeguarding his own interest as opposed to the greater interests
of others.

cases, these two choices are not separable. Consider, for instance, the case that Theron Pummer (2016, p. 83) entitles *Arm Donor*. In this case, you have exactly the following three alternatives: (A1) place an arm on Track 1 at *t* and thereby sacrifice that arm to save the life of the one individual who would otherwise be hit by the train barreling down that track, (A2) place an arm on Track 100 (which is 20 feet apart from Track 1, making it impossible to place an arm on each track) at *t* and thereby sacrifice that arm to save the lives of the hundred individuals who would otherwise be hit by the train barreling down that track, and (A3) refrain from placing an arm on either track at *t* and thereby safeguard your arms while allowing 101 lives to be lost.

But it seems to me that my solution works equally well in this sort of case. Again, we should just deny 6.14. Moreover, on maximalism about reasons, we can plausibly deny that you have more moral reason to take alternative A1 than to take alternative A3. For it seems that the morally best maximal option that entails your taking A3 (the one in which you subsequently dedicate all your resources, including both your arms, to making the world as morally good as possible) will be morally better than the morally best maximal option that entails your taking A1 (the one in which you subsequently dedicate all your resources, including your only arm, to making the world as morally good as possible). For it's plausible to suppose that the loss of an arm would seriously curtail your ability to make the world better.[30]

Last, it's a merit of my solution that it doesn't require that one's altruistic acts always be maximally effective. That is, it doesn't imply that if you're going to donate some of your income to charity, you must donate it to the most effective charity available. To illustrate, suppose that Leilani donates 10 percent of her income to the Pūnāwai Program, which provides Native Hawaiians with emergency financial assistance. And let's assume that the Pūnāwai Program does much less good with Leilani's donation than the Against Malaria Foundation would have. Has Leilani done anything wrong? On my view, it depends.

On one possibility, Leilani has no good reason to prefer providing Native Hawaiians with emergency financial assistance to providing families living in sub-Saharan Africa with insecticide-treated mosquito nets. Imagine, then, that the only reason she chose to donate to the Pūnāwai Program is that her name is Hawaiian and, because of this, she thought that it would

---

30. If you deny this, then I can just say the same thing about this case that I said about *Burning Building II*. That is, I can say that there is no permissible maximal option in which you have attitudes that move you to save the one rather than the hundred.

be "neat" if she gave to the first Hawaiian charity that she could find on the internet. Assume, then, that she has no special connection to Hawaii or to Native Hawaiians beyond the fact that she has a Hawaiian name, which was given to her only because her parents conceived her while honeymooning in Hawaii. In such a case, it seems that she was not permitted to give to the Pūnāwai Program, for she had, it seems, no sufficiently good maximal option that entailed both her preferring to give her income to the Pūnāwai Program and her doing as she preferred to do in this instance.

But there's another possibility. Suppose that Leilani is Native Hawaiian and that her family was saved from financial ruin by the assistance provided by the Pūnāwai Program. Suppose, then, that she prefers giving her income to the Pūnāwai Program, because she feels that she has an obligation of solidarity to her fellow Native Hawaiians as well as an obligation to give back to her Native Hawaiian community. In that case, it seems that she was permitted to donate her income to the Pūnāwai Program, for it seems that she had a sufficiently good maximal option that entailed both her preferring to give her income to the Pūnāwai Program and her acting as she preferred to act.

So, a virtue of my solution to the all or nothing problem is that it implies that whether one is required to be maximally effective in making an altruistic self-sacrifice depends on what sorts of attitudes could motivate one to be less than maximally effective and whether such motives would be morally permissible.

§6.5 Maximalism and the Basic Belief

So far, we've seen three good reasons to favor maximalism about reasons over omnism about reasons: maximalism about reasons is immune to three problems to which omnism about reasons is susceptible—the inheritance problem, the intuition problem, and the all or nothing problem. But maximalism about reasons has another advantage: it helps us to account for what Joseph Raz (2000) calls *the basic belief*—the deeply entrenched commonsensical belief that, in many typical choice situations, the relevant reasons do not require performing one particular act-type but instead permit performing any of a variety of different act-types, such as watching TV, painting the fence, volunteering for Oxfam, reading the newspaper, or working on a book.[31]

---

31. As Raz states things, the basic belief is the belief "that most of the time people have a variety of options such that it would accord with reason for them to choose any one of them and it would not be against reason to avoid any of them" (2000, p. 100). But, interpreted literally,

Raz calls this the *basic* belief, because it seems to be sufficiently well entrenched in our common-sense thinking that we should give it "credence unless it can be shown to be incoherent or inconsistent with some of our rightly entrenched views" (2000, p. 100). Common sense would seem to hold, for instance, that I could now (this morning), in accordance with reason, do any of the following: watch TV, read a novel, volunteer for Oxfam, work on this book, play with my daughter, or prepare for my next lecture. (Call this case: *This Morning*.) But how do we account for this? It seems that there could be such a broad-ranging set of permissions only if the weight of the reasons for performing each act-type in the set were on a par with one another, and yet it is hard to believe that this is the case. And it is especially hard to believe this if we accept omnism's MORE-REASON. Let me explain.

The reason it's so hard to believe that, for instance, the reasons favoring my watching TV are on a par with either the reasons favoring my working on this book or the reasons favoring my volunteering for Oxfam is that it's hard to believe that watching TV is anywhere near as good as these other two options. It seems that on any plausible account of what ultimately matters, my watching TV will not be anywhere near as good as either my working on this book or my volunteering for Oxfam. Of course, there may come a time when I am just too exhausted to do anything but relax. At that point, it could be that my best present alternative is to recharge myself by doing something as mindless and relaxing as watching TV. But, as a matter of fact, I am not now anywhere near that point. Nonetheless, it seems perfectly permissible for me to stop working on this book, get up, and go either watch some TV or volunteer for Oxfam—or, at least, it does so as long as we assume that I will, in the future, have plenty of other opportunities to work productively on this book. Moreover, it seems perfectly permissible for me to continue working on this book and to forgo the opportunity either to watch some TV or to volunteer for Oxfam—or, at least, it does so as long as we assume that I will have plenty

---

this seems too weak to capture the belief that Raz has in mind. For I take it that Raz doesn't mean to be discussing the belief that we always have a variety of options that would accord with reason given that there are always countless permissible ways of performing a required act-type. For instance, suppose that reason requires that I push a certain button with my right index finger. Even so, I'll have a variety of options that would accord with reason given that there are countless permissible ways for me to push that button with my right index finger. I can do so as quickly as possible or not as quickly as possible. I can do so while singing the national anthem or while keeping quiet. I can do so while tapping my foot or while not tapping foot. And so on and so forth. I take it, then, that Raz has in mind the belief that there is often a variety of different act-types that we could perform that would all accord with reason, such as watching TV, painting the fence, volunteering for Oxfam, reading the newspaper, or working on a book.

of other opportunities in the future both to relax and to promote the happiness of others.

So how do we account for my having the option of spending this morning in any of several alternative ways (including spending it watching TV) when some of these options are far better than others? For how could it be that the relevant reasons permit my performing an option that's far worse than some other available alternative? I believe that at least part of the solution rests with our rejecting omnism's MORE-REASON and accepting maximalism's MORE-REASON instead. For once we make this substitution, we find that our evaluative focus shifts from the goodness of each of the nonmaximal options regarding how to spend the morning to the goodness of each of the optimal maximal options that entail performing these nonmaximal options. And when it comes to assessing maximal options, which involve the performance of various types of acts over time, it often doesn't matter in what order these types of acts are performed so long as the same approximate balance among the various types is achieved. For instance, it does not matter whether I work on this book this morning and watch TV this afternoon or watch TV this morning and work on this book this afternoon.

Of course, it could have mattered, as it would have had there been a rugby game on this morning that I wanted to watch live. But in many instances (including this one, let's assume), it does not matter in which order I perform two particular tasks so long as I perform both of them. So, where the order does not matter and where we are comparing a number of maximal options that all involve the same (or roughly the same) proportion of, say, relaxing acts, altruistic acts, and career-furthering acts, just in different temporal sequences, we find that they are all equally well supported by reason. And, given this, we should conclude that whereas some of my optimal maximal options will entail my spending the morning working on this book, others will entail my spending it watching TV. So, although I need to spend some of my time relaxing in order to keep from getting burned out, and although I need to spend some of my time working on this book in order to finish it by the deadline, I don't need to spend any particular occasion doing one or the other. Consequently, the best maximal option that entails my spending this occasion watching TV could be just as good as the best maximal option that entails my spending this occasion working on this book.[32]

---

32. I first explored this sort of solution in PORTMORE 2011.

Of course, from the fact that the best maximal option that entails my watching TV this morning and working on this book this afternoon (call this $M_{TV\text{-}b}$, where the subscripted '$TV\text{-}b$' indicates that the order is to watch TV first and work on this *book* second) is just as good as the best maximal option that entails my working on this book this morning and watching TV this afternoon (call this $M_{b\text{-}TV}$), it does not follow that my spending this morning watching TV (call this N_{TV}) is just as good as my spending it working on this book (call this N_b). For, as a matter of fact, it may be that I would not perform $M_{TV\text{-}b}$ or any other permissible maximal option if I were to perform N_{TV}. That is, it may be that if I were to spend this morning watching TV, I would, then, continue watching TV for the rest of the day. And let's assume that it would be quite bad for me to spend the entire day watching TV (call this $M_{TV\text{-}TV}$). So, if we accept omnism's MORE-REASON, we would have to deny that I have just as much reason to spend the morning watching TV as to spend it working on this book. For watching TV this morning would result in my spending the entire day watching TV, which is much worse than my spending the day working on this book in the morning and watching TV in the afternoon. And my spending the day working on this book in the morning and watching TV in the afternoon is what would happen, we'll suppose, if I were to spend the morning working on this book.

But just because my watching TV this morning would, as a matter of fact, result in my watching TV the entire day does not mean that I don't have the option of watching TV this morning and working on this book in the afternoon. For suppose that the only reason that I would not work on this book this afternoon if I were to watch TV this morning is that I am presently disposed to respond inappropriately to my reasons; consequently, I am about to form the irrational intention to spend the entire day watching TV. And assume that all this is true despite the fact that I have at present the capacity to respond appropriately to my reasons and thereby come to form the rational and efficacious intention to stop watching TV by the afternoon so as to start working on this book. Given these assumptions, it follows that the best maximal option that entails my watching TV this morning (viz., $M_{TV\text{-}b}$) is just as good as the best maximal option that entails my working on this book this morning (viz., $M_{b\text{-}TV}$)—see Table 6.5. So, in this case, maximalism's MORE-REASON implies, contrary to omnism's MORE-REASON, that I have just as much reason to spend the morning watching TV (performing N_{TV}) as I do to spend the morning working on this book (performing N_b).

Table 6.5 My Options in *This Morning*

Nonmaximal Options	Reasons Ranking on Maximalism	Evaluative Ranking
N_{TV}: Spend the morning watching TV	Tied for most reason	Worst
N_b: Spend the morning working on this book	Tied for most reason	Best
Maximal Options	**Reasons Ranking on Maximalism**	**Evaluative Ranking**
$M_{TV\text{-}TV}$: Spend both the morning and the afternoon watching TV	Least reason	Worst
$M_{TV\text{-}b}$: Spend the morning watching TV and the afternoon working on this book	Tied for most reason	Tied for best
$M_{b\text{-}TV}$: Spend the morning working on this book and the afternoon watching TV	Tied for most reason	Tied for best

We can say the same thing about the various other options that are seemingly permissible, such as spending the morning volunteering for Oxfam or playing with my daughter. I'm permitted to spend this morning doing that sort of activity so long as there is a permissible maximal option that entails my spending this morning doing that sort of activity. And since what matters is often not when I do a particular sort of activity but whether I strike an appropriate balance among various sorts of activities, it's plausible to think that there is. Thus, in contrast to the omnist, the maximalist has no trouble explaining why the relevant reasons permit my performing any of numerous alternative options this morning, including the options of spending it watching TV, working on this book, volunteering for Oxfam, or playing with my daughter.

Although it had initially seemed unlikely that I would have just as much reason to perform N_{TV} as to perform N_b, this was only because we were implicitly assuming omnism's MORE-REASON. That is, we were implicitly assuming that how much reason there is to perform a nonmaximal option is a function of how good that option is and not, as maximalism's MORE-REASON supposes, a function of how good the optimal maximal options that entail it are. And when it comes to maximal options that entail performing a sequence of acts over an extended period of time as opposed to individual acts performed at some rather discrete time, we find that it's much more common for them to be equally well supported by reasons than we might have initially thought. For the order in which a sequence of acts is performed is often irrelevant to how good that sequence is. So, whereas the omnist has great difficulty in accounting for how I could have roughly just as much reason to spend this morning watching TV as to spend it working on this book, the maximalist has no trouble at all. Thus, adopting maximalism's MORE-REASON helps us to account for the basic belief and thereby has an advantage over omnism's MORE-REASON.[33]

§6.6 Objections to Maximalism about Reasons

At this point, readers may wonder whether they must accept maximalism about reasons even if I'm right about these problems for omnism about reasons. That is, they may wonder whether these two views exhaust the possibilities. Admittedly, they don't. And, unfortunately, I don't have the space here to consider all the possible alternatives. Yet, it seems sufficient for my purposes to argue merely that maximalism about reasons is more plausible than omnism about reasons. After all, the theories of reasons that philosophers have offered to date have all been formulated as versions of omnism about reasons. That is, they have all taken the following form: for any subject S and any (maximal or nonmaximal) option of hers φ, S has a reason (or a T reason) to φ if and only if S's φ-ing has property P. Of course, they differ on what 'P' stands for—whether, say, it stands for the "property of promoting S's interests" or "the property of advancing some element in S's subjective motivational set" (B. WILLIAMS 1981), but they all take for granted in their formulations that we are to assess all options (maximal and nonmaximal) in terms of whether they have this property. Indeed, they don't even distinguish between maximal and nonmaximal options in their formulations. Given this, I'm not ignoring

---

33. It is important to note, though, that I am claiming only that adopting maximalism's MORE-REASON *helps* us to account for the basic belief. Admittedly, maximalism's MORE-REASON cannot be used to account for our basic-belief-type intuitions in what are known as "small improvement cases," cases in which we think that there is an option both before and after there has been a small improvement in either the number and/or the strength of the reasons in support of only one of the options—see PORTMORE 2011 (pp. 157–191) for more on this. But even if maximalism's MORE-REASON is not the entire solution to the problem of accounting for the basic belief, it is, as I have argued, an important part of the solution.

any proffered views in neglecting to consider other alternatives. I'm ignoring only those views that no one has formulated. And it seems reasonable for me to do so. In any case, to argue that the philosophical orthodoxy is wrong seems significant enough. And that omnism about reasons is the philosophical orthodoxy is, I think, demonstrated by the fact that problems such as the intuition problem, the all or nothing problem, and the problem of accommodating the basic belief don't even get off the ground unless we assume omnism about reasons. And yet in the literature on these problems no one else has even noted the possibility that we could solve these problems by rejecting omnism about reasons. It seems that everyone has just presupposed omnism about reasons.

In any case, I can't establish even the comparatively modest thesis that maximalism about reasons is more plausible than omnism about reasons merely by showing, as I believe that I have, that omnism about reasons is subject to three critical problems to which maximalism about reasons is immune. For it could be that maximalism about reasons is subject to some equally serious problems to which omnism about reasons is immune. And, in that case, maximalism about reasons wouldn't have any net advantage over omnism about reasons. Thus, I need to consider whether maximalism about reasons is subject to any equally serious problems. So I'll now consider and rebut the four main worries that one might have about maximalism about reasons.

§6.6.1 Incorrect explanation

One worry about maximalism about reasons is that, in certain cases, it may seem to have counterintuitive implications regarding why a subject ought to do something. To illustrate, imagine that I have a reason to relieve some of my current stress and that I can do so by presently engaging in any sort of manual activity—that is, any activity that involves working with my hands. And assume that, with regard to relieving my stress, it doesn't matter what the activity is so long as it involves working with my hands. Clearly then, I have a reason to sculpt a statue, for sculpting a statue involves working with my hands. Yet, it doesn't seem as though the reason that I have to work with my hands derives from the reason that I have to sculpt a statue just because sculpting a statue entails working with my hands. So, isn't this a clear counterexample to maximalism about reasons?

No, it is not. Contrary to what this objection assumes, maximalism doesn't hold that if sculpting a statue entails working with my hands, the reason that I have to work with my hands derives from the reason that I have to sculpt a statue. Rather, maximalism holds that if sculpting a statue is a maximal option that entails the nonmaximal option of working with my hands, then the reason that I have to work with my hands derives from the reason that I have to sculpt a statue. But sculpting a statue is not a maximal option. After all, sculpting a statue is entailed by the evaluatively distinct option of sculpting a statue while verbally abusing someone on speaker phone. So, maximalism about reasons doesn't imply that the reason that I have to work with my hands derives from the reason that I have to sculpt a statue. Rather, it implies that both the reason that I have to sculpt a statue and the reason that I have to work with my hands derive from the reason that I have to perform some maximal option that entails my doing these things. In other words, it implies that I have a reason to work with my hands in virtue of the fact that I have a reason to perform some maximal option in which I work with my hands on this occasion—that reason being that my doing so would relieve some of my current stress. And it implies that I have a reason to sculpt a statue in virtue of the fact that I have a reason to perform some maximal option in which I sculpt a statue on this occasion—again, that reason being that my doing so would relieve some of my current stress. But there's nothing counterintuitive about these implications. Although it may seem a bit strange to think that the reason to work with my hands is grounded in the reason that I have to perform some maximal option that entails working with my hands, this is just because we're not used to thinking about maximal options. And refer back to §4.6.3 for why, despite its being unusual, we need to appeal to maximal options in grounding our reasons for performing nonmaximal options.

§6.6.2 Incorrect weights

Another worry is that maximalism about reasons seems to have counter-intuitive implications regarding the weights of a subject's reasons (see, e.g., GERT 2014). To illustrate, suppose that the best maximal option that entails my watching TV this morning and volunteering for Oxfam this afternoon (viz., $M_{TV\text{-}o}$) is slightly better than the best maximal option that entails my volunteering for Oxfam this morning and watching TV this afternoon (viz., $M_{o\text{-}TV}$). Assume that this is because I'll enjoy the day slightly more if I perform $M_{TV\text{-}o}$ as opposed to $M_{o\text{-}TV}$. And assume that, as a matter of fact, I will, come this afternoon, choose to spend the afternoon watching TV regardless of what I did in the morning. Assume, though, that this is only because I am at present forming the intention to spend the afternoon watching TV regardless of how I spend the morning. So, assume that if I were instead to form the conditional intention to spend the afternoon volunteering for Oxfam if I spend the morning watching TV, I would volunteer for Oxfam in the afternoon if I were to watch TV this morning. Nevertheless, given that I'm not at present forming this intention, I would not volunteer this afternoon if I were to watch TV this morning.

Given that, in this case, the best maximal option in which I watch TV this morning is slightly better than the best maximal option in which I volunteer for Oxfam this morning (that is, given that $M_{TV\text{-}o}$ is slightly better than $M_{o\text{-}TV}$), maximalism about reasons implies that I have slightly more reason to spend the morning watching TV than to spend it volunteering for Oxfam. And it implies this despite the fact that I would, we'll suppose, save two additional lives if I were to spend the morning volunteering for Oxfam. Of course, the only reason that I would save two additional lives by spending the morning volunteering for Oxfam is that I'm not now forming the intention that I ought to form: the intention to volunteer for Oxfam in the afternoon if I spend the morning watching TV.

Admittedly, this implication will seem counterintuitive to some. But the same is true of maximalism's implication that the repressible Professor Procrastinate ought to accept the invitation to write the review even though he would, as a matter of fact, not write the review even if he were to accept. I believe, then, that whether, and to what extent, these implications seem counterintuitive just depends on whether, and to what extent, we find such nonactualist verdicts counterintuitive. And I've argued that we should, upon reflection, find them perfectly acceptable. We should, for instance, think that the repressible Professor Procrastinate ought to accept even though, given that he's going to fail to resolve to write, he wouldn't write if he were to accept. Now, in the case of my deciding how to spend this morning, we're likewise to imagine that my tendency to continue to watch TV in the afternoon if I were to watch TV in the morning is presently repressible. Thus, we're to assume that I would volunteer for Oxfam this afternoon if I were, this morning, to respond appropriately to my reasons and start watching TV with the intention of volunteering for Oxfam in the afternoon. And if I did this, I would save just as many lives as I would if I were to spend the morning volunteering for Oxfam. And it's odd to think that how much reason I have to do something depends on what intentions I'm going to form. For instance, it's odd to think that how much reason I have to do something depends on whether I'm going to form the intention to do that thing. So, upon reflection, I think that we should accept that I have more reason to spend the morning watching TV than to spend it volunteering for Oxfam. In any case, I think that whether one is willing to accept this just depends on whether one is willing to accept that the fact that I must spend the morning watching TV in order to perform my best option (i.e., $M_{TV\text{-}o}$) constitutes an instrumental reason for me to spend the morning watching TV even if my doing so would not, in fact, increase the chances that I'll perform my best maximal option. And this is the issue to which I now turn.

§6.6.3 Incorrect account of instrumental reasons

Some worry that maximalism about reasons has counterintuitive implications regarding when there is an instrumental reason to do something—an *instrumental reason* to φ being a reason that a subject has to φ in virtue of the fact that her φ-ing is a necessary means to her bringing about some end that she has reason to bring about. Maximalism about reasons holds that if a subject's φ-ing is a necessary means to her bringing about some end that she has reason to bring about, then she has an instrumental reason to φ regardless of whether her φ-ing increases the objective probability that she'll achieve that end. But this will seem counterintuitive to some. For several philosophers have argued that the fact that a subject's φ-ing is a necessary means to her bringing about some end that she has reason to bring about constitutes an instrumental reason for her to φ only if her φ-ing would make it more objectively likely that she'll achieve that end (see, e.g., KOLODNY 2018). That is, they accept something along the following lines.

> **Probabilism:** For any subject S, any proposition *p* such that she has a reason to see to it that *p*, and any option of hers φ that is a necessary means to her seeing to it that *p*, S has a reason (specifically, an instrumental reason) to φ only if S's φ-ing would increase the objective probability that *p*—that is, only if the objective probability that *p* on the condition that S φs is greater than the objective probability that *p* on the condition that S doesn't φ.

To illustrate, consider again *Professor Procrastinate* and assume that his tendency to procrastinate is presently repressible. According to maximalism about reasons, Professor Procrastinate has an instrumental reason to accept the invitation in virtue of the fact that this is a necessary means to his performing an optimal maximal option—that is, a maximal option that entails his both accepting and writing. Thus, on maximalism about reasons, the fact that he must accept in order to perform his best option (i.e., accepting and writing) provides him with an instrumental reason for accepting. But note that since it's a fact that Professor Procrastinate would not write even if he were to accept, his accepting doesn't increase the objective probability that he'll accept and write. Indeed, it's stipulated that he's not going to write regardless of whether or not he accepts. So the objective probability that he'll write (even on the condition that he accepts) is zero. Thus, probabilism implies that Professor Procrastinate doesn't have an instrumental reason to accept.

Now, I find this implication quite counterintuitive, but people like Kolodny don't. Let me try, then, to bring out some of probabilism's less palatable implications using the following case.

Two Pills: The time is t_1, and Kazumi is suffering from a very painful medical condition. If she isn't cured at t_4, she'll suffer from chronic pain for the rest of her life. The pain won't be so bad as to make her life not worth living, but her life will be much better if she's cured. There are exactly two pills—P1 and P2—available to her. If she takes only P1 at t_3, she'll be cured at t_4. But, given the way the two pills interact, if she takes both P1 and P2 at t_3, she'll die at t_4 (thereby missing out on thirty years of life worth living). And if she does anything else (e.g., takes only P1 at some other time besides t_3, takes only P2 at t_3, or takes neither P1 nor P2 at t_3), she'll be rendered incurable and suffer from chronic pain for her remaining thirty years. Assume that although Kazumi is, at t_1, a rational being with the capacity to respond appropriately to her reasons, she is going to form at t_2 the irrational intention to commit suicide by taking both pills at t_3. Consequently, if she were to take P1 at t_3, she would also take P2 at t_3. Nevertheless, if she were at t_1 to exercise her capacity to respond appropriately to her reasons to good effect and thereby form at t_2 the rational intention to take only P1 at t_3, she would do so and live happily ever after. See Table 6.6.

According to probabilism, Kazumi doesn't have (at t_1) an instrumental reason to take P1 at t_3 even though all the following hold: (1) she has a very strong reason to bring it about that she's cured, (2) her taking P1 at t_3 is a necessary means to her bringing it about that she's cured, and (3) she'll be cured as a result of her taking P1 at t_3 so long as she presently exercises her capacity to respond appropriately to her reasons and thereby forms at t_2 the intention to take only P1 at t_3. Given that she's not presently exercising her capacity to respond appropriately to her reasons and so is going to form at t_2 the irrational

Table 6.6 Kazumi's Options in *Two Pills*

Option	Outcome	Ranking
Take P1 at t_3	She dies at t_4	Worst
Take only P1 at t_3	She's cured at t_4	Best
Take both P1 and P2 at t_3	She dies at t_4	Worst
Do anything besides the above	She suffers chronic pain from t_4	2nd Best

intention to take both pills at t_3, her taking P1 at t_3 would not increase the objective probability that she'll be cured. In fact, given the way that she's going to respond to her reasons, there is zero objective chance that she'll be cured whether she takes P1 at t_3 or not.

But I find it counterintuitive to think that Kazumi has at t_1 no instrumental reason to take P1 at t_3 just because she isn't going to respond appropriately to her reasons and form at t_2 the intention to cure herself by taking only P1 at t_3. For why would the fact that she isn't going to respond appropriately to her reasons affect what her reasons are? It seems to me that whether a subject has a reason to take the necessary means to her ψ-ing depends not at all on either whether she intends to ψ or whether she's going to exercise her capacity to respond appropriately to her reasons and form the intention to ψ. So, it seems to me that we should reject probabilism. Therefore, the fact that maximalism about reasons conflicts with probabilism is no reason to reject maximalism about reasons.

Probabilism is, I admit, getting at something. Whether taking the necessary means to an end makes it more objectively likely that the end will be achieved is often relevant. It's just not always relevant, as probabilism supposes. Thus, I would think that following does a better job of capturing the relevance of a means probabilizing the end for which it is necessary.

> **Rationalist Probabilism:** For any subject S, any proposition p such that she has a reason to see to it that p, and any option of hers φ that is a necessary means to her seeing to it that p, S has a reason (specifically, an instrumental reason) to φ only if S's φ-ing would increase either (1) the objective probability that p or (2) the objective probability that p on the condition that she appropriately exercises her rational control at present and forms the appropriate intentions.

So, I think that what you ought to do depends on what intentions you ought to form, not on what intentions you will in fact form. Given that Kazumi ought to form the intention to cure herself, she has a reason to take P1, which will probabilize her curing herself so long as she forms this intention.

§6.6.4 Incorrect account of reasons
to perform acts with side effects

A final worry concerning maximalism about reasons is that it has counterintuitive implications in the following sort of case.

> *Getting Groceries:* I need some groceries. Assume, then, that I have a reason to perform any maximal option that entails my getting the groceries that I need: that reason being that my getting the groceries that I need would increase my happiness and that such an increase would be noninstrumentally good. Now, the only means that I have of getting these groceries is to drive to the grocery store in my car. But, unfortunately, I don't have the option of driving to the grocery store in my car without wearing down my tires. Thus, all the maximal options that entail my getting groceries entail my wearing down my tires. However, there would be nothing noninstrumentally good about my wearing down my tires.[34]

According to maximalism about reasons, I have a reason to perform a given nonmaximal option if and only if there is a maximal option that I have a reason to perform that entails my performing that nonmaximal option. It follows that in *Getting Groceries*, I have a reason to wear down my tires. For it's stipulated both that I have a reason to perform any maximal option that entails my getting the groceries and that any such maximal option entails wearing down my tires. Yet it seems counterintuitive to think that I have a reason to wear down my tires.

Or does it? Of course, it certainly seems counterintuitive to think that, for any act-token that's an instance of the my-wearing-down-my-tires type, I have a reason to perform that act-token. For I certainly don't have any reason

---

34. I thank David Sobel for pressing me to address this sort of example.

to take an electric sander to my tires even though this would be a token instance of the my-wearing-down-my-tires type. But note that maximalism about reasons doesn't imply that, for any act-token that's an instance of the my-wearing-down-my-tires type, I have a reason to perform that act-token. Rather, it implies only that I have a reason to perform an act-type that entails my wearing down my tires—specifically, the getting-groceries act-type. The reason that getting groceries entails wearing down my tires is that I don't have the option of getting groceries without wearing down my tires. And this is because the only means I have of getting groceries is to drive to the grocery store in my car, which necessarily involves wearing down my tires given the laws of nature.

It's important, then, to realize that there are at least two interpretations of the thought that I have a reason to wear down my tires.

(I_1) There exists an act-type that I have a reason to perform that entails my wearing down my tires. In other words, there is some instance of the my-wearing-down-my-tires type that I have reason to perform.

(I_2) For any act-token that's an instance of the wearing-down-my-tires type, I have a reason to perform that act-token. In other words, I have reason to perform any instance of the my-wearing-down-my-tires type.

I'm not sure whether, in ordinary conversation, I_1 or I_2 would be the standard interpretation of the thought in question. Regardless, maximalism about reasons only supports I_1. And whereas I_2 is quite counterintuitive, I don't see anything counterintuitive about I_1. So I don't think that maximalism about reasons has any counterintuitive implications in this sort of case.

§6.7 Conclusion

I've argued that we should accept maximalism about reasons as opposed to omnism about reasons. As we've seen, omnism about reasons is subject to three significant problems. First, the omnist is committed to OMNISM ABOUT MOST CONSEQUENTIALIST REASON, which is problematic because, in accepting it, she's forced to reject either REASONS INHERITANCE or OPTIMIFIC NONINHERITANCE, both of which are difficult to deny. Indeed, given the coherence of *The Injection*, she can't reject OPTIMIFIC NONINHERITANCE. And she can't reject REASONS INHERITANCE if she wants to give a unified and systematic account of the various sorts of inferences that it validates. Second, the omnist's account of when a subject has more moral reason to φ than to ψ commits her to denying at least one of the following: THREAT BETTER THAN NO THREAT, SELF-INTEREST TRUMPS LIVES, and SELF-INTEREST DOESN'T TRUMP CLEAN HANDS. And no matter which she denies, she'll have to deny one of our considered moral intuitions. Third, the omnist about reasons is committed to 6.14—that is, to the view that, for any subject S and any two of her alternative options φ and ψ, if S's ψ-ing is morally better than S's φ-ing, then S has more moral reason to ψ than to φ. And unfortunately, this leads to the all or nothing problem, where she has to reject at least one of 6.10–6.13, all of which are difficult to deny. By contrast, we can avoid all three problems simply by accepting maximalism about reasons instead. We have, then, at least three good reasons for preferring maximalism about reasons to omnism about reasons.

Last, I've argued that maximalism about reasons helps us to account for the basic belief and has no problems of its own. So, it seems that we should accept maximalism about reasons as opposed to omnism about reasons. And this is fortunate, because although combining maximalism about statuses with omnism about reasons would have forced us to reject the plausible ought-most-reason view, we can accept this plausible view by combining maximalism about statuses with maximalism about reasons. For, on maximalism about reasons, a subject always has most reason to do what maximalism about statuses holds that she ought to do.

CHAPTER 7

Which, if Either, Are We to Assess Directly in Terms of What Ultimately Matters

OUR OPTIONS OR THEIR PROSPECTS?

I'VE ARGUED THAT we should accept rationalist maximalism. It holds that the only options whose deontic statuses are a function of their own goodness are maximal options. The deontic statuses of nonmaximal options, by contrast, are a function of the goodness of the maximal options that entail them. And, as I've noted in previous chapters, the goodness of our options is determined by whatever ultimately matters, whether that be utility, friendship, obedience to God, respect for people's autonomy, all of these, some of these, or none of these. So rationalist maximalism tells us how the goodness of our options determines the deontic statuses of our options, but it doesn't tell us how the things that ultimately matter determine the goodness of our options. There are, as I see it, two possibilities: (1) they do so *directly* in that we assess the goodness of our options directly in terms of the things that ultimately matter or (2) they do so *indirectly* in that we first assess the goodness of outcomes (or prospects) in terms of what ultimately matters and then assess the goodness of our options in terms of how their outcomes (or prospects) compare to each other in terms of what ultimately matters. The first is nonteleological; the second, teleological. In this chapter, I'll expand on these two possibilities and argue for teleology.

§7.1 A Case Study: Teleology, Deontology, Nonteleology, and Agent-Centered Constraints

What determines whether a theory is teleological is whether it holds that how a subject's options rank ultimately depends on how their outcomes or prospects rank. Whereas teleology holds that it does, nonteleology denies this. Thus, as I'll be using these terms, a theory is *teleological* if and only if it holds that, for any option, the goodness (or badness) of that option ultimately and solely depends on the extent to which its outcome or prospect is to be preferred (or dispreferred) to those of its alternatives.[1] And a theory is *nonteleological* if and only if it's not teleological.[2]

There's much to explain here. First, an option's *outcome* is the way the world would be if that option were performed. This, of course, includes not only its causal consequences but everything that would be the case if it were performed. However, there may not be any one way that the world *would* be if an option were performed but only several different ways that it *could* be. And, in that case, we need to talk about its prospect as opposed to its outcome. The prospect of an option is a probability distribution consisting in the set of mutually exclusive and jointly exhaustive ways the world could be if that option were performed, with each possibility assigned a probability such that the sum of these probabilities equals 1. And, to save space, I will, hereafter, talk only of prospects. For we can represent an option's outcome as a prospect in which the probability distribution consists in just one possible world with a probability of 1.

Second, I'll remain neutral on whose preferences are relevant in determining the extent to which one prospect is to be preferred to another. They could be those of the actual subject or those of some hypothetical subject— an impartial spectator, perhaps. Moreover, the relevant preferences could be those that the given subject actually has or those that she would have in some hypothetical situation. And the relevant hypothetical situation could either be descriptively defined (e.g., the situation in which she is fully informed and

---

1. Thus, although W. D. Ross (1930) would allow that the goodness of some options ultimately and solely depends on the extent to which its outcome or prospect is to be preferred (or dispreferred) to those of its alternatives, he counts as a nonteleologist given that he thinks that the goodness of other options directly depends (at least, in part) on other things, such as justice, fidelity, and nonmaleficence.

2. Here, I follow the editors of the *Encyclopedia Britannica* (2017), who write: "Teleological ethics, (teleological from Greek *telos*, 'end'; *logos*, 'science'), theory of morality that derives duty or moral obligation from what is good or desirable as an end to be achieved."

has followed some procedure) or normatively defined (e.g., the situation in which she has all and only the preferences that she ought to have).

Third, it's important to note that what's relevant in determining whether a theory is teleological is what it holds *ultimately* grounds an option's goodness. To illustrate, consider a theory that holds both that what ultimately makes an option sufficiently good is that God does not forbid it and that God forbids all and only those options that have a prospect that's to be dispreferred to that of some alternative. This theory would be nonteleological even though it holds that whether an option is sufficiently good depends on whether its prospect is to be dispreferred to that of some alternative. It's nonteleological because it holds that whether an option is sufficiently good *ultimately* depends not on whether its prospect is to be dispreferred to that of some alternative but on whether God forbids it.

Fourth, it's important to note that the notion of an option's goodness is distinct from that of its prospect's goodness. And this is what allows for the possibility of non-teleology. For the nonteleologist can hold, for instance, that a subject's committing murder (say, to prevent two others from each committing murder) is worse than her refraining from doing so even though the prospect of her doing so is better than that of her refraining from doing so. Only the teleologist insists that the goodness of an option must track the goodness of its prospect such that if the prospect of φ-ing is better than that of ψ-ing, φ-ing must itself be better than ψ-ing.

Having made these clarifications, we can return to the question of whether the things that ultimately matter determine the goodness of our options either directly as the nonteleologist supposes or indirectly as the teleologist supposes. And, for the sake of argument, I'll be supposing that our not violating agent-centered constraints is something that ultimately matters. I pick this supposition because I'll be arguing for teleology, and teleology is generally thought to be inhospitable to agent-centered constraints. Thus, my hope is to show that even if something such as our not violating agent-centered constraints is what ultimately matters, we should still endorse teleology.

And let me clarify that there is an *agent-centered constraint* against a subject's performing an act of a certain type if and only if there are some possible circumstances in which it would be impermissible for her to perform an act of that type even though her doing so would both minimize the total instances of actions of that type and have no other morally relevant implications (SCHEFFLER 1985, p. 409). Thus, common-sense morality includes an agent-centered constraint (hereafter, simply "constraint") against breaking a promise given that it prohibits one from breaking a promise even so as to prevent two others from each breaking comparable promises—or, at least, it does so as long as the implications of each of these promise-breakings are otherwise morally equivalent. And it's important to distinguish between violating a constraint and merely infringing upon it. A subject *infringes* upon a constraint against her performing an act of a certain type if and only if she performs an act of that type. Thus, if a subject breaks a promise, she thereby infringes upon common-sense morality's constraint against breaking a promise. But it doesn't follow that she has violated that constraint. A *violation* of a constraint is just an impermissible infringement of that constraint, and not all infringements of a constraint are impermissible. After all, constraints can have thresholds. A constraint has a *threshold* if and only if merely performing an act of that kind is insufficient to count as having violated that constraint. For instance, common-sense morality's constraint against breaking a promise has a threshold that permits breaking a promise when necessary to produce more than a certain amount of good. Thus, a subject violates common-sense morality's constraint against breaking a promise only if she breaks a promise that fails to meet this threshold for the production of goodness. More generally, then, a subject violates (as opposed to merely infringes upon) a constraint against her performing an act of a certain type if and only if she performs an act of that type that fails to meet the applicable thresholds (THOMSON 1986, p. 51).

Now, it seems—at least, on common-sense morality—that one of the things that ultimately matters is our not violating constraints. But the mere fact that common-sense morality includes such constraints and, thus, takes constraints to be relevant in determining the goodness of our options does not itself determine whether it is teleological or nonteleological. To know whether common-sense morality is teleological or not, we need to know whether the things that ultimately matter determine the goodness of our options either directly or indirectly.

To illustrate, first consider the following nonteleological approach to how constraints determine the goodness of our options.

The Strict Nonteleological Approach

For any subject S and any option of hers φ,

(1) S's φ-ing is sufficiently good (and, thus, objectively permissible) only if, in φ-ing, she would not violate a constraint.[3]

---

3. Note that the things that ultimately matter in determining the goodness of our options

(2) In the event that in φ-ing, she would violate a constraint, φ's degree of badness is directly proportional to the importance of the constraint that she would thereby violate.

This approach is nonteleological, because it holds that the goodness of an option is determined not by how its prospect ranks on some preference ordering, but rather by whether it would constitute the violation of a constraint and, if so, by how important that constraint is.

And now compare this to the following teleological approach to how constraints determine the goodness of our options.

The Normative Teleological Approach

For any subject S and any option of hers φ,

(1) S's φ-ing is sufficiently good (and, thus, objectively permissible) if and only if she has no alternative option ψ such that she ought to prefer its prospect to that of her φ-ing.

(2) The degree to which φ is good or bad is directly proportional to the intensity with which she ought to prefer or disprefer its prospect to those of its alternatives.

(3) She ought, other things being equal, to prefer that she violates as few constraints as possible, that others violate as few constraints as possible, that she and others take as little objective risk of violating a constraint as possible, that the constraints that she and others violate—or even objectively risk violating—are of as little importance as possible, that she doesn't risk disaster for the sake of making things only slightly expectedly better, etc.

On this view, facts about whether an option would constitute the violation of a constraint are directly relevant only in determining how the prospects of a subject's options rank in terms of the preferences that she ought to have—and

---

are not themselves either teleological or nonteleological. Even constraints, which until very recently have been exclusively associated with nonteleological theories, are not themselves nonteleological. As the literature on both consequentializing and deontologizing has shown, we can take any remotely plausible set of deontic verdicts, features, or considerations and incorporate them into either a teleological or a nonteleological framework—see, for instance, DREIER 1993, HURLEY 2013, LOUISE 2004, PORTMORE 2011, and SACHS 2010. Thus, the teleological/nonteleological distinction comes into play only when considering whether the things that ultimately matter determine the statuses of our options either directly or indirectly—that is, either before or after assessing their prospects.

it's because this ranking is in terms of the preferences that she ought to have as opposed to those that she actually has (or would have under some descriptively defined hypothetical situation) that I call this the *normative* teleological approach. Thus, the goodness of a given option is ultimately determined by how good its prospect is as compared to those of its alternatives in terms of whatever ultimately matters. And this is what makes the view teleological: the assessment of the option's prospect in terms of its desirability given what ultimately matters is prior to the assessment of the option's goodness. In other words, what makes a view teleological as opposed to nonteleological is that it takes the evaluation of prospects to be prior to the evaluation of their associated options.[4]

Note, then, that a *constraint-accepting theory*—a theory that holds that there are some constraints—can be teleological. For instance, on the normative teleological approach just described, there would be a constraint against my committing murder if I ought to prefer the prospect of my refraining from committing a murder to the prospect of my committing that murder to prevent more numerous others from each committing comparable murders. But what's even more surprising is that, on my definition of "teleology," a deontological theory can be teleological. For, as I see it, a *deontological theory* is just a constraint-accepting theory that holds that constraints are ultimately grounded in our duty to respect people and their capacity for rational, autonomous decision making. And this is just the duty to have certain attitudes toward them—for example, a duty to regard them as ends-in-themselves as opposed to "mere sites for the realization of value" (LAZAR 2017, p. 582).[5] Thus, a teleologist can be a deontologist by holding that the explanation for why, say, I ought to prefer the prospect of my refraining from committing a murder to the prospect of my committing that murder so as to prevent more numerous others from each committing comparable murders lies with

---

4. Admittedly, then, the way that I draw the teleological/non-teleological distinction differs from the way that some others do (e.g., RAWLS 1971, pp. 24–30), as these others take the distinction to be between views that, on the one hand, hold that the good is prior to the right and views that hold, on the other hand, that the right is prior to the good. I've never quite understood this way of drawing the distinction given that we can talk about the rightness of an option depending on its goodness in a way that's independent of the goodness of its outcome or prospect.

5. Of course, people are sites for the realization of value; they're just not *mere* sites for the realization of value. And this means that we should not view a person merely as a potential location for the addition or subtraction of value or disvalue such that one should add or subtract a certain amount of value or disvalue (e.g., pleasure or pain) from her whenever doing so would maximize the total amount of value overall. For more on this idea, see LAZAR 2017.

the fact that I ought to respect my would-be murder victim and her capacity for rational, autonomous choice—and I'm assuming that my having this attitude is incompatible with my intentionally killing her *without her consent*. This view would be teleological because it holds that the reason I ought to refrain from committing murder is grounded in the fact that I ought to prefer the prospect of my refraining from doing so to the prospect of my doing so. And yet, it's deontological because what ultimately grounds this constraint against my committing murder is the fact that I ought to respect people and their capacity for rational, autonomous decision making. Thus, it's this duty of respect that explains why I should prefer the prospect of my refraining from committing a murder to the prospect of my committing that murder to prevent more numerous others from each committing comparable murders, which, in turn, explains why I should not commit this murder. So, as I see things, whether a theory is deontological depends on whether it accepts that there are agent-centered constraints that are grounded in a duty to have certain attitudes toward rational, autonomous decision makers—for example, a duty to regard them as ends-in-themselves as opposed to "mere sites for the realization of value" (LAZAR 2017, p. 582). By contrast, whether a theory is teleological depends on something entirely different: whether it holds that the goodness of an option's prospect is explanatorily prior to the goodness of that option or vice versa.

The point of all this is to suggest that, on my definition of "teleology," teleology shouldn't seem nearly as controversial as it would if I had defined it in a way that rendered it incompatible with the deontological idea that there are agent-centered constraints that are ultimately grounded in our duty to respect people and their capacity for rational, autonomous decision making.[6] Of course, teleology is also compatible with the idea that there are no constraints and that utility is the only thing that ultimately matters. So what this means is that you should be open to endorsing teleology whether your proclivities lie with Kantian deontology, maximizing act-utilitarianism, or anything in between.

Now, supposing that we hold, as common-sense morality does, that one of the things that ultimately matters is our not violating any constraints, we still need to figure out whether this is something that we use to assess options first and prospects second, or vice versa. In the remainder of this chapter, I'll argue

---

6. I owe the excellent idea that we should define deontology along these lines as well as the idea that a deontologist, so defined, could be a teleologist (in my sense) to Jake Zuehl, who suggested them to me via email in May 2017.

that teleology has it right—the things that ultimately matter determine the goodness of our options only indirectly via our first determining how their prospects rank. I'll argue that the teleological approach is preferable to the nonteleological approach, because only it has the resources to plausibly account for cases in which it's indeterminate whether a given option would constitute a constraint-violation.[7]

§7.2 Ignorance versus Indeterminacy

Sometimes it's unclear whether an agent would violate a constraint by performing a given option. To illustrate, consider the following.

> *The Questionable Vest:* A suspected terrorist named Apollyon has just walked into a crowd of twenty people, and it appears that he might be wearing an explosive vest. Alexandra is the only police officer in the area. She has an easy shot at Apollyon, but she's uncertain whether the vest that he's wearing is an explosive one. If she takes the shot now (that is, at t) and the vest isn't an explosive one, she will have killed him unnecessarily. But if she takes the shot and the vest is an explosive one, she will have neutralized a genuine threat to the twenty. Let's call the evidential probability for Alexandra (and us) that the vest is an explosive one $Evi\text{-}Pr(E)$.[8] And let's assume that there is a constraint against killing someone who is a nonthreat. We have to ask, then: "Would Alexandra violate this constraint if she were to shoot Apollyon at t?" See Figure 7.1.

Unfortunately, there's no clear answer to this question. Alexandra would violate this constraint by shooting Apollyon at t if and only if Apollyon is a nonthreat. And he is a nonthreat if and only if his vest isn't an explosive one. The problem is that Alexandra doesn't know whether it is or not.

---

7. In PORTMORE 2011, I provide several other reasons for adopting a teleological approach. Some of these have to do with teleology's ability to give the most plausible account of our practical reasons (see chap. 3) and others have to do with teleology's ability to give the most plausible account of our intuitions concerning the permissibility of infringing upon a constraint in order to minimize one's own infringements upon that constraint (see chap. 4, especially §4.3).

8. Recall that the evidential probability that p for a given subject is the degree to which her body of evidence supports the proposition that p.

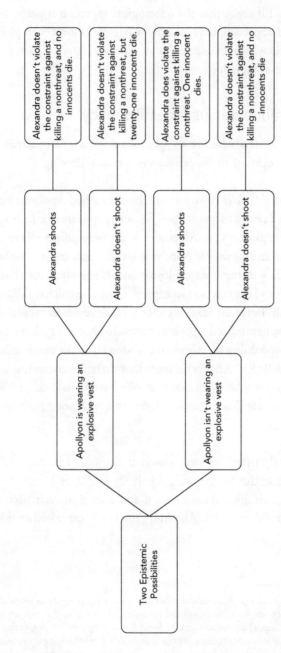

FIGURE 7.1 *The Questionable Vest*

Nevertheless, the vest either is or isn't an explosive one. So there's an answer to this question; it's just that Alexandra doesn't know what it is.

In *The Questionable Vest*, then, there is a determinate answer concerning whether Alexandra's shooting Apollyon at *t* would constitute a constraint-violation. So there is a determinate answer concerning whether her shooting him at *t* would be a sufficiently good (and, thus, objectively permissible) option. It's just that the answer is unknown to those of us who are ignorant of whether Apollyon's vest is an explosive one or not. Thus, this sort of case (which I'll call a *case of ignorance*) poses a problem for neither the normative teleological approach nor the strict nonteleological approach. Both can just say that Alexandra's shooting Apollyon at *t* is sufficiently good only if Apollyon's vest is an explosive one.

But in other types of cases, our uncertainty as to whether an agent's φ-ing would constitute a constraint-violation stems not from our limited knowledge of the world but from something indeterminate about the world itself. These are *cases of indeterminacy*, and there are two subsets of such cases: (1) cases in which the agent has φ-ed and whether this constitutes a constraint-violation depends on whether some event would have occurred had she not φ-ed, and (2) cases in which the agent has not φ-ed and whether her φ-ing would have constituted a constraint-violation depends on whether some event would have occurred had she φ-ed. In the first type of case, the relevant event is the indeterminate act of another agent. I call these *cases of indeterminate agency*, because, in these cases, we are to assume that these acts are not causally determined. Admittedly, it may be that all human acts are, in fact, causally determined. Even so, it's at least possible for there to be acts that are not causally determined, and so a moral theory should be able to assess such acts given that a moral theory is meant to give necessary and sufficient conditions for an act's having various deontic statuses. To illustrate, consider the following.

> *The Questionable Man:* A man named Abaddon has been kidnapped by terrorists, outfitted with an explosive vest, thrown into a crowd of twenty people, and told that unless he uses the trigger mechanism to detonate the vest they're going to kill his brother. In fact, though, they don't have his brother. Shamira knows all this and is the only police officer in the crowd. She has an easy shot at Abaddon. If she takes the shot now (that is, at *t*), only Abaddon will be killed. If she doesn't take the shot now, she could instead try to convince Abaddon that he's being lied to and that he should just give up, but she would thereby

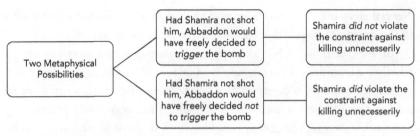

FIGURE 7.2 *The Questionable Man*

risk everyone's being killed. For if she doesn't take the shot at *t* and Abaddon subsequently decides to trigger the vest, everyone will die. Now, Abaddon's behavior is not causally determined. Thus, it is not determined whether he will trigger the vest if he is not shot at *t*. As it happens, though, Shamira shoots Abaddon at *t*. So Abaddon dies, and everyone lives. All we can say, then, is that the objective probability that he would have pulled the trigger (that is, 'P') had he not been killed at *t* (that is, '¬K') is *Obj-Pr*(P|¬K). And let's assume that there is a constraint against killing someone unless doing so is necessary to prevent that someone from killing others.[9] We have to ask, then: "Did Shamira violate this constraint in shooting Abaddon at *t*?" See Figure 7.2.

Again, there's no clear answer to the question. But, in this case, that lack of clarity isn't due to our ignorance. In this case, the relevant sort of probability is objective, not evidential. And, in contrast to evidential probability, objective probability is both mind- and subject-independent. The objective probability that some event will (or would) occur is the percentage of time that that event will (or would) occur under identical causal circumstances— circumstances where the causal laws and histories are exactly the same. Thus, if the laws of nature are deterministic, the objective probability that any event will occur given a certain causal history is always either 0 or 1. However, if the laws of nature are indeterministic, then there will be at least one possible

9. I'm assuming (as you should—at least, for the sake of argument) that, since Abaddon was outfitted with the vest and thrown into the crowd against his will, he hasn't forfeited his right not to be killed unnecessarily. Also, it's important to note that, for my purposes, you needn't agree that there is a constraint against killing someone unless doing so is actually necessary to prevent that someone from killing others or that this is the only constraint that's relevant with respect to assessing Shamira's action. For my point is only to illustrate certain challenges that arise given certain views about what the relevant constraints are.

event such that the objective probability of its occurrence lies somewhere between 0 and 1. Assume, then, that the objective probability that Abaddon would have pulled the trigger had he not been shot and killed at t—that is, $Obj\text{-}Pr(P|\neg K)$—lies somewhere between 0 and 1.[10] So, in this case, it is not merely that we do not know whether Shamira's shooting Abaddon at t saved the twenty. Rather, it's that there is no fact of the matter as to whether it did or not. For there is no fact of the matter as to what Abaddon would have done had he not been shot at t.[11] Thus, we can't say whether, in shooting Abaddon at t, Shamira violated the constraint against killing unnecessarily but only that the objective probability that she did equals: $1 - Obj\text{-}Pr(P|\neg K)$.

Given this indeterminacy regarding whether Shamira's act constituted the violation of a constraint, it's not at all clear what such a constraint-accepting theory (i.e., a theory that holds both that there is such a constraint against killing unnecessarily and that this is the only constraint that's relevant in assessing Shamira's action) should say about the goodness of Shamira's act. Moreover, it's not clear whether it would be better for such a theorist to take a teleological or a nonteleological approach to dealing with this problem. That said, it's clear enough that the strict nonteleological approach won't do. It implies that Shamira's shooting Abaddon at t was sufficiently good only if, in doing so, she did not violate a constraint. But whether she did or not just depends on what Abaddon would have done had he not been shot, and there's just no fact of the matter about this. Thus, the strict nonteleological approach implausibly implies that regardless of what $Obj\text{-}Pr(P|\neg K)$ was, there is no fact of the matter about whether Shamira's shooting Abaddon at t was sufficiently good or not. Yet, if $Obj\text{-}Pr(P|\neg K)$ was sufficiently high (say, greater than 0.99999), it seems clear that Shamira's shooting Abaddon at t was sufficiently

---

10. Buchak (2013B) would deny this. But see Furlong 2017 for a persuasive reply.

11. Consider the following three counterfactuals:

CF_a If Abaddon had not been shot at t, he either would or would not have subsequently triggered the bomb.
CF_b If Abaddon had not been shot at t, he would have subsequently triggered the bomb.
CF_c If Abaddon had not been shot at t, he would not have subsequently triggered the bomb.

On the assumption that Abaddon's behavior is not causally determined, there seems to be nothing about the world that makes either CF_b or CF_c true. Thus, I'm assuming that we should accept something like the Lewis-Stalnaker semantics for counterfactuals, where although CF_a is true, neither CF_b nor CF_c is true. Either they are both false (as they are on Lewis's theory) or they both have indeterminate truth values (as they do on Stalnaker's theory). See Lewis 1973 and Stalnaker 1984. Here, I'm relying on interpretations of Lewis and Stalnaker given in Hare 2011 and Vessel 2003.

good and, thus, objectively permissible. For, in that case, Shamira took only a minuscule risk of violating a constraint in doing something that was exceedingly likely to save twenty lives.

Perhaps, though, there is some alternative nonteleological approach with more plausible implications. In subsequent sections, I'll be considering such alternatives. But before I do, it is important to note that this problem involving indeterminacy arises even if determinism is true. To illustrate, consider the following slightly revised version of a case presented in Chapter 2.

> *Teeing Off 2:* Ka'eo is playing a round of golf and is about to tee off on the second hole when an evil demon presents him with the following dilemma. If he quits the game, refusing to tee off, the demon will do nothing. If he tees off and slices the ball, the demon will kill everyone. If he tees off and doesn't slice the ball, the demon will give everyone a small reward. Although Ka'eo has complete control over whether he tees off, he doesn't, when teeing off, have complete control over whether he slices. Indeed, let's say that the objective probability that he would slice the ball on any given occasion in which he were to tee off is $Obj\text{-}Pr(S|T)$. In the end, though, he chooses not to tee off. Finally, let's assume that there is a constraint against doing what would result in others being killed. We have to ask, then, "Would Ka'eo have violated this constraint had he teed off?"[12]

In cases like this one (and I call these *cases of counterfactual openness*), the reason that there is no fact of the matter as to whether the consequents of the relevant counterfactuals would obtain in the relevant antecedent worlds (an *antecedent world* being a world in which the given antecedent is true) is that their antecedents are underspecified and the subject lacks the ability to further specify the antecedents in a way that would determine whether the consequents would obtain in those antecedent worlds. To illustrate, consider that, in *Teeing Off 2*, the relevant counterfactuals are

CF_1 If Ka'eo had teed off, he would have sliced the ball.
CF_2 If Ka'eo had teed off, he would not have sliced the ball.

---

12. This example is inspired by similar ones in HARE 2011 and VESSEL 2003.

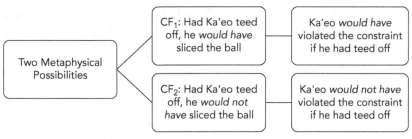

FIGURE 7.3 *Teeing Off 2*

If CF_1 is true, then Ka'eo would have violated the constraint had he teed off. And if CF_2 is true, then Ka'eo would not have violated the constraint had he teed off. See Figure 7.3. But which of these is true? Clearly, they can't both be true. Since they have the same antecedent and logically incompatible consequents, one will be false if the other is true. But which one is true?

Interestingly, it seems that neither is true. Either they're both false or they both have indeterminate truth values. This is because there is no fact of the matter as to whether Ka'eo would have sliced the ball had he teed off. To accept this, we don't need to assume indeterminism. Nor do we need to hold that there is more than just one actual future. We need to accept only both that (1) the antecedents in CF_1 and CF_2 are underspecified given that there are many ways for Ka'eo to tee off (only some of which would result in his slicing the ball) and that (2) Ka'eo lacks complete control over whether or not he tees off in a way that results in his not slicing the ball.[13]

Of course, all this is compatible with both of the following being true.

CF_3 If Ka'eo had teed off by hitting the ball with a 10.9° launch angle, a 2.501° closed clubface angle, a 0.102° out-to-in club-path, and an angular velocity of 15.011 radians per second, he would have sliced the ball.

---

13. I am assuming the contrapositive of the principle that "S is required to φ" implies "S has (complete) control over whether or not she φs"—that is, I'm assuming that if an agent does not have complete control over whether or not she φs, then she cannot be required to φ (or not to φ). She can, at most, be required to *try* to φ (or not to φ)—see Chapter 3. And I'm also assuming that it is implausible to treat this case in the way that epistemicists treat vagueness, claiming that there are some unknown features of this context that determine the relevant dimensions of similarity according to which the world in which Ka'eo tees off and slices the ball is closer to the actual world than any world in which he tees off and doesn't slice the ball (or vice versa). See HARE 2011 (n. 6).

CF$_4$ If Ka'eo had teed off by hitting the ball with a 10.8° launch angle, a 2.489° closed clubface angle, a 0.099° out-to-in club-path, and an angular velocity of 14.998 radians per second, he would not have sliced the ball.

Ka'eo lacks the ability to determine whether he slices the ball. For whether he slices the ball depends on very minute differences with respect to the club-path, launch angle, clubface angle, and angular velocity with which he hits the ball, and he doesn't have the ability to determine these factors with anywhere near the degree of precision necessary to ensure that he doesn't slice the ball. So we can't say whether, had he teed off, he would have violated the constraint. All we can say is that the objective probability that, had he teed off, he would have hit the ball in one of the precise ways that would have resulted in his slicing the ball is *Obj-Pr*(S|T). Just as with *The Questionable Man*, this is a case where our uncertainty about whether an agent's φ-ing would have constituted a constraint-violation is not the result of our failure to know some relevant fact, but is, rather, the result of there being no fact of the matter for us to know.

§7.3 Indeterminacy and Subjective Rightness

Unfortunately, nonteleologists have so far ignored the problem that cases of indeterminacy pose for something like the strict nonteleological approach; they've done so simply because they've failed to consider such cases. Consequently, they've been content to stick with approaches such as the strict nonteleological approach when it comes to giving an account of whether an option is sufficiently good and, thus, objectively permissible. Of course, a number of nonteleologists (e.g., ABOODI ET AL. 2008, ALEXANDER 2016, ISAACS 2014, LAZAR 2018, and SPECTOR 2016) have considered cases of ignorance and have, therefore, realized that they need to supplement their account of objective permissibility with an account of subjective permissibility.[14] For,

---

14. These nonteleologists call themselves deontologists, but, unlike me, they take deontology to be incompatible with teleology. More important, they all seem to deny that how a subject's options rank in terms of their goodness ultimately depends on how their outcomes (or prospects) rank on some preference ordering. Thus, they are all nonteleologists, as I define the term. And I hope to convince these self-professed deontologists that they must embrace teleology if they want to endorse a constraint-accepting theory that can adequately deal with cases of indeterminacy. What's more, I hope to convince them that they can embrace teleology while also accepting the deontological idea that constraints are grounded in our duty to respect the rational, autonomous choices of others.

as cases of ignorance illustrate, an option that is sufficiently good (and, thus, objectively permissible) can be an insufficiently good bet (and, thus, subjectively impermissible).[15] For instance, suppose that in *The Questionable Vest*, the evidential probability (for Alexandra) that Apollyon's vest is an explosive one is extremely high. In that case, shooting him could be a good bet and, thus, subjectively permissible even if it turns out that his vest is not an explosive one, making it objectively impermissible to shoot him.

Given that nonteleologists have developed sophisticated accounts of subjective permissibility in order to deal with cases of ignorance, we may wonder whether these accounts of subjective permissibility might somehow be adapted to give accounts of objective permissibility that can, unlike the strict nonteleological view, adequately deal with cases of indeterminacy. I will argue that they can't. As I'll show presently, the two best proffered nonteleological strategies for determining the subjective permissibility of an act that subjectively risks a constraint-violation are ill-equipped to handle cases of indeterminacy.[16] These two are Yoaav Isaac's knowledge approach and Seth Lazar's decision-theoretic approach.

I'll start with the former.

The Knowledge Nonteleological Approach

For any subject S and any option of hers φ,

(1) S's φ-ing is a sufficiently good bet (and, thus, subjectively permissible) only if she knows that she would not violate a constraint by φ-ing.

---

15. An option is a *sufficiently good bet* for a subject if and only if it is what a conscientious person of her abilities, capacities, and epistemic position might do in her circumstances and it is what she would do in her circumstances if this option were her only sufficiently good bet, where a *conscientious person* is a person who is appropriately concerned with whatever ultimately matters.

16. Recall that whereas a maximal option is objectively permissible if and only if it is a sufficiently good option, a maximal option is subjectively permissible if and only if it is a sufficiently good bet. And note that although I think that these are the two best proffered nonteleological strategies for determining subjective permissibility, I don't think that either is adequate—at least, not as an account of subjective permissibility, as I've defined it. As I've defined it, the following is a conceptual truth: if a subject believes that she is subjectively permitted to φ, then she is subjectively permitted to intend to φ. But since neither of these views accounts for the fact that a subject can be uncertain about what her options are, these views will, in certain cases, imply that a subject is subjectively permitted to φ even though she is not subjectively permitted to intend to φ given that she doesn't believe that she has the option of φ-ing. Nevertheless, whether their accounts are plausible accounts of subjective permissibility doesn't matter for my purposes. For I'm concerned only with whether there might be some way to adapt them so as to provide plausible accounts of objective permissibility.

(2) Assuming that she doesn't know that she would not violate a constraint by φ-ing, how bad a bet her φ-ing is will be directly proportional to how far below the threshold required for knowledge her level of confidence actually is (Isaacs 2014, p. 104).[17]

Admittedly, this approach is well-equipped to deal with cases such as *The Questionable Vest*. On this approach, whether Alexandra's shooting Apollyon is a sufficiently good bet depends (in part) on whether she knows that the vest is an explosive one. If, on the one hand, she does, then it may be a sufficiently good bet and, so, subjectively permissible.[18] If, on the other hand, she doesn't, it's an insufficiently good bet, so it is subjectively impermissible. And since one can be less than 100 percent certain that p and still know that p, whether Alexandra is subjectively permitted to shoot him depends on whether her credence that the vest is an explosive one is sufficiently high for her to know that it's an explosive one. Thus, we get a nonarbitrary and relatively high threshold for the subjective permissibility of her shooting him. And that all seems quite plausible.

But in cases of indeterminacy as opposed to cases of ignorance (cases such as *The Questionable Man* as opposed to *The Questionable Vest*), it's impossible for the agent to ever know that her φ-ing would not constitute a constraint-violation. This is because in such cases it is never true that her φ-ing would not constitute a constraint-violation (the proposition that her φ-ing would not constitute a constraint-violation is, in such a case, always either false or of an indeterminate truth value), and knowledge that p requires that p be true. This means that the knowledge approach implies that it's always subjectively impermissible for an agent to φ in such a case. And this is highly counterintuitive. To illustrate, consider that, in *The Questionable Man*, the knowledge approach implies that even if Shamira knew that the objective probability that Abaddon would trigger the vest (killing the twenty) if she didn't shoot him at

---

17. Isaacs doesn't exactly endorse this approach, as he is not committed to a constraint-accepting theory. He argues only that this is the best approach for a constraint-accepting theorist to take. Also, Isaacs's account doesn't include clause 2. For he doesn't say how to determine how bad a subjectively impermissible option is. Nevertheless, clause 2 seems a natural extension of his account.

18. One attraction of this approach is that it doesn't require Alexandra to be certain that Apollyon's vest is an explosive one in order to be subjectively justified in shooting him, for, plausibly, knowledge doesn't require certainty.

t was 0.99999, it was still subjectively impermissible for her to have shot him at *t*.[19] And this is quite implausible.

Isaacs assumes that it is "fairly easy to see what a [constraint-accepting theory] ... demands of an omniscient agent" (2014, p. 95). But if cases such as *The Questionable Man* and *Teeing Off 2* are coherent, this assumption is mistaken. For in such cases, there is just no fact of the matter as to whether the agent would violate a constraint by φ-ing. And adding that the agent is omniscient is of no help when whether her φ-ing would constitute a constraint-violation is unknowable. What's more, this assumption leads Isaacs to adopt the knowledge approach, which, we've seen, counterintuitively implies that it is always subjectively impermissible to take an objective risk of violating a constraint, no matter how small that risk.

Perhaps, though, Seth Lazar's approach will fare better. His approach is as follows.

The Decision-Theoretic Nonteleological Approach

Let's stipulate that the expected deontic utility of a subject's φ-ing is a probability distribution consisting in the set of mutually exclusive and jointly exhaustive possibilities concerning the determinate degree of goodness/badness that her φ-ing would have on each possibly correct nonteleological account of objective rightness, with each possibility assigned an epistemic probability such that the sum of those probabilities equals 1.

Now, for any subject S and any option of hers φ,

(1) S's φ-ing is a sufficiently good bet (and, thus, subjectively permissible) if her φ-ing would maximize expected deontic utility.

(2) Assuming that her φ-ing wouldn't maximize expected deontic utility, how bad a bet her φ-ing is, other things being equal, directly proportional to how big the difference is between the amount of expected deontic utility associated with it and the amount of expected deontic utility associated with an optimal alternative (LAZAR 2018).[20]

---

19. Given the indeterminacy involved, it is not true that Abaddon would have triggered the vest if Shamira hadn't shot him at *t*. Nonetheless, it is, we'll suppose, true that the objective probability that he would have triggered the vest if she hadn't shot him at *t* was 0.99999.

20. Lazar's account doesn't include the second clause. For he doesn't say how to determine how bad a bet a given subjectively impermissible option is. Nevertheless, this clause seems to be a natural extension of his account. Also, I use the term "deontic utility" instead of his term "moral

Here, it's important to note both that some objectively permissible acts are better than others—for instance, saving two people is, other things being equal, better than saving just one even if both are sufficiently good. Also, some objectively impermissible acts are worse than others—for instance, murdering a child is, other things being equal, worse than telling an inconsequential lie even if both are insufficiently good. With this in mind, I can illustrate how the approach works using *The Questionable Vest*. And, to keep things simple, let's assume that the strict nonteleological approach is the correct nonteleological account of objective rightness, and that, on this account, Alexandra's failing to shoot Apollyon at t has a determinate degree of goodness of 0 if the vest is not an explosive one and a determinate degree of badness of -10 if it is. Further assume that her shooting him at t has a determinate degree of badness of -18 if the vest is not an explosive one and a determinate degree of goodness of $+10$ if it is. Last, assume both that the evidential probability (for her) that the vest is an explosive one is 0.8 and that the evidential probability (for her) that the vest is not an explosive one is 0.2. So the expected deontic utility of her failing to shoot him at t is $(0.2 \times 0) + (0.8 \times -10) = -8$. And the expected deontic utility of her shooting him at t is $(0.2 \times -18) + (0.8 \times 10) = -1$. Thus, she did the subjectively right thing in shooting him at t.

What allows for this approach to be nonteleological is that the term "deontic utility" is being used simply as a formal construct for representing an interval ranking of options in terms of their determinate degrees of goodness/badness on the correct account of objective rightness. As he puts it, "The order of explanation runs like this: the objective right determines the objective 'good', the probability-weighted expectation of which determines the subjective right. So, the right remains prior to the good" (LAZAR 2018). So, if what determines the subjective permissibility of a subject's options are their comparative expected deontic utilities, and what determines their comparative expected deontic utilities is a probability distribution over the various possible determinate degrees of goodness/badness each could have, then the approach is nonteleological so long as the assessment of an option's degree of goodness/badness is itself nonteleological. And it will be nonteleological so long as it denies what all teleological theories accept: that every option has its degree of goodness/badness solely and ultimately in virtue of how its prospect ranks

---

utility," but the terms refer to the same thing: the degree to which an option is good/bad on the correct nonteleological account of objective permissibility. Larry Alexander (2016) and Horacio Spector (2016) also suggest that nonteleologists should take a decision-theoretic approach to subjective permissibility, but I focus on Lazar's account since it seems the most developed.

in comparison to those of its alternatives on some preference ordering.[21] So, whereas a nonteleological theory might hold that how bad your φ-ing solely and ultimately depends on how important the constraint that it violates is, a teleological theory would instead hold that how bad your φ-ing is depends solely and ultimately on how its prospect ranks in comparison to those of its alternatives on some preference ordering. So, provided Lazar adopts a nonteleological account of the goodness/badness of an option (such as the strict nonteleological approach), his approach will be nonteleological.

To keep his approach nonteleological, Lazar must assume that we can give a plausible account of an act's degree of goodness/badness without appeal to how its prospect ranks in comparison to those of its alternatives. And if Lazar could adopt something like the strict nonteleological approach, that wouldn't be a problem. But, as we've seen, the strict nonteleological approach is untenable because it cannot adequately deal with cases of indeterminacy. So the nonteleologist must hope to find some more plausible account of the goodness/badness of options that doesn't appeal to their prospects. But, as I'll argue in the next two sections, this can't be done if there is even the possibility of indeterminacy with respect to whether certain acts constitute constraint-violations. And this is, I'll argue, entirely possible.[22] So, if I'm right, it just isn't plausible to combine a decision-theoretic approach to subjective permissibility with a nonteleological approach to objective permissibility. I'll argue that we should instead combine a decision-theoretic approach to subjective permissibility with a decision-theoretic approach to objective permissibility, ending up with a teleological theory.

---

21. Here, I follow people like Alexander and Moore (2015) in the way that I distinguish nonteleological theories from teleological (or consequentialist) theories. They write: "Non-teleological theories are best understood in contrast to consequentialist [or teleological] ones. Consequentialists hold that choices—acts and/or intentions—are to be morally assessed solely by the states of affairs they bring about. . . . In contrast, . . . non-teleological theories judge the morality of choices by criteria different from the states of affairs those choices bring about." See also PORTMORE 2011 (p. 34), where I write: "Consequentialism [or teleology] is the view that an act's deontic status is determined by how its outcome [or prospect] ranks relative to those of the available alternatives on some evaluative ranking."

22. Thus, it's important to note that my argument doesn't depend on the metaphysical claim that there is indeterminacy in the actual world. Rather, my argument depends only on the modal claim that there are possible worlds in which there is indeterminacy with respect to whether certain possible acts violate certain possible constraints. And such possible worlds are, I believe, relevant in assessing accounts of what the fundamental right- and wrong-makers are. For such accounts are supposed to tell us what would make an act right or wrong, not only in our actual world but also in any possible world. Perhaps, Lazar disagrees given what he says in note 26 of LAZAR 2018.

§7.4 Indeterminacy and Objective Rightness

We can't assume that we won't have to deal with uncertainty when it comes to giving an account of objective permissibility.[23] For uncertainty stems not only from our ignorance of the world but also from the possibility that the world is itself indeterminate. Thus, our theories of objective rightness must be prepared to handle cases of indeterminacy. In this and the next section, I argue that teleological theories of objective rightness can more plausibly deal with such cases than their nonteleological counterparts can.

Perhaps, the simplest way for the nonteleologist to deal with the possibility of indeterminacy is to take the following approach.

The Obstinate Nonteleological Approach: For any subject S and any option of hers φ, if there is no fact of the matter as to whether, by φ-ing, S violated a constraint, then there was neither a fact of the matter as to whether S's φ-ing was sufficiently good (at least assuming that there was nothing else that was sufficient to make S's φ-ing insufficiently good) nor a fact of the matter as to how good/bad her φ-ing was either.

But this approach has counterintuitive implications. To illustrate, suppose again that in *The Questionable Man*, the objective probability that Abaddon would have triggered the vest had he not been shot at t was 0.99999. In that case, it seems quite counterintuitive to deny that Shamira did the objectively right thing in shooting him at t, for not doing so would have been far too risky (objectively risky, that is). Yet, on the obstinate approach, we must deny that what Shamira did was objectively permissible. We must hold instead that there is just no fact of the matter as to whether what she did was objectively permissible. This seems unacceptable.[24]

---

23. Larry Alexander makes this assumption in attempting to deal with cases where the agent risks violating a constraint. He (2016) writes: "The realm of 'risk' is the realm of belief and culpability. The realm of facts is the realm of moral permissibility and impermissibility." But, as I argue, he is wrong to assume that risk/uncertainty is only in our minds and not also in the world itself. In some cases, there is no fact about whether an agent would have violated a constraint had she φ-ed; there is only a certain objective probability (lying between zero and one) that she would have.

24. Note that in cases of indeterminacy such as *The Questionable Man*, there is at least a fact of the matter regarding the objective probability that there was a constraint violation even if there is no fact of the matter regarding whether there was a constraint violation. But there are also *cases of vagueness*—cases where it's borderline whether a constraint was violated. To illustrate, imagine that it's borderline whether you violated the constraint against breaking promises by

The lesson, I take it, is that in many cases of indeterminacy whether it is objectively permissible for S to φ depends on the objective probability that S would, by φ-ing, violate a constraint. If the objective probability is sufficiently high, it will be objectively impermissible for S to φ. But if it is sufficiently low, it will be objectively permissible for S to φ. Of course, this leaves open the question of just how high or low the objective probability of violating a constraint needs to be for it to be permissible for S to φ. Perhaps it should be no greater than zero. If so, the nonteleologist should adopt the following approach.

The Zero-Risk Nonteleological Approach

For any subject S and any option of hers φ,

(1) S's φ-ing was sufficiently good only if the objective probability that, by φ-ing, she violated a constraint was no greater than 0.

(2) How good/bad her φ-ing was is directly proportional to how low/high the objective probability was that, by φ-ing, she would violate a constraint.

This is not an absolutist view. For one *violates* (as opposed to merely *infringes upon*) a constraint against performing instances of a certain act-type by φ-ing if and only if φ is an instance of that act-type that fails to satisfy the applicable thresholds (THOMSON 1986, p. 51).[25] Thus, if there is a constraint against breaking a promise that permits doing so in order to produce at least *n* amount of good, then one violates this constraint only if one breaks a promise without producing at least that much good. But even if not absolutist, the view is still too restrictive. Suppose again that, in *The Questionable Man*, the objective probability that Abaddon would have triggered the vest had he not

φ-ing. Perhaps the constraint against breaking promises has an imprecise threshold and your φ-ing lies within this imprecise threshold region. Or, perhaps, your words were vague or ambiguous and so it's unclear whether you must refrain from φ-ing in order to fulfill your promise. Or, perhaps, your level of intoxication when you made the promise was neither clearly high enough to prevent your words from being binding nor clearly low enough to make your words binding. Assuming, then, that we should not be moral epistemicists about such cases (and see J. R. G. WILLIAMS 2016 for significant worries concerning moral epistemicism), we may have to concede that there is neither a fact of the matter regarding whether you violated the constraint against breaking promises by φ-ing nor a fact of the matter regarding what the objective probability was that you violated the constraint against breaking promises by φ-ing. And if that's right, perhaps we should say that there is just no fact of the matter as to whether your φ-ing was sufficiently good. Still, we should definitely not say this about cases of indeterminacy, as I've shown above.

25. One infringes upon a constraint against performing instances of a certain act-type by φ-ing if and only if φ is an instance of that act-type.

been shot at t was 0.99999. In that case, the objective probability that, by shooting Abaddon at t, Shamira violated the constraint against killing unnecessarily was very low: 0.00001. Yet, because this very low number is greater than 0, the zero-risk nonteleological approach implies that her act was objectively impermissible. This is implausible. When enough is at stake, a very small objective risk of violating a constraint will be worth taking. The problem with the zero-risk nonteleological approach, then, is that it implausibly insists that no such objective risk is ever worth taking.[26]

The lesson is that the objective probability that S's φ-ing would violate a constraint needs to be higher than zero. Perhaps, then, the nonteleologist should replace the zero-risk nonteleological approach with the following.

The Nonindividualistic Nonteleological Approach
For any subject S and any option of hers φ,

(1) S's φ-ing was sufficiently good only if the objective probability that, by φ-ing, S violated a constraint was no greater than T ($0 < T \leq 1$).
(2) How good/bad her φ-ing was is directly proportional to how far below/above T that objective probability was.

But consider that constraints are often grounded in rights. For instance, corresponding to the constraint against killing a person unnecessarily is that person's right not to be killed unnecessarily. And it seems that individuals, not the mere mereological sums of individuals, are the bearers of rights. This suggests that there is a problem with the above approach, for it counterintuitively implies that what's morally relevant is whether S's φ-ing has a greater than T chance of violating someone or other's rights rather than whether S's φ-ing imposes a greater than T chance on some individual that her rights will be violated. To illustrate the problem, consider what I'll call *Two Questionable Men*, which is exactly like *The Questionable Man* except that, in this case, Abaddon has a partner, Chesed, who can also trigger the vest. In this case, assume that Shamira can kill both (thereby neutralizing the threat that each of them poses to the twenty) by firing a single shot at a certain angle at t that will pass through Abaddon and then hit Chesed. Assume that with respect to each of Abaddon and Chesed, the objective probability that killing him is unnecessary to prevent him from killing the twenty is 0.02. Last, assume that

---

26. For a more detailed discussion of this and other problems with the zero-risk approach, see HUEMER 2010.

T equals 0.03. So the probability that Shamira's firing the shot would violate someone or other's right is the probability that it would violate Abaddon's right plus the probability that it would violate Chesed's right minus the probability that it would violate both of their rights—that is, $[0.02 + 0.02 - (0.02 \times 0.02)] = 0.036$.[27] Since 0.036 is greater than T (which is 0.03), this approach implies that it was wrong for Shamira to have fired the shot.[28] But given that individuals, not the mere mereological sums of individuals, are the bearers of rights, it seems that what matters is the sort of risk of a rights-violation the agent imposed on each individual, not the sort of risk of a rights-violation the agent "imposed" on some mereological sum of individuals. Thus, it seems that if the relevant threshold is at 0.03, it should, contrary to what this approach implies, be permissible for Shamira to take the shot.

The lesson, here, is that nonteleologists should take a more individualistic approach (ABOODI ET AL. 2008), such as the following.

The Individualistic Nonteleological Approach
For any subject S and any option of hers φ,

(1) S's φ-ing was sufficiently good only if there was no one such that the objective probability that she violated a constraint against treating that person a certain way by φ-ing was greater than T ($0 < T \leq 1$).
(2) How good/bad her φ-ing was is directly proportional to how far above/ below T that objective probability was.

The problem with this view lies with its fixed threshold. For it seems that how averse we should be to risking the violation of a particular constraint depends on how important that constraint is. And not all constraints are equally important. For it is not as important to avoid risking the violation of a constraint against breaking a relatively trivial promise as it is to avoid risking the violation of a constraint against killing an innocent person. Thus,

---

27. I'm assuming that Abaddon's and Chesed's propensities are uncorrelated.

28. Although, as we've just seen, this approach implies that it is impermissible for Shamira to fire one shot that would kill both Abaddon and Chesed, it implies that it is permissible for Shamira to fire two shots—one at Abaddon (at an angle that won't hit Chesed after passing through Abaddon) and one at Chesed—and thereby kill them each with a separate shot. Since, in the two-shot case, each act of taking a shot has only a 0.02 chance of violating someone or other's rights, each act would be permissible. Now, the fact that this approach implies that whether it is permissible for Shamira to kill both Abaddon and Chesed depends on whether she uses one or two shots to do so seems unacceptable. For more on this, see JACKSON & SMITH 2006 (pp. 275–278).

it's implausible to have one threshold of risk for each and every type of constraint. Instead, we need a sliding risk-threshold that adjusts depending on how important the constraint in question is. Thus, the nonteleologist should, it seems, adopt something like the following instead.

> **The Sliding Risk-Threshold Nonyeleological Approach:** For any subject S and any option of hers φ, S's φ-ing was (or would have been) sufficiently good only if there was no one such that the objective probability that S violated (or would have violated) a constraint of a degree of importance D_n (D_n ranging from 0 to 10) against treating that person a certain way by φ-ing was greater than T_n (T_n ranging from 0 to 1), where T_n is inversely proportional to D_n such that, as D_n increases, T_n decreases.[29]

On this view, if a constraint is very important (with, say, a D_n of 9.0), then the objective probability that S would have violated it by φ-ing must be very low—perhaps, lower than 0.01—for S's φ-ing to have been objectively permissible. But if a constraint is not very important (with, say, a D_n of 1.0), then the objective probability that S would have violated it by φ-ing need be only somewhat low—perhaps, just lower than 0.05—for S's φ-ing to have been objectively permissible.

This approach has at least two problems. One problem is that it has counterintuitive implications, because it doesn't account for the fact that how many people will be subject to a given risk is morally relevant. For instance, it can be permissible to impose a tiny risk on just one person, but impermissible to impose that same small risk on a billion people. Yet, this approach denies this. It implies that if T_n is 0.01 for the constraint against killing, then just as it would be permissible to take a 1 percent chance of killing a single person, it would likewise be permissible to take a 1 percent chance of killing a billion people.[30] This is quite implausible.

Another problem with this approach is that it seems arbitrary. To illustrate, suppose that the advocates of this approach insist that T_n is 0.01 for the constraint against killing. We should ask them, Why is the threshold at

---

29. This sort of approach has been suggested by Kagan (1989, p. 89). See also Thomson's discussion of risk in her 1990. (Note that I leave out a clause about what, on this view, determines how good or bad an option is both because I'm uncertain about how best to do so on such an approach, and because what I'm going to say about the view doesn't hang on this.)

30. This point has been made both by Huemer (2010, pp. 345–347) and Sobel (2012, p. 52).

1 percent and not at either 1.01 percent or 0.99 percent? Now, the most natural answer is that it's because 1 percent is the tipping point where increasing the percentage by any amount tips the balance of reasons from being in favor of taking the risk (and, thus, φ-ing) to being in favor of not taking the risk (and, thus, not φ-ing). But, for this explanation to work, the reasons for φ-ing and not φ-ing must be commensurable. And although we can certainly take them to be commensurable on a teleological view, it's not clear that we can do so on a nonteleological view. On a teleological view, the reasons for φ-ing and the reasons for not φ-ing both have to do with the desirability of their prospects; so, presumably, they're commensurable in terms of this. But, on a nonteleological view, only the reasons for φ-ing (those having to do with the chance that φ-ing has of doing good) have to do with the desirability of its prospect. The reasons for not φ-ing (those having to do with the chance that φ-ing would result in a constraint-violation) have to do with the kind of dignity or inviolability that the potential victim has, which is meant to be above all price in the sense of being incommensurable with the desirability of prospects. And if it isn't above all price, then it's unclear what would make it a nonteleological view rather than a teleological view that ranks all prospects in terms of their expected price. Given all this, it's not clear how the nonteleologist can claim that the 1 percent threshold marks the tipping point where the weight of the reasons for preferring the prospect of φ-ing exactly balances out with the weight of the reasons for not risking a constraint-violation against a potential victim with a certain moral status. If they're incommensurable, they can't balance each other out. It seems, then, that the above approach is unacceptably arbitrary.[31]

So, we've seen that given the indeterminacy in our world, the nonteleologist needs to deal with uncertainties even when it comes to providing an account of objective rightness. And the problem is that there are many disparate factors to consider in determining objective rightness, and it's not clear how we're supposed to weigh each against the other when many of these factors seem to be incommensurable on a nonteleological view. There's the probability that S's φ-ing will be an instance of a certain constrained act-type (for instance, an instance of unnecessary killing). There's the probability that S's φ-ing will produce more than n amount of good. There's the probability that S's φ-ing will impose a greater than n risk of harm on any one person. And there's the probability that S's φ-ing will impose a certain risk on more than n people.

---

31. I borrow this sort of argument from ELLIS 1992. See also ALEXANDER 2000.

Unlike the teleologist, the nonteleologist denies that we can just assign a certain degree of desirability to each of these factors and then rank the actions in terms of their overall desirability—that is, their price. So it's unclear how the nonteleologist can take all these factors into account.

Perhaps, though, the solution for the nonteleologist is to have an absolute constraint against performing act-types while embedding all the relevant factors/thresholds within the description of the act-type itself. That way, she can maintain that there are just certain ways in which people cannot be treated and that the constraints themselves specify what these ways are. It would, then, just be a brute fact about people that they have the sort of status that, say, constrains us from killing them for the sake of saving fewer than n lives but not for the sake of saving n or more lives (see, e.g., KAMM 2007). Thus, the nonteleologist can avoid having to weigh these competing factors against each other by adopting the following approach.

The Embedded Version of the Strict Nonteleological Approach:
For any subject S and any option of hers φ, S's φ-ing is insufficiently good (and, thus, objectively impermissible) if, in φ-ing, she would infringe upon a constraint, where each constraint C_n prohibits the performance of some very specific kind of act K_n such that an act counts as an instance of K_n if and only if there is a greater than T_i chance of its being an instance of a certain type of act (for instance, an instance of an unnecessary killing), a less than T_j chance of its producing at least n amount of good, a greater than T_k chance of harming any individual, a less than T_l chance of harming n or more individuals, etc.

To my mind, this approach is problematically ad hoc. Of course, others may feel differently. But even those others should concede that the following will be problematically ad hoc. Imagine, then, that I could have φ-ed and that the following two embedded constraints seem to be the only relevant constraints:

C_1 For any subject S and any option of hers φ, S's φ-ing is insufficiently good (and, thus, objectively impermissible) if there is a greater than a 5 percent chance that φ would be an instance of K_1 that has less than a 100 percent chance of producing at least 100 units of goodness.

C_2 For any subject S and any option of hers φ, S's φ-ing is insufficiently good (and, thus, objectively impermissible) if there is a greater than a 5 percent chance that φ would be an instance of K_2 that has less than a 100 percent chance of producing at least 100 units of goodness.

And let's assume that performing an instance of K_1 is, other things being equal, just as bad as performing an instance of K_2—which is what explains why they have the same threshold of being wrong unless they have a 100 percent chance of producing at least 100 units of goodness. Further suppose that my *x*-ing would produce 100 units of goodness, has a 4.9 percent chance of being an instance of both K_1 and K_2, and has a 95.1 percent chance of being an instance of neither K_1 nor K_2. Thus, in *x*-ing, I would be taking less than a 5 percent chance of violating either C_1 or C_2 (which are the constraints against performing instances of K_1 and K_2, respectively). So, according to the embedded approach, it is objectively permissible for me to *x*. But this is counterintuitive. If it would be wrong for me to take a 5 percent chance of infringing on just one of two equally important constraints, then it should also be wrong to take a slightly smaller chance (that is, a 4.9 percent chance) of infringing upon them *both*. After all, it would seem that infringing on them both would be twice as bad as infringing on just one of the two, and so not worth the risk even if it's a slightly reduced risk. The problem with the embedded approach, then, is that it holds that the threshold for the permissibility of an act that risks violating a constraint is the same whether the act carries the risk of violating one or two equally important constraints.

To avoid such counterintuitive implications, the embedded approach will need to deny that C_1 and C_2 are the only relevant constraints and claim that there is the following meta-constraint.

mC_1 For any subject S and any option of hers φ, S's φ-ing is insufficiently good (and, thus, objectively impermissible) if there is a greater than a 2.5 percent chance that φ is an instance of both K_1 and K_2 that has less than a 100 percent chance of producing at least 100 units of goodness.

But now, it seems likely that mC_1 won't be the only meta-constraint, for we'll need a meta-constraint for each pair of equally important constraints. For instance, we'll need to consider the possibility that my *x*-ing has a

2.4 percent chance of violating both mC_1 and some other equally important meta-constraint: mC_2. And we'll need a *meta*–meta-constraint (i.e., m^2C_1) to tell us when we are permitted to take such a chance. Moreover, we'll need a meta-meta-meta-constraint (i.e., m^3C_1) to tell us when we are permitted to take a chance on violating two equally important meta-meta-constraints. And so on and so forth. Surely, postulating such levels upon levels of meta-constraints is problematically ad hoc.

To sum up, then, we've seen that to avoid counteractive implications, the nonteleologist must make many complex and seemingly ad hoc moves. And I see no reason to adopt such a complex and seemingly ad hoc approach, when there is clearly a simpler and non–ad-hoc approach to accounting for our intuitions about when it is objectively permissible to risk violating a constraint. That approach is, I'll argue in the next section, a teleological one. Moreover, it is one that is compatible with the deontological idea that constraints are ultimately grounded in our duty to respect people and their capacity for rational, autonomous decision making. So I see no reason to settle for an ad hoc nonteleological approach.

§7.5 A Teleological Approach

I've argued that the correct moral theory is going to be teleological. More formally, the argument has been as follows.

(7.1) There is a type of act X such that, for any subject S, there is a constraint against S's X-ing. [Assumption]

(7.2) There is a possible world in which a particular subject S_1 performs a particular act X_1 and there is just no fact of the matter as to whether she violated the constraint against X-ing in performing X_1. [Assumption based on the coherence of cases such as *The Questionable Man* and *Teeing Off 2*]

(7.3) The correct moral theory must provide us with a criterion of objective rightness that tells us what determines whether S_1 was objectively wrong in performing X_1. [Assumption]

(7.4) Such a criterion must hold that what determines whether S_1 was objectively wrong in performing X_1 is either ($Poss_1$) whether the prospect of S_1's X_1-ing was outranked by that of her performing some alternative on the relevant preference ordering or ($Poss_2$) whether something else is true. [From the law of excluded middle]

(7.5) If $Poss_1$, then the correct moral theory is teleological. [Analytic]

(7.6) If Poss₂, then the correct moral theory will either be ad hoc or have significant counterintuitive implications. [From the arguments above]

(7.7) The correct moral theory will neither be ad hoc nor have significant counterintuitive implications. [Assumption]

(7.8) Therefore, the correct moral theory is teleological. [From 7.1–7.7]

Of course, many teleologists (such as act-utilitarians) will just deny 7.1. But my argument isn't directed at them. Rather, my argument is directed at those who endorse some constraint-accepting theory and think that they must adopt some nonteleological approach in order to accommodate their deontological intuitions. I've argued that they're mistaken. Indeed, I've argued that the best way to accommodate their deontological intuitions is to adopt a teleological approach to constraints.

What will this teleological approach look like? Well, on perhaps the simplest version of the teleological approach, an option is objectively permissible if and only if it maximizes expected deontic utility, where performing an act of a certain kind (for instance, an act of unnecessary killing) has a certain deontic disutility, performing an act that produces a certain amount of good has a certain deontic utility, performing an act that imposes a specific risk on a certain set of individuals has a certain deontic disutility per individual, etc. But this version of the teleological approach assumes that we should always prefer the option with the greatest expected deontic utility. That is, it assumes that deontic utility is the only thing that ultimately matters and that, consequently, maximizing expected deontic utility is the only thing that derivatively matters. Perhaps, though, avoiding a significant risk of there being a lot of deontic disutility is something that itself ultimately matters. If so, we should perhaps prefer an option with less expected deontic utility if choosing that option ensures that we end up choosing an option with a decent amount of deontic utility and not some option with a lot of deontic disutility.³² In other words, we should perhaps be risk averse and prefer an option with less expected deontic utility if choosing that option ensures that we don't take any substantial risks of a disaster occurring. So, in order to allow for such possibilities, I suggest that we adopt the slightly more complex teleological approach that was given in the opening to this chapter.

---

32. See BUCHAK 2013A for why it may be rational to sometimes prefer a prospect (or gamble) with suboptimal expected utility.

The Normative Teleological Approach

For any subject S and any option of hers φ,

(1) S's φ-ing is objectively/subjectively permissible if and only if she has no alternative option ψ such that she ought to prefer its objective/subjective prospect to that of her φ-ing.

(2) How good or bad φ is as an option/bet is directly proportional to the intensity with which she ought to desire or be averse to its objective/subjective prospect.

(3) She ought, other things being equal, to prefer that she violates as few constraints as possible, that others violate as few constraints as possible, that she and others take as little objective risk of violating a constraint as possible, that the constraints that she and others violate—or even objectively risk violating—are of as little importance as possible, that she doesn't risk disaster for the sake of making things only slightly expectedly better, etc.[33]

This seems to be an attractive approach to dealing with indeterminacy and the problems that nonteleology had with it. Consider, for instance, the ease with which this approach can account for the fact that constraints have thresholds. The teleologist need only claim (and plausibly so) that, at some point, the agent-neutral reason that one has to want a prospect with more pleasure or fewer overall infringements of a constraint outweighs the agent-relative reason that one has to want to avoid infringing upon that constraint oneself. Likewise, this approach can with similar ease account for why some constraints are more stringent than others, such that one can permissibly infringe upon one but not the other in instances where one must violate one or the other. For instance, the teleologist can hold that, other things being equal, one ought to prefer performing an act of one kind to performing an act of some other kind. The teleologist could, for instance, hold that the agent-relative reason that one has to want to avoid committing murder outweighs, other things being equal, the agent-relative reason one has to want to avoid

---

33. The difference between subjective and objective prospects is that whereas the former is calculated in terms of evidential probabilities, the latter is calculated in terms of objective probabilities. As formulated above, this approach will result in a very demanding moral theory, one where agents are never permitted to perform an act with a suboptimal prospect. But see the literature on consequentializing, especially PORTMORE 2011, on how such a teleological approach could be revised to avoid being overly demanding.

breaking a rather trivial promise. This view has no trouble with the idea that taking a risk of infringing upon a billion people's rights is much worse than taking a slightly higher risk of infringing upon just one person's rights. And it can even account for its being permissible to take a slightly greater risk of infringing upon only one of a person's rights while it's being impermissible to take a slightly smaller risk of infringing upon two or more of that same person's rights. Last, it can account for why we shouldn't risk a moral catastrophe merely for the sake of making things slightly expectedly better.

So, when it comes to a case such as *The Questionable Man*, this approach tells us to look both at the objective prospect of Shamira's shooting Abaddon at t (call this P_S) and at the objective prospect of Shamira's refraining from shooting Abaddon at t (call this P_R) and then to determine which one Shamira ought to prefer. On the teleological approach, her shooting him at t was objectively permissible if either she should have preferred P_S to P_R or should have been indifferent between the two. But, if she should have preferred P_R to P_S, then her shooting him at t was objectively impermissible. So we get a very simple and unified approach to accounting for objective rightness in cases of indeterminacy. We just rank the agent's options in terms of her reasons for preferring their prospects and hold that their deontic statuses are a function of this preference ordering.

§7.6 Rationalist Teleological Maximalism

We've seen that constraint-accepting theorists can have a difficult time accounting for the status of a subject's φ-ing when it's unclear whether she violated a constraint in φ-ing. The difficulty arises because there are just so many disparate factors that need to be weighed against each other, and it's unclear how nonteleologists can do so in a way that's neither ad hoc nor arbitrary. They also have difficulty accounting for the fact that we may have reason to be risk averse such that sometimes we should prefer a less risky prospect with less expected deontic utility to a more risky prospect with more expected deontic utility. Now, nonteleologists such as Larry Alexander, Horacio Spector, and Seth Lazar take the solution to this difficulty to lie with our adopting a decision-theoretic approach that appeals to expected deontic utility. And such an approach does indeed seem a promising approach in accounting for subjective permissibility. But these professed nonteleologists can remain nonteleologists while adopting such a decision-theoretic approach to subjective permissibility only if they define the relevant notion of deontic utility in terms of a nonteleological account of objective rightness.

But I've argued that our uncertainty with respect to whether a subject has violated a constraint in φ-ing can stem not only from our limited knowledge of the actual world but also from the indeterminacy that's inherent in certain possible worlds. And this means that constraint-accepting theorists will need to find a way to deal with such uncertainty even when it comes to giving an account of objective rightness. And we find that, again, a difficulty arises, because, again, there are many disparate factors that need to be weighed against each other in determining objective rightness. And, again, a decision-theoretic approach seems to provide a promising solution to this difficulty—one that's neither ad hoc nor arbitrary. But this time we can't remain nonteleological and adopt a decision-theoretic approach, because this time we can't appeal to a nonteleological account of objective rightness in defining the relevant notion of deontic utility if what we're doing is giving an account of objective rightness in terms of expected deontic utility. It seems, then, that the most plausible approach for the constraint-accepting theorist is a teleological one.

So if we want rationalist maximalism to plausibly account for the possibility that our not violating constraints is something that ultimately matters (and I do), then we should adopt a teleological version of rationalist maximalism. In doing so, we needn't give up any of our common-sense intuitions, such as the intuition that it's impermissible for a subject to break a promise even to prevent two others from each breaking comparable promises.[34] And we needn't give up the deontological idea that constraints are ultimately grounded in our duty to respect people and their capacity for rational, autonomous decision making. What's more, we can, I've argued, provide a more unified and systematic account for some of our common-sense intuitions by adopting a teleological theory.

Last, teleology is itself an attractive view. For it is through our actions that we attempt to affect the way the world goes. Whenever we face a choice of what to do, we also face a choice of which of various possible worlds to attempt to actualize. Moreover, whenever we act intentionally, we act with the aim of making the world go a certain way. The aim needn't be anything having to do with the causal consequences of the act. The aim could be nothing more than to bring it about that one performs the act in question. For instance, one could intend to run merely for the sake of bringing it about that one runs. The fact remains, though, that for every intentional action there is some end

---

34. For more on this, see the literature on consequentializing, especially PORTMORE 2011.

at which the agent aims. It's natural, then, to think that the agent ought to act so as to make the world go as she ought to aim for it to go. And if there's no fact of the matter as to whether the world would go this way, then she ought, it seems, to perform the act whose prospect she ought to prefer to that of each of the available alternatives. This very simple and intuitive idea is normative teleology, and it is, I believe, something that every plausible theory about what we ought to do should accommodate. Thus, it's natural to suppose that our practical theories should all take a teleological approach, telling us to perform the option whose prospect we should prefer to that of all the available alternatives.

For all these reasons, I believe that we should accept rationalist teleological maximalism, which is the conjunction of rationalism, maximalism, and the normative teleological theory described above.

CHAPTER 8

Rationalist Teleological Maximalism

RATIONALIST TELEOLOGICAL MAXIMALISM conjoins the following three views.

Rationalism: For any event *e*, any subject S, any time *t*, and any later time *t′*, *e*-ing at *t′* is, as of *t*, an option for S if and only if she has at *t* rational control over whether she will *e* at *t′*.

Normative Teleology: For any subject S and any option that she has as of time *t*, the extent to which φ is good (or bad) ultimately and solely depends on the extent to which she ought, as of *t*, to prefer (or disprefer) its prospect to those of its alternatives given what ultimately matters.[1]

Maximalism: For any maximal option M that a subject S has as of *t*, the deontic status of S's M-ing depends on how M's goodness (or badness) compares to that of the alternative maximal options available to her as of *t*. And, for any nonmaximal option N that S has as of *t*, the deontic status of S's N-ing depends on how the maximal options available to her as of *t* that entail her N-ing compare to those that don't.

In the preceding chapters, I argued for rationalist teleological maximalism by arguing for each of these three views individually. In this chapter, I'll illustrate how these three views operate together to determine the deontic statuses

---

1. This is *normative* teleology given that it holds that the relevant preferences are not those that the subject actually has (or would have in some descriptively defined hypothetical situation) but those that she *ought* to have.

of our options. I'll describe some of rationalist teleological maximalism's main virtues. And I'll explain why it's important to work out the structure of our normative theories.

§8.1 An Illustration of How Rationalist Teleological Maximalism Works

To illustrate how rationalist teleological maximalism ("RTM" for short) works, let's return to the famous case of *Professor Procrastinate*.

> Professor Procrastinate receives an invitation to review a book. He is the best person to do the review, has the time, and so on. The best thing that can happen is that he says yes and then writes the review when the book arrives. However, suppose it is further the case that were Procrastinate to say yes, he would not in fact get around to writing the review. Not because of incapacity or outside interference or anything like that, but because he would keep on putting the task off.... Moreover, we may suppose, [his saying yes and never writing the review] is the worst that can happen. It would lead to the book not being reviewed at all. (JACKSON & PARGETTER 1986, p. 235)

Like all versions of the opting-for-the-best view, RTM holds that for some relevant subset of his options, Professor Procrastinate ought to perform his best option. So it's crucial to determine both what his options are and which subset of them is the relevant one. Given RTM's commitment to rationalism, his options at t_0 (t_0 being the present time—the time just subsequent to his having received the invitation) consist in all and only those events that are at t_0 under his rational control. Thus, whether Professor Procrastinate has at t_0 the option of, say, accepting and writing depends on whether he has at t_0 rational control over whether he will both accept and write. And that, we've seen, depends on whether his tendency to procrastinate is presently repressible or not.[2] On the one hand, if it's presently repressible (and call this case *The Repressible Procrastinate*), then he has at t_0 the option of both accepting and writing. For, in that case, we're to assume that if he were at t_0 to exercise

---

2. Recall that his tendency to procrastinate is presently repressible if he will later refrain from procrastinating so long as he, at present, appropriately exercises his rational capacities and, thereby, resolves not to procrastinate later on. Otherwise, his tendency is presently irrepressible.

Table 8.1 Options and Utilities in *The Repressible Procrastinate*

Option	Description	Utility
O_1	Accept	−10
O_2	Don't accept	22
O_3	Accept and then write	25
O_4	Accept and then don't write	−10
O_5	Don't accept and then write	15
O_6	Don't accept and then don't write	22

his rational capacities appropriately, he would immediately form both (1) the intention to accept and write and (2) the resolution to resist the anticipated temptation to procrastinate when the book arrives. Furthermore, we're to assume that his forming these attitudes at present would be sufficient (holding everything else fixed) to ensure that he both accepts the invitation presently and then writes the review when the book arrives.

If, on the other hand, his tendency to procrastinate is presently irrepressible (and call this case *The Irrepressible Procrastinate*), then no matter how he exercises his rational capacities at t_0 (and, thus, no matter what acts and attitudes he now forms and performs), he will not write the review. And, in that case, we must deny that he has at t_0 rational control over whether he writes the review. Thus, given its commitment to rationalism, RTM implies that, in *The Irrepressible Procrastinate*, Professor Procrastinate lacks at t_0 the option to both accept and write.

So, in *The Repressible Procrastinate*, RTM holds that Professor Procrastinate's options at t_0 include all the following: (O_1) accept, (O_2) don't accept, (O_3) accept and write, (O_4) accept and don't write, (O_5) don't accept and write, and (O_6) don't accept and don't write. See Table 8.1. But, in *The Irrepressible Procrastinate*, RTM insists that we strike both O_3 and O_5 from the list of his options given that neither is, at present, under his rational control in the case where his tendency to procrastinate is presently irrepressible. See Table 8.2. Of course, Professor Procrastinate would, in both cases, likely have many other options besides those listed, including, say, that of accepting while tapping his right foot. But, to simplify our discussion of things, I'll just stipulate that in *The Repressible Procrastinate*, his options at t_0 consist in all and only O_1–O_6 and that in *The Irrepressible Procrastinate*, his options at t_0 consist in all and only O_1, O_2, O_4, and O_6. And, to further simplify things, I'll

Table 8.2 Options and Utilities in *The Irrepressible Procrastinate*

Option	Description	Utility
O_1	Accept	−10
O_2	Don't accept	22
O_4	Accept and then don't write	−10
O_6	Don't accept and then don't write	22

assume that utility is the only thing that ultimately matters and that counterfactual determinism is true such that there is a determinate fact about how much utility each option would produce. Indeed, I'll assume that the utilities are as stated in both Table 8.1 and Table 8.2.[3]

Given rationalism and the utilities stated in both Table 8.1 and Table 8.2, we know both what Professor Procrastinate's options are and which ones are better than the others in terms of what ultimately matters—which we're assuming is just utility. But we still need to know which of his options have their deontic statuses in virtue of their own goodness and which, if any, have their deontic statuses in virtue of the goodness of the options that entail them. Of course, given RTM's commitment to maximalism, the answer is that only maximal options have their deontic statuses in virtue of their own goodness. And maximal options, you'll recall, are those that are entailed only by evaluatively equivalent options. Thus, O_1 is not a maximal option given that it is entailed by O_3, which is evaluatively distinct from it. And the same holds for O_2, for it is entailed by O_5, which is evaluatively distinct from it. But O_3–O_6 are maximal options, for each is entailed only by itself, and an option is always evaluatively equivalent to itself. Therefore, O_3–O_6 are the only options that have their deontic statuses in virtue of their own goodness (that is, their own utility). And, of course, O_3 is the best of the lot in that it would produce

---

3. Procrastinate's accepting and not writing would be quite bad in that it would result in the book's not being reviewed at all—hence, −10 utiles. And his accepting would also result in −10 utiles given that he would, in fact, not write if he were to accept. His not accepting, by contrast, would be relatively good in that it would result in the book's being reviewed by the second-best person, the result being 22 utiles. Of course, given that Procrastinate is the best person for the job, his accepting and writing would be even better, producing 25 utiles. Last, Procrastinate's not accepting and writing would be worse than his not accepting and not writing, given that it would be pointless for him to write a review that won't be published. And it won't be published if he doesn't accept. Hence, his not accepting and writing would result in only 15 utiles, as compared to the 22 utiles that would result from his not accepting and not writing.

25 utiles, which is more than any alternative maximal option would. So, in *The Repressible Procrastinate,* RTM implies that Professor Procrastinate ought to perform O_3 (that is, he ought to accept and write). And, since his performing O_3 entails his performing O_1 (that is, his accepting), RTM also implies that he ought to accept, and this is true despite the fact that his accepting would result in −10 utiles. He ought to accept despite the fact that this would, in fact, result in −10 utiles, both because he must accept in order to maximize utility and because he can accept without the risk of a bad result.[4] To do so, he need only accept while resolving not to procrastinate, thereby ensuring that 25 utiles will result. And we're assuming that he has now the relevant sort of control over whether he will accept while resolving not to procrastinate.

Thus, on RTM, we assess whether the repressible Professor Procrastinate ought to accept, not by looking to the utility of his accepting (which is −10 utiles) and how that compares to the utility of *its* alternatives (and one of its alternatives—viz., not accepting—has a utility of 20), but by looking to the utility of the best maximal option that entails his accepting (and that's his accepting and writing, which has a utility of 25) and how that compares to the utility of the best maximal option that doesn't entail his accepting (and that's his not accepting and not writing, which has a utility of 22).

However, in *The Irrepressible Procrastinate,* things are different, as O_3 isn't an option in this case. Consequently, Professor Procrastinate's best maximal option in this case is O_6 (that is, his not accepting and not writing). And since O_6 entails O_2 (that is, his not accepting), RTM implies that he should not accept. Thus, RTM yields different answers in these two cases given that Professor Procrastinate has rational control over whether he writes in the one but not the other.

To further deepen our understanding of how RTM works, I'll now turn to a more complicated case. I call it *The Indeterminate Procrastinate.* In this case, Professor Procrastinate accepts the invitation to write the review without re-solving to write the review and, yet, by a fluke ends up writing the review any-way. There was, we'll assume, a very good chance that he wouldn't write the review given his lack of resolve. Indeed, let's assume both that counterfactual determinism is false and that the objective probability that he would have

---

4. The claim that he ought to accept does not imply that he ought to perform just any instance of the accepting type. It doesn't, for instance, imply that he ought to accept without resolving not to procrastinate. Instead, he ought to accept while resolving not to procrastinate. Thus, Professor Procrastinate's doing what he ought to do (that is, accepting) needn't result in −10 utiles. It's just that given that he's not going to respond appropriately to his reasons and resolve not to procrastinate, his accepting will, as a matter of fact, result in −10 utiles.

written the review given his lack of resolve to do so was only 0.1. Yet, had he resolved to write, the objective probability that he would have written would have been 0.9. So it was quite lucky that he ended up writing despite his lack of resolve to do so. Moreover, we'll assume that he could have easily resolved to write, as this was entirely under his rational control at the time. Indeed, had he exercised his rational capacities appropriately, he would have accepted while resolving to write.

And, to keep things as simple as possible, let's again assume that utility is the only thing that ultimately matters.[5] Of course, given that we're dealing with indeterminacy and, thus, with objective probabilities, there won't always be a fact of the matter as to how much utility would result from Professor Procrastinate's performing a given option. But each option will have an expected utility. Moreover, the expected utility of an option will be something that matters even if it isn't something that ultimately matters. Recall that we're assuming that only utility ultimately matters. Thus, maximizing expected utility matters only because utility matters and maximizing expected utility is the most likely way to succeed in maximizing utility. In any case, I'll be assuming that the goodness of Professor Procrastinate's options are directly proportional to their expected utilities.[6] And I'll stipulate that in *The Indeterminate Procrastinate*, Professor Procrastinate's complete set of options and their expected utilities are as depicted in Table 8.3.

RTM implies that in *The Indeterminate Procrastinate*, Professor Procrastinate ought not to have accepted (that is, he ought not to have performed O_7). Although his accepting happened to turn out well, resulting in 25 utiles, it was too objectively risky to be what he objectively ought to have done. In any case, given RTM's commitment to maximalism, O_7's deontic status isn't a function of its own goodness. It is instead a function of the goodness of the maximal options that entail it. For, given maximalism, only Professor Procrastinate's maximal options (that is, only O_8–O_{10}) have their deontic statuses in virtue of their own goodness.[7] And since neither of the

---

5. If utility is the only thing that ultimately matters, then avoiding significant risks of producing a lot of disutility matters only insofar as those risks affect the calculation of expected utilities.

6. Since not all options will have a determinate utility in this case, we can't compare his options in terms of what ultimately matters. Instead, we must compare them in terms of what derivatively matters: expected utility.

7. O_7 is a nonmaximal option, because it is entailed by O_9, which is evaluatively distinct from it. And each of O_8–O_{10} is a maximal option, because each is entailed only by itself (and, again, an option is always evaluatively equivalent to itself).

Table 8.3 Options, Utilities, and Expected Utilities
in *The Indeterminate Procrastinate*

Option	Description	Utility	Expected Utility
O_7	Accept	25	$(0.1 \times 25) + (0.9 \times -10) = -6.5$
O_8	Don't accept	Indeterminate	$(1.0 \times 22) = 22$
O_9	Accept while resolving to write	Indeterminate	$(0.9 \times 25) + (0.1 \times -10) = 21.5$
O_{10}	Accept without resolving to write	25	$(0.1 \times 25) + (0.9 \times -10) = -6.5$

two maximal options that entail his accepting (that is, neither O_9 nor O_{10}) is as good as the one maximal option that entails his not accepting (viz., O_8), it follows that, in *The Indeterminate Procrastinate*, Professor Procrastinate should not have accepted. And, interestingly, this means that what Professor Procrastinate did (viz., accepting while not resolving to write) was objectively impermissible despite the fact that it happened to result in the best possible outcome: the one with 25 utiles.[8]

To sum up, then, the way we determine on RTM whether a given option is one that the subject in question ought, as of *t*, to perform is as follows. First, we determine which possible events are, as of *t*, options for her. These, according to RTM, are all and only those that are, at *t*, under her rational control. Second, we figure out which of these options are maximal and which of them are nonmaximal—that is, which are entailed only by evaluatively equivalent options and which are also entailed by evaluatively distinct options. Third, we evaluate the prospects of the maximal options to determine which, if any, is to be preferred to all the rest given what ultimately matters. Thus, if utility is the only thing that ultimately matters, we look at how much utility each possible world in a given prospect has and what the probability of each possible world's obtaining is. And if one of these prospects is to be preferred

---

8. As Caspar Hare (2011) has rightly pointed out, there are at least two distinct ways of thinking about the objective ought: the first is to think of what you objectively ought to do as "what an omniscient, rational creature with appropriate interests would want you to do [or will be glad that you did]" and the second is to think of what you objectively ought to do as what you have "most reason to do" (p. 190). Clearly, I'm thinking of the objective ought in the second, action-guiding way. For it is in this sense that it was objectively wrong for Professor Procrastinate to have accepted without resolving to write even though an omniscient, rational creature with the appropriate interests will, knowing how things turned out, be glad that he did accept.

to all the rest, then its option is, according to RTM, her best maximal option. Fourth, we conclude that a given option is one that she ought, as of t, to perform if and only if it is entailed by her best maximal option as of t. Thus, in *The Indeterminate Procrastinate*, Professor Procrastinate ought, as of t, to have accepted if and only if his best maximal option as of t (viz., O_8) entailed his accepting, and it didn't. So, in *The Indeterminate Procrastinate*, Professor Procrastinate ought not to have accepted, as he did.

Hopefully, this summary along with the above three illustrations is sufficient to make it reasonably clear how RTM works. In any case, I think that we'll achieve even greater clarity as we consider, in the next section, some of RTM's many virtues.

§8.2 Rationalist Teleological Maximalism's Many Virtues

In this section, I'll explain RTM's virtues by elucidating which virtues are brought to the table by each of RTM's three components, starting with maximalism. Adopting maximalism is, I've argued, crucial to solving many otherwise intractable problems, including the problem of act versions (§4.1–§4.2), the latitude problem (§4.4), the inheritance problem (§6.2), the intuition problem (§6.3), the all or nothing problem (§6.4), and the problem of accounting for the basic belief (§6.5). Of course, there is no point to my reiterating these arguments here. Instead, I'll explain the general virtue that allows maximalism to solve these problems. That virtue is that maximalism has us take into account the entailment relations between our options, which is something that omnism has us ignore. So, whereas omnism insists that we are never to perform a suboptimal option, maximalism recognizes that sometimes we must do so in order to perform our best option, because, given the entailment relation that obtains between certain options, performing our best option (e.g., the option of accepting and writing) can necessitate performing a suboptimal option (e.g., the option of accepting). To illustrate, let's again assume that utility is the only thing that ultimately matters. And let's again consider *The Repressible Procrastinate* and the issue of what he should do. Omnism would have us focus solely on the utility of each of his options and how each compares to that of its alternatives—again, see Table 8.1. Thus, omnism implies that he ought not to accept, since the utility of his accepting (i.e., −10 utiles) is less than that of the alternative of his not accepting (i.e., 22 utiles). Moreover, omnism implies that he ought to accept and write, since the utility of his accepting and writing (i.e., 25 utiles) is greater than that of every alternative (the best alternative being his not accepting and not writing, which has a utility of 22 utiles). Thus, omnism implies both that he ought to accept and write and that he ought not to accept. But, of course, it's impossible for him to plan both (1) on accepting and writing and (2) on not accepting, for his accepting and writing entails his accepting. Thus, omnism holds that, when it comes to assessing each of our options and whether we ought to perform them, we are just to ignore the fact that the performance of certain options entails the performance of others. And, on the face of it, that seems to be a mistake, for it leads us to implications such as the above, where a subject ought to plan on φ-ing and, yet, ought also to plan on not ψ-ing even though she knows that she doesn't have the option of φ-ing without ψ-ing. Maximalism, by contrast, has the virtue of recognizing that when assessing what we ought to do, we need to consider, not only how each of our options fares in terms of what ultimately matters, but also how they relate to each other—in particular, to the fact that performing some options entails performing others. And it is this virtue that enables RTM to solve the sorts of problems listed above.

Next, consider RTM's commitment to rationalism. By itself, this commitment has the virtue of allowing RTM to avoid the problems associated with what's known as *exclusively act-oriented theories*. But, when combined with maximalism, it has the additional virtue of allowing RTM to solve the sorts of problems that only what's known as *attitude-dependent theories* can solve. I'll consider each of these in turn, explaining the relevant terminology in the process.

A theory is exclusively act-oriented if and only if it requires subjects only to perform and to refrain from performing certain voluntary acts. Such theories have at least three problems. First, they cannot require subjects to form (nonvoluntarily) various reasons-responsive attitudes but only to act voluntarily so as to cause themselves to form these attitudes. Thus, such theories can't require me to want what's best for my daughter, but only to do what might cause me to want what's best for her. And such views cannot account for our intuition that I should want what's best for my daughter without having to perform some intentional act so as to cause myself to want this. RTM, by contrast, can require me to "do" anything that's under my rational control, including requiring me to form a desire for what's best for my daughter.[9]

---

9. Recall that, throughout this book, I use the verbs "do" and "perform" such that believing, desiring, intending, etc. all count as things that a subject "does" and "performs."

Second, exclusively act-oriented theories can't accommodate the intuitive idea that I can be required to perform mixed acts, such as that of giving a sincere apology. An exclusively act-oriented theory can require me to say the words "I'm sorry," but it can't require me to offer a sincere apology, since that not only involves my saying these words but also feeling contrite while I do, and feeling contrite is not something I can do voluntarily. Fortunately, given its commitment to rationalism, RTM can require me to offer a sincere apology—for example, to feel contrite while expressing this feeling using the words "I'm sorry." Given that both feeling contrite and saying the words "I'm sorry" are under my rational control, RTM can require that I do both.

Third, exclusively act-oriented theories can't accommodate our intuition that, in the case of *Slice and Patch Go Golfing* from Chapter 5, Dr. Slice and Dr. Patch are each guilty of a moral mistake. Since each doctor performed all and only those voluntary acts that they ought to have performed, an exclusively act-oriented theory must deny that either of them is guilty of a moral mistake. But this is highly counterintuitive. Fortunately, RTM can hold that each doctor had not only an obligation to do what would, in the given situation, maximize utility, but also an obligation to form the intention to do, in all situations, whatever would maximize utility (and let's assume, again, that utility is the only thing that ultimately matters). And it's because our intentions are just as much under our rational control as our voluntary acts are that RTM can hold that each doctor was not only obligated to stay away from the hospital but also obligated to form the intention to do whatever would maximize utility and, thus, to form the conditional intention to do his part to save the patient on the condition that he knows that his doing so would maximize utility.

So, one virtue of RTM is that by endorsing rationalism, it avoids being exclusively act-oriented and the problems associated with that. But another related virtue is that, in endorsing rationalism in conjunction with maximalism, RTM becomes an attitude-dependent theory, which is especially advantageous. A theory is *attitude-dependent* if and only if it holds that the deontic status of an action can depend on what reasons-responsive attitudes the agent ought (or is obligated) to form and to refrain from forming. What makes RTM attitude-dependent is that it holds both that (1) we must first evaluate the entire set of things over which a subject exerts rational control, where this includes the nonvoluntary formation of certain reasons-responsive attitudes as well as the performance of certain intentional acts, and that (2) only then can we evaluate an individual act by considering the deontic statuses of the sets that entail them. And, because RTM evaluates acts as parts of such attitude-including sets, the deontic status of an act can depend on what reasons-responsive attitudes the agent ought (or is obligated) to have.

To illustrate, recall the case of Leilani from §6.4. She chose to donate to the Pūnāwai Program even though she knew that she could produce more utility by instead donating to the Against Malaria Foundation. And, as I noted in §6.4, it seems that whether she was permitted to act as she did depends on what attitudes she ought to have had. For suppose that she was right in caring more about providing Native Hawaiians with emergency financial assistance than about producing as much utility as possible. Assume, then, that she's a Native Hawaiian and that the best prospects for the Native Hawaiian community depend on the continued solidarity of its members, which in turn depends on their giving each other preferential support. In that case, it seems that she was indeed permitted to donate to the Pūnāwai Program. For in that case she had a permissible maximal option in which she cared more about helping her fellow Native Hawaiians than she did about producing as much utility as possible and, as a consequence, chose to donate to the Pūnāwai Program instead of the Against Malaria Foundation.

But now consider the following alternative possibility. On this alternative, Leilani has no more of a special tie to Native Hawaiians than she does to sub-Saharan Africans. Assume, then, that she chose to donate to the Pūnāwai Program only because she thought it would be "neat" to give to a Native Hawaiian charity given that her name happens to be Hawaiian. Thus, what motivated her choice was that she cared more about doing something "neat" than about producing the considerably greater sum of utility that would have resulted from her choosing instead to donate to the Against Malaria Foundation. And, in that case, it seems that she acted impermissibly. For it seems that she had no permissible maximal option that entailed her caring more about doing something "neat" than about producing a considerably greater sum of utility and, as a consequence, chose to donate to the Pūnāwai Program instead of the Against Malaria Foundation. Thus, the deontic status of Leilani's action depends on what reasons-responsive attitudes she ought to have had—specifically, on what she ought to have cared about most: doing something "neat," helping Native Hawaiians, or maximizing utility. And for a theory to account for this it must be attitude-dependent, which RTM is in virtue of its commitment to both rationalism and maximalism.[10]

---

10. In another paper, I explain how adopting an attitude-dependent theory can help us solve the self-torturer puzzle—see PORTMORE MANUSCRIPT.

The last component of RTM is its teleology. On a teleological theory, the extent of an option's goodness ultimately depends on the extent to which its prospect is to be preferred to those of its alternatives in terms of whatever ultimately matters. The virtue of such a theory is that it is able to handle cases in which it is indeterminate whether an option is best in terms of what ultimately matters. To illustrate, consider again *The Indeterminate Procrastinate* and assume that utility is the only thing that ultimately matters. And, given this assumption, it follows that an option is best in terms of what ultimately matters *only if* it is better than every alternative in terms of how much utility it produces. Now, suppose we want to know whether Professor Procrastinate performed his best option in accepting without resolving to write (that is, in his performing O_{10})—see Table 8.3. Of course, we know that his doing so resulted in 25 utiles. But to know whether this was his best option, we need to know whether there was any alternative that would have produced at least as much utility. For if he had such an alternative, his accepting without resolving to write could not have been his best option. But, unfortunately, there's just no fact of the matter about whether there was such an alternative. For there is no fact of the matter about how much utility he would have produced had he performed the alternative of accepting while resolving to write. For the only facts are of the following sort: there was a 0.1 objective chance that his accepting while resolving to write would have resulted in −10 utiles and a 0.9 objective chance that it would have resulted in 25 utiles. So, if we have to assess the goodness of our options directly in terms of what ultimately matters, then there can be no fact of the matter concerning whether his accepting without resolving to write was his best option and, thus, *the* option that he ought to have performed.

But what such cases show, I believe, is that we shouldn't try to assess the goodness of our options without first assessing the goodness of their prospects. Thus, we shouldn't try to assess, say, whether O_9 is better than O_{10} in terms of what ultimately matters, for this seems impossible given both that we're assuming utility is the only thing that ultimately matters and that O_9 doesn't have a utility, but only an expected utility. So, instead, we should try to assess only whether O_9's prospect (call it P_9) is preferable to O_{10}'s prospect (call it P_{10}) in terms of what ultimately matters. And P_9 is better than P_{10} in terms of what ultimately matters—namely, utility. For, in terms of utility, a prospect consisting of a 0.9 chance of 25 utiles and a 0.1 chance of −10 utiles (that is, P_9) is preferable to a prospect consisting of a 0.1 chance of 25 utiles and a 0.9 chance of −10 utiles (that is, P_{10}). And, since O_9's prospect is preferable to O_{10}'s prospect in terms of what ultimately matters, we should conclude, given teleology, that O_9 is better than O_{10}. Therefore, we should think that Professor Procrastinate's did not do what he ought to have done in performing O_{10}.

Thus, it seems that if utility is something that ultimately matters, we need to be teleologists, for we cannot always evaluate options in terms of their own utilities. As we've seen, some options don't even have a utility. And, in such cases, we can't assess our options directly in terms of what ultimately matters (that is, utility) but must instead assess their prospects in terms of what ultimately matters and then assess our options in terms of their prospects. Of course, one could try to resist this argument for teleology by arguing that utility isn't something that ultimately matters. One could, for instance, argue that the sorts of things that ultimately matter are not things such as utility but only things such as constraint-violations. But, as I've shown in Chapter 7, there isn't always a fact about whether performing an option would entail a constraint-violation. For I've argued that just as it can be indeterminate how much utility would result from an option's being performed, it can also be indeterminate whether a constraint-violation would result from an option's being performed. So, even when it comes to the sorts of features that we most closely associate with nonteleological theories (viz., constraints), it seems that we must first evaluate prospects, not options, in terms of such features.

Of course, another way to resist this argument for teleology would be to argue that what ultimately matters is not things such as utility and constraint-violations but things such as expected utility and the risk of a constraint-violation. But this, I believe, is implausible.

For one, it seems that expected utility matters only because utility matters. And, thus, it's utility, not expected utility, that *ultimately* matters. For instance, we should be glad (not sad) that, in *The Indeterminate Procrastinate*, Professor Procrastinate performed O_{10} and as a result produced 25 utiles. After all, the only reason that we, not knowing how things would turn out, may have wanted him to perform O_8 instead was that performing O_8 was expected to produce more utility. But, as a matter of fact, performing it would have produced less.

For another, it seems that the risk of a constraint-violation matters only because constraint-violations matter. And, thus, it's constraint-violations, not the risk of a constraint-violation, that *ultimately* matters. We care about the risk of violating someone's rights only because we care that this someone's rights not be violated. Thus, it's prospects, not options, that will need to be evaluated directly in terms of the things that ultimately matter. Thus, we'll need to evaluate an option in terms of its prospect for producing utility rather than evaluate it in terms of its own utility. For there may be no fact of the matter about what its utility is. And we'll need to evaluate an option in terms of its prospect for resulting in a constraint-violation rather than evaluate that option in terms of whether it itself would constitute a constraint-violation. For there may be no fact of the matter about whether it would constitute a constraint-violation. It seems, then, that what ultimately matters is always going to be something such as X rather than the probability of X. And since, regardless of what 'X' stands for, it could be indeterminate whether X would obtain if some option were performed, we'll have to evaluate prospects, not options, in terms of what ultimately matters. And teleology has the virtue of allowing us to do just that.

To sum up, then, I've argued that each of RTM's three components has its own virtue and that these virtues allow RTM to solve many problems that otherwise seem intractable.

§8.3 On What Matters and the Importance of Structure

In a sense, this book has been about what doesn't matter, for I have, for the most part, set aside the issue of what ultimately matters so as to focus on issues concerning what structure our normative theories should take. Because of this, I once considered entitling the book *On What Doesn't Matter*, as a play on Derek Parfit's *On What Matters*. But, in the end, I decided against it. For one, it seemed a bit too cheeky. For another, I don't want to suggest that this book is about something that doesn't matter. It just hasn't been about what *ultimately* matters. Nevertheless, this book is different from most other books in practical philosophy. Most of these other books deal with normative questions by arguing that something does or doesn't ultimately matter. For instance, a book on animal ethics typically argues that we ought to change the way we treat nonhuman animals because their interests ultimately matter and matter just as much as our interests do. And a book on population ethics might argue that we ought, other things being equal, to favor population policies that would increase the number of happy people because bringing additional happy people into existence is something that ultimately matters.

But I have taken a different tack. I have argued that the key to addressing certain normative questions lies in setting aside controversial issues concerning what ultimately matters and focusing instead on certain structural questions—questions about what kinds of events are to be normatively assessed, which of these events have their deontic statuses in virtue of their own goodness and which have them in virtue of their relations to those events that do, and whether we are to assess the goodness of events directly in terms of what ultimately matters or only indirectly by first assessing their prospects in terms of what ultimately matters. And I've tried to make the case that answering these structural questions matters more than answering the question of what ultimately matters when it comes to solving certain puzzles about what we ought to do: puzzles involving supererogation, indeterminate outcomes, overdetermined outcomes, predictable future misbehavior, and the like.

GLOSSARY

Accountable—For a subject to be responsible in the accountability sense for having φ-ed is for her to be praiseworthy or blameworthy for having φ-ed, thereby making her the appropriate target of either retributive attitudes (such as guilt and indignation) or meritorious attitudes (such as [deontic] pride and admiration) in virtue of her having φ-ed. See *guilt, responsible, deontic pride, retributive attitude*, and *meritorious attitude*. Contrast with *attributable*.

Act-consequentialism—Act-consequentialism is the view that holds that (1) an option is permissible if and only if there is no alternative option whose prospect is better than its prospect, that (2) if an option is permissible, it is in virtue of the fact that there is no alternative option whose prospect is better than its prospect, and that (3) what ultimately matters is only the (impersonal) goodness of the world such that one prospect is better than another if and only if the one has more expected (impersonal) goodness than the other. See *prospect, consequentialism*, and *alternative*. Contrast with *rule-consequentialism*.

Actualism—For any subject S and any act φ that she could possibly perform, S ought to φ if and only if there is no alternative act that she could possibly perform, ψ, such that what would actually happen if she were to ψ is at least as good as what would actually happen if she were to φ. See *could possibly perform*. Contrast with *possibilism*.

Act-utilitarianism—Act-utilitarianism is the view that combines act-consequentialism with welfarism. See *welfarism* and *act-consequentialism*.

Agent-centered constraint (or simply "constraint")—There is an agent-centered constraint against a subject's performing an act of a certain type if and only if there are some possible circumstances in which it would be impermissible for her to perform an act of that type even though her doing so would both minimize the total instances of actions of that type and have no other morally relevant implications (SCHEFFLER 1985, p. 409).

Alternative members—For any two options, φ and ψ, of the set O, φ and ψ are alternative members of O if and only if <φ and ψ> is not itself a member of O.

Alternative options—Two options, φ and ψ, are alternative options if and only if <φ-ing and ψ-ing> is not an option. See *option*. Contrast with *distinct options*.

Antecedent world—An antecedent world is any possible world in which the antecedent of the given counterfactual is true. Thus, an antecedent world with respect to the counterfactual "If Gandhi hadn't been assassinated, then the British Indian Empire never would have been partitioned into modern-day India and Pakistan" is any possible world in which Gandhi hadn't been assassinated.

Appropriate (in the alethic sense—i.e., the sense of being fitting and correct)—It would be appropriate (in the alethic sense) for a subject to φ if and only if she has the option of φ-ing and the thoughts implicated by her φ-ing are all true. Thus, it would be appropriate for me to fear the animal in my yard if and only if I have the option of fearing this animal and the thought implicated by this attitude (i.e., the thought that this animal is a danger to me) is true. See *thought*.

Attitude dependent—A normative theory is attitude dependent if and only if it holds that the deontic status of an action can depend on what reasons-responsive attitudes the agent ought (or is obligated) to form or to refrain from forming. See *deontic status* and *reasons-responsive attitudes*.

Attitudes—See *reasons-responsive attitudes*.

Attributable—For a subject to be responsible in the attributability sense for having φ-ed is for her to have expressed her values, character, and/or commitments in φ-ing, thereby making her the appropriate target of various aretaic judgments (e.g., the judgment that she is selfish, cruel, or cowardly) in virtue of her having φ-ed. See *responsible*. Contrast with *accountable*.

Basic belief—The basic belief is the deeply entrenched common-sensical belief that in many typical choice situations, the relevant reasons do not require performing one particular act-type, but instead permit performing any of a variety of different act-types, such as gardening, watching TV, volunteering for Oxfam, reading the newspaper, or working on a book.

Best bet—An option is a subject's best bet if and only if it is what it would make most sense for a conscientious person of her abilities, capacities, and epistemic position to do in the given circumstances. Thus, an option is a subject's best bet if and only if it is the option that she subjectively ought to perform. See *bet, subjective ought*, and *conscientious person*.

Best option—An option is a subject's best option if and only if it is both sufficiently good and better than every alternative option. Thus, an option is a subject's best option if and only if it is the option that she objectively ought to perform. See *option, objective ought*, and *alternative option*.

Bet—A bet is an option with uncertain or indeterminate outcomes of unequal desirability. See *option*.

Better option—For any subject S and any two of her options φ and ψ, φ is better than ψ if and only if φ is better than ψ in terms of whatever ultimately matters—that is, better in terms of whatever she should ultimately be concerned with at the time.

Thus, if she should ultimately be concerned with only how much utility there is, then her φ-ing is better than her ψ-ing if and only if her φ-ing would produce more utility than her ψ-ing would. See *option* and *matters*.

Cases of counterfactual openness—A case of counterfactual openness is a case in which there is no fact of the matter concerning whether a subject would have violated a constraint had she φ-ed, because neither of the following two counterfactuals is true: (CF_V) if she had φ-ed, she would have violated that constraint, and $(CF_{\neg V})$ if she had φ-ed, she would not have violated that constraint. In such cases, neither counterfactual is true, because their shared antecedent is underspecified and the subject lacks the ability to further specify the antecedent in a way that would determine which of their two consequents would obtain in the antecedent world. See *antecedent world* and *agent-centered constraint*.

Cases of ignorance—A case of ignorance is a case in which we are uncertain about whether a subject's φ-ing constitutes a constraint-violation because we're ignorant of some relevant facts. See *agent-centered constraint*.

Cases of indeterminacy—A case of indeterminacy is a case in which we are uncertain about whether a subject's φ-ing constitutes a constraint-violation, because there is no fact of the matter concerning whether her φ-ing constitutes a constraint-violation. See *violates* and *agent-centered constraint*.

Cases of indeterminate agency—A case of indeterminate agency is a case where there is no fact of the matter concerning whether a subject violated a constraint in φ-ing, because whether she violated a constraint in φ-ing depends on what some other agent would have done had she not φ-ed and there is no fact of the matter as to what that other agent would have done had she not φ-ed given that the other agent's actions are not causally determined. See *violates* and *agent-centered constraint*.

Cases of vagueness—A case of vagueness is a case where there seems to be no fact of the matter concerning whether a subject violated a constraint in φ-ing, because her φ-ing is a borderline case of a constraint-violation—that is, a case that is neither a clear case of a constraint-violation nor a clear case of a non–constraint-violation. See *violates* and *agent-centered constraint*.

Complete control—A subject's control over whether she φs is complete if and only if, holding everything else fixed, whether she φs just depends on how she exercises her control such that the objective probability that she'll φ will be 1 if she exercises her control in certain ways and will be 0 otherwise. See *control* and *objective probability*. Contrast with *partial control*.

Conscientious person—A conscientious person is one who is appropriately concerned with what ultimately matters. See *matters*.

Consequences—The consequences of a subject's φ-ing is the way the world would be if she were to φ, where the way the world would be if she were to φ depends, in part, on what she would in fact simultaneously and subsequently do if she were to φ.

Consequentialism—The view that what ultimately matters is only the (impersonal) goodness of the world such that an option is good/bad in virtue of its consequences being (impersonally) good/bad. Moreover, the degree to which an option is good/bad is in strict proportion to how (impersonally) good/bad its consequences are. See *option, matters*, and *consequences*.

Consistency requirement on beliefs and intentions—A subject ought to be such that the set consisting of the propositional contents of all her beliefs and all her intentions is logically consistent (J. ROSS 2009, p. 244).

Constraint-accepting theory—A constraint-accepting theory, which needn't be nonteleological, includes at least one agent-centered constraint. See *agent-centered constraint*.

Constraint-violation—See *violates*.

Continualism—A subject has at t the option of φ-ing at t' if and only if whether she φs at t' depends (in the right way) on her continually trying, from t onward, to φ at t'. See *option*.

Control—For a subject to have, at present, control over whether an event e occurs is for her to have the present ability/power to determine whether e occurs—or, if not to determine whether e occurs, then, at least, to affect the objective probability that e will occur. See *objective probability*. Contrast with *complete control* and *partial control*.

Could possibly perform—For any subject S and any act x, x-ing at t' is, as of t, something that S could possibly perform if and only if there exists a schedule of available intentions from t onward such that, if S's intentions were to follow this schedule, S would x at t'.

Counterfactual determinism—Counterfactual determinism is the view that, for any possible event e, there is some determinate fact as to what the world would be like if e were to occur.

Decisive reason—A subject has decisive reason to φ if and only if her reasons are such as to make her obligated to φ. Contrast with *most reason* and *sufficient reason*.

Deontic inheritance—For any subject S and any two of her options φ and ψ, if S ought to φ and S's φ-ing entails S's ψ-ing, then S ought to ψ. Contrast with *evaluative inheritance*.

Deontic noninheritance—It is not the case that for any subject S and any two of her options φ and ψ, if S ought to φ and S's φ-ing entails S's ψ-ing, then S ought to ψ. Contrast with *evaluative noninheritance*.

Deontic pride—Deontic pride is a specific sort of pride. To take deontic pride in having φ-ed is, in part, to have both (1) the thought that one's having φ-ed reveals that one is good or superior in a way that could potentially result in a gain of honor, respect, or esteem and (2) the thought that one is good or superior in that one deserves to experience the pleasantness of this feeling in virtue of having responded as one ought to have responded in φ-ing. (Deontic pride is the positive analogue of guilt.) See *thought*. Contrast with *guilt* and *pride*.

Deontic status—A deontic status is any status such as the following: wrong, optional, obligatory, permissible, supererogatory, that which ought to be done, etc. Contrast with *evaluative status*.

Deontic utility—Deontic utility is a measure of how good an option is in terms of whatever ultimately matters. See *option* and *matters*. Contrast with *expected deontic utility*.

Deontology—A theory is deontological if and only if it is a constraint-accepting theory that holds that constraints are ultimately grounded in our duty to respect people and their capacity for rational, autonomous decision making. See *agent-centered constraints* and *constraint-accepting theory*.

Deserves—To say that a subject (morally) deserves X is to say that, as a matter of justice and in virtue of her possessed characteristics and/or prior activities, she merits X in a certain sense. The relevant sense in which she merits X is the one such that the world in which she gets X while meriting X in this sense is, other things being equal, morally better than the world in which she gets X without meriting X in this sense.

Diachronic View—A subject has at t the option of φ-ing at t' if and only if whether she φs at t' depends (in the right way) on how she exerts her control from t onward. See *option*. Contrast with *synchronic view*.

Directive ought—A directive ought is an ought that directs some subject to perform an option, implying that she has reason to perform that option—e.g., "Doug ought to run faster." See *option*. Contrast with *evaluative ought*.

Directly responsible—When a subject is responsible for having φ-ed, but not in virtue of being responsible for anything else, she is directly responsible for having φ-ed. See *responsible*. Contrast with *indirectly responsible*.

Distinct options—Two options, φ and ψ, are distinct options if and only if it is not the case that each entails the other. Thus, <kissing> and <kissing passionately> are distinct options even though they are not alternative options. See *entails*. Contrast with *alternative options*.

Entails (in the performance sense as opposed to the logical sense)—For any subject S and any two of her options φ and ψ, S's φ-ing entails S's ψ-ing if and only if S doesn't have the option of φ-ing without ψ-ing. And, to save words, I will sometimes say "φ-ing entails ψ-ing" instead of "S's φ-ing entails S's ψ-ing." See *option*.

Enticing reason—Let 'T' stand for something such as "moral," "rational," or "prudential." A T-ly enticing reason to φ is a reason for φ-ing that has some T-ly favoring strength but no T-ly requiring strength. See *reason for, favoring strength*, and *requiring strength*. Contrast with *requiring reason*.

Evaluative inheritance—For any subject S and any two of her options φ and ψ, if φ is S's best option and S's φ-ing entails S's ψ-ing, then ψ is also S's best option. See *option*. Contrast with *deontic inheritance*.

Evaluative noninheritance—It is not the case that, for any subject S and any two of her options φ and ψ, if φ is S's best option and S's φ-ing entails S's ψ-ing, then ψ is also S's best option. See *option*. Contrast with *deontic noninheritance*.

Evaluative ought—An evaluative ought is an ought that doesn't imply that there is a subject who has a reason to perform some option. Such an ought implies only that something is good or desirable—e.g., "There ought to be world peace" or "It ought to be that Doug runs faster." See *option*. Contrast with *directive ought*.

Evaluative status—An evaluative status is any status such as the following: good, bad, better, worse, best, worst, sufficiently good, insufficiently good, etc. Contrast with *deontic status*.

Evaluatively distinct option—For any two options φ and ψ, φ and ψ are evaluatively distinct if and only if they are not evaluatively equivalent. See *option*. Contrast with *evaluatively equivalent options*.

Evaluatively equivalent options—For any two options φ and ψ, φ and ψ are evaluatively equivalent if and only if they are equivalent in terms of whatever ultimately matters such that each is no better or worse than the other. So, if the only thing that ultimately matters is how much utility there is, and if I'll maximize utility if and only if I think of a number greater than 10, then my thinking of 11 is evaluatively equivalent to my thinking of 12. See *option* and *matters*. Contrast with *evaluatively distinct options*.

Evidential probability—For any proposition *p*, the evidential probability that *p* for a given subject is the degree to which her body of evidence supports *p*.

Exclusively act-oriented—A normative theory is exclusively act-oriented if and only if it directs subjects only to perform and to refrain from performing certain voluntary acts.

Expected deontic utility—The expected deontic utility of a subject's φ-ing is a probability distribution consisting in the set of mutually exclusive and jointly exhaustive possibilities concerning φ's deontic utility, with each possibility assigned a probability such that the sum of those probabilities equals 1. See *deontic utility*.

Expected utility—The expected utility of a subject's φ-ing is a probability distribution consisting in the set of mutually exclusive and jointly exhaustive possibilities concerning φ's utility, with each possibility assigned a probability such that the sum of those probabilities equals 1. See *utility*.

Externalism—According to externalism, a subject could have a reason to φ even if she could not come to φ via a sound deliberative route from the motivations that she already has. Contrast with *internalism*.

Favoring strength—Let 'T' stand for something such as "moral," "rational," or "prudential." One reason, R_1, has more T-ly favoring strength than another, R_2, if and only if both (1) R_1 would make it T-ly better to do anything that R_2 would make it T-ly better to do and (2) R_1 would make it T-ly better to do some things that R_2 would not make it T-ly better to do. See also *requiring strength*.

Fitting attitude—An attitude that has *X* as its intentional object is fitting if and only if it accurately represents *X*. Thus, the belief that *p* is fitting if and only if *p* is true, for beliefs represent their intentional objects as being true. Likewise, the intention to φ is fitting if and only if φ is choiceworthy, for intentions represent their intentional objects as being choiceworthy. In other words, it would be fitting for a subject to have a certain attitude if and only if it would be appropriate (in the alethic sense) for her to have this attitude. See *appropriate* and *reasons-responsive attitudes.* Contrast with *fortunate attitude.*

Fittingness reasons—For any subject S, any option φ, and any fact *p*, the fact that *p* is a fittingness reason for S to φ if and only if it is fitting for S to φ at least in part because *p*. See *option.* Contrast with *pragmatic reasons.*

Fortunate attitude—It would be fortunate for a subject to have a certain attitude if and only if it would be good if she were to have this attitude. See *reasons-responsive attitudes.* Contrast with *fitting attitude.*

Guilt—To feel guilty for having φ-ed is, in part, to have the thought that one deserves to experience the unpleasantness of this feeling in virtue of having violated a legitimate demand by φ-ing. (Guilt is the negative analogue of deontic pride.) See *thought.* Contrast with *deontic pride.*

Imperfect duty—An imperfect duty is a duty to adopt a certain end and, derivatively, to live one's life in any of the ways that's consistent with having done so. Contrast with *perfect duty.*

Imperfect duty of beneficence—The imperfect duty of beneficence is the duty both "to make the happiness of others a serious, major, continually relevant, life-shaping end" (HILL 2002, p. 206) and to live one's life in any of the ways that's consistent with having done so.

Impermissible—For any option φ, a subject's φ-ing is impermissible if and only if her φ-ing is not permissible and, thus, is wrong/prohibited. And note that all options are either permissible or impermissible. See *option* and *deontic status.* Contrast with *permissible.*

Indirectly responsible—When a subject is responsible for having φ-ed in virtue of being responsible for something else, she is only indirectly responsible for having φ-ed. See *responsible.* Contrast with *directly responsible.*

Infringes—A subject infringes upon a constraint against her performing an act of a certain type if and only if she performs an act of that type. See *agent-centered constraint.* Contrast with *violates.*

Instrumental reason—For any option φ, a subject has an instrumental reason to φ if and only if she has a reason to φ in virtue of the fact that her φ-ing is a necessary means to her bringing about some end that she has reason to bring about.

Intention-guiding—To say that a subject's obligation to φ is intention-guiding is to say that it necessitates there being some option ψ (where ψ may or may not be identical to φ) such that she's obligated to form the intention to ψ and her ψ-ing entails her φ-ing. See *option.*

Internalism—According to internalism, a subject has a reason to φ only if she could come to φ via a sound deliberative route from the motivations that she already has. Contrast with *externalism.*

Irrepressible—For any option φ, a subject's tendency to φ is presently irrepressible if and only if she will not refrain from φ-ing even if she appropriately exercises her rational capacities at present, resolving not to φ. Contrast with *repressible.*

Joint satisfiability—If a subject is both obligated to φ and obligated to ψ, then she has the option of both φ-ing and ψ-ing (KIESEWETTER 2018). See *option*. Contrast with *obligation dilemma*.

Justifying strength—Let 'T' stand for something such as "moral," "rational," or "prudential." One reason, R_1, has more T-ly justifying strength than another, R_2, if and only if both (1) R_1 would make it T-ly permissible to do anything that R_2 would make it T-ly permissible to do, and (2) R_1 would make it T-ly permissible do some things that R_2 would not make it T-ly permissible to do (GERT 2003, pp. 15–16). Thus, for any two alternative options φ and ψ, a reason to φ can make it T-ly permissible to ψ if it has more T-ly justifying strength than the reason one has to ψ has T-ly requiring strength, and it can do so without being a T reason for one to refrain from ψ-ing. For instance, the reason I have to spend my surplus income on myself can morally justify my not instead donating it to a charity, and it can do so without being a moral reason for me to spend this income on myself. See *moral reason, surplus income*, and *alternative option*. Contrast with *requiring strength*.

Latitude problem—The latitude problem is the problem that some theories have in yielding counterintuitive implications regarding what's supererogatory in instances where the duty that the subject goes beyond the call of is one that allows for a lot of latitude in how she is to comply with it. See *supererogatory*.

Matters—What ultimately matters for a given subject at a given time is just whatever she ought to care about noninstrumentally at that time. Thus, if one of the things that a subject should ultimately care about at present is that she doesn't take the present opportunity to violate anyone's rights, then one thing that ultimately matters (at least, relative to her at this moment) is that she doesn't take the present opportunity to violate anyone's rights. And this view is to be contrasted with, say, the view that what she should ultimately care about at present is her minimizing her rights violations over time such that she should perform now an option that would violate someone's rights if that would minimize her rights violations over time. On this contrasting view, then, what ultimately matters for her at present is, not that she doesn't take the present opportunity to violate anyone's rights, but that she acts now so as to minimize her rights violations over time.

Maximal option—A maximal option is a maximally evaluatively specific option—that is, an option that is entailed only by evaluatively equivalent options (which, of course, includes itself). See *option*. Contrast with *nonmaximal option*.

Maximalism—For any maximal option M that a subject S has as of time t, the deontic status of S's M-ing depends on how M's goodness (or badness) compares to that of the alternative maximal options available to her as of t. And, for any nonmaximal option N that S has as of t, the deontic status of S's N-ing depends on how the goodness (or badness) of the maximal options available to her as of t that entail her N-ing compare to the maximal options available to her as of t that don't. See *entails, deontic status, maximal option*, and *nonmaximal option*. Contrast with *omnism, nullusism*, and *nonnullusism*.

Maximalism about reasons—(**A-REASON**) For any subject S and any maximal option of hers M, S has a reason (or a T reason—where 'T' stands for some adjective, such as "moral" or "prudential," that refers to some type of normative domain) to M if and only if there is something good (or something T-ly good) about S's M-ing. And, for any subject S and any nonmaximal option of hers N, S has a reason (or a T reason) to N if and only if there is a maximal option M_x such that S has a reason (or a T reason) to M_x and S's M_x-ing entails S's N-ing. (**MORE-REASON**) For any subject S and any two of her maximal options M_x and M_y, S has more reason (or more T reason) to M_x than to M_y if and only if M_x is better (or T-ly better) than M_y. And, for any subject S and any two of her nonmaximal options N_x and N_y, S has more reason (or more T reason) to N_x than to N_y if and only if the best maximal option that entails her N_x-ing is better (or T-ly better) than the best maximal option that entails her N_y-ing. (**MOST-REASON**) For any subject S and any maximal option of hers M, S has most reason (or most T reason) to M if and only if M is better (or T-ly better) than every alternative maximal option. And, for any subject S and any nonmaximal option of hers N, S has most reason (or most T reason) to N if and only if there is a maximal option M_x such that S has most reason (or most T reason) to M_x and S's M_x-ing entails S's N-ing. See *entails, best option, more reason, most reason, maximal option,* and *nonmaximal option.* Contrast with *omnism about reasons.*

Maximalism about statuses—(**OUGHT**) For any maximal option M, a subject ought to M if and only if M is her best maximal option. And, for any nonmaximal option N, she ought to N if and only if there is a maximal option that she ought to perform whose performance entails N-ing. (**PERMI**) For any maximal option M, a subject is permitted to M if and only if M is one of her sufficiently good maximal options. And, for any nonmaximal option N, she is permitted to N if and only if there is a maximal option that she is permitted to perform whose performance entails N-ing. (**SUPER**) For any maximal option M_x, a subject's M_x-ing is supererogatory if and only if there is an alternative maximal option M_y such that: (a) she is both permitted to M_x and permitted to M_y, and (b) her M_x-ing is better than her M_y-ing. And, for any nonmaximal option N_x, her N_x-ing is supererogatory if and only if both: (a) in N_x-ing, she does not merely minimally or merely partially satisfy some necessary condition for performing a permissible maximal option, and (b) there is an alternative nonmaximal option N_y such that (i) she is both permitted to N_x and permitted to N_y, and (ii) her N_x-ing is better than her N_y-ing (The relevant deontic statuses are the objective ones. Also, I leave implicit the relevant grounding clauses. For instance, I leave implicit that if a subject ought to M, this is in virtue of the fact that M is her best maximal option.) See *entails, supererogatory, best option, deontic status, alternative option, merely minimally satisfies,* and *merely partially satisfies.* Contrast with *omnism about statuses.*

Maximally evaluatively specific option—See *maximal option.*

Maximally specific option—A maximally specific option is an option that is entailed by no distinct option. In other words, it's an option that is entailed only by itself. See *distinct option.* Contrast with *non–maximally specific option.*

Merely minimally satisfies—In φ-ing, a subject merely minimally satisfies some necessary condition for performing a permissible maximal option if and only if, although her φ-ing satisfies this condition, it is no better for her to φ than to perform any alternative option that would satisfy this condition.

Merely partially satisfies—In φ-ing, a subject merely partially satisfies some necessary condition for performing a permissible maximal option if and only if her φ-ing is a proper subset of some set of options by which she merely minimally satisfies that condition.

Meritorious attitude—A meritorious attitude is one that includes the constitutive thought that someone deserves some reward. See *thought*. Contrast with *retributive attitude*.

Minimalism—(**OUGHT**) For any minimally specific option *m*, a subject ought to *m* if and only if *m* is her best minimally specific option. And, for any non–minimally specific option *n*, she ought to *n* if and only if *n*-ing entails performing a minimally specific option that she ought to perform. (**PERMI**) For any minimally specific option *m*, a subject is permitted to *m* if and only if *m* is one of her sufficiently good minimally specific options. And, for any non–minimally specific option *n*, she is permitted to *n* if and only if *n*-ing entails performing a minimally specific option that's permissible. (The relevant deontic statuses are the objective ones. Also, I leave implicit the relevant grounding clauses. For instance, I leave implicit that, if a subject ought to *m*, this is in virtue of the fact that *m* is her best minimally specific option.) See *entails, deontic status, alternative option, minimally specific option*, and *non–minimally specific option*.

Minimally specific option—A minimally specific option is an option that entails no distinct option. In other words, it's an option that entails only itself. See *option*. Contrast with *non–minimally specific option*.

Mixed acts—Mixed acts are acts that have both a voluntary component and a nonvoluntary component. Examples include acting in good faith, offering a sincere apology, expressing one's gratitude, and diverting a trolley onto the side track with the intention of saving the five on the main track.

Moral failure—A moral failure is a failure to follow one or more of morality's directives—that is, a failure to do all that morality holds that one ought to do.

Moral reason—The fact that *p* is a moral reason for a subject to φ if and only if the fact that *p* is a reason for her to φ and, in virtue of *p*, it is, other things being equal, morally better that she φs. In other words, a moral reason is a reason with morally favoring strength. See *reason for* and *favoring strength*.

Morally best option—An option is a subject's morally best option if and only if it is both sufficiently morally good and morally better than every alternative option. See *alternative option*.

Morally requiring reason—A morally requiring reason is a moral reason that has some morally requiring strength. See *moral reason* and *requiring strength*.

More reason—For any two options φ and ψ, a subject has more reason to φ than to ψ if and only if the set of all the reasons that she has to φ has greater combined favoring strength than the set of all the reasons that she has to ψ. See *favoring strength*.

Most reason—For any option φ, a subject has most reason to φ if and only if she has more reason to φ than to perform any alternative option. See *more reason* and *alternative option*. Contrast with *decisive reason*.

Murder—Murder consists in intentionally killing an innocent person without her consent.

Nonmaximal option—An option φ is a nonmaximal option if and only if it is not a maximal option. See *option*. Contrast with *maximal option*.

Nonmaximally specific option—An option φ is a nonmaximally specific option if and only if it is not a maximally specific option. See *distinct option*. Contrast with *maximally specific option*.

Nonminimally specific option—An option φ is a nonminimally specific option if and only if it is not a minimally specific option. See *option*. Contrast with *minimally specific option*.

Nonnormative possibility—A nonnormative possibility is a possibility such as the possibility that a subject's φ-ing would maximize utility or the possibility that a subject has the option of φ-ing. Contrast with *normative possibility*.

Nonnullusism—According to nonnullusism (*nonnullus* meaning "not none" or "some" in Latin), only some options are to have their deontic statuses assessed in terms of their own goodness. See *option* and *deontic status*. Contrast with *omnism, maximalism,* and *nullusism*.

Nonteleology—A theory is nonteleological if and only if it is not teleological. Contrast with *deontology* and with *teleology*.

Normative possibility—A normative possibility is a possibility such as the possibility that what makes an option best is that it maximizes utility or the possibility that what makes a bet best is that it maximizes expected utility. Contrast with *nonnormative possibility*.

Nullusism—According to nullusism (*nullus* meaning "none" in Latin), no option is to have its deontic status assessed in terms of its own goodness. Thus, for any subject S and any option of hers φ: (**OUGHT**) S ought to φ if and only if φ is entailed by her best maximal option, (**PERMI**) S is permitted to φ if and only if φ is entailed by one of her sufficiently good maximal options, and (**SUPER**) S's φ-ing is supererogatory if and only if φ is entailed by some maximal option M_x with an alternative maximal option M_y such that (1) she is morally permitted both to M_x and to M_y, and (2) her M_x-ing is better than her M_y-ing. (The relevant deontic statuses are the objective ones. Also, I leave implicit the relevant grounding clauses. For instance, I leave implicit that if a subject ought to φ, this is in virtue of the fact that φ is entailed by her best maximal option.) See *entails, maximal option,* and *deontic status*. Contrast with *omnism, maximalism,* and *nonnullusism*.

Objective gamble—An objective gamble is an act of risk-taking in which the risk is measured in terms of the objective probability that some unwelcomed event will occur. See *objective probability*. Contrast with *subjective gamble*.

Objective ought—What a subject objectively ought to do depends solely on the facts concerning what her options are, how they relate to each other, what ultimately matters, and how her options compare in terms of whatever ultimately matters. Substantively speaking, for any event φ, a subject objectively ought to φ if and only if φ is appropriately related to her best option. (One possibility is that φ's being appropriately related to her best option consists in φ's being identical to her best option, but another possibility is that φ's being appropriately related to her best option consists in φ's being entailed by her best option.) Contrast with *subjective ought*.

Objective probability—The objective probability that some event will (or would) occur is the percentage of the time that it will (or would) occur under identical causal circumstances—circumstances where the causal laws and histories are exactly the same. Contrast with *evidential probability*.

Obligation dilemma—An obligation dilemma is a situation in which a subject is both obligated to φ and obligated to ψ but does not have the option of <φ-ing and ψ-ing>. See *option*. Contrast with *tragic dilemma* and *joint satisfiability*.

Obligatory—For any option φ, a subject's φ-ing is obligatory if and only if she is permitted to φ but not to perform any alternative to φ. And note that all permissible options are either optional or obligatory. Also, note that all obligatory options ought to be performed. See *option, permissible, deontic status*, and *ought to be performed*. Contrast with *optional*.

Omnism—According to omnism (*omni* meaning "all" in Latin), all options are to have their deontic statuses assessed in terms of their own goodness. Thus, for any option φ, the deontic status of φ depends on how φ's goodness compares to that of its alternatives. See *entails, option*, and *deontic status*. Contrast with *maximalism, nullusism*, and *nonnullusism*.

Omnism about reasons—(A-REASON) For any subject S and any option of hers φ, S has a reason (or a T reason) to φ if and only if there is something good (or T good) about S's φ-ing. (MORE-REASON) For any subject S and any two of her options φ and ψ, S has more reason (or T more reason) to φ than to ψ if and only if φ is better (or T-ly better) than ψ. (MOST-REASON) For any subject S and any option of hers φ, S has most reason (or most T reason) to φ if and only if φ is better (or T-ly better) than every alternative option. See *entails, option, best option, more reason*, and *most reason*. Contrast with *maximalism about reasons*.

Omnism about statuses—For any subject S and any option of hers φ, (OUGHT) S ought to φ if and only if φ is her best option, (PERMI) S is permitted to φ if and only if φ is one of her sufficiently good options, and (SUPER) S's φ-ing is supererogatory if and only if there is some alternative option ψ such that (1) she is both permitted to φ and permitted to ψ and (2) her φ-ing is better than her ψ-ing. (The relevant deontic statuses are the objective ones. Also, I leave implicit the relevant grounding clauses. For instance, I leave implicit that if a subject ought to φ, this is in virtue of the fact that φ is her best option.) See *entails, supererogatory, deontic status*, and *alternative option*. Contrast with *maximalism about statuses*.

Optimal—An option is optimal if and only if there is no alternative option that is better than it. See *option, better option*, and *alternative option*. Contrast with *optimific*.

Optimific—An option is optimific if and only if it is better than every alternative option. See *option, better option*, and *alternative option*. Contrast with *optimal*.

Optimific noninheritance—It is not the case that, for any subject S and any two options φ and ψ, if S's φ-ing would have optimific consequences and S's φ-ing entails S's ψ-ing, then S's ψ-ing would have optimific consequences.

Option—An option for a subject is any member of the set such that, for any possible event *e*, whether her *e*-ing has a deontic status depends on whether *e* is a member of this set.

Optional—For any option φ, a subject's φ-ing is optional if and only if she is both permitted to φ and permitted to refrain from φ-ing. And note that all permissible options are either optional or obligatory. See *option, permissible*, and *deontic status*. Contrast with *obligatory*.

The Opting-for-the-Best View—There is a set of events, which is a proper subset of all possible events and which I call the set of S's options (or 'O' for short) such that, for any subject S and any possible event *e*, whether S's *e*-ing has a deontic status depends on whether *e* is a member of O, and, if it is a member of O, then what particular deontic status it has depends on how it compares to the alternative members of O such that, for any member φ of a certain subset (perhaps, a proper subset) of O, (**OUGHT**) S ought to φ if and only if φ is the best member of this subset of O; (**PERMI**) S is permitted to φ if and only if φ is one of the sufficiently good members of this subset of O; and (**SUPER**) S's φ-ing is supererogatory if and only if there is some alternative member of this subset of O, ψ, such that (1) she is both permitted to φ and permitted to ψ and (2) her φ-ing is better than her ψ-ing. [I leave implicit that the word "objectively" should modify each deontic status. I also leave implicit that for each bi-conditional, the right side grounds the left side.] See *option, supererogatory, deontic status*, and *alternative member*.

Ought-Most-Reason View—For any subject S and any option of hers φ, S ought to φ if and only if S has most reason to φ—that is, if and only if S has more reason to φ than to perform any alternative option. See *option, most reason*, and *alternative option*.

Ought to Be performed—For any option φ, a subject ought to φ if and only if she is permitted to φ and her φ-ing is better than every alternative to φ. Thus, a subject ought to φ if and only if she ought to φ. Now, all obligatory options ought to be performed, and some, but not all, optional options ought to be performed. The optional options that ought to be performed are those that are better than each of its alternatives. See *option, permissible*, and *deontic status*.

Outcome—The outcome of a subject's φ-ing is the possible world that would be actual if she were to φ. If there is no determinate way the world would be if she were to φ (if, say, counterfactual determinism is false), then her φ-ing doesn't have *an* outcome, but only a prospect. See *counterfactual determinism*. Contrast with *prospect*.

Partial control—A subject's control over whether she φs is merely partial if and only if, holding everything else fixed, how she exercises her control determines, not whether she will φ, but only the objective probability between 0 and 1 that she'll φ. See *control* and *objective probability*. Contrast with *complete control*.

Perfect duty—A perfect duty is a duty that doesn't derive from a duty to adopt a certain set of ends. Contrast with *imperfect duty*.

Permissible—For any option φ, a subject's φ-ing is permissible if and only if her φ-ing is not wrong/prohibited/impermissible. See *option* and *deontic status*. Contrast with *impermissible*.

Permission inheritance—For any subject S and any two of her options φ and ψ, if S is permitted to φ and S's φ-ing entails S's ψ-ing, then S is permitted to ψ. See *option*.

Personal control—A subject's control over her φ-ing is personal if and only if this control makes her φ-ing intelligible to her in terms of her reasons and her capacity for responding to them and not merely in terms of cause and effect. See *control*. Contrast with *subpersonal control*.

Possibilism (also known as *schedulist possibilism*)—For any subject S and any maximal act MA_x that she could possibly perform, S ought to MA_x if and only if there is no alternative maximal act that she could possibly perform, MA_y, such that what would actually happen if she were to MA_y is at least as good as what would actually happen if she were to MA_x. And for any subject S and any nonmaximal act NA that she could possibly perform, S ought to NA if and only if there is a MA_x that she ought to perform that entails her NA-ing. See *could possibly perform*. Contrast with *actualism*.

Pragmatic reasons—For any subject S, any option of hers φ, and any fact p, the fact that p is a pragmatic reason for S to φ if and only if the fact that p is a reason for S to φ and it would be good if S were to φ at least in part because p. See *option*. Contrast with *fittingness reasons*.

Preference ordering—A preference ordering is a cardinal ranking of some set of outcomes or prospects according to some entity's actual or hypothetical preferences, and, being a cardinal ranking, it will convey not only which prospects are (or should be) preferred to which others but also by how much each is (or should be) preferred.

Pride—To take pride in X is, in part, to have the thought that X reveals that one is good or superior in a way that could potentially result in a gain of honor, respect, or esteem. (Pride is the positive analogue of shame.) See *thought*. Contrast with *shame* and *deontic pride*.

Principle of Moral Harmony—According to this principle, a moral theory is correct if and only if the agents who satisfy it, whoever and however numerous they may be, are guaranteed to produce the morally best world that they could (in the relevant sense) together produce. See *satisfy*.

Principle of Rationalist Moral Harmony (RMH)—According to this principle, a moral theory is correct if and only if the agents who satisfy it, whoever and however numerous they may be, are guaranteed to produce the morally best world that they could together produce by each of them, at present, responding appropriately to their reasons. See *satisfy*. Contrast with *principle of strict moral harmony*.

Principle of Schedulist Moral Harmony (SMH)—According to this principle, a moral theory is correct if and only if the agents who satisfy it, whoever and however numerous they may be, are guaranteed to produce the morally best world that they could together produce by their following a certain schedule of intention-formations whereby each of them forms (or doesn't form) certain intentions at certain times. See *satisfy*. Contrast with *principle of reasonable moral harmony*.

Probabilism—For any subject S, any proposition *p* such that she has a reason to see to it that *p*, and any option of hers φ that is a necessary means to her seeing to it that *p*, S has a reason (specifically, an instrumental reason) to φ only if S's φ-ing would increase the objective probability that *p*—that is, only if the objective probability that *p* on the condition that S φs is greater than the objective probability that *p* on the condition that S doesn't φ. See *option* and *instrumental reason*.

Problem of act versions—The problem of act versions is the problem posed by the fact that the following three seemingly plausible propositions are jointly inconsistent: (1) for any subject S and any option of hers φ, S ought to φ if and only if φ is her best option; (2) for any subject S and any two of her options φ and ψ, if S ought to φ and S's φ-ing entails (or, in other words, is a version of) S's ψ-ing, then S ought to ψ; and (3) it is not the case that for any subject S and any two events φ and ψ, if φ is S's best option and S's φ-ing entails S's ψ-ing, then ψ is S's best option. In other words, it's the problem posed by the fact that omnism, deontic inheritance, and evaluative noninheritance are all seemingly plausible but jointly incompatible. See *option, best option, omnism, deontic inheritance*, and *evaluative noninheritance*.

Problem of overdetermination—This is the problem of accounting for our intuition that there has been a moral failure in cases of overdetermination such as *Slice and Patch Go Golfing*, and solving the problem involves identifying what the moral failure is, who committed it, and why it counts as a moral failure. See *moral failure*.

Prohibition dilemma—A prohibition dilemma is a situation in which a mutually exclusive and jointly exhaustive set of options are all impermissible. See *option*. Contrast with *obligation dilemma*.

Proper subset—For any two sets A and B, if every member of A is also a member of B, but not every member of B is also a member of A, then A is a proper subset of B. Contrast with *subset*.

Propositional content—The propositional content of a subject's intention to φ is the proposition that she will φ, and the propositional content of a subject's belief that *p* is the proposition that *p*.

Prospect—The prospect of a subject's φ-ing is the probability distribution consisting in the mutually exclusive and jointly exhaustive set of possible worlds that could be actualized by her φ-ing, with each possibility assigned an objective probability such that the sum of those objective probabilities equals 1. See *objective probability*. Contrast with *outcome*.

Rational capacities—For any option φ, a subject has, as of time *t*, the relevant rational capacities with respect to whether she φs at some later time *t'* if and only if she is inherently so structured that, under a suitably wide range of conditions, she would recognize the considerations that count for and against her φ-ing at *t'* and either φ or refrain from φ-ing at *t'* depending on which response these considerations make appropriate. See *option*.

Rational control—Rational control is the sort of control that we exert directly over our reasons-responsive attitudes (such as our beliefs, desires, and intentions) and indirectly over those things that we influence via such attitudes (such as our voluntary actions). My tentative proposal is that for any event *e*, a subject has, as of time *t*, rational control over whether she *e*-s at some later time *t'* if and only if she has, as of *t*, the relevant rational capacities and whether she *e*-s at *t'* depends (and in the right way) on whether and how she exercises these capacities at *t*. See *control, rational capacities*, and *reasons-responsive attitudes*.

Rationalism—For any subject S and any event *e*, S has at time *t* the option of *e*-ing at a later time *t'* if and only if she has, as of *t*, rational control over whether she *e*-s at *t'*. See *option, control*, and *rational control*. Contrast with *tryism, schedulism, voluntarism*, and *volitionalism*.

Reactive attitudes—These attitudes are formed in reaction to a subject's having φ-ed, and they include the following: pride, guilt, anger, regret, shame, remorse, gratitude, contrition, frustration, resentment, indignation, satisfaction, and disappointment. See also *retributive attitudes* and *meritorious attitudes*.

Reason for—Let 'T' stand for something such as "moral," "rational," or "prudential." For any subject S, a T reason for S to φ is a fact that counts in T-ly favor of her φ-ing—that is, it's a reason with some T-ly favoring strength with respect to her φ-ing. Consequently, a T reason for S to φ plays at least one of the following two functional roles: (FR1) it could make it the case that S T-ly ought to φ and/or (FR$_2$) it could make it the case that S is T-ly required to φ. See *favoring strength*.

Reasons inheritance—For any subject S and any two options φ and ψ, if S has a T (or most T) reason to φ and S's φ-ing entails S's ψ-ing, then S has a T (or most T) reason to ψ. See *option, entails*, and *most reason*.

Reasons-responsive attitudes—Reasons-responsive attitudes include all and only those mental states that a rational subject will tend to have, or tend not to have, in response to her awareness of reasons (or apparent reasons)—facts (or what are taken to be facts) that count for or against the attitudes in question.

Relevantly informed—A subject is relevantly informed if and only if she knows all the relevant facts—that is, all the facts that are relevant to determining what the deontic and evaluative statuses of her options are. See *options, deontic status*, and *evaluative status*.

Repressible—For any option φ, a subject's tendency to φ is presently repressible if and only if she will refrain from φ-ing so long as she appropriately exercises her rational capacities at present, resolving not to φ. See *rational capacities*. Contrast with *irrepressible*.

Requiring strength—Let 'T' stand for something such as "moral," "rational," or "prudential." One reason, R_1, has more T-ly requiring strength than another, R_2, if and only if both (1) R_1 would make it T-ly impermissible to do anything that R_2 would make it T-ly impermissible to do, and (2) R_1 would make it T-ly impermissible do some things that R_2 would not make it T-ly impermissible to do (GERT 2003, pp. 15–16). Requiring strength is, like enticing strength, a type of favoring strength. See *enticing strength* and *favoring strength*. Contrast with *justifying strength*.

Resolution—A resolution to φ consists in both a first-order intention to φ and a second-order intention not to let that first-order intention be deflected by anticipated temptation not to φ—see Holton 2009 (pp. 11–12).

Response constraint—(RC1) For any option φ, any subject S, and any proposition *p*, the fact that *p* constitutes a genuine reason for S to φ only if both (a) S has the capacity to know or otherwise adequately cognize this fact and (b) her adequately cognizing this fact could, via the exercise of her rational capacities, directly cause her to φ—that is, without doing so via the intermediary step of causing her to form the intention to φ. And (RC2), for any principle P that directs a subject to φ based on certain facts that putatively constitute decisive reason for her to φ, P states a genuine obligation only if both (a) she has the capacity to know or otherwise adequately cognize these facts and (b) her adequately cognizing these facts could, via the exercise of her rational capacities, directly cause her to φ. See *rational capacities* and *decisive reason*.

Responsible—For a subject to be responsible for having φ-ed is for her to be the appropriate target of normative assessment in virtue of her having φ-ed. See *accountable* and *attributable*.

Resultant moral luck—Resultant moral luck occurs when one's degree of accountability for φ-ing is affected by events over which one lacks control and that determine the results of one's φ-ing. An example would be where an assassin's degree of accountability for intentionally lining up a headshot with her sniper rifle and then pulling the trigger is affected by whether or not a bird happens to unexpectedly fly into the path of the bullet, thereby preventing the assassin from killing her intended target. See *control* and *accountability*.

Retributive attitude—A retributive attitude is one that includes the constitutive thought that someone deserves to suffer some burden. (I take guilt, resentment, and indignation to all be retributive attitudes. For, as I see it, a thought that's constitutive both of my feeling guilt for having φ-ed and of your feeling resentment and/or indignation for my having φ-ed is the thought that I deserve to suffer the unpleasantness of feeling guilt in the recognition that I have, in φ-ing, violated some legitimate demand.) See *deserves* and *thought*. Contrast with *meritorious attitude*.

Rule-consequentialism—Rule-consequentialism is the view that holds (1) that an option is permissible if and only if it accords with the best code of rules; (2) that, if an option is permissible, it is in virtue of the fact that it accords with the best code of rules; and (3) that what ultimately matters is only the (impersonal) goodness of the world such that one option or code of rules is better than another if and only if the one has more expected goodness than the other. See *option* and *consequentialism*. Contrast with *act-consequentialism*.

Satisfy—An agent satisfies a normative theory if and only if she complies with all the theory's directives, doing everything that the theory says that she ought to do, where this includes everything that she's required to do and whatever else it would be morally best to do, including any morally best acts that are supererogatory.

Schedulism—For any subject S and any event *e*, S has at time *t* the option of *e*-ing at a later time *t'* if and only if whether she *e*-s at *t'* depends (in the right way) on her having certain intentions from *t* onward—that is, on her having a certain schedule of intentions from *t* onward. See *option*. Contrast with *tryism, rationalism, voluntarism*, and *volitionalism*.

Shame—To feel ashamed of *X* is, in part, to have the thought that *X* reveals that one is substandard in a way that could potentially result in a loss of honor, respect, or esteem. (Shame is the negative analogue of pride.) See *thought*. Contrast with *pride*.

Subjective gamble—A subjective gamble is an act of risk-taking in which the risk is measured in terms of the evidential probability (relative to the agent) that some unwelcome event will occur. See *evidential probability*. Contrast with *objective gamble*.

Subjective ought—For any option φ, a subject subjectively ought to φ if and only if we can legitimately expect (in the normative, and not necessarily the probabilistic, sense of "expect") her to intend to φ—assuming, that is, that she believes that whether she φs is controlled by her intentions. Thus, it's a conceptual truth that a subject who believes that she subjectively ought to φ will intend to φ if she's conscientious. Substantively speaking, a subject subjectively ought to φ if and only if φ is an option for her that constitutes her best bet. See *option, conscientious*, and *best bet*. Contrast with *objective ought*.

Subpersonal control—A subject's control over her φ-ing is subpersonal if and only if this control makes her φ-ing intelligible to her merely in terms of cause and effect, and not in terms of her reasons or her capacity for responding to them. See *control*. Contrast with *personal control*.

Subset—For any two sets A and B, if every member of A is also a member of B, then A is a subset of B. (This allows that A can be a subset of B even if A and B each contain all the same members.) Contrast with *proper subset*.

Sufficient reason—A subject has sufficient reason to φ if and only if her reasons are such as to make her permitted to φ. Contrast with *decisive reason*.

Sufficiently good bet—An option is a sufficiently good bet for a subject if and only if it is what a conscientious person of her abilities, capacities, and epistemic position might do in her circumstances and it is what she would do in her circumstances if this option were her only sufficiently good bet. See *option* and *conscientious person*.

Sufficiently good option—An option is a sufficiently good option if and only if it is good enough both in terms of how it compares to the alternative options and in terms of whatever the relevant noncomparative standards are. See *option* and *alternative option*.

Supererogation inheritance—For any subject S and any two of her options φ and ψ, if S's φ-ing is supererogatory and S's φ-ing entails S's ψ-ing, then S's ψ-ing is also supererogatory. See *option, entails*, and *supererogatory*.

Supererogatory—For any option φ, a subject's φ-ing is supererogatory if and only if her φ-ing is optional and better than some permissible alternative. In other words, her φ-ing is supererogatory if and only if, in φ-ing, she goes beyond the call of duty, exceeding what's minimally required of her. See *option, optional, permissible*, and *deontic status*. Contrast with superperfecterogatory.

Superperfecterogatory—A subject's φ-ing is superperfecterogatory if and only if, in φ-ing, she goes beyond the call of perfect duty—that is, if and only if, in φ-ing, she does more than what her perfect duties require of her (SINNOTT-ARMSTRONG 2005, p. 204). See *perfect duty*. Contrast with *supererogatory*.

Surplus time and resources—Our surplus time and resources are whatever time and resources that we have in excess of what's necessary to ensure a sufficient degree of our own happiness and moral virtue.

Synchronic View—A subject has at *t* the option of φ-ing at *t'* if and only if whether she φs at *t'* depends (in the right way) merely on how she exerts her control at *t*. Contrast with *diachronic view*.

Teleology—A theory is teleological if and only if it holds that, for any option, the goodness (or badness) of that option ultimately and solely depends on the extent to which its outcome or prospect is to be preferred (or dispreferred) to those of its alternatives. Contrast with *nonteleology*.

Thought—For a subject to have the thought that *p* is only for it to strike her that *p* in the same way that it can strike her that the lines in a Müller-Lyer illusion are unequal in length even while she believes that they are equal in length. Thus, unlike having the belief that *p*, having the thought that *p* needn't include a disposition to assent to *p*.

Threshold—For any constraint against performing an act of a certain kind, that constraint has a threshold if merely performing an act of that kind (that is, merely infringing upon that constraint) is insufficient to count as having violated that constraint. For instance, if a subject counts as having violated a constraint against performing acts of a certain kind if and only if she performs an act of that kind that doesn't produce at least n amount of goodness, then that constraint has a threshold. See *violates, infringes*, and *agent-centered constraint*.

Tryism—For any subject S and any event e, S has at time t the option of e-ing at a later time t' only if she would e at t' if she were to try to e at t. See *option*. Contrast with *rationalism, schedulism, voluntarism*, and *volitionalism*.

Ultimately matters—See *matters*.

Utility—Utility is a theoretical construct that's used as a measurement of how much well-being something produces or possesses.

Version—For any two options φ and ψ, a subject's φ-ing (e.g., kissing passionately) is a version of her ψ-ing (e.g., kissing) if and only if her φ-ing entails her ψ-ing but not vice versa. See *option* and *entails*.

Violates—A subject violates (as opposed to merely infringes upon) a constraint against her performing an act of a certain type if and only if she performs an act of that type that fails to satisfy all the applicable thresholds (THOMSON 1986, p. 51). See *agent-centered constraint*. Contrast with *infringes*.

Volitional control—Volitional control is the sort of control that we exert directly over our deliberate, voluntary actions (such as intentionally using one's arms to rotate the car's steering wheel) and indirectly over those things that we manipulate via such actions (such as the turning of the car that one's driving). My tentative proposal is that, for any option φ, a subject has, as of time t, volitional control over whether she φs at some later time t' if and only if she has, as of t, the capacity to form the volition to φ at t' for whatever reason she takes to be sufficient for doing so and whether she φs at t' depends (and in the right way) on whether and how she exercises this capacity at t—specifically, on whether she exercises it at t so as to form the volition to φ at t'. See *option, control*, and *voluntary act*. Contrast with *rational control*.

Volitionalism—For any subject S and any event e, S has at time t the option of e-ing at a later time t' if and only if she has, as of t, volitional control over whether she e-s at t'. See *option, control*, and *volitional control*. Contrast with *tryism, schedulism, rationalism*, and *voluntarism*.

Voluntarism—For any subject S and any event e, S has at time t the option of e-ing at a later time t' if and only if she has, as of t, voluntary control over whether she e-s at t'. See *option, control*, and *voluntary control*. Contrast with *tryism, schedulism, rationalism*, and *volitionalism*.

Voluntary act—A voluntary act is one over which its agent exerts voluntary control. See *voluntary control*.

Voluntary control—A subject has voluntary control over whether she φs at t' if and only if she has both volitional control over whether she φs at t' and rational control over whether she forms the volition to φ at t'. See *control, rational control*, and *volitional control*.

Welfarism—Welfarism is the view that one prospect is better than another if and only if its utility (or expected utility) is greater than the other's. See *utility* and *expected utility*.

Wrong—A subject's φ-ing is wrong if and only if φ is an option that she's not permitted to perform. See *option*.

REFERENCES

Aboodi, R., A. Borer, and D. Enoch. (2008). "Deontology, Individualism, and Uncertainty: A Reply to Jackson and Smith." *Journal of Philosophy* 105: 259–272.

Adams, R. M. (1985). "Involuntary Sins." *Philosophical Review* 94: 1–31.

Alexander, L. (2016). "The Means Principle." *SSRN University of San Diego School of Law Legal Studies Research Paper Series*, Research Paper No. 14-138. Retrieved January 20, 2016, from SSRN: http://ssrn.com/abstract=2378608.

Alexander, L. (2000). "Deontology at the Threshold." *San Diego Law Review* 37: 893–912.

Alexander, L. and M. Moore. (2015). "Deontological Ethics." In E. N. Zalta (ed.), *The Stanford Encyclopedia of Philosophy* (Spring Edition), http://plato.stanford.edu/archives/spr2015/entries/ethics-deontological/.

Archer, A. (2016A). "Moral Obligation, Self-Interest and the Transitivity Problem." *Utilitas* 28: 441–464.

Archer, A. (2016B). "The Supererogatory and How Not to Accommodate It: A Reply to Dorsey." *Utilitas* 28: 179–188.

Arpaly, N. (2006). *Merit, Meaning, and Human Bondage: An Essay on Free Will.* Princeton, NJ: Princeton University Press.

Arpaly, N. (2003). *Unprincipled Virtue: An Inquiry into Moral Agency.* New York: Oxford University Press.

Austin, J. L. (1956). "Ifs and Cans." *Proceedings of the British Academy* 42: 107–132.

Baier, K. (1958). *The Moral Point of View.* Ithaca, NY: Cornell University Press.

Bergström, L. (1966). *The Alternatives and Consequences of Actions.* Stockholm: Almqvist & Wiksell.

Björnsson, G. (2017). "Review of Rik Peels, Responsible Belief: A Theory in Ethics and Epistemology." *Notre Dame Philosophical Reviews.*

Bradley, B. (2006). "Against Satisficing Consequentialism." *Utilitas* 18: 97–108.

Bratman, M. E. (2009). "Intention, Belief, Practical, Theoretical." In S. Robertson (ed.), *Spheres of Reason*, pp. 29–62. Oxford: Oxford University Press.

Bratman, M. E. (2007). *Structures of Agency.* New York: Oxford University Press.

Bratman, M. E. (1987). *Intention, Plans, and Practical Reason*. Cambridge, MA: Harvard University Press.

Broome, J. (2013). *Rationality through Reasoning*. Chichester, UK: Wiley-Blackwell.

Broome, J. (2004). "Reasons." In R. J. Wallace, P. Pettit, S. Scheffler, and M. Smith (eds.), *Reasons and Value: Themes from the Moral Philosophy of Joseph Raz*, pp. 91–118. Oxford: Clarendon Press.

Brown, C. (2018). "Maximalism and the Structure of Acts." *Noûs* 52: 752–771.

Buchak, L. (2013A). *Risk and Rationality*. Oxford: Oxford University Press. Kindle edition.

Buchak, L. (2013B). "Free Acts and Chance." *Philosophical Quarterly* 63: 20–28.

Bykvist, K. (2002). "Alternative Actions and the Spirit of Consequentialism." *Philosophical Studies* 107: 45–68.

Cariani, F. (2013). "'Ought' and Resolution Semantics." *Noûs* 47: 534–558.

Carlson, E. (1999A). "The Oughts and Cans of Objective Consequentialism." *Utilitas* 11: 91–96.

Carlson, E. (1999B). "Consequentialism, Alternatives, and Actualism." *Philosophical Studies* 96: 253–268.

Carlsson, A. B. (2017). "Blameworthiness as Deserved Guilt." *Journal of Ethics* 21: 89–115.

Carlsson, A. B. (2015). *Ignorance and Control: Essays on Moral Blameworthiness*. PhD dissertation, University of Oslo.

Castañeda, H.-N. (1981). "The Paradoxes of Deontic Logic: The Simplest Solution to All of Them in One Fell Swoop." In R. Hilpinen (ed.), *New Studies in Deontic Logic*, pp. 37–85. Dordrecht: D. Reidel.

Castañeda, H.-N. (1974). *The Structure of Morality*. Springfield, IL: Charles Thomas.

Castañeda, H.-N. (1968). "A Problem for Utilitarianism." *Analysis* 28: 141–142.

Chang, R. (2016). "Comparativism: The Grounds of Rational Choice." In E. Lord and B. Maguire (eds.), *Weighing Reasons*, pp. 213–240. Oxford: Oxford University Press.

Chappell, R. Y. (2012). "Fittingness: The Sole Normative Primitive." *Philosophical Quarterly* 62: 684–704.

Clarke, R. (2016). "Moral Responsibility, Guilt, and Retributivism." *Journal of Ethics* 20: 121–137.

Clarke, R. (2013). "Some Theses on Desert." *Philosophical Explorations* 16: 153–164.

Cohen, Y. and T. Timmerman (2016). "Actualism Has Control Issues." *Journal of Ethics and Social Philosophy* 10: 1–18.

Copp, D. (2008). "'Ought' Implies 'Can' and the Derivation of the Principle of Alternate Possibilities." *Analysis* 68: 67–75.

Copp, D. (2003). "'Ought' Implies 'Can,' Blameworthiness, and the Principle of Alternate Possibilities." In D. Widerker and M. McKenna (eds.), *Moral Responsibility and Alternate Possibilities*, pp. 265–299. Burlington, VT: Ashgate.

Copp, D. (1997A) "Defending the Principle of Alternate Possibilities: Blameworthiness and Moral Responsibility." *Noûs* 31: 441–456.

Copp, D. (1997B). "The Ring of Gyges: Overridingness and the Unity of Reason." *Social Philosophy and Policy* 14: 86–106.

Curran, A. (1995). "Utilitarianism and Future Mistakes: Another Look." *Philosophical Studies* 78: 71–85.

D'Arms, J. and D. Jacobson. (2003). "The Significance of Recalcitrant Emotion (or, Anti-Quasijudgmentalism)." *Philosophy* 52 (Supp): 127–145.

D'Arms, J. and D. Jacobson. (2000). "The Moralistic Fallacy: On the 'Appropriateness' of the Emotions." *Philosophy and Phenomenological Research* 61: 65–90.

Dancy, J. (2004). "Enticing Reasons." In R. J. Wallace, P. Pettit, S. Scheffler, and M. Smith (eds.), *Reasons and Value: Themes from the Moral Philosophy of Joseph Raz*, pp. 91–118. Oxford: Clarendon Press.

Darwall, S. (2013). "Morality's Distinctiveness." In S. Darwall (ed.), *Morality, Authority, and Law: Essays in Second-Personal Ethics I*, pp. 3–19. Oxford: Oxford University Press.

Darwall, S. (2010). "But It Would Be Wrong." *Social Philosophy and Policy* 27: 135–157.

Darwall, S. (2006). *The Second-Person Standpoint: Morality, Respect, and Accountability.* Cambridge, MA: Harvard University Press.

Dorsey, D. (2016). *The Limits of Moral Authority.* Oxford: Oxford University Press.

Dorsey, D. (2013A). "The Supererogatory, and How to Accommodate It." *Utilitas* 25: 355–382.

Dorsey, D. (2013B). "Consequentialism, Cognitive Limitations, and Moral Theory." In M. Timmons (ed.), *Oxford Studies in Normative Ethics*, vol. 3, pp. 179–202. Oxford: Oxford University Press.

Drayson, Z. (2014). "The Personal/Subpersonal Distinction." *Philosophy Compass* 9: 338–346.

Dreier, J. (1993). "Structures of Normative Theories." *Monist* 76: 22–40.

Editors of *Encyclopedia Britannica.* (2017). "Teleological Ethics." *Encyclopedia Britannica.* Retrieved June 6, 2017, from https://www.britannica.com/topic/teleological-ethics.

Ellis, A. (1992). "Deontology, Incommensurability, and the Arbitrary." *Philosophy and Phenomenological Research* 52: 855–875.

Estlund, D. (FORTHCOMING). *Utopophobia: On the Limits (If Any) of Political Philosophy.* Princeton, NJ: Princeton University Press.

Estlund, D. (2017). "Prime Justice." In K. Vallier and M. Weber (eds.), *Political Utopias*, pp. 35–55. Oxford: Oxford University Press.

Ewing, A. C. (1948). *The Definition of Good.* London: Routledge and Kegan Paul.

Feldman, F. (1986). *Doing the Best We Can: An Essay in Informal Deontic Logic.* Dordrecht: D. Reidel.

Feldman, F. (1980). "The Principle of Moral Harmony." *Journal of Philosophy* 77: 166–179.

Fischer, J. M. (2006). *My Way: Essays on Moral Responsibility.* New York: Oxford University Press.

Fischer, J. M. (2003). "'Ought-Implies-Can,' Causal Determinism and Moral Responsibility." *Analysis* 63: 244–250.

Fischer, J. M. (1994). *The Metaphysics of Free Will: An Essay on Control*. Oxford: Wiley-Blackwell.

Fischer, J. M., and M. Ravizza. (1998). *Responsibility and Control: A Theory of Moral Responsibility*. Cambridge: Cambridge University Press.

Foot, P. (1985). "Utilitarianism and the Virtues." *Mind* 94: 196–209.

Forcehimes, A. T. and L. Semrau (2015). "The Difference We Make: A Reply to Pinkert." *Journal of Ethics & Social Philosophy*, www.jesp.org. (September Discussion Note).

Frankfurt, H. G. (1969). "Alternate Possibilities and Moral Responsibility." *Journal of Philosophy* 66: 829–839.

Furlong, P. (2017). "Libertarianism, the Rollback Argument, and the Objective Probability of Free Choices." *Pacific Philosophical Quarterly* 98: 512–532.

Gert, J. (2014). "Perform a Justified Option." *Utilitas* 26: 206–217.

Gert, J. (2012). *Normative Bedrock: Response-Dependence, Rationality, and Reasons*. Oxford: Oxford University Press.

Gert, J. (2007A). "Normative Strength and the Balance of Reasons." *Philosophical Review* 116: 533–562.

Gert, J. (2007B). "Reply to Tenenbaum." *Canadian Journal of Philosophy* 37: 463–476.

Gert, J. (2004). *Brute Rationality: Normativity and Human Actions*. Cambridge: Cambridge University Press.

Gert, J. (2003). "Requiring and Justifying: Two Dimensions of Normative Strength." *Erkenntnis* 59: 5–36.

Gibbard, A. (1990). *Wise Choices, Apt Feelings: A Theory of Normative Judgment*. Cambridge, MA: Harvard University Press.

Gibbons, J. (2013). *The Norm of Belief*. Oxford: Oxford University Press.

Gibbons, J. (2010). "Things That Make Things Reasonable." *Philosophy and Phenomenological Research* 81: 335–361.

Goldman, H. S. [now H. M. Smith]. (1978). "Doing the Best One Can." In A. I. Goldman and J. Kim (eds.), *Values and Morals*, pp. 185–214. Dordrecht: D. Reidel.

Goldman, H. S. [now H. M. Smith]. (1976). "Dated Rightness and Moral Imperfection." *Philosophical Review* 85: 449–487.

Goldstein, S. (2016). "A Preface Paradox for Intention." *Philosophers' Imprint* 16: 1–20.

Gomberg, P. (1989). "Consequentialism and History." *Canadian Journal of Philosophy* 19: 383–403.

Graham, A. (2014). "A Sketch of a Theory of Moral Blameworthiness." *Philosophy and Phenomenological Research* 88: 388–409.

Gustafsson, J. E. (2014). "Combinative Consequentialism and the Problem of Act Versions." *Philosophical Studies* 167: 585–596.

Haji, I. (1997). "Frankfurt-Pairs and Varieties of Blameworthiness: Epistemic Morals." *Erkenntnis* 47: 351–377.

Hare, C. (2011). "Obligation and Regret When There Is No Fact of the Matter about What Would Have Happened if You Had Not Done What You Did." *Noûs* 45: 190–206.

Harman, E. (2015). "The Irrelevance of Moral Uncertainty." In R. Shafer-Landau (ed.), *Oxford Studies in Metaethics*, vol. 10, pp. 53–79. Oxford: Oxford University Press.

Harwood, S. (2003). "Eleven Objections to Utilitarianism." In L. Pojman (ed.), *Moral Philosophy: A Reader*, 3rd ed., pp. 179–192. Indianapolis: Hackett.

Hieronymi, P. (2008). "Responsibility for Believing." *Synthese* 161: 357–373.

Hieronymi, P. (2014). "Reflection and Responsibility." *Philosophy & Public Affairs* 42: 3–41.

Hieronymi, P. (2006). "Controlling Attitudes." *Pacific Philosophical Quarterly* 87: 45–74.

Hieronymi, P. (2004). "The Force and Fairness of Blame." *Philosophical Perspectives* 18: 115–148.

Hill, T. E. Jr. (2002). *Human Welfare and Moral Worth*. Oxford: Oxford University Press.

Holton, R. (2009). *Willing, Wanting, Waiting*. Oxford: Oxford University Press.

Hooker, B. (2000). *Ideal Code, Real World*. Oxford: Oxford University Press.

Horton, J. (2017). "The All or Nothing Problem." *Journal of Philosophy* 114: 94–104.

Howard-Snyder, F. (1999). "Response to Carlson and Qizilbash." *Utilitas* 11: 106–111.

Howard-Snyder, F. (1997). "The Rejection of Objective Consequentialism." *Utilitas* 9: 241–248.

Huemer, M. (2010). "Lexical Priority and the Problem of Risk." *Pacific Philosophical Quarterly* 91: 332–351.

Hurley, P. (2017). "Why Consequentialism's 'Compelling Idea' Is Not." *Social Theory and Practice* 43: 29–54.

Hurley, P. (2013). "Consequentializing and Deontologizing: Clogging the Consequentialist Vacuum." In M. Timmons (ed.), *Oxford Studies in Normative Ethics*, vol. 3, pp. 123–153. Oxford: Oxford University Press.

Hursthouse, R. (1991). "Virtue Theory and Abortion." *Philosophy and Public Affairs* 20: 223–246.

Isaacs, Y. (2014). "Duty and Knowledge." *Philosophical Perspectives* 28: 95–110.

Jackson, F. (2014). "Procrastinate Revisited." *Pacific Philosophical Quarterly* 95: 634–647.

Jackson, F. (1991). "Decision-Theoretic Consequentialism and the Nearest and Dearest Objection." *Ethics* 101: 461–482.

Jackson, F. and R. Pargetter (1986). "Oughts, Actions, and Actualism." *Philosophical Review* 95: 233–255.

Jackson, F. and M. Smith. (2016). "The Implementation Problem for Deontology." In E. Lord and B. Maguire (eds.), *Weighing Reasons*, pp. 279–291. Oxford: Oxford University Press.

Jackson, F. and M. Smith. (2006). "Absolutist Moral Theories and Uncertainty." *Journal of Philosophy* 103: 267–283.

Johnson, R. N. (1999). "Internal Reasons and the Conditional Fallacy." *Philosophical Quarterly* 49: 53–71.

Kagan, S. (1989). *The Limits of Morality*. Oxford: Oxford University Press.

Kamm, F. M. (2007). *Intricate Ethics*. Oxford: Oxford University Press.

Kamm, F. M. (1985). "Supererogation and Obligation." *Journal of Philosophy* 82: 118–138.

Kavka, G. (1983). "The Toxin Puzzle." *Analysis* 43: 33–36.

Kelly, T. (2002). "The Rationality of Belief and Some Other Propositional Attitudes." *Philosophical Studies* 110: 163–196.

Khoury, A. C. (2018). "The Objects of Moral Responsibility." *Philosophical Studies* 175: 1357–1381.

Kierland, B. (2006). "Cooperation, 'Ought Morally,' and Principles of Moral Harmony." *Philosophical Studies* 128: 381–407.

Kiesewetter, B. (2018). "Contrary-to-Duty Scenarios, Deontic Dilemmas and Transmission Principles." *Ethics* 129: 98–115.

Kiesewetter, B. (2017). *The Normativity of Rationality*. Oxford: Oxford University Press.

Kiesewetter, B. (2016). "You Ought to Φ Only If You May Believe that You Ought to Φ." *Philosophical Quarterly* 66: 760–782.

Kiesewetter, B. (2015). "Instrumental Normativity: In Defense of the Transmission Principle." *Ethics* 125: 921–946.

Killoren, D. and B. Williams (2013). "Group Agency and Overdetermination." *Ethical Theory and Moral Practice* 16: 295–307.

King, A. (2014). "Actions that We Ought, But Can't." *Ratio* 27: 316–327.

Kneer, M. and E. Machery (2019). "No Luck for Moral Luck." *Cognition* 182: 331–348.

Kolodny, N. (2018). "Instrumental Reasons." In D. Star (ed.), *The Oxford Handbook of Reasons and Normativity*, pp. 731–763. Oxford: Oxford University Press.

Kolodny, N. (2005). "Why Be Rational?" *Mind* 114: 509–563.

Kolodny, N. and J. MacFarlane (2010). "Ifs and Oughts." *Journal of Philosophy* 107: 115–143.

Lazar, S. (2018). "In Dubious Battle: Uncertainty and the Ethics of Killing." *Philosophical Studies* 175: 859–883.

Lazar, S. (2017). "Deontological Decision Theory and Agent-Centered Options." *Ethics* 127: 579–609.

Lewis, D. (1973). *Counterfactuals*. Oxford: Blackwell.

Lord, E. and B. Maguire. (2016). "An Opinionated Guide to the Weight of Reasons." In E. Lord and B. Maguire (eds.), *Weighing Reasons*, pp. 3–24. Oxford: Oxford University Press.

Louise, J. (2004). "Relativity of Value and the Consequentialist Umbrella." *Philosophical Quarterly* 54: 518–536.

Maier, J. (2014). "Abilities." In E. N. Zalta (ed.), *The Stanford Encyclopedia of Philosophy* (Fall Edition), http://plato.stanford.edu/archives/fall2014/entries/abilities/.

Marušić, B. (2015). *Evidence and Agency: Norms of Belief for Promising and Resolving*. Oxford: Oxford University Press.

McHugh, C. (2017). "Attitudinal Control." *Synthese* 194: 2745–2762.

McHugh, C. (2014). "Exercising Doxastic Freedom." *Philosophy and Phenomenological Research* 88: 1–37.

McHugh, C. (2012). "Epistemic Deontology and Voluntariness." *Erkenntnis* 77: 65–94.

McKenna, M. (2012). *Conversation and Responsibility*. Oxford: Oxford University Press.

McMahan, J. (2018). "Doing Good and Doing the Best." In P. Woodruff (ed.), *The Ethics of Giving: Philosophers' Perspectives on Philanthropy*, pp. 78–102. New York: Oxford University Press.

McNamara, P. (2014). "Deontic Logic." In E. N. Zalta (ed.), *The Stanford Encyclopedia of Philosophy* (Winter Edition), http://plato.stanford.edu/archives/win2014/entries/logic-deontic/.

Mellema, G. (1991). "Supererogation and the Fulfilment of Duty." *Journal of Value Inquiry* 25: 167–175.

Mill, J. S. (1991). [1861]. *Utilitarianism*. In J. M. Robson (ed.), *Collected Works of John Stuart Mill*, vol. 10, pp. 203–259. London: Routledge.

Morris, H. (1976). "Guilt and Suffering." In his *On Guilt and Innocence: Essays in Legal Philosophy and Moral Psychology*, pp. 89–110. Berkeley: University of California Press.

Nair, S. (2016). "Conflicting Reasons, Unconflicting 'Ought's." *Philosophical Studies* 173: 629–663.

Naylor, M. (1984). "Frankfurt on the Principle of Alternate Possibilities." *Philosophical Studies* 46: 249–258.

Nelkin, D. K. (2016). "Accountability and Desert." *Journal of Ethics* 20: 173–189.

Nelkin, D. K. (2011). *Making Sense of Free Will and Responsibility*. New York: Oxford University Press.

Noggle, R. (2009). "Give Till It Hurts? Beneficence, Imperfect Duties, and a Moderate Response to the Aid Question." *Journal of Social Philosophy* 40: 1–16.

Parfit, D. (2011A). *On What Matters*, vol. 1. Oxford: Oxford University Press.

Parfit, D. (2011B). *On What Matters*, vol. 2. Oxford: Oxford University Press.

Parfit, D. (1984). *Reasons and Persons*. Oxford: Oxford University Press.

Peels, R. (2017). *Responsible Belief: A Theory in Ethics and Epistemology*. New York: Oxford University Press.

Pereboom, D. (2014). *Free Will, Agency, and Meaning in Life*. Oxford: Oxford University Press.

Pereboom, D. (2007). "Hard Incompatibilism." In D. Pereboom, J. M. Fischer, R. Kane, and M. Vargas, *Four Views on Free Will*, pp. 85–125. New York: Blackwell.

Pettit, P. and C. List (2011). *Group Agency: The Possibility, Design, and Status of Corporate Agents*. New York: Oxford University Press.

Pinkert, F. (2015). "What If I Cannot Make a Difference (and Know It)." *Ethics* 125: 971–998.

Portmore, D. W. (MANUSCRIPT). "What's a Rational Self-Torturer to Do?"

Portmore, D. W. (FORTHCOMING). "Control, Attitudes, and Accountability." *Oxford Studies in Agency and Responsibility*.

Portmore, D. W. (2018). "Maximalism and Moral Harmony." *Philosophy and Phenomenological Research* 96: 318–341.

Portmore, D. W. (2017A). "Uncertainty, Indeterminacy, and Agent-Centered Constraints." *Australasian Journal of Philosophy* 95: 284–298.

Portmore, D. W. (2017B). "Transitivity, Moral Latitude, and Supererogation." *Utilitas* 29: 286–298.

Portmore, D. W. (2017C). "Maximalism vs. Omnism about Permissibility." *Pacific Philosophical Quarterly* 98: 427–452.

Portmore, D. W. (2017D). "Maximalism vs. Omnism about Reason." *Philosophical Studies* 174: 2953–2972.

Portmore, D. W. (2016). "Review of Dale Dorsey's The Limits of Moral Authority." *Notre Dame Philosophical Reviews*, https://ndpr.nd.edu/news/71274-the-limits-of-moral-authority/.

Portmore, D. W. (2013). "Perform Your Best Option." *Journal of Philosophy* 110: 436–459.

Portmore, D. W. (2012). "Imperfect Reasons and Rational Options." *Noûs* 46: 24–60.

Portmore, D. W. (2011). *Commonsense Consequentialism: Wherein Morality Meets Rationality*. New York: Oxford University Press.

Pummer, T. (2016). "Whether and Where to Give." *Philosophy & Public Affairs* 44: 77–95.

Quinn, W. (1990). "The Puzzle of the Self-Torturer." *Philosophical Studies* 59: 70–90.

Rawls, J. (1971). *A Theory of Justice*. Cambridge, MA: Belknap Press.

Raz, J. (2011). *From Normativity to Responsibility*. Oxford: Oxford University Press.

Raz, J. (2000). *Engaging Reason: On the Theory of Value and Action*. Oxford: Oxford University Press.

Regan, D. (1980). *Utilitarianism and Co-operation*. New York: Oxford University Press.

Rinard, S. (2018). "Equal Treatment for Belief." *Philosophical Studies*, https://doi.org/10.1007/s11098-018-1104-9.

Robertson, S. (2008). "Not So Enticing." *Ethical Theory and Moral Practice* 11: 263–277.

Robinson, M. (2012). "Modified Frankfurt-type Counterexamples and Flickers of Freedom." *Philosophical Studies* 157: 177–194.

Rosen, G. (2015). "The Alethic Conception of Moral Responsibility." In R. Clarke, M. McKenna, and A. M. Smith (eds.), *The Nature of Moral Responsibility: New Essays*, pp. 65–87. Oxford: Oxford University Press.

Ross, A. (1941) "Imperatives and Logic." *Theoria* 7: 53–71.

Ross, J. (2012). "Actualism, Possibilism, and Beyond." In M. Timmons (ed.), *Oxford Studies in Normative Ethics*. vol. 2, pp. 74–96. Oxford: Oxford University Press.

Ross, J. (2009). "How to Be a Cognitivist about Practical Reason." In R. Shafer-Landau (ed.), *Oxford Studies in Metaethics*, vol. 4, pp. 243–282. Oxford: Oxford University Press.

Ross, W. D. (1930). *The Right and the Good*. Oxford: Oxford University Press.

Rulli, T. (2016). "Conditional Obligations." Working manuscript.

Sachs, B. (2010). "Consequentialism's Double-Edge Sword." *Utilitas* 22: 258–271.

Scanlon, T. M. (2013). "Giving Desert Its Due." *Philosophical Explorations* 16: 101–116.

Scanlon, T. M. (2008). *Moral Dimensions. Meaning, Permissibility and Blame.* Cambridge, MA: Harvard University Press.

Scanlon, T. M. (1998). *What We Owe to Each Other.* Cambridge, MA: Belknap Press.

Scheffler, S. (1985). "Agent-Centred Restrictions, Rationality, and the Virtues." *Mind* 94: 409–419.

Schroeder, M. (2007). *Slaves of the Passions.* Oxford: Oxford University Press.

Shah, N. (2006). "A New Argument for Evidentialism." *Philosophical Quarterly* 56: 481–498.

Shoemaker, D. (2015). *Responsibility from the Margins.* Oxford: Oxford University Press.

Shpall, S. (2016). "The Calendar Paradox." *Philosophical Studies* 173: 801–825.

Singer, P. (2009). *The Life You Can Save.* New York: Random House.

Sinnott-Armstrong, W. (2015). "Consequentialism." In Edward N. Zalta (ed.), *Stanford Encyclopedia of Philosophy* (Summer 2015), http://plato.stanford.edu/archives/sum2015/entries/consequentialism/.

Sinnott-Armstrong, W. (2005). "You Ought to Be Ashamed of Yourself (When You Violate an Imperfect Moral Obligation)." *Philosophical Issues* 15: 193–208.

Sinnott-Armstrong, W. (1984). "'Ought' Conversationally Implies 'Can.'" *Philosophical Review* 93: 249–261.

Skorupski, J. (1999). *Ethical Explorations.* Oxford: Oxford University Press.

Smilansky, S. (1996). "Responsibility and Desert: Defending the Connection." *Mind* 105: 157–163.

Smith, A. M. (2015). "Attitudes, Tracing, and Control." *Journal of Applied Philosophy.* 32: 115–132.

Smith, A. M. (2012). "Attributability, Answerability, and Accountability: In Defense of a Unified Account." *Ethics* 122: 575–589.

Smith, A. M. (2005). "Responsibility for Attitudes: Activity and Passivity in Mental Life." *Ethics* 115: 236–271.

Smith, M. (2006). "Moore on the Right, the Good and Uncertainty." In T. Horgan and M. Timmons (eds.), *Metaethics after Moore*, pp. 133–148. New York: Oxford University Press.

Smith, M. (2003). "Rational Capacities, or: How to Distinguish Recklessness, Weakness, and Compulsion." In S. Stroud and C. Tappolet (eds.), *Weakness of Will and Practical Irrationality*, pp. 17–38. Oxford: Clarendon Press.

Snedegar, J. (2016). "Reasons, Oughts, and Requirements." In R. Shafer-Landau (ed.), *Oxford Studies in Metaethics*, vol. 11, pp. 183–211. Oxford: Oxford University Press.

Snedegar, J. (2015). "Contrastivism about Reasons and Oughts." *Philosophy Compass* 10: 379–388.

Snedegar, J. (2014). "Deontic Reasoning across Contexts." In F. Cariani, D. Grossi, J. Meheus, and X. Parent (eds.), *Deontic Logic and Normative Systems*, pp. 208–223. Switzerland: Springer International.

Sobel, D. (2012). "Backing Away from Libertarian Self-Ownership." *Ethics* 123: 32–60.

Southwood, N. and D. Wiens. (2016). "'Actual' Does Not Imply 'Feasible'." *Philosophical Studies* 173: 3037–3060.

Spector, H. (2016). "Decisional Nonconsequentialism and the Risk Sensitivity of Obligation." *Social Philosophy and Policy* 32: 91–128.

Stalnaker, R. (1984). *Inquiry*. Cambridge, MA: MIT Press.

Star, D. (2015). *Knowing Better: Virtue, Deliberation, and Normative Ethics*. Oxford: Oxford University Press.

Steup, M. (2008). "Doxastic Freedom." *Synthese* 161: 375–392.

Steup, M. (2001). *Knowledge, Truth, and Duty: Essays on Epistemic Justification, Responsibility, and Virtue*. Oxford: Oxford University Press.

Strawson, P. F. (2008). *Freedom and Resentment and Other Essays*. London: Routledge.

Streumer, B. (2003). "Does 'Ought' Conversationally Implicate 'Can'?" *European Journal of Philosophy* 11: 219–228.

Sverdlik, S. (2011). *Motive and Rightness*. Oxford: Oxford University Press.

Swanson, E. (2014). "Ordering Supervaluationism, Counterpart Theory, and Ersatz Fundamentality." *Journal of Philosophy* 109: 289–310.

Talbert, M. (2017). "Omission and Attribution Error." In D. Nelkin and S. Rickless (eds.), *The Ethics and Law of Omissions*, pp. 17–35. Oxford: Oxford University Press.

Talbert, M. (2016). "Symmetry, Rational Abilities, and the Ought-Implies-Can Principle." *Criminal Law and Philosophy* 10: 283–296.

Tenenbaum, S. (2007). "Brute Requirements: A Critical Notice of J. Gert's Brute Rationality." *Canadian Journal of Philosophy* 37: 153–172.

Tessman, L. (2015). *Moral Failure: On the Impossible Demands of Morality*. New York: Oxford University Press.

Thomson, J. J. (1990). *The Realm of Rights*. Cambridge, MA: Harvard University Press.

Thomson, J. J. (1986). "Some Ruminations on Rights." In W. Parent (ed.), *Rights, Restitution, and Risk: Essays in Moral Theory*, pp. 49–65. Cambridge, MA: Harvard University Press.

Timmerman, T. (2015A). "Does Scrupulous Securitism Stand-up to Scrutiny? Two Problems for Moral Securitism and How We Might Fix Them." *Philosophical Studies* 172: 1509–1528.

Timmerman, T. (2015B). "Sometimes There Is Nothing Wrong with Letting a Child Drown." *Analysis* 75: 204–212.

Timmerman, T. and Y. Cohen. (2016). "Moral Obligations: Actualist, Possibilist, or Hybridist?" *Australasian Journal of Philosophy* 94: 672–686.

Timmons, M. (2013). *Moral Theory: An Introduction*, 2nd ed. Lanham, MD: Rowman & Littlefield.

Unger, P. (1996). *Living High and Letting Die*. Oxford: Oxford University Press.

Vallentyne, P. (1992). "Moral Dilemmas and Comparative Conception of Morality." *Southern Journal of Philosophy* 30: 117–124.

Vallentyne, P. (1989). "Two Types of Moral Dilemmas." *Erkenntnis* 30: 301–318.

van Inwagen, P. (1978). "Ability and Responsibility." *Philosophical Review* 87: 201–224.

Vargas, M. (2013). *Building Better Beings*. Oxford: Oxford University Press.

Vessel, J.-P. (2016). "Against Securitism, the New Breed of Actualism in Consequentialist Thought." *Utilitas* 28: 164–178.

Vessel, J.-P. (2010). "Supererogation for Utilitarianism." *American Philosophical Quarterly* 47: 299–319.

Vessel, J.-P. (2003). "Counterfactuals for Consequentialists." *Philosophical Studies* 112: 103–125.

Wallace, R. J. (1994). *Responsibility and the Moral Sentiments*. Cambridge, MA: Harvard University Press.

Watson, G. (2004). *Agency and Answerability*. Oxford: Oxford University Press.

Watson, G. (1996). "Two Faces of Responsibility." *Philosophical Topics* 24: 227–248.

Way, J. (2012). "Transmission and the Wrong Kind of Reason." *Ethics* 122: 489–515.

Wedgwood, R. (2017). *The Value of Rationality*. Oxford: Oxford University Press.

Wedgwood, R. (2011). "Defending Double Effect." *Ratio* 24: 384–401.

Wedgwood, R. (2007). *The Nature of Normativity*. Oxford: Oxford University Press.

White, S. J. (2017). "Transmission Failures." *Ethics* 127: 719–732.

Widerker, D. (2003). "Blameworthiness and Frankfurt's Argument against the Principle of Alternative Possibilities." In D. Widerker and M. McKenna (eds.), *Moral Responsibility and Alternate Possibilities*, pp. 265–299. Burlington, VT: Ashgate.

Widerker, D. (2000). "Frankfurt's Attack on Alternative Possibilities: A Further Look." *Philosophical Perspectives* 14: 181–201.

Widerker, D. (1991). "Frankfurt on 'Ought Implies Can' and Alternative Possibilities." *Analysis* 51: 222–224.

Wiland, E. (2005). "Monkeys, Typewriters, and Objective Consequentialism." *Ratio* 18: 252–360.

Williams, B. (1981). "Internal and External Reasons." In his *Moral Luck*, pp. 101–113. Cambridge: Cambridge University Press.

Williams, B. (1995). "Internal Reasons and the Obscurity of Blame." In his *Making Sense of Humanity: And Other Philosophical Papers 1982–1993*, pp. 35–45. Cambridge: Cambridge University Press.

Williams, J. R. G. (2016). "Vagueness as Indecision." *Proceedings of the Aristotelian Society* 90: 287–309.

Wolf, S. (2011). "Blame Italian Style." In R. J. Wallace, R. Kumar, and S. R. Freeman (eds.), *Reasons and Recognition: Essays on the Philosophy of T. M. Scanlon*, pp. 332–347. New York: Oxford University Press.

Wolf, S. (1980). "Asymmetrical Freedom." *Journal of Philosophy* 77: 151–166.

Young, L., S. Nichols, and R. Saxe. (2010). "Investigating the Neural and Cognitive Basis of Moral Luck: It's Not What You Do but What You Know." *Review of Philosophy and Psychology* 1: 333–349.

Zimmerman, M. J. (2017). "Prospective Possibilism." *Journal of Ethics* 21: 117–150.

Zimmerman, M. J. (2002). "Taking Luck Seriously." *Journal of Philosophy* 99: 553–576.

Zimmerman, M. J. (1996). *The Concept of Moral Obligation*. Cambridge: Cambridge University Press.

Zimmerman, M. J. (1987). "Luck and Moral Responsibility." *Ethics* 97: 374–386.

Index

Tables, figures, and boxes are indicated by an italic *t*, *f*, and *b* following the page number. Notes are indicated by 'n.' following the page number.